HEGEL ON TRAGEDY

ANNE PAOLUCCI was born in Rome. She received her B.A. from Barnard College and her M.A. from Columbia University. In 1951–52 she held a Fulbright to Italy where she studied at the University of Rome. At present she is a member of the English Department of The City College of New York. She has contributed articles to the *Romanic Review* and the *Shakespeare Quarterly* and has written poetry for a number of magazines, among them the *Kenyon Review*. With her husband, Henry Paolucci, she translated Machiavelli's *Mandragola*. She has been made a Woodbridge Honorary Fellow in English and Comparative Literature at Columbia University for 1961–62.

HENRY PAOLUCCI was born in New York City and received his B.S.S. from The City College of New York, his M.A. and Ph.D. from Columbia University. He was a Columbia Traveling Fellow in 1948–49 at the University of Florence and held a Fulbright to Italy. He is an Assistant Professor of History at Iona College and a Lecturer in Greek and Roman history at The City College of New York. He has contributed to the *Columbia-Viking Desk Encyclopedia* and the *Encyclopedia Americana,* and has edited *The Enchiridion of St. Augustine* and *The Achievement of Galileo* (with Professor James Brophy). He has also translated Beccaria's *On Crimes and Punishments* (with Professor Vito Caporale).

HEGEL

ON TRAGEDY

Edited, *with an Introduction, by*

ANNE AND HENRY PAOLUCCI

Anchor Books
Doubleday & Company, Inc.
Garden City, New York
1962

"Hegel's Theory of Tragedy" from *Oxford Lectures on Poetry* by A. C. Bradley, reprinted by permission of Macmillan & Co. Ltd.

Material from Hegel's *The Phenomenology of the Mind,* translated by J. B. Baillie, reprinted by permission of George Allen & Unwin, Ltd.

Material from Hegel's *The Philosophy of Fine Art,* translated by F. P. B. Osmaston, reprinted by permission of G. Bell & Sons Ltd.

Material from Hegel's *Lectures on the Philosophy of Religion,* translated by E. B. Speirs and J. Burdon Sanderson, reprinted by permission of Routledge & Kegan Paul Ltd.

Material from *Hegel's Lectures on the History of Philosophy,* edited and translated by E. S. Haldane, reprinted by permission of Routledge & Kegan Paul Ltd.

TABLE OF CONTENTS

INTRODUCTION   xi
BIBLIOGRAPHICAL NOTE   xxxiii

CHAPTER I

TRAGEDY AS A DRAMATIC ART   1
1. Drama as a Poetic Work of Art   2
   a. The Principle of Dramatic Poetry   2
   b. Dramatic Composition   9
   c. The Relation of the Dramatic Composition to the
      General Public   22
2. Composition and External Representation of Dramatic Works of Art   30
   a. The Reading and Recitation of Dramatical Com-
      positions   32
   b. The Art of the Actor   36
   c. The Theatrical Art Which Is More Independent
      of Poetical Composition   41
3. Types of Dramatic Poetry and the Chief Phases of
   Their Historical Development   44
   a. The Principle of Tragedy, Comedy, and the
      Drama, or Social Play   45
   b. The Difference between Ancient and Modern
      Dramatic Poetry   58
   c. The Concrete Development of Dramatic Poetry
      and Its Types   62

CHAPTER II

DRAMATIC ACTION AND CHARACTER   97
1. Appropriate World Condition   98
2. Situation and Collision   112

3. Action and Individuality   129
  a. Universal Forces of Action   132
  b. Individuals in Action   138
  c. Character   152

CHAPTER III

DRAMATIC MOTIVATION AND LANGUAGE   165
1. Myth and Motivation in Classical Drama   168
  a. Conflict between the Old and New Gods   169
  b. Survival of the Natural Divinities in the Hu-
     manized Gods   182
  c. The Classical Ideal and Its Dissolution   187
2. Subjective Motives of Romantic Drama   192
  a. Honour   194
  b. Love   196
  c. Fidelity   203
  d. The Self-Subsistency of Romantic Character   206
3. Notes on Language   217
  a. The Metaphor   221
  b. The Simile   224
  c. Verbal Expression   231

CHAPTER IV

ETHICS AND TRAGEDY   237
1. Self-Consciousness and the Social Order   237
  a. Pleasure and Necessity   242
  b. The Law of the Heart, and the Frenzy of Self-
     Conceit   246
  c. Virtue and the Course of the World   254
2. Objective Spirit: the Ethical Order   259
  a. The Ethical World   260
  b. Ethical Action   274
3. The Spiritual Work of Art   286
  a. The Earliest Language of Spirit: Epic   288
  b. The Higher Language: Tragedy   291
  c. The Self-Conscious Language: Comedy   298

CHAPTER V

HISTORICAL, RELIGIOUS, AND PHILOSOPHICAL SUBSTANCE
OF TRAGEDY   303
1. Necessity and Freedom in the Pantheon of Gods   304
   a. Formless Necessity   308
   b. Posited Necessity or the Particular Gods   311
   c. The Beautiful Form of the Divine Powers   313
2. Art as Worship in the Religion of Humanity   318
   a. Inner Feeling or Subjective Attitude   319
   b. Worship as Service   327
   c. Service as Reconciliation   337
3. Tragedy and the Impiety of Socrates   345
   a. The Attacks   347
   b. The Trial   351
   c. Socrates and the Tragic End of Greece   364

APPENDIX: A. C. BRADLEY:
   "Hegel's Theory of Tragedy"   367
INDEX   389

INTRODUCTION

> Since Aristotle dealt with tragedy, and, as usual, drew
> the main features of his subject with those sure and
> simple strokes which no later hand has rivaled, the
> only philosopher who has treated it in a manner both
> original and searching is Hegel.
>
> A. C. Bradley

Hegel's writings on tragedy are scattered throughout his work.
In bringing the chief of them together for the first time in
one volume, the editors have sought to make them available
to a wider audience than heretofore. Lifted out of the larger
contexts of Hegelian thought in which they originally appeared, Hegel's statements on tragedy acquire a new importance, especially for students of literature.

Since the publication of Bradley's lecture on "Hegel's Theory of Tragedy" in 1909,[1] references to Hegel have become
almost a commonplace in English and American dramatic
criticism. But these are rarely accompanied by clear indications
that the critics have actually read the relevant pages. One
prominent critic, for instance, has cautiously ascribed to
"Hegel, or his interpreters" an analysis of the *Antigone* of
Sophocles that seems to him merely to have "clouded the issue."[2] Of course, not all scholars who reject Hegel's view of
tragedy do so without having read him. Some of his severest
critics have apparently searched through all his writings and
come away dissatisfied, wondering what could have led Bradley to attribute such importance to them. One such scholar,
Israel Knox, author of the lengthiest critique of Hegel's aesthetics in English, has in fact boldly challenged Bradley's interpretation of Hegel. According to Knox, Bradley read Hegel
too literally, and was therefore "inclined to accept much that
is really in conflict with his own views."[3] One must realize,
Knox explains, that Hegel doesn't always mean what he says.
His "apparent denial of guilt or innocence in tragedy," for ex-

ample, is very deceptive. Bradley accepts it literally, when in fact, Knox asserts, it needs to be very carefully interpreted in a "typically" Hegelian sense, as a doctrine "permeated with a vicious moralism—with a flaming justification of the socio-political and historico-cultural *status quo*,"[4] insisting on "the rightness and rationality of the human sacrifice upon the altar of some Moloch principle."[5]

If Knox's view is correct, it has been to Hegel's advantage that his writings have remained relatively inaccessible. On the other hand, in reading this sharp rejection of Bradley's literal interpretation, one cannot help being reminded of Bosanquet's sobering remark, in his own critique of Hegel, that for all of us, in varying degrees, "the hardest of all lessons in interpretation is to believe that great men mean what they say. We are below their level, and what they actually say seems impossible to us, till we have adulterated it to suit our own imbecility."[6]

It remains a fact, however, that, on the whole, English and American literary scholars have not been persuaded, even by Bradley's emphatic acknowledgment of his own indebtedness, of the value of examining the Hegelian texts for themselves. As a consequence, the brilliant analyses and interpretations that inspired the Oxford lectures on *Hamlet, Othello, King Lear, Macbeth,* and the character of Falstaff have not yet become, as they long ago should have, a part of the common currency of Shakespearean criticism. In marked contrast, Hegel's interpretations of the chief writers of Germany, France, Italy, and Spain have had a pervasive influence among literary scholars in those countries. His pages on Dante, for instance, have been a focal point of interest for all important Italian critics since the time of De Sanctis; and even his summary judgments on the artistry of Petrarch, Boccaccio, Ariosto, Tasso, and Machiavelli have been analyzed, elaborated, and disputed by a multitude of scholars in the course of the past century. Yet it is not in his appraisals of Dante or Petrarch, Goethe or Schiller, Racine or Molière, Virgil or Homer, or even the Greek tragedians, that Hegel has been most penetrating and original. His best pages are on Shakespeare. Indeed, in his *Philosophy of Fine Art,* which surveys the realms of architecture, sculpture, painting, and music, as well as literature, it is, as Professor Carl J. Friedrich has noted, the dra-

matic world of Shakespeare that "appears to be the very pin-
nacle of aesthetic achievement."[7]

The writings collected here ought to be of considerable interest to all who are concerned with the enjoyment and critical appreciation of great literature. Of course, there is the
difficulty of the Hegelian language—but a literary generation
addicted as ours has been to deciphering the verbal puzzles of
modern poetry and exploring the mazes of existentialist frus-
tration should not be seriously troubled by that. It is, after
all, merely the difficulty of permanent and universal intelligibility. Often a work that one generation, or one group of
specialists, finds transparently easy proves to be, for every
other, either impossibly obscure or unworthy of being read at
all. Hegel's works have not suffered such a fate. Scholars of
every generation since his time, and specialists in every field,
have found stimulation and enlightenment in his pages.

The extent of Hegel's influence, not only on such philosophers as Hartmann, Dilthey, Husserl, Heidegger, F. H. Bradley, Bosanquet, Cassirer, Gentile, and Croce, who have shaped
their intellectual careers around his thought, but also on historians, theologians, jurists, political scientists, economists, anthropologists, sociologists, and revolutionaries, almost exceeds
belief.

"His ideas," Professor Morris R. Cohen wrote, "dominate
our evolutionary social sciences as well as most diverse schools
of philosophy and theology. We can see this in the dialectic
materialism of the orthodox Marxism which is disturbing the
world, as well as in the Oxford idealism of our Anglo-American
thought. . . . Above all, Hegel still fashions our concepts of
the history of social institutions, art, religion, and philosophy."[8] Professor Friedrich has written, more specifically:

Hegel's influence on existentialism, on Kierkegaard and
Jaspers, on Heidegger and Sartre, is tremendous. His influence on Dewey is well-known. . . .[9] Max Weber's
crucial categories of "understanding" and of "ideal types,"
derived from the methodological work of Rickert and
Windelband, are Hegelian, especially in their teleological
implications. Similarly, the work of Toynbee is rooted
in Hegel's philosophy of history, and indeed closer

to Hegel than some of the intervening work in this field. . . . Finally, the work of the cultural anthropologists, such as Ruth Benedict, is derived from Hegel's philosophy.[10]

In his last years, George Santayana lamented the fact that he had not devoted his period of graduate study to Hegel; such study, he wrote, "would have knit my own doctrine together at the beginning of my career, as I have scarcely had the chance of doing at the end. My warhorse would not have been so much blinded and hidden under his trappings."[11] And the virulently anti-Hegelian Bertrand Russell, who has done more than anyone else since Schopenhauer to popularize the impression that Hegel's writing is often "muddle-headed nonsense," has himself acknowledged that, in his intellectually formative years, he was inspired by Hegel to pursue simultaneously the studies in the theoretical and practical or social sciences that have attracted world-wide attention to him. The Hegelian inspiration, he wrote, "survived the change in my philosophy. The moment had had a certain importance. . . ."[12]

The key to this extraordinary influence lies in Hegel's language—the language, that is, of his dialectical method, which he shaped in his effort to break down the barriers—as we like to phrase it today—between the specialized academic disciplines, and to exhibit their interdependence. The extent of his influence is both a clear indication and an accurate measure of the success of his effort. Whatever difficulties one may encounter in the language of that method are worth encountering and overcoming. For the methodical language is in itself a valuable tool, an instrument of analysis and learning that, as Sidney Hook has observed, "may be taken over, with some modifications, whether one is a professed Hegelian or not."[13]

But of all Hegel's philosophic writings, those on dramatic literature offer the least difficulty. Hegel treats the subject no less methodically than he treats other subjects; yet in this sphere, as in no other, he had the advantage of a philosophic language already adequately shaped by the continuous influence of Aristotle's *Poetics* on literary criticism.

Hegel arrives at his main discussion of tragedy, in *The Philosophy of Fine Art*, only after an extensive survey of the entire realm of artistic beauty. A word should be said here about some of the main points of that survey, for the discussion of tragedy is bound to suggest questions that can be answered only in terms of the whole aesthetic system.

One such question, which at once touches the heart of Hegel's conception of tragedy, has to do with the relation of art to religion and philosophy in the Hegelian system. The charge is sometimes advanced that Hegel's conception of tragedy is vitiated by his low estimation of the entire province of art, which he subordinates first to religion and ultimately to philosophy. Croce, reviewing the case against him, remarks that Hegel's attitude seems to parallel Plato's. Both philosophers had a very lively aesthetic sense and were fervent lovers of art, but—

> just as the Greek philosopher, obeying what he presumed to be the command of religion, condemned mimesis and the Homeric poetry so dear to him; so the German philosopher, unwilling to free himself from the logical exigencies of his system, declared the mortality of art, or rather its very death, already suffered. . . . Hegel's Aesthetics is, therefore, a funeral eulogy: he recalls the successive forms of art, reviews the progressive stages of their internal evolution, and arranges them all in the tomb, with an epitaph inscribed above it by Philosophy.[14]

Croce is sympathetic in pressing the point, but other critics have seized upon it to accuse Hegel of an aesthetic insensitivity that must disqualify him as a competent judge of "living" masterpieces of art.

The question hinges on what Hegel means by the "death" of art—an important question here, for it amounts to asking what he means by "tragedy."

According to Hegel, the highest kind of art (but only the highest) reaches a moment in its development when it ceases to be of primary concern to the civilization that has produced it. It is the moment when great tragedians have come and gone, and Comedy, the universal dissolvent, has already made its appearance. Societies that reach that point, Hegel asserts, find that they require something other than art to satisfy their deepest longings. And he arrives at this conclusion, not because the "exigencies of his system" drive him to it, but because of the incontrovertible record of cultural history. There have been periods in which an entire civilization has dedicated almost all its spiritual energy to the creation and enjoyment of art. The fifth century B.C. in Athens was one such period. The high renaissance, though inwardly distracted by Christianity, was another. But such periods have been rare; according to Hegel, there have been only these two, one of which produced the Greek tragedians, the other, Shakespeare. In the Near East, in China and India, among the Hebrews, Christians, and Mohammedans, art has always been subordinated to religion. And when, as in fourth-century Greece and the post-renaissance period of modern times, religion has not prevailed over art, both have had to submit themselves, finally, to the criticism and discipline of rationalistic science or speculative philosophy. Once the critical or scientific attitude of mind comes to prevail in a civilization, no arguments in favor of the superiority of art or religion can alter the accomplished historical fact.

It is only in this historical sense that art may be said to perish by being absorbed into religion or, ultimately, into philosophy. In the literal sense it can never perish, for, according to Hegel, it is one of the three "moments of Absolute Spirit" that transcend the historical process. Like religion and philosophy, art has its roots in history, in human worldly experience which encompasses the activities of *making, behaving,* and *explaining.* All peoples *make, behave,* and *explain;* all peoples develop manual skills, customary norms of behavior, and imaginative "meanings" for things. In rare corners of the world, where principles of reason have come to be rigorously applied in the ordering of human experience, *making* has developed into technology or productive science; customary norms of behavior have been rationalized into ethics or practical science; and imaginative explanations have been systematized into philosophic understanding or theoretic science.

But the perfection of these three basic human activities by no means ends there. There is a level of *making, behaving,* and *explaining* that transcends the discipline of reason. On that level men act as if moved by a higher-than-human faculty that transforms technical skill into fine or inspired art, ethical norms of behavior into divine commandments, and scientific

knowledge into God-centered wisdom or theology. In the first
of these, the divinity that inspires all three arrests attention
with its supreme beauty; in the second, it graciously compels
worship as the highest good; in the third, it reveals itself to
the fullest satisfaction of the highest faculty of man, as the
ultimate explanation, the source of all things—all being, all
beauty, all goodness, all truth. Each of these is an absolute
moment of the Spirit, and the third, the moment of absolute
philosophic contemplation, may be said to surpass the other
two only in the sense that it grasps or comprehends them in
a higher unity. When philosophy is emptied of its high aesthetic or religious content, it becomes—Hegel never wearies of
saying—an empty intellectual exercise. From this point of view,
it is meaningless to charge that Hegel depreciates the value of
art. What he says simply means, in effect, that when creative
power is nearest to omnipotence, when it is most divine, it
must say with Prospero:

> This rough magic
> I here abjure. . . . I'll break my staff,
> Bury it certain fathoms in the earth,
> And deeper than did ever plummet sound
> I'll drown my book.[15]

Another question that is likely to arise in reading Hegel's
discussion of tragedy has to do with the meaning of the terms
"classical" and "romantic" as applied to ancient and renaissance tragedy, respectively. The difficulty consists in an apparent ambiguity of usage. We find, on the one hand, that *romantic* and *classical,* together with the term *symbolic,* are used
by Hegel as broad designations for types of artistic expression,
distinguished according to the diverse relationships that may
obtain between artistic content and form. On the other hand,
Hegel uses the same words to characterize the several arts in
their particularity, and to distinguish various phases of their
historical development. For example, he classifies poetry as a
characteristically romantic art—a designation it shares with
painting and music. Sculpture is the classical art par excellence, and architecture, the characteristically symbolic art.
These Hegelian designations are simple enough in themselves.
The possibility of ambiguity occurs when we read subse-

quently that poetry, though characteristically romantic, has passed, historically, through symbolic and classical phases before attaining in modern times that precise relationship between content and form that defines the romantic type of artistic expression. Thus, Greek tragedy is romantic in comparison with Greek sculpture, yet classical in comparison with Shakespearean tragedy.

Once the Hegelian terms have been clearly understood, the double classification is seen to be logically consistent as well as remarkably suited to its purpose, which is to comprehend in an orderly scheme, and with the maximum economy of means, the myriad details of the historical legacy of fine art. The scheme has been criticized, yet, oddly enough, not as too restrictive but as unnecessarily pliant in accommodating itself to the empirical character of its richly varied subject matter. "Here," Bosanquet has written in reply to this criticism, "as often happens, the wealth of Hegel's knowledge and industry has disconcerted his critics and even his followers."[16]

Hegel himself had examined carefully the various schemes of classification that have been or might be used in ordering the details of art-history in a meaningful way. His own formulation, based on an analysis of the various possible relations between content and form in artistic expression, embraces them all—in the way that a universal law of gravitation embraces particular laws of mechanics—and at the same time extends beyond their widest reaches to comprehend a multitude of particulars and varieties of artistic experience they do not touch. For students of tragedy, the formulation is of special importance, because it is in terms of the relation between content and form that Hegel reveals the essence of tragedy and justifies his appraisal of it as the highest form of art.

"The artistic consciousness," Hegel begins, laying the foundation for his classification, "no less than the religious . . . and we may even include the impulse of scientific inquiry, have originated in *wonder*."[17] It is when man has somehow torn himself away from his early, practical involvement in his natural surroundings that the facts of nature begin to astonish him and become, for his consciousness, something outside himself, within which he vaguely discerns, or tries to discern, a subjective presence, a personal consciousness like his own. Nature at once excites and frustrates this vague discernment; and in the feeling of wonder that man experiences in being thrust back by nature, art discovers its source. It is a source intimately associated with primitive religious experience. For religion, too, has its beginning, not in mere adoration of external fact, but in an imaginative discernment of willful, thoughtful personality pervading the things of sky and earth. In this sense art is, writes Hegel, "by virtue of its power to create forms cognate with its own substance, the *first* interpreter of religious consciousness."[18]

In the earliest type of art, the primitive artistic pantheism characteristic of the East, the ideal content—which is the inspiring divinity or "mighty presence" in nature—can receive only the vaguest form of representation, because it is itself only vaguely conceived in the artistic imagination. No material that the artist can lay his hands on, no sensory form that anything in nature can suggest to him, is vague enough to represent adequately the vague impression of power he has in mind. To express his imperfect intuition even approximately, he must either distort what he uses into some monstrously unrealistic shape or somehow charge its commonplace form with suggestiveness. In either case artistic content and form remain reciprocally inadequate. And such reciprocal inadequacy, according to Hegel, precisely defines the symbolic type of art, "with its aspiration, its disquiet, its mystery and its sublimity."[19]

This type of art, which makes use of any and every kind of material and shape discernible in earth or sky to represent the all-pervading divinity of nature, has found its most satisfactory medium of expression in architecture—the characteristically symbolic art which prevailed in all the extra-classical and pre-classical civilizations of the ancient world. Architecture's task, writes Hegel, "lies in so manipulating external inorganic nature that it becomes cognate to mind, as an artistic outer world."[20] But architecture does not build for its own sake; it reshapes the substances of external nature for the expression or manifestation of nature's god. In its culminating form, as we find it in primitive Greece, it actually "levels a space for the god, gives form to his external surroundings, and builds him his temple as a fit place for the concentration of spirit, and for its direction to the mind's absolute objects."[21] In civilizations where sculpture, in the strict sense, has not developed to any degree of perfection, architectural construction sometimes takes on the aspects of a colossal statue. But even then it remains symbolic in significance, directing the mind away from itself.

In classical art, as Hegel conceives it, the reciprocal inadequacy of content and form that characterizes symbolic art is overcome. To pass beyond symbolic expression, the artistic consciousness must first attain a true notion or, more precisely, an "adequate idea" of the free spiritual character of the divinity it had vaguely conceived of as submerged in the plurality of natural things. Then it must recognize that the human figure is the only form in nature at all adequate to represent or "embody" such a spiritual content. "Personification and anthropomorphism," writes Hegel, "have often been decried as a degradation of the spiritual; but art, in so far as its end is to bring before perception the spiritual in sensuous form, must advance to such anthropomorphism, as it is only in its proper body that mind is adequately revealed to sense."[22]

Sculpture has proved to be, historically, the most satisfactory artistic medium for the ideal or classical type of artistic expression. Like architecture, it is a spatial, three-dimensional art; but unlike architecture, which respects the mechanical properties of the external matter it employs, sculpture "strikes and permeates the inert mass" animating it with "spiritual individuality."[23] When the symbolic temple of architecture is ready, the classical hand of sculpture provides, in the idealized figure of man, an embodiment of divinity itself. In the perfect adequacy of content and form that characterizes Greek sculpture, Hegel asserts, the classical type of art "attained the highest excellence of which the sensuous embodiment of art is capable."[24]

Yet art can aim higher. The ideal content of the classical type is not all we know or all we need to know. The godlike figures of Greek sculpture reveal nothing of the inner, self-conscious life of "spiritual individuality." Their eyes are vacant, unresponsive to the world about them. Try as he may, the conscious beholder cannot look into these figures, eye to eye, as into a conscious soul. To express the inner, self-conscious life[25] of the divinity embodied in classical sculpture—or, rather, to attempt to express it—is the task of romantic art.

The romantic type of art, Hegel explains, "destroys the completed union of the Idea and its reality" attained in the classical type, and "recurs, though in a higher phase, to that difference and antagonism of two aspects which was left unvanquished by symbolic art."[26] Its content, the inner world of spirit, has a "significance which goes beyond the classical form of art and its mode of expression."[27] In its efforts to represent this new content, romantic art finds the materials of three-dimensional space, as they present themselves objectively to consciousness, inadequate. It attempts, therefore, to strip them of their "immediate material guise,"[28] so that they may be used to reveal rather than embody the higher spiritual content. In romantic art, Hegel writes, the solid unity of sculpture breaks up and the diversified interior life of spirit, with its perception, feeling, and thought, is revealed to human consciousness by means of color, musical sound, and, finally, the spoken or written word, used as "the mere indication of inward perceptions and ideas."[29] To the extent that it succeeds in dematerializing its means of expression, romantic art "must be considered as art transcending itself."[30]

Historically, painting, music, and poetry have been the characteristic forms of romantic art. Painting makes use of material substances for its expression, but its true medium is reflected light, or color, which it attempts to separate as much as possible from the mechanical and spatial qualities of external existence. By compressing the three dimensions of space into a plane surface, it provides a "mirrored" view of the sensory world—a view that can contain within its relatively small limits the broad expanse of land and sea and sky; the forms and countenances of man in every posture and mood; animals, plants, inanimate objects, the world of human art, as well as abstract associations of color and line. "All this diversity of material," Hegel writes, "is capable of entering into the varied content of painting . . . if only some allusion to an element of mind endows it with affinity to thought and feeling."[31]

In music, the second romantic art, the dimensions of space are dissolved into tones that have only temporal extension.

Music puts aside the perspective and coloring of human perception in order to express the rhythm and stress of inward life, finding "utterance in its tones for the heart with its whole gamut of feelings and passions."[32] It has content, but not in the sense that the plastic arts have. Externally, it conforms, like architecture, to quantitative laws that strictly regulate the conjunction and succession of its tones, yet it does not present an enduring form for the conscious mind to contemplate from without. The swiftly evanescent world of tones, writes Hegel, "directly penetrates through the ears of man to the depths of his soul, attuning the same in concordant emotional sympathy."[33] Music is, in essence, the most subjective, the most inward of the arts, and, therefore, the most romantic.

But, for Hegel, the most spiritual mode of representation of the romantic art type is poetry, the art of speech, which unites in itself the subjectivity of music and the objectivity of the plastic arts. It uses sounds as a medium of expression, but does not, like music, treat them as fixed tonal qualities. The sounds of poetry are conventional signs that can communicate artistic impressions only when correctly interpreted. Poetry is least dependent of all the arts on external sensuous means of expression, and yet it can represent for the imagination "an objective world, in which the determinateness of sculpture and painting is not altogether absent, and is capable of unfolding all the conditions of an event, a succession or interchange of emotional states, passions, conceptions and the settled course of human conduct with more thoroughness than any other art."[34] It can present a canvas of color and line for the inner eye richer than that of painting. To the inner ear it can sing melodies that are sweeter than the finest known to the sensual ear. And, finally, on its highest level of development, poetry can call the very world of architecture into objective existence before us and people it with figures of living flesh whose gestures are animated painting and whose cadenced speech is the sublimest song of thought and feeling.

The universal art of poetic utterance, T. S. Eliot has reminded us—in terms reminiscent of Hegel's distinctions—has three voices. "The first voice," Eliot explains, "is the voice of the poet talking to himself—or to nobody." The second "is the voice of the poet addressing an audience, whether large or small"; and the third is the poet's voice "when he is saying, not what he would say in his own person, but only what he can say within the limits of one imaginary character addressing another."[35] Hegel, in his long discussion of the subject, reverses the order of the first two voices—or, rather, holds to the traditional sequence, based on the historical experience of most nations, in which the narrative or epic voice comes first, followed by the subjective or lyrical voice, and finally the dramatic, which is a synthesis of the two.

Poetic narration has a wide range, but its culminating form is the Epos. In the Epos, the poet or minstrel sets before us the full compass of a grand action, enriched by "association with the organically complete world of a nation and an age."[36] The epic poet, though he has imagined it all in his mind's eye, does not present his story as a creation of his own fantasy. His artistic consciousness is submerged in the spirit of a people or an age. He retires from sight, and his epic subject, with its pageant of divine and heroic figures, is left standing before us with an objectivity at once architectural, sculptural, and pictorial.

In lyric poetry, the poet is wrapped up in himself, unwilling to absorb or to be absorbed in the national consciousness. He descends from the objectivity of the epic world into his own private domain and speaks to relieve the passions pent up in his heart. But genuine lyric utterance does not merely provide an outlet for the passions: "it creates therefrom an object which is purified from all mere contingency of the passing mood; an object in which the soul-life in this deliverance returns once more to itself freely and with self-conscious satisfaction, and remains there at home."[37] If the poet has acquired sufficient mastery of his language, the original spontaneous overflow of emotion is transmuted, through tranquil recollection, into a universal poetic song.

In the third voice of poetry, the dramatic, we have, as in epic poetry, writes Hegel, "an action expanded to our view in its conflicts and issues; spiritual forces come to expression and battle; the element of contingency is everywhere involved, and human activity is either brought into contact with the energy of an omnipotent destiny, or a directive and world-ruling Providence." But instead of being presented to us as "an event of the past resuscitated by the narrative alone," the action of drama "is made to appear as actually realized in the particular volition, morality or immorality of the specific characters depicted, which thereby become central in the principle of *lyric* poetry."[38]

Historically, dramatic poetry has divided itself into three kinds: tragedy, comedy, and the so-called drama of real life, which is a sort of mean between the other two. In the last two, dramatic poetry dissolves itself into the common prose of ordinary existence; but it does so, according to Hegel, only after having attained, in tragedy, the highest phase of development to which art in general can aspire.

One final point remains to be discussed here: the question of Hegel's "preferences" in tragic literature and their bearing on his definition of the principle of tragedy. A. C. Bradley has remarked that Hegel's discussion of the subject in the closing section of *The Philosophy of Fine Art* (the first selection in this volume) leaves, "rightly or wrongly, the impression that to his mind the principle is more adequately realized in the best classical tragedies than in modern works."[39] The key to this preference, Bradley suggests, is to be found in Hegel's distinction between classical and romantic art. According to Bradley, Hegel taught that the classical art of Greece, in which "beauty held a position such as it never held before and will not hold again," is art par excellence, and modern or romantic art, with its "boundless subjectivity," its emphasis on motives of personal honor, loyalty, and passion, and its "fuller admission of common and un-beautiful reality into the realm of Beauty," is essentially defective in comparison. If the reader thinks through the implications of Hegel's notion of romantic art, Bradley concludes, "he will see how all this is connected with those characteristics of modern tragedy which Hegel regards as necessary and yet as, in part, drawbacks."[40]

Bosanquet, however, has maintained that the opposite is correct. "It has been said," he wrote, "that Hegel's classification is a descending series. This is not so; the romantic arts are the culmination of art as such, though it is mere truth to say that they are not the culmination of beauty in the narrow sense."[41] Bradley, of course, was aware of Hegel's high esti-

mate of Shakespeare, and he cautioned readers not to conclude
from what Hegel said about classical and romantic art that
"the advantage was all on one side," or that Hegel "considered this or that ancient poet greater than this or that modern."[42] Nevertheless, largely as a consequence of Bradley's essay, Hegel's alleged preference for *Antigone* ("his favorite
tragedy," one critic remarks simply[43]) has become notorious;
and his supposedly low estimate of the characterizations of
modern tragic heroes has led one scholar to write absurdly:
"[Hegel] objects to Shakespeare's characters because they are
vessels driven by passion and hate and love and doubt and
fear and desire."[44]

The question—and the difficulty for Bradley, clearly—turns
upon that apparent ambiguity in Hegel's scheme of classification touched upon earlier in this Introduction. Tragedy as a
whole, ancient and modern, is, according to Hegel, essentially
a romantic art. Historically, however, it has passed through a
symbolical and a classical phase of development before attaining its ultimate, thoroughly romantic form of expression. No
notable literary works were produced in the primitive symbolic phase, which should be classed as a form of religious
worship rather than as a form of art in the proper sense. In
the second phase, among the Greeks of the fifth century B.C.,
tragedy attained a beauty of literary expression as nearly
"classical" as its essentially romantic content could allow. But,
Hegel remarks, the Greek tragedians themselves seem to have
felt, in a vague way, that for the fullest realization of all the
possibilities of tragedy, something beyond the ideal beauty of
classical expression was required.

Stressing this point, Hegel notes that the Greeks developed
two distinct types of tragic situation: one dealing with the
opposition "between ethical life in its social universality and
the family as the natural ground of moral relations";[45] the
other exploring the dilemma of moral responsibility incurred
for deeds committed in fact but not with conscious intent by a
person evidently acting "under the directing providence of the
gods."[46] It is important to bear this distinction in mind, for in
popular criticism of Hegel, attention is often focused on the
first type of situation—that is, on the opposition of social and
moral values—and then illustrations are drawn from plays in-

volving the second, in order to demonstrate the alleged nar-
rowness of Hegel's view.

The first type is best represented, Hegel asserts, in the *Antigone* of Sophocles. Defining with precision his estimate of
that play, he writes: "Of all that is noble in the ancient and
modern world—I know pretty nearly all of it, and it is right
and possible to know it—the *Antigone* appears to me, from
this point of view, the most excellent, the most satisfying work
of art."[47] It is most satisfying, artistically, as an example of the
first type because, he explains, each of its protagonists, Creon
as well as Antigone, is in a tragic situation: both acknowledge
a double obligation—on the one hand, to respect their family
ties, and on the other, to respect their social obligations as
rulers or offspring of rulers. That is to say, the tragic conflict
is not the opposition between the protagonists, as many critics
have imagined; on the contrary, "imminent in the life of both"
is the value each combats, and "they are seized and broken
by that very bond which is rooted in the compass of their own
social existence."[48]

Having defined the point of view of the *Antigone,* Hegel considers the second type of tragic situation explored by the
Greeks: the dilemma of personal responsibility for deeds done
under external constraint—in which, he says, there is a "real
approach to our modern point of view." Identifying the masterpiece of this second type, Hegel is no less emphatic than
in his praise of the *Antigone.* "The most perfect example of
this in ancient drama," he writes, "is to be found in the ever
admirable *Oedipus at Colonus.*" In Hegel's judgment, the
hero of that play, attempting to resolve his dreadful moral dilemma, "resembles Adam, losing his happiness when he obtains the knowledge of good and evil." Oedipus assumes full
moral responsibility for all that he has done and chooses to live
among the Erinyes, or Furies, until all the disruption in him
is extinguished and his soul is purified. What makes the play
almost modern in its point of view, Hegel explains, is the emphasis on psychological reconciliation worked out by Oedipus
"in and for himself," through his own "essential character."[49]

Nevertheless, there remains an essential difference between
ancient and modern tragedy; and in spelling out that difference, Hegel unequivocally declares his ultimate preference. He

notes, first of all, that from the "point of view of our profounder modern consciousness of right and wrong," the crimes
of Oedipus and of other ancient tragic heroes do not appear
as "deeds for which the true personality of the perpetrator
was responsible." It is not easy for us to feel at home with heroes who "have no desire to avoid the blame" for deeds done
unintentionally, and who, without revealing the psychological
motivation, make it "a point of honor . . . that they are
guilty."[50] The modern point of view insists on the distinction
between the subjective attitude of self-conscious individuality
and the "objective significance of the fact accomplished."[51]
There are, here and there in Greek literature—especially in Euripides—instances of characters who reflect and vacillate in
forming their resolves, examining their consciences and weighing their motives. But in the "supreme results of ancient tragedy," Hegel reminds us, the truly heroic personalities invariably identify their individuality "with an ethical pathos which
is substantive." This is never the case in the best examples of
modern tragedy. The great romantic heroes make their tragic
decisions in the complex depths of personality, where the
sanctions of moral law or social responsibility have no compelling power. Whether morally justified, or wrong and criminal in their deeds, they invariably act as they do, not out of
interest in the "ethical vindication of the truly substantive
claims, but for the simple reason that they are the kind of men
they are."[52] According to Hegel, the highest mastery in the
representation of fully developed characters of this sort was
attained by the English dramatists of the renaissance; and
among these modern masters, "soaring above the rest at an
almost unapproachable height, stands Shakespeare."[53]

Shakespeare, Hegel asserts, has revealed in his great heroes
and heroines the innermost essence of tragic experience. Exploring the extreme limits of evil and folly, as well as moral
nobility, he has endowed his characters with a degree of intelligence and imagination that "makes them free artists" in
themselves, capable of contemplating their own lives as works
of art. Because of the incomparable universality of his characterizations and the variety of situations included in the "infinite embrace of his world-stage,"[54] Shakespeare's works have
gained entrance everywhere, except in those rare quarters

where national conventions of art are too narrow and specific. On this point of universality and variety, Hegel makes a telling comparison: "A similar position of advantage, such as that we allow to Shakespeare, would be attributable to the tragedies of the ancients, if we did not, apart from our changed habits in respect to scenic reproduction and certain aspects of the national consciousness, make the further demand of a profounder psychological penetration and a greater breadth of particular characterization."[55]

But the tragedies of Shakespeare do not all equally satisfy the profounder requirements of the modern point of view. In *Macbeth*, for instance, the disposition of the tragic hero who listens to the "equivocal sisters of fate," allowing himself to be driven to crime by their "double-tongued" promises and false admonitions, hardly differs from that of ancient Oedipus or Orestes, both sent to destruction by oracular and evidently divine utterances. Indeed, according to Hegel, in only one of Shakespeare's great plays is the modern, romantic point of view consistently maintained throughout. Its hero has a type of consciousness that is much purer than Macbeth's, "which believes in witches,"[56] and much more sober, thorough, and solid than that of the ancient heroes, who put their trust in the frenzy of priestesses, or in the voices of trees and birds, or in dreams. This purer type of consciousness cannot allow itself to be lifted out of its moral dilemma by external determinations. Its tragic self-mistrust, therefore, finds no relief. In attempting to represent such self-consciousness, "with all the intimate traits of its evolution," in "self-destructive conflict with circumstances,"[57] Shakespeare produced the work that is for Hegel the supreme masterpiece of all human art: that insoluble psychological enigma, that "Mona Lisa" of literature, as T. S. Eliot calls it[58]—the tragedy of *Hamlet*.

A word about the selection of materials reprinted in the following chapters.

The first chapter contains Hegel's most mature discussion of tragedy as a dramatic art, drawn from the concluding section of *The Philosophy of Fine Art*. According to Bradley, it is in these pages that the German philosopher "seems to touch the essence of tragedy."[59] The second and third chapters are made up of readings from other parts of the same work, in which Hegel examines the actions, characters, and motivating thoughts and sentiments in the masterpieces of ancient and modern tragedy. He reviews the familiar Aristotelian ideas on these subjects and, without exaggerating their significance, defends them where he can against a narrowly literal interpretation that would make them seem no longer applicable. Diction, the fourth element of poetic drama distinguished by Aristotle, is treated at great length by Hegel; but only in the passages reprinted at the close of the third chapter does his discussion relate specifically to tragedy.

The readings in the fourth chapter approach the subject from a different point of view. As Bradley observes, Hegel's study of tragedy is penetrating and original precisely because he comes to it, as Aristotle came, not with a merely literary interest, but with profound philosophic regard for the problems of personality and for the ethical, political, and religious implications of the actions presented by the great tragedians. In the fourth chapter, therefore, readings from the *Philosophy of Right* and the *Phenomenology of Mind* are introduced, selected to emphasize their bearing on the ethical significance of tragedy. Although the discussion there is supported by illustrations from Sophocles as well as Shakespeare, its searching analysis of the interior life makes it especially important for the interpretation of modern tragedy.

In the fifth chapter the subject is approached from the religious aspect. Hegel's discussion of the role of the pantheon of gods, and, especially, of Necessity, in Greek tragedy is presented in selections drawn from the *Philosophy of History* and the *Lectures on the Philosophy of Religion*. The chapter closes with one of the most moving passages in the entire corpus of Hegelian writings: his brilliant analysis, in the *Lectures on the History of Philosophy*, of the moment in Western history when tragedy passed from the stage to enter historical reality, in the trial and death of Socrates.

The Appendix reprints A. C. Bradley's essay on "Hegel's Theory of Tragedy." The reader who comes to it after having read Hegel himself should readily appreciate its importance; he will probably also admire Bradley's candor in insisting at the close that the value of his criticisms and suggestions "is trifling, compared with that of the theory which they attempt to strengthen and to which they owe their existence."[60]

NOTES TO INTRODUCTION

1. A. C. Bradley, "Hegel's Theory of Tragedy," *Oxford Lectures on Poetry*, London, 1950, pp. 69–95.
2. D. W. Lucas, *The Greek Tragic Poets*, London, 1950, p. 125.
3. Israel Knox, *The Aesthetic Theories of Kant, Hegel and Schopenhauer*, New York, 1936, p. 184.
4. *Ibid.*, p. 109.
5. *Ibid.*, pp. 110–11.
6. *The Introduction to Hegel's Philosophy of Fine Art*, tr. Bernard Bosanquet, London, 1905, p. xix.
7. *The Philosophy of Hegel*, ed. Carl J. Friedrich, New York, 1953, p. lix.
8. Morris B. Cohen, "Hegel's Rationalism," *The Philosophical Review*, vol. XLI, no. 3, May 1932, p. 283.
9. Friedrich, p. xvi.
10. *Ibid.*, pp. lxii–lxiii.
11. George Santayana, *Persons and Places, The Middle Span*, New York, 1945, p. 153.
12. Bertrand Russell, *Introduction to Mathematical Philosophy*, London, 1956, p. 11.
13. Sidney Hook, "The Contemporary Significance of Hegel's Philosophy," *The Philosophical Review*, vol. XLI, no. 3, May 1932, p. 240.
14. Benedetto Croce, *Estetica*, Bari, 1912, pp. 352–53 (eds.' translation).
15. *The Tempest*, act V, sc. 1, 11:50–57.
16. Bernard Bosanquet, *A History of Aesthetic*, London, 1949, p. 352.
17. *The Philosophy of Fine Art*, tr. F. P. B. Osmaston, London, 1920, vol. II, p. 23.
18. *Ibid.*, pp. 25–26.
19. Bosanquet, *Introduction*, p. 184.
20. *Ibid.*, p. 196.
21. *Ibid.*, p. 197.
22. *Ibid.*, pp. 185–86.
23. *Ibid.*, pp. 198–99.
24. *Ibid.*, p. 187.
25. "*Die selbstbewusste Innerlichkeit.*"
26. Bosanquet, *Introduction*, p. 187.
27. *Ibid.*, p. 188.
28. *Fine Art*, III, p. 221.
29. Bosanquet, *Introduction*, p. 202.

30. *Ibid.*, p. 190.
31. *Ibid.*, pp. 204–5.
32. *Ibid.*, p. 206.
33. *Fine Art*, III, p. 347.
34. *Fine Art*, IV, p. 5 (adapted).
35. T. S. Eliot, "Three Voices of Poetry," *Types of Literature,* ed. Francis Connolly, New York, 1955, p. 690.
36. *Fine Art*, IV, p. 111.
37. *Ibid.*, p. 194.
38. *Ibid.*, p. 104.
39. Bradley, p. 76.
40. *Ibid.*, p. 94.
41. Bosanquet, *Aesthetic*, p. 354.
42. Bradley, p. 94.
43. René Wellek and Austin Warren, *Theory of Literature,* New York, 1949, p. 20.
44. Knox, p. 115.
45. *Fine Art*, IV, p. 318.
46. *Ibid.*, p. 319.
47. *Ibid.*, p. 324 (adapted).
48. *Ibid.*, p. 324.
49. *Ibid.*, pp. 325–26.
50. *Ibid.*, pp. 319–21.
51. *Ibid.*, p. 319.
52. *Ibid.*, p. 335.
53. *Ibid.*, p. 337.
54. *Ibid.*, p. 337.
55. *Ibid.*, p. 273.
56. *The Phenomenology of Mind,* tr. J. B. Baillie, London, 1910, p. 740.
57. *Fine Art*, IV, p. 340.
58. T. S. Eliot, *Selected Essays 1917–1932,* New York, 1932, p. 124.
59. Bradley, p. 85.
60. *Ibid.*, p. 92.

BIBLIOGRAPHICAL NOTE

The following is a list of the translations from which the selections reprinted in the present volume are taken:

THE PHILOSOPHY OF FINE ART, tr. F. P. B. Osmaston. London: G. Bell and Sons, Ltd., 1920. (Four volumes.) Vols. I, II, IV.

LECTURES ON THE PHILOSOPHY OF RELIGION, tr. E. B. Speirs and J. Burdon Sanderson. London: Kegan Paul, Trench, Trübner, & Co., Ltd., 1895. (Three volumes.) Vol. II.

HEGEL'S LECTURES ON THE HISTORY OF PHILOSOPHY, ed. and tr. E. S. Haldane. London: Routledge & Kegan Paul Ltd., 1955 (reprinted). (Three volumes.) Vol. I.

THE PHILOSOPHY OF HISTORY, tr. J. Sibree. New York: The Colonial Press, 1899.

THE PHENOMENOLOGY OF MIND, tr. J. B. Baillie. London: George Allen & Unwin Ltd.; New York: The Macmillan Company, 1910 (revised edition, 1931).

HEGEL'S PHILOSOPHY OF RIGHT, tr. T. M. Knox. Oxford: The Clarendon Press, 1942.

A. C. Bradley, OXFORD LECTURES ON POETRY. London: Macmillan and Co. Ltd., 1950.

The selection from Osmaston's translation of *The Philosophy of Fine Art* reprinted in the first chapter has been revised in a number of places to bring it into closer accord with the meaning of the German text. A few conspicuous errors have been corrected elsewhere; but, on the whole, the other selections are reproduced as found in the translations listed—except for slight modifications, consistent with the German texts, which we have introduced to facilitate transitions.

A letter in superscript ([a]) marks the beginnings of selections, and the precise source in each case is identified in the footnote.

HEGEL ON TRAGEDY

CHAPTER I

TRAGEDY
AS A DRAMATIC ART

[a]Drama, because it elaborates its content as well as its form into an altogether perfect whole, must be regarded as the highest phase of poetry and of art generally. For in contrast to every other sort of sensuous *materia,* whether it be stone, wood, colour, or tone, that of human speech is the only medium fully adequate to the presentation of spiritual life; and further, among the particular types of the art of articulate speech, dramatic poetry is the one in which we find the objective character of the Epos essentially united to the subjective principle of the Lyric. In other words, it presents an action completed in the past as actually happening before us, both as emanating from the inner life of a self-directed character and as determined in its outcome by the substantial nature of purposes, individuals, and collisions. This mediation of the epic art through the inner life of the subject displayed before us in action does not, however, permit the drama to describe the external aspects of local condition and environment, nor yet the action and event itself in the way that they are described in the epic. Consequently, in order that the entire art-product may receive the full animation of life, we require its complete scenic representation. And finally, the action itself, regarded in the full complexus of its internal and external reality, is adaptable to quite distinctive interpretation, the pervading principle of which provides, in addition to the Tragic

[a] *The Philosophy of Fine Art,* tr. F. P. B. Osmaston. London: 1920. Vol. IV, pp. 248–348.

and Comic, a third main classification of types of dramatic poetry.

Starting then from the vantage of these general observations we may indicate the course of our inquiry as follows:

First, we propose to consider the dramatic composition, both in its general and more detailed features, in the contrast it presents to epic and lyrical poetry.

Secondly, our attention will be directed to its scenic presentation and the conditions of this necessity.

Thirdly, we shall pass under review the different types of dramatic poetry as we find them realized in the concrete facts of past history.

1. DRAMA AS A POETIC WORK OF ART

What we have, in the first instance, to define more emphatically is the poetic aspect of the dramatic composition as such, that is to say in its independence of the fact that the same is necessarily presented to our direct vision on the stage. Our investigation of this will do well to concentrate itself on the following points:

First, there is the general principle of dramatic poetry.

Secondly, we have the several specific types of dramatic composition.

Thirdly, there is the relation which obtains between these and the public audience.

a. The Principle of Dramatic Poetry

The demand of the drama, in the widest sense, is the presentation of human actions and relations in their actually visible form to the imaginative consciousness, that is to say, in the uttered speech of living persons, who in this way give expression to their action. Dramatic action, however, is not confined to the simple and undisturbed execution of a definite purpose, but depends throughout on conditions of collision, human passion and characters, and leads therefore to actions and reactions, which in their turn call for some further resolution of conflict and disruption. What we have consequently before us are definite ends individualized in living personalities and situations pregnant with conflict; we see these as they are asserted and maintained, as they work in co-operation or opposition—all in a momentary and kaleidoscopic interchange of expression—and along with this, too, the final result presupposed and issuing from the entirety of this interthreading and conflicting skein of human life, movement, and accomplishment, which has none the less to work out its tranquil resolution. The mode of poetical composition adapted to this novel type of content can be, as already suggested, no other than a mediating union of the principles of epic and lyrical art respectively.

(1) The *first* point of importance we have to settle to our satisfaction is that of the *time* at which dramatic poetry is able to assert itself in all its predominance. Drama is the product of an already essentially cultured condition of national life. It already presupposes as essentially a feature of past history not only the primitive poetic period of the genuine Epos, but also the independent personal excogitation of lyrical rapture. The bare fact that, while combining these two points of view, it is satisfied with neither sphere in its separation proves that this is so. And in order that we may have this poetic combination the free self-consciousness of human aims, developments and destinies must be already fully alert and awake, must have attained, in short, a degree of culture such as is only possible in the intermediate and later epochs of a nation's development. For this reason, too, the greatest exploits and events of a nation's primitive history are rather of an epic than a dramatic type. Such are features of the national existence for the most part related to communities outside it, such as the Trojan war, or the wave of popular migration, as illustrated in the Crusades, or the national resistance to a common enemy, as was the case in the war of Greece against Persia. It is only at a later stage that we meet with the more stable independence of single heroes, who create for themselves and out of themselves in their isolation definite ends, and carry through the undertakings they imply.

(2) We may add the following remarks upon the nature of

this *mediation* between the opposed principles of *epic* and *lyric poetry*.

The Epos already makes an action visible to our imaginative sense. It is, however, here presented as the substantive entirety of a national spirit under the form of definite events and exploits of external life, in which personal volition, the individual aim and the externality of vital conditions, together with the obstructions which such external facts present, are retained in an equal balance. In the Lyric, on the contrary, it is the individual person, which is emphasized in the independence of his subjective life and as such expressed.

(a) In combining these two points of view drama has in the *first* place, following in this respect the Epos, to bring before our vision an event, action, or practical affair. But above all in everything that is thus presented the factor of bare externality must be obliterated, and in its place the self-conscious and active personality is posited as the paramount ground and vital force. The drama, in short, does not take exclusive refuge in a lyrical inwardness as opposed to an external world, but propounds such a life in and through *its* external realization. And in virtue of this the event does not appear to proceed from external conditions, but rather from personal volition and character; it receives in fact its dramatic significance exclusively in its relation to subjective aims and passions. At the same time the individual is not left exclusively rooted in his self-exclusive independence; he comes to his own through the peculiar nature of the conditions in which he is placed, and subject to which his character and purpose become the content of his volitional faculty, quite as much so in fact as in virtue of the nature of the particular purpose itself in its opposition to and conflict with other ends. Consequently the dramatic action in question must submit to a process of development and collision with other forces, which themselves, on their own account, and even in a contrary direction to that willed and intended by the active personality, effect the ultimate course of the events through which the personal factor, in its essential characteristics of human purpose, personality, and spiritual conflict, is asserted. This substantive or objective aspect, which is enforced along with the individual character, in other respects acting independently from its own ideal resources, is no other than the very point of view which we find effective and vital in the principle of dramatic poetry, when it coincides with that of the epic composition.

(b) However much, therefore, we may have as a centre of attraction the inwardness of particular men and women, nevertheless dramatic composition cannot rest content with the purely lyrical conditions of the emotional life; nor can the poet of such merely limit his sympathy to the dusty record of exploits that are already complete, or, speaking generally, merely describe the experience of enjoyment or other states of emotional or contemplative life. The drama, on the contrary, has to exhibit situations and the spiritual atmosphere that belongs to them as definitely motived by the individual character, which is charged with specific aims, and which makes these an effective part of the practical content of its volitional self-identity. The definition of emotional life, therefore, in the drama passes into the sphere of impulse, the realization of personality by means of active volition, in a word, effective action; it passes out of the sphere of pure ideality, it makes itself an object of the outer world, and inclines itself to the concrete facts of the epic world. The external phenomenon, however, instead of attaining existence in the bare fact of an event, is here, in the view of the acting character himself, charged with the opinions and aims he forms on his own account. Action is here the executed will, which as such is at the same time *recognized*, recognized, that is, not merely in its origin and point of departure from the inner feeling, but also in respect to its ultimate purpose. In other words, all that issues from the action, issues, so far as the personality in question is concerned, from himself, and reacts thereby on his personal character and its circumstances. This constant relation of the entire complexus of external condition to the inwardness itself of the self-realized and self-realizing individuality, who is at once the basis and assimilating force of the entire process, marks the point where dramatic poetry falls in line with the truly lyrical principle.

(c) It is only when thus regarded that human action asserts itself as *action* in the supreme sense, that is, as actual execution of ideal intentions and aims with the realization of which the individual agent associates himself as with himself, discovers himself and his satisfaction therein, and thereupon further takes his stand with his entire being in all that proceeds from it as a constituent of the objective world. A character which is dramatic plucks for himself the fruit of his own deeds.

Inasmuch, however, as the interest, in a dramatic sense, restricts itself to the personal aim, whose hero the active personality is, and it is only necessary in the artistic work to borrow from the external world so much as is bound in an essential relation to this purpose, which originates in self-conscious life, for this reason the drama is *primarily* of a more abstract nature than the epic poem. For on the one hand the action, in so far as it reposes in the self-determination of character, and is deducible from this vital source and centre, does not presuppose the epic background of an entire world through all the varied aspects and ramifications of its positive realization, but is concentrated in the simpler definition of circumstance subject to which the individual man is absorbed in his immediate purpose and carries the same to accomplishment. And from a further point of view we have not here the type of personality which asserts its development to our vision in the *entire complexity* of national qualities as such are displayed by the epic, but rather character viewed in *direct* relation to its action, character which possesses a *definite* end directed to spirit life in its universality. This end or purpose, this eventual fact on which it depends, is placed in a more exalted position than is possible to the extension of the purely individual life, which appears inclusively as living organ and animating vehicle of the same. A more widely extended unveiling of character under the most varied aspects which are present either in no connection at all or only in a more remote one to its action, as we find it concentrated on *one* single point of interest would be a superfluity; consequently in this respect, too, that is, in its relation to the active personality, dramatic poetry ought to be more simply concentrated than epic poetry. The same generalization is applicable to the number and variety of the characters represented. For in virtue of the fact, as previously insisted, that the movement of the drama is not thrown upon the background of a national existence essentially complete in its envisagement of every conceivable variety of class, age, sex, activity, and so forth, but on the contrary, rivets our attention throughout on *one* fundamental purpose and its achievement, a realization of objective fact so extended and intricate as this would not merely be ineffective, but would actually impair the result proposed. At the same time, however, and *secondly*, the end and content of an action is only dramatic by reason of the fact that on account of its defined character, in the distinctive qualities of which the particular personality itself can alone lay hold of it under equally definite conditions, it calls into being in other individuals other objects and passions opposed to it. This pathetic excitant may, no doubt, in each separate active agent, assume the form of spiritual, ethical, and divine forces, such as duty, love to fatherland, parents, wife, relations, and the like. If, however, this essential content of human feeling and activity is to assert itself as dramatic it must in its specialization *confront* us as distinct ends, so that in every case the action will inevitably meet with obstruction in its relation to other active individuals, and fall into subjection to changing conditions and contradictions, which alternately prejudice the success of their own particular fulfilment. The genuine content, the essential operative energy throughout may therefore very well be the eternal forces, the essentially explicit ethical State, the gods of vital reality, in a word the divine and the true, but it is not these in the might of their tranquillity, in that condition, so to speak, wherein the unmoved gods abide, saved from all action, as some serene figures of sculpture self-absorbed in a state of blessedness. What we have here is the divine in its community, as content, that is, and object of human personality, as concrete existence in its realization, invited to act and charged with movement.

If, however, as above described, the godlike presence constitutes the most vital objective truth in the external precipitate of human action, then, *thirdly*, the deciding factor in the course and original departure of such an evolution and conflict cannot reside with particular individuals, which are placed in a relation of opposition to one another; it must be referred to the divine presence itself, regarded as essential totality: and for this reason, the drama, it matters not in what form it may be shaped, will have to propound to us the vital energy of a principle of Necessity which is essentially self-supporting, and capable of resolving every conflict and contradiction.

(3) Consequently, we have before everything else the demand made on the dramatic *poet* in his creative capacity, that to the fullest extent his intelligence is awake to that ideal and universal substance which is at the root of human ends, conflicts, and destinies. He must fully acquaint himself with all the contradictions and developments which the particular action will, under the proposed conditions, necessarily involve and display. He must not merely be aware of them in so far as they originate in personal passion and the specific characterization of particular individuals, or as he finds such related to the actual content of human designs and resolves; but also in so far as they are simply referable to the external relations and circumstances of concrete life. And, along with this, it should be within his powers to recognize what the real nature of these paramount forces are, which apportion to man the just guerdon of his achievements. The rightful claim, no less than the wrongful misuse of the passions, which storm through the human heart, and excite to action, must lie disclosed to him with equal clarity, in order that precisely in those cases where the ordinary vision can only discover the ascendancy of obscurity, chance, and confusion, he, at least, will find revealed the actual self-accomplishment of what is the essence of reason and truth itself. It follows, therefore, that the dramatic poet ought as little to confine his efforts to the indefinite exploration of the depths of emotional life, as the one-sided retention of any single exclusive mood, or any limited partiality in the type of his sense-perception and spiritual outlook generally. He ought, rather, to exclude nothing from his vision that may be embraced by the widest expansion of Spirit conceivable. And this is so because the spiritual powers which are exclusively distinct in the mythological Epos, and which, by virtue of the many-sided aspects of *actual individualization* tend to lose the *clear definition* of their significance, assert themselves in dramatic poetry in consonance with their simple substantive content as pathos altogether, and as apart from individual characters. The drama is, in fact, the resolution of the one-sided aspect of these powers, which discover their self-stability in the dramatic character. And this is so whether, as

in tragedy, they are opposed to such in hostility, or, as in comedy, they are displayed within these characters themselves, without further mediation, in a condition of resolution.

b. Dramatic Composition

In discussing the drama as a concrete work of art, I propose to emphasize, briefly, the following fundamental points:

First, there is the unity of the same viewed in contrast to that of the Epos and the lyric poem.

Secondly, we have to consider the articulation of its parts and their development.

Thirdly, there is the external aspect of diction, dialogue, and verse-measure.

(1) What we have in the first instance to observe and, from the broadest point of view, to establish with regard to the unity of the drama, is connected with a remark made in a previous passage to the effect that dramatic poetry, in contradistinction to the Epos, must be more strenuously self-concentrated. For, although the Epic makes a specific event its centre of unity, this is none the less expanded over a wide and manifold field of the national existence, and may break up into very various episodes and the independent presentation which belongs to each as parts of the entire panorama. An analogous appearance of merely general connection, on grounds which are converse to the above, is permissible to certain types of lyrical poetry. Inasmuch, however, as in dramatic poetry, from one point of view, that epic foundation, as we have seen, falls away—and as, otherwise regarded, the individual characters do not find their expression under the insulation proper to lyric expression, but rather assert in such a way their mutual relations to one another, by means of the opposed features of their characterization and aims, that it is just this personal relation which constitutes the ground of their dramatic realization—it follows, as by a law of necessity, that the synthetic unity of the entire composition is of a more stringent character. Now this more restricted homogeneity is quite as much objective as it is ideal in its nature. It is objective relatively to the features of the practical content of the objects,

which the different characters carry out in a condition of conflict. It is ideal or subjective in virtue of the fact that this essentially substantive content appears in dramatic work as the
passion of particular characters, so that the ill-success or
achievement, fortune or misfortune, victory or defeat, essentially affect the individuals, whom such concern, in their actual
intention.

The more obvious laws of dramatic composition may be
summarized in the time-honoured prescription of the so-called
unities of place, time, and action.

(a) The inalterability of one exclusive *locale* of the action
proposed belongs to the type of those rigid rules, which the
French in particular have deduced from classic tragedy and
the critique of Aristotle thereupon. As a matter of fact, Aristotle merely says[1] that the duration of the tragic action should
not exceed at the most the length of a day. He does not mention the unity of place at all; moreover, the ancient tragedians
have not followed such a principle in the strict sense adopted
by the French. As examples of such a deviation, we have a
change of scene both in the "Eumenides" of Aeschylus and the
"Ajax" of Sophocles. To a still less extent can our more modern dramatic writing, in its effort to portray a more extensive
field of collision, *dramatis personae* of whatever kind and incidental event, and, in a word, an action the ideal explication
of which requires, too, an external environment of greater
breadth, subject itself to the yoke of a rigid identity of scene.
Modern poetry, in so far, that is, as its creations are in harmony with the romantic type, which as a rule displays more
variety and caprice in its attitude to external condition, has
consequently freed itself from any such demand. If, however,
the action is in truth concentrated in a few great motives, so
that it can avoid complexity of external exposition, there will
be no necessity for considerable alternation of scene. Indeed,
the reverse will be a real advantage. In other words, however
false such a rule may be in its purely conventional application, it contains at least the just conception that the constant
transition of scene, without any particular reason why we
should have one more than another, is obviously quite inad-

[1] Poet., c. 5.

missible. The dramatic concentration of the action ought necessarily to assert itself also in this external aspect, and thus
present a contrast to the Epos, which is permitted in the most
varied way to adapt itself to the fresh expatiation in the form
of the spatial condition and its changes. Moreover, from a further point of view, the drama is not, as the Epos, composed
exclusively for the imaginative sense, but for the direct vision
of our senses. In the sphere of the pure imagination we can
readily pass from one scene to another. In a theatrical representation, however, we must not put too great a strain on the
imaginative faculty beyond the point which contradicts the ordinary vision of life. Shakespeare, for example, in whose tragedies and comedies there is a very frequent change of scene,
had posts put up with notices attached to them indicating the
particular scene on view. A device of this kind is a poor sort
of affair, and can only impair the dramatic effect. For this reason the unity of place is at least commendable to the extent
that its intelligibility and convenience are *primâ facie* assured,
in so far, that is, that all confusion is thus avoided. But after
all, no doubt, much may still be trusted to the imagination,
which would conflict with our ordinary perception and notion
of probability. The most convenient course in this, as in other
matters, is a happy mean; in other words, while not wholly
excluding the claim of purely natural fact and perception, we
may still permit ourselves considerable license in our attitude
to both.

   (b) The unity of *time* is a precisely similar case. In the
pure realm of imaginative idea we may no doubt, with no
difficulty, combine vast periods of time; in the direct vision of
perception we cannot so readily pass over a few years. If the
action is, therefore, of a simple character, viewed in its entire
content and conflict, we shall do best to concentrate the time
of such a conflict, from its origin to its resolution, in a restricted
period. If, on the contrary, it demands character richly diversified, whose development necessitates many situations which,
in the matter of time, lie widely apart from one another, then
the formal unity of a purely relative and entirely conventional
duration of time will be essentially impossible. To attempt to
remove such a representation from the domain of dramatic
poetry, on the *primâ facie* ground that it is inconsistent with

the strict rule of time-unity would simply amount to making the prose of ordinary facts the final court of appeal, as against the truth of poetic creation. Least of all need we waste time in discussing the purely empirical probability that as audience we could, in the course of a few hours, witness also, directly through our sense, merely the passage of a short space of time. For it is precisely in the case where the poet is most at pains to illustrate this conclusion that, from other points of view, he well-nigh invariably perpetrates the most glaring improbabilities.

(c) In contrast, unity of *action* is the one truly inviolable rule. The true nature, however, of this unity may be a matter of considerable dispute. I will therefore develop my own views of its significance at greater length.

Every action must without exception have a *distinct* object which it seeks to achieve. It is through his action that man enters actively into the concrete actual world, in which also the most universal subject-matter is in its turn accepted in the poetic work and defined under more specific manifestation. From this point of view, therefore, the unity will have to be sought for in the realization of an end itself essentially definite, and carried under the particular conditions and relations of concrete life to its consummation. The circumstances adapted to dramatic action are, however, as we have seen, of a kind that the individual end meets with obstructions at the hands of other personal agents, and this for the reason that a contradictory end stands in its path, which in its turn equally strives after fulfilment, so that it is invariably attached to the reciprocal relation of conflicts and their devolution. Dramatic action in consequence rests essentially upon an action that is involved with *resistance;* and the genuine unity can only find its *rationale* in the entire movement which consists in the assertion of this collision relatively to the definition of the particular circumstances, characters, and ends proposed, not merely under a mode consonant to such ends and characters, but in such a way as to resolve the opposition implied. Such a resolution has, precisely as the action itself has, an external and an inside point of view. In other words, on the one side, the conflict of the opposed *ends* is finally composed; and on the other the particular *characters*, to a greater or less extent, have committed their entire volitional energy and being to the undertaking they strive to accomplish. Consequently the success or misadventure of the same, the complete or partial execution, the inevitable disaster or the secure union effected with intentions that are apparently opposed to their extent, so determine even the destiny of the character in question, that it is inextricably involved with that which it was impelled to commit to such activity. A true end is therefore only then consummated, where the object and interest of the action, around which all revolves, are identified with the individuals concerned, and absolutely united to them. And depending on whether the difference and opposition of the dramatic characters assumes a simple form or branches out in various accessory episodes and individuals, the unity, again may be of a more severe or a less stringent nature. Comedy, for instance, in the many-sided features of its worked-out intrigue does not require such deliberate self-concentration as tragedy does, which is as a rule motived on grandiose and simple lines. Romantic tragedy, however, is also in this respect more varied and less consistent in its unity than is classic tragedy. And even where there is more license the relation of the episodes and supplementary characters must be throughout recognizable; and the entirety of the piece should also naturally and without strain fit in with and help to complete the conclusion. So, for example, in "Romeo and Juliet," the discord between the families, which lies outside the lovers and their object and destiny, is no doubt the base on which the action is shaped, though not the actual matter on which all actually depends. Shakespeare consequently devotes the necessary, if also wholly subordinate attention to the final issue of this conflict in his conclusion. In the same way in "Hamlet" the fortunes of Denmark remain a subsidiary interest, though with the entrance of Fortinbras they are apparently considered, and are settled at last satisfactorily.

No doubt in the particular end, which resolves the colliding factors, the possibility of fresh interests and conflicts may be presented; it is, however, the *one* collision with which the action is concerned, which has to discover its final adjustment in the essentially independent composition. Of this type are the three tragedies of Sophocles borrowed from the Theban cycle of myths. The first contains the discovery by Oedipus of the murderer of Laius; the second his peaceful death in the home of the Eumenides; the third the fate of Antigone. And, despite this connection, every one of the three is equally an intrinsically complete whole independent of the other two.

(2) *Secondly*, with regard to the mode of development of a dramatic composition, there are three points to consider, in which drama differs from the epic and the song: namely, extent, technique of progression, and division into scenes and acts.

(a) We have already seen that the embrace of a drama is not so extensive as the demand of the Epos implies. I propose, therefore—over and above the two features already discussed of that world-condition, which is necessarily implied in the complete picture of the epic, and the more simple collision which is an equally essential constituent of the content of drama—merely to advert to the further ground, that in the drama the greater part of everything that the muse of the epic poet has to describe and linger over as servant of our imaginative vision, is omitted altogether from the scenic reproduction. And, further, in the case of drama it is not actual exploit, but the exposition of personal passions which is here the main thing. This personal life, however, in contrast to the expanse of the phenomenal world, is concentrated in simple emotions, sentences, decisions, and the like; and here, too, as distinct from the collateral display of epic narration and its historical part, it gives effect to the principle of lyric absorption and the origination and expression in present time of passion and idea. Dramatic poetry is, however, not satisfied with merely *one* situation; it presents the ideal world of emotional life or intelligence in active self-assertion as a totality of circumstances and ends of very various character, which expresses taken together, all that, if viewed relatively to its activity, passes in such an inward world. In comparison with the lyrical poem, the drama reaches out to and is completed in a far more extensive embrace of subject-matter. To summarize this comparative relation we may say, perhaps, that dramatic poetry stands as a mean between the wide embrace of the Epopaea and the concentrated compression of the Lyric.

(b) Yet more important than this aspect of external exten-

sion is the nature of the *dramatic progression* as opposed to
the mode of the epic's devolution. The form of the epic objectivity demands throughout, as we have seen, a lingering
style of description, which may along with this become more
intense and pointed in its display of active obstruction. It is
possible that we may at first blush incline to the view that,
inasmuch as other ends and characters resist the main end and
principal character in dramatic exposition, dramatic poetry is
entitled to accept this sort of pause and obstacle as an essential feature of its principle. As a matter of fact just the reverse
is the case. The true dramatic progression is a *continuous*
movement *onwards* to the final catastrophe. This is clear from
the simple fact that it is in *collision* that we find the emphatic
turning point. In consequence of this we have the twofold view
of, in the first place, a general strain towards the outbreak of
this conflict, and, secondly, the necessity implied in this discord and contradiction of views, ends, and activities, that they
should find some resolution to which they are driven forwards.
By this we by no means assert that mere celerity of forward
movement is simply in itself beautiful in the dramatic sense.
On the contrary, the dramatic poet should allow himself room
to supply every situation on its own account with all the motives which it truly implies. Episodical scenes, however, which
only impede the action are contrary to the nature of the drama.

(c) As a final point, we may divide the course of the dramatic work most naturally by simply following the stages implied in the notion of dramatic movement itself. In this connection Aristotle[2] long ago remarked that a whole is that
which possesses a beginning, a middle, and a conclusion. He
further defined a beginning as that which, of itself necessary,
does not issue from something else, and out of which something other than itself issues and proceeds. The end is the reverse of this, namely, that which originates from something
else, either of necessity, or mainly so at least, but which does
not itself lead to further consequence. The middle is that which
both issues from something else, and also is that from which
something else proceeds.

Now no doubt in the reality of our experience every action

[2] Poet., c. 7.

includes many presuppositions which make it a difficult matter to decide the exact point where we may find the true commencement. In so far, however, as dramatic action rests essentially on a definite state of collision, the right point of departure
will lie in the situation, out of which the future devolution of
that conflict, despite the fact that it has not as yet broken out,
will none the less in its further course issue. The end, on the
contrary, will then be attained, when the resolution of the discord and its development is secured in every possible respect.
In the midway condition between origination and end we have
the conflict of ends, and the struggle of individual persons in
collision. These different sections are, in dramatic plots, the
phases or moments of the action, and the definition of this is
admirably indicated by the *acts* of the piece. They are now of
course more or less equivalent to pauses of time, and a prince
on one occasion, who was either in a hurry, or wished the action to proceed without interruption, blamed his chamberlain
openly that such a pause occurred. With regard to their *number, three* such acts for every kind of drama is the number that
will adapt itself most readily to intelligible theory. Of these
the *first* discloses the appearance of the collision, which is
thereupon emphasized in the *second* with all the animation of
conflicting interests as the positive difference of such discord
and its progression, until, *finally*, driven as it were upon the
very apex of its contradiction, it is necessarily resolved. We
may cite—as an appropriate analogue of this division which
the nature of such an action suggests—from ancient drama, in
which no doubt the dramatic articulation is as a rule less distinct, the trilogies of Aeschylus, in which each part is nevertheless rounded out to form a single and completely exclusive
whole. In modern poetry the Spaniards mainly follow a division into three acts. The English, French, and Germans, on
the contrary, for the most part divide the entire play into *five*
acts, in which the initial exposition is assigned to the first, the
three next are occupied with the various aggressions and reactionary effects, the complex intentions and conflicts of the
opposed parties; and it is not until the fifth that we reach the
entire resolution of such contending forces.

(3) The third and final important aspect we have to investigate in our present connection is the nature of the *external*

means, in so far as the employment of the same by dramatic art can be held distinct from and independent of the actual scenic representation that is otherwise essential to its complete display. An account, first, of the specific nature of dramatically effective diction, secondly, of the distinguishing features of the monologue, dialogue, and the like, and, lastly, of verse measure, will be all that is necessary here. As we have more than once insisted, in the drama the principal aspect is not the actual happening, but the exposition of the ideal spirit of the action, not merely in respect to the *dramatis personae* and their passion, pathos, resolve, interaction, and mediation, but also relatively to the universal essence of the action in its conflict and destiny. It is this ideally pregnant spirit, in so far as poetry gives embodiment to it in poetic form, which pre-eminently discovers an appropriate expression in the language of poetry, viewing this, as we should, as the most spiritual way of expressing emotions and ideas.

(a) But, moreover, just as the drama combines the principles of the Epos and the Lyric, dramatic diction, too, is compelled both to carry and assert within itself elements that are lyrical and those that are epic. The *lyrical* approach finds its place especially in modern drama, and as a rule in those cases where the personal life is or tends to be self-absorbed, and seeks in its decision and action throughout to retain the self-consciousness of its inward resources. But none the less this unveiling of the individual heart-life, if it is to remain dramatic, ought not merely to be the exploitation of a vague and variable cloud of emotions, memories, and visions; it should keep its relation to the action constant throughout, should make its result identical with that of the different phases of the same.

In contrast to this subjective pathos the epic character of the diction, which we may define as the *objective* pathos, is mainly concerned with the unfolding of what is substantive in dramatic relations, ends, and persons on lines rather directed to the vision of the audience. Such a point of view can also in part assume a lyrical tone, remaining when it does so dramatic only in so far as it does not move entirely in its independent force from the progress of the action and its asserted relation to the same. And over and above this, as a second residue, so to speak, of epic poetry, we may have the records of narrative, descriptions of battles and the like thrown in. But these also, in genuine dramatic composition, ought to be marked with greater compression and animated movement, and, relatively to their presentment as narrative, a necessary connection with the progress of the action should be evident.

In conclusion, genuine dramatic art consists in the expression of individuals in the conflict of their interests and the discord roused between their characters and their transitory passions. It is here that the twofold aspect of lyric and epic poetry will assert its power in true dramatic union: and we have then attached to this the aspect of positive external fact expressed likewise in the medium of language, as where we have, for instance, the departure and entrance of *dramatis personae* as a rule announced beforehand; not unfrequently also their external habit or demeanour is indicated by other persons.

A fundamental distinction over the entire field now under review is the so-called realistic mode of expression, as opposed to a conventional speech of the theatre and its rhetoric. Diderot, Lessing, Goethe, and Schiller also in their youth addressed themselves in modern times above all to this attitude of direct and natural expression. Lessing did so with the powers of a trained and sensitive observation. Schiller and Goethe did so with their predilection for the direct animation of unembellished robustness and force. That men should converse with one another as in the Greek, or with more insistence—and in this latter respect the criticism has a reasonable basis—as in French comedy and tragedy was scouted as contrary to Nature. This type of naturalism, however, may very readily, with its superfluity of merely realistic traits, fall into the other extreme of dryness and prose, in so far, that is, as the characters are not developed in the essential qualities of their emotional life and action, but only as they happen to express themselves in the literal accuracy of their individual life, without indicating therein any more significant self-consciousness or any further sense of their essential position. The more natural the characterization is allowed to remain in this sense the more prosaic it becomes. In actual life men converse and strive with one another before everything else on the mere basis of their *distinct singularity*. If our object is to depict them simply

as such it is impossible that they should also be represented
in their truly substantive significance. And, if we look at the
essence of the matter, this question of crudeness and urbanity
can only be in the last instance treated subject to the above
considerations. In other words while, on the one hand, such
crudeness or coarseness is made to issue from the particular
personality, which yields itself to the immediate suggestions of
an uncultured mind and way of feeling, in the converse treatment, urbanity rises only to a purely abstract and formal
generalization of consideration for others, recognition of the
claims of personality, love, honour, and the like, in which,
however, nothing that is suggestive of a rich and objective
content can be expressed. Between these two extremes of a
purely formal generality and this natural expression of unpol-
ished peculiarities we have the true universal, which is
throughout neither formal nor destitute of individuality, but
finds its concrete realization in a twofold way from the defined
content of character and the objective presence of opinions and
aims. Genuine poetry will therefore consist in the assertion of
what belongs to immediate and actual life as characteristic and
individual in the purifying medium of universality, both aspects being permitted to mediate each other. In this case we
are conscious, even in respect to diction, that without being
wholly banished from the basis of reality and its actual traits
of truth, we are nevertheless carried into another sphere, that
is to say the ideal realm of art. Of this latter character
is the diction of Greek dramatic poetry, the later diction of
Goethe, and in part, too, that of Schiller, and in his own way
Shakespeare's also, although the Englishman, owing to the peculiar conditions of the contemporary stage, is forced in part
now and again to accommodate his verbal language to the
actual ability of the actor.

(b) We may *further* classify the mode of dramatic expression as that of choral interlude, monologue, and dialogue. It
is the ancient drama which has pre-eminently elaborated the
distinction between chorus and dialogue. In our modern drama
this falls away. What, in the classical composition, was presented by the *chorus,* is now rather placed in the mouths of
the leading characters. The choric song expresses, among the
ancients, by way of contrast to the particular characters and

their more personal or more reciprocal conflict, the general or
more impersonal view of the situation, and the emotions it
excites, in a manner which at one time inclines to the objective style of epic narrative, at another to the impulsive movement of the Lyric. In the *monologue*, on the other hand, it is
the isolated individual who, in a given situation of the action,
becomes objective on his own account. Monologues are, therefore, dramatically in their right place at those moments chiefly
when the emotional life is entirely self-concentrated as the result of previous events; when it sums up, as it were, the nature
of the cleft between itself and others, or its own spiritual division; or when it arrives at some sudden decision, or comes
to the final point of resolve on matters already long debated.

The *third* and complete form of the drama, however, is the
dialogue. For in this the *dramatis personae* are mutually able
to express their character and aims, not merely relatively to
their personal attitude to each other, but also to the substantive character of the pathos disclosed; they engage in conflict,
and thereby actually advance the movement of the action. We
may further distinguish in the dialogue between the expression of a pathos that is *subjective* and one that is *objective*. The
first rather appertains to a given passion of more accidental
a nature, whether it be the case in which it is retained essentially in suppression, and is only expressed aphoristically, or
that in which it finds a vent in the most complete and exhaustive explosion. Poets, who endeavour to arouse the full movement of personal emotion by means of poignant scenes, are
exceptionally partial to this type of pathos. Nevertheless, despite all their endeavour to depict personal suffering and un-
restrained passion, or the unreconciled inward dissension of
soul-life, it remains the fact that the human soul, in its depth,
is less affected thereby than it is through a pathos, wherein
at the same time a genuine objective content is evolved. For
this reason the earlier plays of Goethe, despite all the real
penetration of their subject-matter and the natural force of
their dialogue, make on the whole a weaker impression. And,
in the same way, outbreaks of unrelieved distraction and un-
restrained fury, affect a truly healthy sense only in subordinate
degree; and, above all, what is wholly frightful rather chills us
than makes the blood flow. The poet may describe passion

with all the overwhelming power possible. It is ineffective; the heart is merely rent in pieces, and turns aside from it. What we fail to find here is that which art can least dispense with, the positive aspect of reconciliation. The ancient tragedians, therefore, mainly sought for their effect by means of the objective type of pathos; nor is there wanting here genuine human individuality, so far as this was compatible with their art. The plays, also, of Schiller possess this pathos of a great spiritual force, a pathos which is penetrative throughout, and is manifested and expressed everywhere as fundamental to the action. It is, above all, to this circumstance that we may ascribe the lasting effect which the tragedies of Schiller produce even in our own day; I refer in particular to their scenic reproduction. For that which produces a profound dramatic effect of universal and enduring appeal can be only the substantive in action—by which I mean, viewing it as definite content, the ethical substance therein, or, in its more formal aspect, the grandeur of ideal reach and character, in which respect, again, Shakespeare is supreme.

(c) I will, in conclusion, add merely a word or two on the point of *verse-measure*. Dramatic metre is best when it lies midway between the tranquil, uniform flow of the hexameter and the more interrupted and split-up syllabic metres congenial to the Lyric. In this respect the iambic metre is above all others commendable. For the iambus, with the rhythm of its onward movement, which may be either accelerated by anapaests, or be made more solemn and weighty with the spondee, forms a most fitting accompaniment to the march of the action; and in quite a peculiar way the senarius possesses a real tone of noble and restrained emotional force. Among modern authors the Spaniards, with an artistic purpose the reverse of this, adopt trochaeic tetrameters, the effect of which is one of tranquil retardation; a measure which, with its variety of interwoven rhymes and assonances, in part, too, with its alternative absence of rhyme, is admirably adapted to the imaginative exuberance of phantasy, and to the fine-drawn argumentative antitheses, which characterize this poetry and impede rather than advance the action. In a contrast of a similar kind, the French Alexandrine is harmonious with the formal carriage and the declamatory rhetoric of passions, sometimes held in restraint and at others expressed at full heat, the conventional expression of which the art of French drama has tasked itself to elaborate. The more realistic Englishman, whom we Germans too have followed in more recent times, has, on the contrary, retained the iambic metre, which Aristotle long ago defined as τὸ μάλιστα λεκτικὸν τῶν μέτρων.[3] He has, however, not accepted the same in identical form with the Greek trimeter, but substituted a measure of less pathetic character, if capable of the greatest freedom of treatment.

c. The Relation of the Dramatic Composition to the General Public

Although the advantages or defects of diction and metre are important, also, in epic and lyrical poetry, we must nevertheless ascribe a more emphatic effect to them in dramatic compositions, in virtue of the circumstance that we are in this case dealing with opinions, characters, and actions which have to appear before us in all the reality of life itself. A comedy of Calderon, for example, with all the interplay of fantastic wit we may assume, embodied, however, in the kind of diction we associate with this poet, with its logical niceties and its bombast—subject, also, to all the variations of his lyrical metres—would not, we may presume, on the simple ground of this manner of expression, be likely to arouse any general sympathy. It is on account of this visual presence and nearness of approach that the other aspects of the content, apart from that of purely dramatic form, are brought into a far more direct relation to the public before whom they are reproduced. We should like shortly to explain the nature of this.

Scientific compositions and lyrical or epic poems either possess a distinct public, whose interest in such works is associated with their profession, or it is a matter of chance into what hands compositions of this character may fall. If a book does not please anyone it can be neglected, just as a man passes by the picture or statue that he does not like; such works may, in fact, be held to carry to some extent with them the author's

[3] Poet., c. 4. ["the most speakable of metres."]

admission that his book is not written for such. The case is somewhat otherwise with dramatic works. Here we have a distinct public for which the author has to cater, and he is under certain obligations towards it. Such a public possesses the right of applause no less than expressed displeasure; inasmuch as a work is represented before it in its entirety, and the appeal is made that it should be enjoyed with sympathy in a given place and at a stated time. A public of this sort, as in the case of any other public jury, is of a very varied character; it differs in its education, interests, accustomed tastes, and hobbies, so that to secure complete success in certain distinct respects a talent in the display of vulgar effect, or at least a relative shame-facedness in regard to the finest demand of genuine art, may be necessary. No doubt the dramatic poet has always the alternative left him to despise his public. But in that case he obviously fails to secure the very object for which dramatic writing exists. With us Germans, to an exceptional extent, it has become the fashion since the times of Tieck thus to scorn the public. Our German play-writer will express his own particular individuality, but takes no trouble to commend the result to his audience. The ideal of our German egotism is, on the contrary, that every man must turn out something different to that of other people, in order that he may prove his originality. It was owing, in part, to this that Tieck and the brothers Schlegel, men who, from the very nature of their sentimental irony, were quite unable to master the emotional forces and intelligence of their nation and time, fell foul of Schiller, and tried to blacken his poetical reputation on the ground that he did among us Germans manage to strike the right key, and obtain a popularity unsurpassed. With our neighbours, the French, we find the opposite. Their authors write with the present effect on the public always in view, which further, on its own account, is capable of being a keener and less indulgent critic of the author, owing to the fact that a more definite artistic taste is already fixed in France: with us anarchy prevails, and everyone expresses his critical views, applauds or condemns just as he likes, or as his opinions, emotion, and mood may chance to dictate.

Inasmuch, however, as it is an essential part of the definition of the dramatic composition that it should possess the vitality able to command a favourable popular reception, the dramatic poet should submit to the conditions—quite apart, that is, from the accidental circumstances or tendencies of the time—which are likely to secure this result in an artistic form. What these are I will attempt to explain, at least in their more general features.

(1) Now, in the *first* place, the ends, which in a dramatic work come into conflict and are resolved out of such conflict, either possess a general human interest, or at least have at bottom a pathos, which is of a valid and substantive character for the people for whom the poet creates his work. In such a case, however, the universal human quality and what is more definitely national, in so far as either are connected with the substance of dramatic collisions, may lie very widely apart. Compositions which stand in the national life at the very summit of their dramatic art and development may consequently quite fail to be appreciated by another age and nation. We find, for example, in Hindoo lyrical poetry, even in our own time, much that carries with it a real charm, tenderness, and fascinating sweetness. The particular collision, however, around which the action in the "Sakontala" revolves, in other words, the furious curse upon Sakontala of the Brahman, because she does not see him, and omits to make her obeisance, can only strike us as absurd, so much so in fact that, despite all other excellences in this quite exceptionally beautiful poem, we fail to discover any interest in the very culminating crisis of the action. We may affirm very much the same thing of the way in which the Spaniards treat the motive of personal honour with the abstract severity of a logic, the brutality of which outrages most deeply all our ideas and feelings. Let me recall, for example, the attempt made by our own theatrical management to bring upon the stage one of the less famous plays of Calderon entitled "Clandestine Revenge for Clandestine Insult," an attempt condemned to failure from the first on this ground. Another tragedy, which on similar lines portrays a more profound human conflict, "The Physician of his own Honour," under the changed title of "The Intrepid Prince," has after some revision secured more leeway; but this, too, is handicapped by its abstract and unyielding Catholic principle. Conversely, and in an opposite direction, the Shakespearean

tragedies and comedies are appreciated by a public that is constantly increasing. We find here that, despite all their nationality, the universal human interest is incomparably greater. Shakespeare has only failed to secure an entrance where the national conventions of art are so narrow and specific that they either wholly exclude or materially weaken works of the Shakespearean type. A similar position of advantage, such as that we allow to Shakespeare, would be attributable to the tragedies of the ancients, if we did not, apart from our changed habits in respect to scenic reproduction and certain aspects of the national consciousness, make the further demand of a profounder psychological penetration and a greater breadth of particular characterization. So far, however, as the *subject-matter* of ancient tragedy is concerned, it could never at any time fail in its effect. We may, therefore, broadly affirm that, in proportion as a dramatic work accepts for its content wholly specific rather than typical characters and passions, conditioned, that is, exclusively by definite tendencies of a particular epoch of history, instead of mainly concerning itself with human interests substantive in all times, to that extent, despite of all its other advantages, it will be more transitory.

(2) And, *further,* it is necessary that universal human ends and actions of this kind should emphasize their poetic individualization to the point of animated life itself. Dramatic composition does not merely address itself to our sense of vitality, a sense which even the public certainly ought to possess, but it must itself, in all essentials, offer a living actual presence of situations, conditions, characters, and actions.

(a) I have already, in a previous passage of this work, entered into some detail relatively to the aspect of local environment, customs, usages and other matters which affect the visual representation of action. In this respect dramatic individualization ought to be either so thoroughly poetical, vital, and rich with interest that we can discount what is alien to our sense, and feel ourselves attracted to the performance by this vital claim on our attention, or it should not pretend to do more than present such characteristics as external form, which is entirely outshone by the spiritual and ideal characteristics which underlie it.

(b) More important than this external aspect is the vitality of the *dramatis personae*. Such ought not to be merely specific interests personified, which is only too frequently the case at the hands of modern dramatists. Such abstract impersonations of particular passions and aims are wholly destitute of dramatic effect. A purely superficial individualization is equally insufficient. Content and form in such cases, as in the analogous type of allegorical figures, fail to coalesce. Profound emotions and reflections, imposing ideas and language offer no real compensation. Dramatic personality ought to be, on the contrary, vital and self-identical throughout, a complete whole in short, the opinions and characterization of which are consonant with its aims and action. It is not the breadth of particular traits which is here of first importance, but the permeating individuality, which synthetically binds all in the central unity, which it in truth is, and displays a given personality in speech and action as issuing from one and the same living source, from which every characteristic, whether it be of idea, deed or manner of behaviour, comes into being. That which is merely an aggregate of different qualities and activities, even though such be strung together in one string, will not give us the vital character we require. This presupposes from the point of view of the poet himself a creative activity which is instinct with life and imagination. It is to the latter type, for instance, that the characters of the Sophoclean tragedies belong, despite the fact that they do not possess the variety of particular characteristics which distinguish the epic heroes of Homer. Among later writers Shakespeare and Goethe are pre-eminently famous for the vitality of their characterization. The French, on the contrary, particularly in their earlier dramatic compositions, appear to have been rather content to excogitate characters that are little more than the formal impersonations of general types and passions, than to have aimed at giving us true and living persons.

(c) But, *thirdly*, the task of dramatic creation is not completed with the presentment of vital characterization. Goethe's "Iphigenia" and "Tasso" throughout are good enough examples of this poetic excellence—and yet they are not, if we look at them more strictly, by any means perfect examples of dramatic vitality and movement. It is for this reason that Schiller long ago remarked of the "Iphigenia," that it is the ethical content, the heart experience, the personal opinion which is there made the object of the action, and is as such visually reproduced. And unquestionably the display and expression of the personal experience of different characters in definite situations is not by itself sufficient; we must also have real emphasis laid on the collision of the *ultimate ends* involved, and the forward and conflicting movement which such imply. Schiller is consequently of the view that the movement of the "Iphigenia" is not sufficiently disturbed; we are permitted to linger within it too long and easily. He even maintains that it without question inclines to the sphere of epic composition, if we contrast it at least with any strict conception of tragedy. In other words, dramatic effect is action simply as action; it is not the exposition of personality alone, or practically independent of the express purpose and its final achievement. In the Epos play may be permitted to the breadth and variety of character, external conditions, occurrences and events; in the drama, on the contrary, the self-concentration of its principle is most asserted relatively to the particular collision and its conflict. It is thus that we recognize the truth of Aristotle's dictum,[4] that tragic action possesses two sources (αἴτια δύο), opinion and character (διάνοια καὶ ἦθος), but what is most important is the end (τέλος), and individuals do not act in order to display diverse characters, but these latter are united with a common bond of imaginative conception to the former in the interest of the action.

(3) As a matter for our *final* consideration in this place there is the relation in which the *poet* is placed to the general public. Epic poetry in its truly primitive state requires that the poet place wholly on one side his distinctive personality in its contrast to his actually objective work. He offers us the content of that and only that. The lyric poet, on the contrary, deliberately expresses his own emotional life and his personal views of the world.

(a) We might imagine that the poet must perforce withdraw himself in the drama by reason of the very fact that he brings action before us in its sensuous presence, and makes the characters speak and active in their own names, to a

[4] Poet., c. 6.

greater extent than in the Epos, in which he appears at any rate as narrator of the events. Such an impression is only, however, very partially valid. For, as I have already contended, the drama is exclusively referable in its origin to those epochs, in which the personal self-consciousness, both relatively to the general outlook on life and artistic culture, has already reached a high degree of development. A dramatic composition therefore should not, as an epic one does, present the appearance as though it originated from the popular consciousness simply, for the display of which content the poet is merely an instrument of expression which possesses no reference to the poet's personal life; rather what we seek to recognize in the complete work is quite as much the product of the self-aware and original creative force, and by reason of this the art and virtuosity of a genuine poetic personality. It is only thereby that dramatic productions attain to the genuine excellence of their artistic vitality and definition, as contrasted with the actions and events of natural life. It is on this account that where the authorship of dramatic works is a subject of controversy we find such to be nowhere more frequent than where it concerns the primitive Epopaea.

(b) From the opposite point of view the general public too, if it has itself preserved a true sense of meaning of art, will not submit to have placed before it in a drama the more accidental moods and opinions, the peculiar tendencies and the one-sided outlook of this or that individual, the expression of which is more appropriate to the lyric poet. It has a right to demand that in the course and final issue of the dramatic action, whether of tragedy or comedy, what is fundamentally reasonable and true should be vindicated. Being myself convinced of this I have in a previous passage given a place of first importance to the demand that the dramatic poet must in the profoundest sense make himself master of the essential significance of human action and the divine order of the world, and along with this of a power to unfold this eternal and essential foundation of all human characters, passions and destinies in its clarity as also in its vital truth. It is no doubt quite possible that a poet, in rising equal to this demand upon his powers of penetration and artistic achievement, may under particular circumstances find himself in conflict with the restricted and uncultured ideas of his age and nation. In such a case the responsibility for such a disunion does not rest with himself, but is a burden the public ought to carry. He has the single obligation to follow the lead of truth and his own compelling genius, the ultimate victory of which, provided it is of the right quality, is no less assured than that of ultimate truth itself universally.

It is impossible to define closely the limits within which a dramatic poet is entitled to bring his actual personality before the public. I will therefore merely recall attention to the fact in a general way that in many periods of history dramatic poetry, no less than other kinds, is induced to disseminate with a vital impulse novel ideas upon politics, morals, poetry, religion, and the like. So early as Aristophanes we have polemics in those comedies of his youth against the domestic condition of Athens and the Peloponnesian war. Voltaire again frequently endeavours in his dramatic works to popularize his free thought principles. But above all worthy of notice is the effort of our Lessing in his "Nathan" to vindicate his ethical faith against the strait waistcoat of a blockish orthodoxy. In still more recent times too Goethe has in his earliest works challenged the prose of our German life and its defective views of art. Tieck has to some extent followed his lead in this respect. Where personal views of the above type are not only of superior worth, but are further not expressed in such deliberate separation from the action of the drama as to make the latter appear as a mere means for their exploitation, the claims of true art are not likely to suffer injury. If, however, the freedom of the composition is thereby impaired, though no doubt the poet may possibly produce no inconsiderable impression on the public by his introduction of his own predilections into his work; yet, however true they may be, if they are at the same time unable to coalesce with the work as an artistic whole the interest thereby aroused can only be limited to the matters thus handled; it is in fact no true artistic interest at all. The worst case of all is that, however, where a poet with similar deliberation seeks, out of pure flattery and in order to please, to give prominence to some popular prejudice which is entirely false. His sins of commission are in that case twofold, not merely against art, but truth no less.

(c) One further remark may be perhaps admitted in this connection to the effect that among the particular types of dramatic art a more limited measure of indulgence is permitted to tragedy than to comedy in this more free expatiation of the personality of the poet. In the latter type the contingency and caprice of individual self-expression is from the first agreeable to its main principle. Thus we find that Aristophanes frequently makes matters of immediate interest to his Athenian public the subject of his parabases. In portions of these he gives free utterance to his own views upon contemporary events and circumstances, and withal shrewd advice to his fellow citizens. He is at other times concerned to defend himself from the attacks of political opponents and his artistic rivals. Indeed there are passages in which he deliberately eulogizes himself and his peculiarities.

2. COMPOSITION AND EXTERNAL REPRESENTATION OF DRAMATIC WORKS OF ART

Poetry, alone among the arts, completely dispenses with the sensuous medium of the objective world of phenomena. Inasmuch moreover as the drama does not interpret to the imaginative vision the exploits of the past, or express an ideal personal experience to mind and soul, but rather is concerned to depict an action in all the reality of its actual presence, it would fall into contradiction with itself if it were forced to remain limited to the means which poetry, simply as such, is in a position to offer. The present action no doubt belongs entirely to the personal self, and from this point of view complete expression is possible through the medium of language. From an opposite one, however, the movement of action is towards objective reality, and it requires the complete man to express its movement in his corporeal existence, deed and demeanour, as well as the physiognomical expression of emotions and passions, and not only these on their own account, but in their effect on other men, and the reactions which are thereby brought into being. Moreover, in the display of individuality in its actual presence, we require further an external environment, a specific *locale,* in which such movement and action is achieved. Consequently dramatic poetry, by virtue of the fact that no one of these aspects can be permitted to remain in their immediate condition of contingency, but have all to be reclothed in an artistic form as phases of fine art itself, is compelled to avail itself of the assistance of pretty well all the other arts. The surrounding scene is to some extent, just as the temple is, an architectonic environment, and in part also external Nature, both aspects being conceived and executed in pictorial fashion. In this *locale* the sculpturesque figures are presented with the animation of life, and their volition and emotional states are artistically elaborated, not merely by means of expressive recitation, but also through a picturesque display of gesture and of posture and movement, which, in its objective form, is inspired by the inward soul-life. In this respect we may have brought home to us a distinction which recalls a feature I have at an earlier stage indicated in the sphere of music as the opposition implied in the arts of declamation and melody. In other words, just as in declamatory music language in its spiritual signification is the aspect of most importance, to the characteristic expression of which the musical aspect is entirely subordinate, whereas the movement of melody is unfolded freely on its own account in its own specific medium, although it too is able to assimilate the content of language—so also dramatic poetry, on the one hand, avails itself of those sister arts merely as instrumental to a material basis and environment, out of which the language of poetry is in its free domination asserted as the commanding central focus, upon and around which all else really revolves. From the further point of view, however, that which in the first instance had merely the force of an assistant and accompaniment, becomes an object on its own account, and receives the appearance in its own domain of an essentially independent beauty. Declamation passes into song, action into the mimic of the dance, and scenery in its splendour and pictorial fascination itself puts forward a claim to artistic perfection.

In contrasting, then, a contrast frequently insisted upon, and more particularly in recent times, poetry in its simplicity with the external dramatic execution such as we have above described, we may continue the course of our review under the following heads of discussion:

First, there is the dramatic poetry whose object is to restrict itself to the ordinary ground of poetry, and consequently does not contemplate the theatrical representation of its productions.

Secondly, we have the genuine art of the theatre, to the extent, that is, in which it is limited to recitation, play of pose and action, under the modes in which the language of the poet is able throughout to remain the definitive and decisive factor.

Lastly, there is that type of reproduction which admits the employment of every means of scenery, music, and dance, and suffers the same to assert an independent position as against the dramatic language.

a. The Reading and Recitation of Dramatical Compositions

The true sensuous medium or instrument of dramatic poetry is, as we have seen, not only the human voice and the spoken word, but the entire man, who not merely expresses emotions, ideas, and thoughts, but, as vitally absorbed in a concrete action, in virtue of all that he is influences the ideas, designs, the action and behaviour of others, experiences similar effects on himself, or maintains his independent opposition to them.

(1) In contrast to such a definite view, which is based upon the essential character of dramatic poetry itself, it is a feature of modern notions on the subject, particularly so among ourselves, to regard the organization of drama with a view to its theatrical reproduction as unessential and subsidiary, although as a fact all dramatic authors, even when they adopt this attitude of indifference and contempt, entertain the wish and hope to see their compositions on the stage. The result is that the greater number of more recent dramas are unable ever to find a stage, and the simple reason of this is that they are undramatical. We are not of course, therefore, in a position to deny that a dramatic composition may satisfy the conditions of genuine poetry in virtue of its intrinsic worth. What

we affirm is that it is only to an action, the dramatic course of which is admirably adapted to theatrical representation, that we are to attribute such intrinsic dramatic worth. The best authority for such a statement is supplied by the Greek tragedies. It is true that we no longer see these on the contemporary stage, but they do nevertheless, if we regard the facts more closely, completely satisfy us to a real extent precisely on this ground that they were written without reserve for the theatre of their day. What has banished them from the theatre of to-day is not so much the character of their dramatic organization, which differs mainly from that of to-day in its employment of the chorus, as in the nature of national predilections and conditions, upon which for the most part, if we consider their content, they are based, and in which owing to the distance in which they are placed relatively to our own contemporary life we are unable now to feel ourselves at home. The malady of Philoctetes, for instance, the loathsome ulcer on his foot, his ejaculations and outcries, are as little likely to awaken the genuine interest of a modern audience as the arrows of Hercules, about which the main course of that drama revolves. In a similar way, though we may admit the barbaric cruelty of the human sacrifice in the "Iphigenia in Aulis" and "Tauris" in an opera, we find it absolutely necessary in tragedy at any rate that this aspect should be wholly revised as Goethe has in fact done.

(2) The difference, however, thus indicated between ancient and modern customs, which affects the mere perusal of such works, no less than the complete and vital reproduction of them as a whole, has had the further effect of pointing out to us another by-way, in which poets to some extent deliberately fashion their work exclusively for the reader's perusal, and in a manner by which the difficulty above indicated no longer affects the character of such compositions. There are no doubt in this connection isolated points of view, which merely refer to features of external form, which are implied in the so-called knowledge of the stage, and an indifference as to which does not lessen the poetical worth of a dramatical production. To these belong, for example, the careful regulation of the scenic arrangements, that one scene can follow without difficulty after another, though it requires great altera-

tions in the scenery, or that the actor is given sufficient time
to make the necessary change of costume, or to recover from
his previous exertions. A knowledge and aptitude of this nature is neither indicative of any poetical superiority or the reverse; they rather depend upon the naturally varying and conventional arrangements of the theatre. There are, however,
other features relatively to which the poet, in order to be truly
dramatical, must have the animated reproduction visibly present in its substance, must make his *dramatis personae* speak
and act conformably thereto, that is, in complete congruity
with an actually present realization. Viewed in this light
theatrical reproduction is a real test. For in the presence of
the supreme court of appeal of a sound and artistic public the
mere speeches and tirades of our so-called exquisite diction,
if dramatic truth is not thereby asserted, will not hold water.
There are periods, no doubt, in which the public also is corrupted by the culture it is the fashion so highly to praise, I
mean by heads generally overstocked with the current opinions and fancies of the connoisseur and critic. Let it however
only retain its own essentially sterling common sense, and it
will only be satisfied in those cases where characters express
themselves and act precisely as the reality of life no less than
art demands and necessitates. If the poet, on the contrary,
writes exclusively for the single reader he very readily gets no
further than making his characters speak and behave much as
they might do in an epistolary correspondence. If any one thus
gives us the reasons for his aims and what he does, or unbares
his heart in any other respect, instead of that which we should
at once remark thereupon we get between the receipt of the
letter and our immediate reply time for all kinds of reflection
and idea. The imagination opens in this case a wide field of possibilities. In the *actually present* speech and rejoinder we have
to presuppose that as between man and man the volition and
heart, the movement of feeling and decision are more direct,
that in short the dialogue passes on without any such recourse
to considerable reflection, but at once from soul to soul, as eye
to eye, mouth to mouth, and ear to ear. Only in such a case
the actions and speeches are expressed with life from the actual personality, who has no time left him to make a careful
selection of one out of many possibilities. Under this view of

the case it is not unimportant for the poet throughout his composition to keep his eye on the stage, which renders such a direct type of animation necessary. Nay, for myself I go to the length of maintaining that no dramatic work ought to be printed, but rather, as no doubt with the ancients, it should belong to the stage repertory in manuscript form, and only receive quite an insignificant circulation. We should at least in that case limit very considerably the present superabundance of dramas, which it is possible possess the speech of culture, fine sentiments, excellent reflections, and profound thoughts, but which are defective in the very direction which makes a drama dramatical, that is, in the display of action, and the vital movement which belongs to it.

(3) In the mere *perusal* and *reading aloud* of dramatic compositions we find a difficulty in deciding whether they are of a type which would produce the due effect from the stage. Even Goethe, whose experience of stage management in his later years was exceptional, was far from being dependable on this head, a result no doubt mainly due to the extraordinary confusion of our public taste, which is able to accept with approval almost anything and everything. If the character and object of the *dramatis personae* are on their own account great and substantive the manner of composition no doubt presents less difficulty. But as regards the motive force of interests, the various phases in the progress of the action, the suspended interest and development of situations, the just degree in which characters assert their effect on each other, the appropriate force and truth of their demeanour and speech—in all such respects the mere perusal unassisted by a theatrical performance can only in the rarest cases arrive at a reliable decision. Reading a work aloud is only under great qualification a further assistance. Speech in drama requires the presence of separate individuals. The delivery of *one voice*, however artistically it may adapt itself to different shades of tone in alternate or varying change is insufficient. Add to this the fact that in reading aloud we are throughout confronted with the difficulty whether on every occasion the persons speaking should be mentioned or not. Both alternatives are equally open to objection. If the delivery is that of one voice the statement of the names of the characters speaking becomes an indispensa-

ble condition of intelligibility, but by doing so the expression of pathos throughout suffers violence. If, on the other hand, the delivery is vitally dramatic, and we are carried thereby into the actual situation, a further kind of contradiction can hardly fail to appear. For with the satisfaction of our sense of hearing that of sight puts forward a certain claim of its own. For when we listen to an action we desire to see the acting persons, their demeanour and surroundings; the eye craves for a completed vision, and finds instead before it merely a reciter, who sits or stands peacefully in a private house with company. Reading aloud or recitation is consequently always an unsatisfying compromise between the unambitious pretensions of private perusal, in which the aspect of realization is absent entirely and all is left to the imagination, and the complete theatrical presentation.

b. The Art of the Actor

In conjunction with actual dramatic reproduction there is along with music a second practical art, namely, that of *acting*, the complete development of which belongs entirely to more recent times. Its principle consists in this, that while it summons to its assistance dramatic posture, action, declamation, music, dance, and scenery, it accepts as the predominant mark of its effort human speech and its poetical expression. And this is for poetry in its simplest significance the exclusively just relation. For if mere mimicry or song or dance once begin to assume an independent position of their own, poetry viewed as a fine and creative art is degraded to the position of an instrument, and loses its ascendancy over the, in other respects, accompanying arts. We will venture to point out a few characteristic distinctions in this connection.

(1) The primary phase of the art of acting is to be found among the Greeks. Here, as one aspect of the matter, the art of speech is affiliated with that of sculpture. The acting *dramatis persona* stands before us as an objective figure in his entire bodily realization. In so far as here this statuesque figure is animated, assimilates and expresses the content of the poetry, enters into every movement of personal passion and at the

same time asserts it through word and voice, this presentation
is more animated and more spiritually transparent than any
statue or picture.

As to this quality of living animation we may distinguish
two ways of regarding it.

(a) *First*, there is declamation in the sense of artistic
speech. Declamation was not carried far among the Greeks;
intelligibility is here what is of most importance. We desire
to recognize in the tone of the voice and in the quality of the
recitations the characterization of soul-life in its finest shades
and transitions, as also in its oppositions and contrasts, in short,
in its entire concreteness. The ancients, on the contrary, added
a musical accompaniment to declamation, partly to emphasize rhythm, and in part to increase the modulation of the
verbal expression. At the same time it is probable that the
dialogue was either not at all or only very lightly accompanied.
To the reproduction of the choruses, however, the lyric association of music was essential. It is highly probable that sing-
ing, by means of its more definite accentuation of the meaning
of the language used in the choice strophes and antistrophes,
made the same more intelligible; only under such an assumption can I myself understand how it was possible for a Greek
audience to follow the choruses of either Aeschylus or Sophocles. I admit that such choruses might not necessarily present
to a Greek all the difficulties we ourselves experience; at the
same time I confess that, though I know the German language
well and am not wholly destitute of imagination, German lyrics
written in the same style, if declaimed from the stage, with
the full accompaniment of song, would still be far from wholly
intelligible.

(b) A *further* means of interpretation is supplied by the
pose and movement of the body. In this respect it is worth
noticing that with the Greeks the play of facial expression is
entirely absent, by reason of the fact that their actors wore
masks. The facial contour returned an unalterable sculpturesque image, the plastic outlines of which were as unable to
assimilate the varied expression of particular states of soul, as
to reproduce the acting characters, which fought through a
pathos securely fixed and universal in the nature of its dramatic conflict, and neither deepened the substance of this

pathos to the ideal intensity of our modern emotional life, nor
suffered it to expand into all the particularization of the world
of dramatic individualities now in vogue. The action was
equally simple, for which reason we do not possess any tradition of famous Greek mimes. Sometimes the poet himself was
actor; both Sophocles and Aristophanes are examples. To some
extent the mere citizen, who was not strictly a professional
actor at all, took a part in tragedy. As a set-off to such difficulties the choric songs were accompanied with the dance,
a procedure which can only appear frivolous to us Germans
in the view we generally take of the dance. With the Greeks it
belonged as an essential feature to their theatrical performances.

(c) To summarize, then, we find that among the ancients
not only was the poetical claim of language, and the intelligible expression of general emotional states, freely admitted,
but also the external realization received the most complete
elaboration by means of musical accompaniment and the
dance. A concrete unity of this kind gives to the entire presentation a plastic character. What is spiritual is not on its own
account self-concentrated, nor is it expressed under such a
mode of particularization; the main effect is to bring about its
complete affiliation and reconciliation with the external aspect
of sensuous appearance whose correspondent claim is equally
recognized.

(2) In rivalry with music and the dance speech suffers injury, in so far as it ought to remain the *spiritual* expression
of spirit. Our modern art of the theatre has consequently suc-
ceeded in liberating itself from such features. The poet is by
this means exclusively placed in a relation to the actor simply,
who, by his declamation, play of facial expression, and posture, has to represent to vision the poetical work. This relation
of the author to the external material is, however, in its contrast to other arts, quite unique. In painting and sculpture it
is the artist himself, who executes his conceptions in colour,
bronze, or marble; and although musical execution is dependent upon the hands and voices of others, yet the feature thus
added, albeit, of course, the element of soul in the delivery
ought not to be absent, is none the less, to a more or less degree, overwhelmingly mechanical technique and virtuosity.

The actor, on the contrary, appears before us in the entire personality which combines his bodily presence, physiognomy, voice, and so forth, and it is his function to coalesce absolutely with the character he portrays.

(a) In this respect the poet has the right to demand of the actor that he enters with all his faculties into the part he receives, without adding thereto anything peculiar to himself, that, in short, he acts in complete consonance with the creative conception and means of its display supplied by the poet. The actor ought, in fact, to be the instrument upon which the author plays, an artist's brush which absorbs all colours and returns the same unchanged. Among the ancients this was more easily achieved for the reason that declamation, as above stated, was mainly restricted to clarity of meaning, and music looked after the aspect of rhythm, while masks concealed the faces, and, moreover, not much scope was left to the action. Consequently, the actor could without real difficulty conform in his delivery to a universal tragic pathos; and although too, in comedy, portraits of living people such as Socrates, Nicias, Creon, and so forth, had to be represented, in a real measure the masks reproduced characteristic traits with sufficient force, and further we should note that a detailed individualization was less necessary, inasmuch as the comic poets, as a rule, merely introduced such characters in order to represent general tendencies of the time.

(b) The position is different in the modern theatre. Here, to start with, we have no masks or musical accompaniment, but have instead of these the play of facial expression, the variety of pose, and a richly modulated style of declamation. For, on the one hand, human passions, even when they are expressed by the poet in a more general and typical characterization, have none the less to be asserted as part of an inner and personal life; and for the rest our modern characters receive, for the most part, a far more extended compass of particularization, the distinctively appropriate expression of which has in the same way to be placed before us with all the animation of present life. The characters of Shakespeare are, above all, entire men, standing before us in distinctively unique personality, so that we require of our actors that they, for their part, give us back the entire impression of such complete creations. There is no specific rôle here that does not require a definite kind of expression fitted to it, and which covers in fact every feature of its display, whether we regard that which we cannot see or that which we do, whether it be in the tone of the voice, the mode of delivery, gesticulation, or facial expression. For this reason, apart from the nature of the dialogue, the varied character of the pose and gesture, through every possible shade, receives an entirely new significance. In fact, the modern poet leaves to the actor's self-expression here much that the ancients would have expressed in words. Take the example of the final scene of "Wallenstein". The old Octavio has assisted materially in the downfall of Wallenstein. He finds him treacherously murdered by the machinations of Buttler, and at the very moment when the Countess Terzky makes the announcement that she has taken poison, an imperial letter arrives. Gordon, after reading the same, hands it to Octavio with a glance of reproach, adding the words, "To the Lord Piccolomini." Octavio is confounded, and, pained to the heart, glances heavenwards. That which Octavio experiences in this reward for a service, for the bloody issue of which he himself is mainly responsible, is in this passage not expressed in so many words, but is left solely to the gesture of the actor.

(c) Owing to demands of this kind made by our modern art of acting, poetry may, relatively to the material of its presentation, not unfrequently open up difficulties unknown to the ancients. In other words, the actor, being the man he is, possesses, in respect to voice, figure, physiognomical expression, as everybody else, his native peculiarities, which he is compelled to set on one side, either owing to their incompatibility with a pathos of universal import and a really typical characterization, or to bring them into harmony with the more complete personalities of a type of poetry rich in its power of individualization.

Actors claim the title of artists, and receive all the honours of an artistic profession. According to our modern ideas, no taint of any sort, whether ethical or social, is implied in the fact of being a dramatic actor. This view is the right one. The profession demands conspicuous talent, intelligence, perseverance, energy, practice, knowledge, and, indeed, its highest attainment is impossible without the rare qualities of genius. The actor has not only to assimilate profoundly the spirit of the poet and the part he accepts, and to make his own individuality conform entirely to the same, both inwardly and outwardly; he has, over and above this, in many respects to supplement the part with his own creative insight, to fill in gaps, to discover modes of transition, and generally, by his performance, to interpret the poet by making visibly and vitally present and intelligible meanings which lie beneath the surface, or the less obvious touches of a master's hand.

c. The Theatrical Art Which Is More Independent of Poetical Composition

Finally, we have that further, or *third* aspect of the art in its actual employment, where it liberates itself from the exclusive precedency of articulate poetry, and accepts as an independent end what was previously, to a more or less extent, a mere accompaniment or instrument, and elaborates the same on its own account. To carry out this emancipation, music and the dance are quite as much essential features of the dramatic development as the art of the actor simply.

(1) In respect to this change in the art, there are broadly speaking two systems. The first, according to which the performer tends to be simply in spirit and body the living instrument of the poet, we have already referred to. The French, who make much of professional rôles and schools, and are, as a rule, more typical in their theatrical representations, have shown an exceptional fidelity to this system in their tragedy and *haute comédie*. What we may define here as the position of the art of acting reversed consists in this, that the entire creation of the poet now tends to be purely an appendage or frame to and for the natural endowment, technical ability, and art of the actor. It is by no means uncommon to hear actors make the demand that poets should write expressly for them. The sole function of poetical composition is, in this view, to give the artist an opportunity to display and unfold in all its brilliance his emotional powers and art, to let us see the final outcome of his particular individuality. Among the Italians, the *commedia dell' arte* belongs to this type. Here, no doubt,

we have certain definite types of character such as those of the *arlecchino, dottore,* and the like, with appropriate situations and series of scenes; the more detailed execution is, however, almost entirely left to the discretion of the actors. Among ourselves, the dramatic pieces of Iffland and Kotzebue, and many others besides, though in large measure regarded as poetry, unimportant or even bad compositions, nevertheless offer such an opportunity for the creative powers of the actor, who is compelled to initiate and shape something from such generally sketchy and artificial productions, which on account of a vital and independent performance of this kind receive a unique interest exclusively united to one and no other artist. It is here, more especially, that we find our much belauded realistic effects are displayed, a style carried to such lengths that a mere mumble and whisper of articulate speech, quite impossible to follow, will pass as an admirable performance. In protest to such a style, Goethe translated Voltaire's "Tancred" and "Mahomet" for the Weimar stage, in order to compel its actors to drop this vulgar naturalism, and accustom themselves to a more noble exposition. And this is invariably the case with the French, who, even in all the animation of the farce, always keep the audience in view, and throughout address themselves to it. As a matter of fact, mere realism and imitation of our everyday expression is as little exhaustive of the real problem as the mere intelligibility and clever use made of characterization. If an actor seeks to produce a really artistic effect in such cases, he will have to extend his powers to a genial virtuosity similar to that I have described already in a previous passage when referring to musical execution.

(2) A *second* province belonging to the type under consideration is that of the modern *opera,* in the direction, at least, which it more and more is inclined to take. In other words, although in opera, generally speaking, the music is of most importance, which of course possesses a content in partnership with the poetry and the libretto, albeit it treats and executes the same freely as it thinks best, yet in more recent times, and particularly among ourselves, it has become increasingly an affair of luxurious display. It has carried its *accessoires,* in the splendour of its decorations, the pomp of its costumes, the completeness of its choruses and their grouping,

to a degree of independence that throws all else into the shade. It was a magnificence of this kind, sufficiently criticized among ourselves, which Cicero long ago complains of when referring to Roman tragedy. In tragedy, where the poetry is always the most essential thing, such a lavish display of the sensuous side of things is no doubt not in its right place, although Schiller, in his "Maid of Orleans," shows a tendency here to run astray. In the opera, on the contrary, with its sensuous exuberance of song and the melodic, thundering chorus of voices and instruments, we may with more reason admit such an emphasized charm of external embellishment and display. If the decorations are splendid, then the groups and processions, to give point to them, must be equally gorgeous, and everything else must be adapted to the same scale. The subject most suited to a sensuous luxuriance of this kind, which, no doubt, is always some indication of the decline of genuine art, is that part of the entire performance which inclines to the wonderful, fantastic, or fairy tale. Mozart, in his "Magic Flute," has supplied us with an example which is not too extravagant, and is worked out on completely artistic lines. At the same time, we may entirely exhaust all the arts of scenic display, costume, instrumentation and the rest, but the fact remains that, if we are not really in earnest with that part of the content which concerns real dramatic action, the impression upon us can be at the strongest merely that of a perusal of the fairy tale of "The Thousand and One Nights."

(3) The same observations apply to the modern *Ballet*, which above all is most suited to fairy-land and miracle of all kinds. Here, too, we note as one supreme feature, quite apart from the picturesque beauty of the grouping and tableaux, the kaleidoscopic splendour and fascination of the decorations, costumes, and lighting, to an extent that ordinary persons find themselves transported into a world in which common sense and the laws and pressure of our daily life vanish altogether. As a further aspect of these performances, connoisseurs in such subjects will go into ecstasies over the elaborately trained dexterity and virtuosity of legs, which is nowadays an essential feature of the dance. If, however, any more spiritual significance is to flash athwart such mere physical agility, which we have reduced to the final ultimatum of senselessness and

ideal poverty, we ought to have associated with the complete
command over all the executive difficulties implied a real
measure and euphony of movement, a freedom and grace such
as finds a response in the soul; and it is only very rarely that
we do so. As a further element in association with the dance
here, which stands in the place of the choruses and solos of
the opera, we find as real expression of action the Pantomime.
This, however, in proportion as our modern dance has advanced in technical dexterity, has fallen from the rank which
it once possessed, and, indeed, has so deteriorated that the
very thing tends once more to drop out of the modern ballet
altogether, which is alone able to lift the same into the free
domain of art.

3. TYPES OF DRAMATIC POETRY AND THE CHIEF PHASES OF THEIR HISTORICAL DEVELOPMENT

Viewing for a moment the course of our present inquiry in
retrospect, it will be seen that we have, *first*, established the
principle of dramatic poetry in its widest and more specific
characteristics, and, further, in its relation to the general public. *Secondly*, we deduced from the fact of the drama's presenting an action distinct and independent in its actually visible development the conclusion that a fully complete sensuous
reproduction is also essential, such as is for the first time possible under artistic conditions in the theatrical performance.
In order that the action, however, may adapt itself to an external realization of this kind, it is necessary that both in
poetic conception and detailed execution it should be absolutely definite and complete. This is only effected, our *third*
point, by resolving dramatic poetry into *particular types*, receiving their typical character, which is in part one of opposition and also one of mediatory relation to such opposition, from
the distinction, in which not only the end but also the characters, as also the conflict and entire result of the action, are
manifested. The most important aspects emerging from this
distinction, and carrying it into a many-sided historical devel-

opment, are the tragic and the comic, as well as the counter-balancing of both modes of comprehension, which, in dramatic poetry, become for the first time so essentially important that they form the basis of classification of the different types.

In considering more closely the nature of these distinctions we shall do well to discuss their subject-matter in the following order:

First, we must define the general principle of tragedy, comedy, and the so-called drama.

Secondly, we must indicate the character of ancient and modern dramatic poetry, to the contrast between which the distinctive relation of the above-named types is referable in their historical development.

Thirdly, we will attempt, in conclusion, to examine the concrete modes, which these types, though mainly comedy and tragedy, are able to exhibit within the boundary of this opposition.

a. The Principle of Tragedy, Comedy, and the Drama, or Social Play

The essential basis of differentiation among the types of epic poetry is to be found in the distinction whether the essentially substantive displayed in the epic manner is expressed in its universality, or is communicated in the form of objective characters, exploits, and events. In contrast to this, the classification of lyric poetry, in its series of varied modes of expression, is dependent upon the degree and specific form in which the content is assimilated in more or less stable consistency with subjective experience, as its inwardness reveals itself. And, finally, dramatic poetry, which accepts as its centre of significance the collision of aims and characters, as also the necessary resolution of such a conflict, cannot do otherwise than deduce the principle of its separate types from the relation in which *individual persons* are placed relatively to their purpose and its content. The definition of this relation is, in short, the decisive factor in the determination of the particular mode of dramatic schism and the issue therefrom, and consequently presents the essential type of the entire process in its animated

and artistic display. The fundamental points we have to examine in this connection are, speaking broadly, those phases or
features in the process, the mediation of which constitutes the
essential purport of every true action. Such are from one point
of view the substantively sound and great, the fundamental
stratum of the realized divine nature in the world, regarded
here as the genuine and essentially eternal content of individual character and end. And, on its other side, we have the
personal conscious life simply as such in its unhampered power
of self-determination and freedom. Without doubt, essential
and explicit truth is asserted in dramatic poetry; it matters
not in what form it may be manifested from time to time in
human action. The specific type, however, within which this
activity is made visible receives a distinct or, rather, actually
opposed configuration, according as the aspect of substantive
worth or in its opposition thereto, that of individual caprice,
folly, and perversity is retained as the distinctive *modus* of operation either in individuals, actions, or conflicts.

We have therefore to consider the principle in its distinctive relation to the following types:

First, as associated with tragedy in its substantive and
primitive form.

Secondly, in its relation to comedy, in which the life of the
individual soul as such in volition and action, as well as the
external factor of contingency, are predominant over all relations and ends.

Thirdly, in that to the drama, the theatrical piece in the
more restricted use of the term, regarding such as the middle
term between the two first-mentioned types.

(1) With respect to *tragedy,* I will here confine myself to a
consideration of only the most general and essential characteristics, the more concrete differentiation of which can only
be made clear by a review of the distinctive features implied
in the stages of its historical process.

(a) The genuine content of tragic action subject to the *aims*
which arrest tragic characters is supplied by the world of
those forces which carry in themselves their own justification,
and are realized substantively in the volitional activity of mankind. Such are the love of husband and wife, of parents, children, and kinsfolk. Such are, further, the life of communities,

the patriotism of citizens, the will of those in supreme power. Such are the life of churches, not, however, if regarded as a piety which submits to act with resignation, or as a divine judicial declaration in the heart of mankind over what is good or the reverse in action; but, on the contrary, conceived as the active engagement with and demand for veritable interests and relations. It is of a soundness and thoroughness consonant with these that the really tragical *characters* consist. They are throughout that which the essential notion of their character enables them and compels them to be. They are not merely a varied totality laid out in the series of views of it proper to the epic manner; they are, while no doubt remaining also essentially vital and individual, still only the one power of the particular character in question, the force in which such a character, in virtue of his essential personality, has made himself inseparably coalesce with some particular aspect of the capital and substantive life-content we have indicated above, and deliberately commits himself to that. It is at some such elevation, where the mere accidents of unmediated individuality vanish altogether, that we find the tragic heroes of dramatic art, whether they be the living representatives of such spheres of concrete life or in any other way already so derive their greatness and stability from their own free self-reliance that they stand forth as works of sculpture, and thus the lofty tragic characters of the Greeks also interpret the essentially more abstract statues and figures of gods more completely than is possible for any other kind of elucidation or commentary.

Broadly speaking, we may, therefore, affirm that the true theme of primitive tragedy is the godlike. But by godlike we do not mean the Divine, as implied in the content of the religious consciousness simply as such, but rather as it enters into the world, into individual action, and enters in such a way that it does not forfeit its substantive character under this mode of realization, nor find itself converted into the contradiction of its own substance. In this form the spiritual substance of volition and accomplishment is ethical life. For what is ethical, if we grasp it, in its direct consistency—that is to say, not exclusively from the standpoint of personal reflection as formal morality—is the divine in its secular or world realization, the substantive as such, the particular no less than the essential features of which supply the changing content of truly human actions, and in such action itself render this their essence explicit and actual.

(b) These ethical forces, as also the characters of the action, are *distinctively defined* in respect to their content and their individual personality, in virtue of the principle of differentiation to which everything is subject, which forms part of the objective world of things. If, then, these particular forces, in the way presupposed by dramatic poetry, are attached to the external expression of human activity, and are realized as the determinate aim of a human pathos which passes into action, their concordancy is cancelled, and they are asserted *in contrast* to each other in interchangeable succession. Individual action will then, under given conditions, realize an object or character, which, under such a presupposed state, inevitably stimulates the presence of a pathos opposed to itself, because it occupies a position of unique isolation in virtue of its independently fixed definition, and, by doing so, brings in its train unavoidable conflicts. Primitive tragedy, then, consists in this, that within a collision of this kind both sides of the contradiction, if taken by themselves, are *justified;* yet, from a further point of view, they tend to carry into effect the true and positive content of their end and specific characterization merely as the negation and *violation* of the other equally legitimate power, and consequently in their ethical purport and relatively to this so far fall under *condemnation.*

I have already adverted to the general ground of the necessity of this conflict. The substance of ethical condition is, when viewed as concrete unity, a totality of *different* relations and forces, which, however, only under the inactive condition of the gods in their blessedness achieve the works of the Spirit in enjoyment of an undisturbed life. In contrast to this, however, there is no less certainly implied in the notion of this totality itself an impulse to move from its, in the first instance, still abstract ideality, and transplant itself in the real actuality of the phenomenal world. On account of the nature of this primitive obsession, it comes about that mere difference, if conceived on the basis of definite conditions of individual personalities, must inevitably associate with contradiction and collision. Only such a view can pretend to deal seriously with those gods which, though they endure in their tranquil repose and unity in the Olympus and heaven of imagination and religious conception, yet, in so far as they are actual, viewed at least as the energic in the definite pathos of a human personality, participate in concrete life, all other claims notwithstanding, and, in virtue of their specific singularity and their mutual opposition, render both blame and wrong inevitable.

(c) As a result of this, however, an unmediated contradiction is posited, which no doubt may assert itself in the Real, but, for all that, is unable to maintain itself as that which is wholly substantive and verily real therein; which rather discovers, and only discovers, its essential justification in the fact that it is able to *annul* itself as such contradiction. In other words, whatever may be the claim of the tragic final purpose and personality, whatever may be the necessity of the tragic collision, it is, as a consequence of our present view, no less a claim that is asserted—this is our *third* and last point—by the tragic resolution of this division. It is through *this* latter result that Eternal Justice is operative in such aims and individuals under a mode whereby it restores the ethical substance and unity in and along with the downfall of the individuality which disturbs its repose. For, despite the fact that individual characters propose that which is itself essentially valid, yet they are only able to carry it out under the tragic demand in a manner that implies contradiction and with a one-sidedness which is injurious. What, however, is substantive in truth, and the function of which is to secure realization, is not the battle of particular unities, however much such a conflict is essentially involved in the notion of a real world and human action; rather it is the reconciliation in which definite ends and individuals unite in harmonious action without mutual violation and contradiction. That which is abrogated in the tragic issue is merely the *one-sided* particularity which was unable to accommodate itself to this harmony, and consequently in the tragic course of its action, through inability to disengage itself from itself and its designs, either is committed in its entire totality to destruction or at least finds itself compelled to fall back upon a state of resignation in the execution of its aim in so far as it can carry this out. We are reminded of the famous dictum of Aristotle that the true effect of tragedy is to excite and purify *fear* and *pity*. By this statement Aristotle did not mean merely the concordant or discordant feeling with anybody's private experience, a feeling simply of pleasure or the reverse, an attraction or a repulsion, that most superficial of all psychological states, which only in recent times theorists have sought to identify with the principle of assent or dissent as ordinarily expressed. For in a work of art the matter of exclusive importance should be the display of that which is conformable with the reason and truth of Spirit; and to discover the principle of this we have to direct our attention to wholly different points of view. And consequently we are not justified in restricting the application of this dictum of Aristotle merely to the emotion of fear and pity, but should relate it to the principle of the *content,* the appropriately artistic display of which ought to purify such feelings. Man may, on the one hand, entertain fear when confronted with that which is outside him and finite; but he may likewise shrink before the power of that which is the essential and absolute subsistency of social phenomena. That which mankind has therefore in truth to fear is not the external power and its oppression, but the ethical might which is self-defined in its own free rationality, and partakes further of the eternal and inviolable, the power a man summons against his own being when he turns his back upon it. And just as fear may have two objectives, so also may compassion. The first is just the ordinary sensibility—in other words, a sympathy with the misfortunes and sufferings of another, and one which is experienced as something finite and negative. Your countrified cousin is ready enough with compassion of this order. The man of nobility and greatness, however, has no wish to be smothered with this sort of pity. For just to the extent that it is merely the nugatory aspect, the negative of misfortune which is asserted, a real depreciation of misfortune is implied. True sympathy, on the contrary, is an accordant feeling with the ethical claim at the same time associated with the sufferer—that is, with what is necessarily implied in his condition as affirmative and substantive. Such a pity as this is not, of course, excited by ragamuffins and vagabonds. If the tragic character, therefore, just as he aroused our fear when contemplating the might of violated morality, is to awake a tragic sympathy in his misfortune, he must himself essentially possess real capacity and downright character. It is only that which has a genuine content which strikes the heart of a man of noble feeling, and rings through its depths. Consequently we ought by no means to identify our interest in the tragic *dénouement* with the simple satisfaction that a sad story, a misfortune merely as misfortune, should have a claim upon our sympathy. Feelings of lament of this type may well enough assail men on occasions of wholly external contingency and related circumstance, to which the individual does not contribute, nor for which he is responsible, such cases as illness, loss of property, death, and the like. The only real and absorbing interest in such cases ought to be an eager desire to afford immediate assistance. If this is impossible, such pictures of lamentation and misery merely rack the feelings. A veritable tragic suffering, on the contrary, is suspended over active characters entirely as the consequence of their own act, which as such not only asserts its claim upon us, but becomes subject to blame through the collision it involves, and in which such individuals identify themselves heart and soul.

Over and above mere fear and tragic sympathy we have therefore the feeling of *reconciliation*, which tragedy affords in virtue of its vision of eternal justice, a justice which exercises a paramount force of absolute constringency on account of the relative claim of all merely contracted aims and passions; and it can do this for the reason that it is unable to tolerate the victorious issue and continuance in the truth of the objective world of such a conflict with and opposition to those ethical powers which are fundamentally and essentially concordant. Inasmuch as then, in conformity with this principle, all that pertains to tragedy pre-eminently rests upon the contemplation of such a conflict and its resolution, dramatic poetry is—and its entire mode of presentation offers a proof of the fact—alone able to make and completely adapt the tragic, throughout its entire course and compass, to the principle of the art product. And this is the reason why I have only now found occasion to discuss the tragic mode of presentation, although it extends an effective force, if no doubt one of subordinate degree, in many ways over the other arts.

(2) In tragedy then that which is eternally substantive is triumphantly vindicated under the mode of reconciliation. It

simply removes from the contentions of personality the false one-sidedness, and exhibits instead that which is the object of its volition, namely, positive reality, no longer under an asserted mediation of opposed factors, but as the real support of consistency. And in contrast to this in *comedy* it is the purely *personal experience*, which retains the mastery in its character of infinite self-assuredness. And it is only these two fundamental aspects of human action which occupy a position of contrast in the classification of dramatic poetry into its several types. In tragedy individuals are thrown into confusion in virtue of the abstract nature of their sterling volition and character, or they are forced to accept that with resignation, to which they have been themselves essentially opposed. In comedy we have a vision of the victory of intrinsically self-assured subjectivity, the laughter of which resolves everything through the medium and into the medium of such individuality.

(a) The general basis of comedy is therefore a world in which man has made himself, in his conscious activity, complete master of all that otherwise passes as the essential content of his knowledge and achievement; a world whose ends are consequently thrown awry on account of their own lack of substance. A democratic folk, with egotistic citizens, litigious, frivolous, conceited, without faith or knowledge, always intent on gossip, boasting and vanity—such a folk is past praying for; it can only dissolve in its folly. But it would be a mistake to think that any action that is without genuine content is therefore comic because it is void of substance. People only too often in this respect confound the merely *ridiculous* with the true comic. Every contrast between what is essential and its appearance, the object and its instrument, may be ridiculous, a contradiction in virtue of which the appearance is absolutely cancelled, and the end is stultified in its realization. A profounder significance is, however, implied in the comic. There is, for instance, nothing comic in human crime. The satire affords a proof of this, to the point of extreme aridity, no matter how emphatic may be the colours in which it depicts the condition of the actual world in its contrast to all that the man of virtue ought to be. There is nothing in mere folly, stupidity, or nonsense, which in itself necessarily partakes of the comic, though we all of us are ready enough to laugh at it. And as a rule it is extraordinary what a variety of wholly different things excite human laughter. Matters of the dullest description and in the worst possible taste will move men in this way; and their laughter may be excited quite as much by things of the profoundest importance, if only they happen to notice some entirely unimportant feature, which may conflict with habit and ordinary experience. Laughter is consequently little more than an expression of self-satisfied shrewdness; a sign that they have sufficient wit to recognize such a contrast and are aware of the fact. In the same way we have the laughter of mockery, of disdain, of desperation and the like. What on the other hand is inseparable from the comic is an infinite geniality and confidence capable of rising superior to its own contradiction, and experiencing therein no taint of bitterness or sense of misfortune whatever. It is the happy frame of mind, a hale condition of soul, which, fully aware of itself, can suffer the dissolution of its aims and realization. The unexpansive type of intelligence is on the contrary least master of itself where it is in its behaviour most laughable to others.

(b) In considering with more detail the kind of content which characterizes and educes the object of comic action, I propose to limit myself to the following points of general interest.

On the *one* hand there are human ends and characters essentially devoid of substantive content and contradictory. They are therefore unable to achieve the former or give effect to the latter. Avarice, for example, not only in reference to its aim, but also in respect to the petty means which it employs, is clearly from the first and fundamentally a vain shadow. It accepts what is the dead abstraction of wealth, money simply as such, as the *summum bonum*, the reality beyond which it refuses to budge; and it endeavours to master this frigid means of enjoyment by denying itself every other concrete satisfaction, despite the fact too that, in the impotency of its end no less than the means of its achievement, it is helpless when confronted with cunning and treachery, and the like. In such a case then, if anyone identifies *seriously* his personal life with a content so essentially false, to the extent of a man confining the embrace of his existence to that exclusively, and in the result, if the same is swept away as his foot-hold, the more he strives to retain that former foot-hold, the more the life collapses in unhappiness—in such a picture as this what is most vital to the comic situation fails, as it does in every case where the predominant factors are simply on the one side the painfulness of the actual conditions, and on the other scorn and pleasure in such misfortune. There is therefore more of the true comic in the case where, it is true, aims intrinsically mean and empty are meant to be achieved with an appearance of earnest solemnity and every kind of preparation, but where the individual himself, when he falls short of this, does not experience any real loss because he is conscious that what he strove after was really of no great importance, and is therefore able to rise superior with spontaneous amusement above the failure.

A situation which is the reverse of this occurs where people vaguely grasp at aims and a personal impression of real substance, but in their own individuality, as instruments to achieve this, are in absolute conflict with such a result. In such a case what substance there is only exists in the individual's imagination, becomes a mere appearance to himself or others, which no doubt offers the show and virtue of what is thus of material import, but for this very reason involves end and personality, action and character in a contradiction, by reason of which the attainment of the imaged end or characterization is itself rendered impossible. An example of this is the "Ecclesiazusae" of Aristophanes, where the women who seek to advise and found a new political constitution, retain all the temperament and passions of women as before.

We may add to the above two divisions of classification, as a distinct basis for yet *another*, the use made of external accident, by means of the varied and extraordinary development of which situations are placed before us in which the objects desired and their achievement, the personal character and its external conditions are thrown into a comic contrast, and lead to an equally comic resolution.

(c) But inasmuch as the comic element wholly and from the first depends upon contradictory contrasts, not only of ends themselves on their own account, but also of their content as opposed to the contingency of the personal life and external condition, the action of comedy requires a *resolution* with even more stringency than the tragic drama. In other words, in the action of comedy the contradiction between that which is essentially true and its specific realization is more fundamentally asserted.

That which, however, is abrogated in this resolution is not by any means either the *substantive* being or the *personal* life as such.

And the reason of this is that comedy too, viewed as genuine art, has not the task set before it to display through its presentation what is essentially rational as that which is intrinsically perverse and comes to naught, but on the contrary as that which neither bestows the victory, nor ultimately allows any standing ground to folly and absurdity, that is to say the false contradictions and oppositions which also form part of reality. The masculine art of Aristophanes, for instance, does not turn into ridicule what is truly of ethical significance in the social life of Athens, namely genuine philosophy, true religious faith, but rather the spurious growth of the democracy, in which the ancient faith and the former morality have disappeared, such as the sophistry, the whining and querulousness of tragedy, the inconstant gossip, the love of litigation and so forth; in other words, it is those elements directly opposed to a genuine condition of political life, religion, and art, which he places before us in their suicidal folly. Only in more modern times do we find in such a writer as Kotzebue the baseness possible which throws over moral excellence, and spares and strives to maintain that which only exists under a condition of sufferance. To as little extent, however, ought the individual's private life suffer substantial injury in comedy. Or to put it otherwise, if it is merely the appearance and imagined presence of what is substantive, or if it is the essentially perverse and petty which is asserted, yet in the essential self-stability of individual character the more exalted principle remains, which in its freedom reaches over and beyond the overthrow of all that such finite life comprises, and continues itself in its character of self-security and self-blessedness. This subjective life that we above all identify with comic personality has thus become master of all the phenomenal presence of the real. The mode of actual appearance adequate to what is, so to speak, substantive, has vanished out of it; and, if what is essentially without fundamental subsistence comes to naught with its mere pretence of being that which it is not, the individual asserts himself as master over such a dissolution, and remains at bottom unbroken and in good heart to the end.

(3) Midway between tragedy and comedy we have furthermore a *third* fundamental type of dramatic poetry, which is, however, of less distinctive importance, despite the fact that in it the essential difference between what is tragic and comic makes an effort to construct a bridge of mediation, or at least to effect some coalescence of both sides in a concrete whole without leaving either the one or the other in opposed isolation.

(a) To this class we may, for example, refer the *Satyric* drama of the ancients, in which the principal action itself at least remains of a serious if not wholly tragic type, while the chorus of its Satyrs is in contrast to this treated in the comic manner. We may also include in such a class the tragic-comedy. Plautus gives an example of this in his "Amphitryo," and indeed in the prologue, through verses given to Mercury, asserts this fact; the declamation runs as follows:

> Quid contraxistis frontem? Quia Tragoediam
> Dixi futuram hanc? Deus sum: commutavero
> Eamdem hanc, si voltis: faciam, ex Tragoedia
> Comoedia ut sit, omnibus eisdem versibus.
> Faciam ut conmista sit Tragicocomoedia.

He offers us as a reason for this intermixture the fact, that while gods and kings are represented among the *dramatis personae*, we have also in comic contrast to this the figure of the slave Sofia. With yet more frequency in modern dramatic poetry we have the interplay of tragic and comic situation; and this is naturally so, because here, even in tragedy, the principle of subjectivity which is asserted by comedy in all its freedom, from the first has been predominant, forcing into the background the substantive character of the content of ethical forces.

(b) The profounder mediation, however, of tragic and comic composition in a new whole does not consist in the juxtaposition or alteration of these contradictory points of view, but in a mutual accommodation, which blunts the force of such opposition. The element of subjectivity, instead of being exercised with all the perversity of the comic drama, is steeped in the seriousness of genuine social conditions and substantial characters, while the tragic steadfastness of volition and the depth of collisions is so far weakened and reduced that it becomes compatible with a reconciliation of interests and a harmonious union of ends and individuals. It is under such a mode of conception that in particular the modern play and drama arise. The profound aspect of this principle, in this view of the playwright, consists in the fact that, despite the differences and conflicts of interests, passions, and characters, an essentially harmonious reality none the less results from human action. Even the ancient world possesses tragedies which accept an issue of this character. Individuals are not sacrificed, but maintained without serious catastrophe. In the "Eumenides" of Aeschylus, for example, both parties there brought to judgment before the Areopagus, namely Apollo and the avenging Furies, have their claims to honourable consideration vindicated. Also in the "Philoctetes" the conflict between Neoptolemos and Philoctetes is disposed of through the divine interposition of Hercules and the advice he gives. They depart reconciled for Troy. In this case, however, the accommodation is due to a *deus ex machina,* and the actual source of such is not traceable to the personal attitude of the parties themselves. In the modern play, however, it is the individual characters alone who find themselves induced by the course of their own action to such an abandonment of the strife, and to a reciprocal reconciliation of their aims and personalities. From this point of view the "Iphigenia" of Goethe is a genuine model of a play of this kind, and it is more so than his "Tasso," in which in the first place the reconciliation with Antonio is rather an affair of temperament and personal acknowledgment that Antonio possesses the genuine knowledge of life, which is absent from the character of Tasso, and along with this that the claim of ideal life, which Tasso had rigidly adhered to in its conflict with actual conditions, adaptability, and grace of manners, retains its force throughout with an audience merely in an ideal sense, and relatively to actual conditions at most asserts itself as an excuse for the poet and a general sympathy for his position.

(c) As a rule, however, the boundary lines of the intermediate type fluctuate more than is the case with tragedy or
comedy. It is also exposed to a further danger of breaking
away from the true dramatic type, or ceasing to be genuine
poetry. In other words, owing to the fact that the opposing
factors, which have to secure a peaceful conclusion from out
of their own division, are from the start not antithetical to
one another with the emphasis asserted by tragedy; the poet
is for this reason compelled to devote the full strength of his
presentation to the psychological analysis of character, and to
make the course of the situations a mere instrument of such
characterization. Or, as an alternative, he admits a too extensive field for the display of the material aspect of historical or
ethical conditions; and, under the pressure of such material,
he attempts to keep attention alive only through interest in
the series of events evolved. To this class of composition we
may assign a host of our more recent theatrical pieces, which
rather aim at theatrical effect than claim to be poetry. They
do not so much seek to affect us as genuine poetical productions as to reach our emotions generally as men and women;
or they aim on the one hand simply at recreation, and on the
other at the moral education of public taste; but while doing
so they are almost equally concerned to provide ample opportunity to the actor for the display of his trained art and virtuosity in the most brilliant manner.

b. The Difference between Ancient and Modern Dramatic Poetry

The same principle which offered us a basis for the classification of dramatic art into tragedy and comedy also will give
us the essential points of arrest in the history of their development. The progress we find in this course of evolution can only
appear after we have placed these particular moments in the
process side by side for comparison and analysis. They subsist, in short, in the notion of dramatic action, with the result
that on the one hand the entire composition and its theatrical
execution emphasizes what is *substantive* in the ends, conflicts, and characters, and on the other that the *personal* factor

of conscious and individual life constitutes the focal centre throughout.

(1) With regard to such an inquiry we may at once in the present work, which does not attempt to include an exhaustive history of art, leave out altogether those origins of dramatic art which we find among Oriental peoples. Despite the considerable progress made by Eastern poetry in the epic and certain types of lyrical composition the entire world-outlook of such peoples nevertheless from the first excludes an artistic development favourable to dramatic art. And the reason is that to genuine *tragic* action it is essential that the principle of *individual* freedom and independence, or at least that of self-determination, the will to find in the self the free cause and source of the personal act and its consequences, should already have been aroused; and we may observe that to a still more emphatic degree is this free claim of the personal life and its self-recognized *imperium* a necessary condition to the appearance of comedy. In the East we find in neither case such a condition satisfied. In particular remoteness from any and every attempt at real dramatic self-expression is that imposing sublimity of Mohammedan poetry, although from a certain point of view it is capable with real power of vindicating the claim of individual independence. But it necessarily fails, because it is an equally essential assumption of it that the One substantive Power overrules every created being and determines his irreversible destiny, and with all the more irresistible fatality in proportion as such a spirit is asserted. The justification of a particular content of individual action and of a personal life which explores its own most intimate substance, in the sense that dramatic art presupposes, is here impossible; indeed it is precisely in Mohammedanism that the subjugation of the individual self to the will of God is the more abstract in proportion as the One predominant Power, who rules the universe, is more abstractly conceived in his universality, and in the last instance will not tolerate one shred of particularity to remain. We consequently only find origins of dramatic composition among the Chinese and Hindoos. But here, too, so far as our present scanty evidence carries us, these do not so much amount to the execution of any free and individual action; they merely reflect the animated life of events and

emotions under the mode of definite situations, which are displayed in their course as they actually happen.

(2) The true beginning of dramatic poetry we have consequently to seek among the Hellenes, with whom for the first time and in every respect the principle of free individuality renders the perfect elaboration of the classic type of art possible. Compatibly with this type of art, however, and in its relation to human action, individuality is only so far asserted as it directly demands the free animation of the essential content of human aims. That which pre-eminently is of valid force in ancient drama, therefore, whether it be tragedy or comedy, is the universal and essential content of the end, which individuals seek to achieve. In tragedy this is the ethical claim of human consciousness in view of the particular action in question, the vindication of the act on its own account. And in the old comedy, too, it is in the same way at least the general public interests which are emphasized, whether it be in statesmen and the mode in which they direct the State, questions of peace or war, the general public and its moral conditions, or the condition of philosophy and its decline. And it is owing to this that here neither the varied exposition of inner spirit and exceptional character, nor the equally exceptional plot and intrigue can obtain the fullest play, nor does the main interest revolve so much around the fate of individuals. In the place of this interest for such particular aspects of the drama above all else sympathy is evoked and claimed for the simple conflict and issue of the essential powers of life, and for the godlike manifestations of the human heart, as distinctive representatives of which the heroes of tragedy are set before us in much the same way as that in which the figures of comedy make visible the general perversity of mankind, to the expression of which, in the reality of the actual present, even the fundamental institutions of public life have been corrupted.

(3) In *modern* romantic poetry, on the contrary, it is the individual passion, the satisfaction of which can only be relative to a wholly personal end, generally speaking the destiny of some particular person or character placed under exceptional circumstances, which forms the subject-matter of all importance.

From such a point of view the poetic interest consists in that greatness of characters, who, in virtue of their imaginative power or their disposition and talents, display a spiritual elevation over their situations and actions no less than over the entire wealth of their spirit, and show it as the real substance of political forces, though often, too, these may be obstructed and, indeed, annihilated in the stress of particular circumstances and the current of events; and we may add that in the greatness of such natures it is not infrequent to find that a power of recovery is further contained. With regard to the particular content of the action in this style of composition it is not therefore the ethical vindication and necessity, but rather the isolated individual and his conditions to which our interest is directed. From a standpoint such as this, therefore, a fundamental motive will arise in such qualities as love and ambition; indeed, crime itself is not excluded. But in the latter case we may easily find rocks ahead difficult indeed to clear. For an out and out criminal, and irrevocably so when he is weak and a thoroughly mean scamp, as is the hero in Müllner's drama, "Crime," is something more than a sorry sight. What we require therefore above all in such cases is at least the formal greatness of character and power of the personal life which is able to ride out everything that negates it, and which, without denial of its acts or, indeed, without being materially discomposed by them, is capable of accepting their consequences. And on the other side we find that those substantive ends, such as patriotism, family devotion, loyalty, and the rest, are by no means to be excluded, although for the individual persons concerned the main question of importance is not so much the substantive force as their own individuality. But in such cases as a rule they rather form the particular ground upon which such persons, viewed in the light of their private character, take their stand and engage in conflict, rather than have supplied what we may regard as the real and ultimate content of their volition and action.

And further, in conjunction with a personal self-assertion of this type we may have presented the full extension of individual idiosyncrasy, not merely in respect to the internal simply, but also in relation to external circumstances and conditions, within which the action proceeds. And it is owing to this that in contrast to the simple conflicts which characterize more classical dramatic composition, we now meet with the variety and exuberance of the characters dramatized, the unforeseen surprises of the ever new and complicated developments of plot, the maze of intrigue, the contingency of events, and, in a word, all those aspects of the modern drama which claim our attention, and the unfettered appearance of which, as opposed to the overwhelming emphasis attached to what is essentially most fundamental in the content, accentuates the type of romantic art in its distinction from the classic type.

But again, even in the cases above indicated, and despite all this apparently untrammelled particularity, the whole ought to continue to be both dramatic and poetical. In other words, on the one hand, the harshness of the collision, which has to be fought through, ought to be visibly obliterated, and on the other, pre-eminently in tragedy, the predominant presence of a more exalted order of the world, whether we adopt the conception of Providence or Fatality, ought to plainly discover itself in and through the course and issue of the action.

c. The Concrete Development of Dramatic Poetry and Its Types

Within the essential distinctions of conception and poetical achievement which we have just considered the different types of dramatic art assert themselves, and, for the first time in such association, and in so far as their development follows either one or the other direction, attain a really genuine completeness. We have, therefore, in concluding the present work, still to concentrate our inquiry upon the concrete mode under which they receive such a configuration.

(1) Excluding as we shall do for the reasons already given from our subject-matter the origins of such poetry in Oriental literature, the material of first and fundamental importance which engages our attention, as the most valuable phase of genuine tragedy no less than comedy, is the dramatic poetry of the *Greeks*. In other words, in it for the first time we find the human consciousness illuminated with that which in its general terms the tragic and comic situation essentially is; and

after these opposed types of dramatic outlook upon human action have been securely and beyond all confusion separated from each other, we mark first in order tragedy, and after that comedy, rise in organic development to the height of their achievement. Of such a successful result the dramatic art of Rome merely returns a considerably attenuated reflection, which does not indeed reach the point secured by the similar effort of Roman literature in epic and lyrical composition. In my examination of the material thus offered my object will be merely to accentuate what is most important, and I shall therefore limit my survey to the tragic point of view of Aeschylus and Sophocles, and to Aristophanes so far as comedy is concerned.

(a) Taking, then, tragedy first, I have already stated that the fundamental type which determines its entire organization and structure is to be sought for in the emphasis attached to the substantive constitution of final ends and their content, as also of the individuals dramatized and their conflict and destiny.

In the tragic drama we are now considering, the general basis or background for tragic action is supplied, as was also the case in the Epos, by that world-condition which I have already indicated as the *heroic*.[5] For only in heroic times, when the universal ethical forces have neither acquired the independent stability of definite political legislation or moral commands and obligations, can they be presented in their primitive jucundity as gods, who are either opposed to each other in their personal activities, or themselves appear as the animated content of a free and human individuality. If, however, what is intrinsically ethical is to appear throughout as the substantive foundation, the universal ground, shall we say, from which the growth of personal action arrests our attention with equal force in its disunion, and is no less brought back again from such divided movement into unity, we shall find that there are two distinct modes under which the ethical content of human action is asserted.

First, we have the simple consciousness, which, in so far as it wills its substantive content wholly as the unbroken iden-

[5] See Chapter II.

tity of its particular aspects, remains in undisturbed, uncriticized, and neutral tranquillity on its own account and as related to others. This undivided and, we may add, purely
formal state of mind in its veneration, its faith, and its happiness, however, is incapable of attaching itself to any definite
action; it has a sort of dread before the disunion which is
implied in such, although it does, while remaining itself incapable of action, esteem at the same time that spiritual courage which asserts itself resolutely and actively in a self-
proposed object, as of nobler worth, yet is aware of its inability
to undertake such enterprise, and consequently considers that
it can do nothing further for such active personalities, whom
it respects so highly, than contrast with the energy of their decision and conflict the object of its own wisdom, in other words,
the substantive ideality of the ethical Powers.

The *second* mode under which this ethical content is asserted is that of the individual pathos, which urges the active characters with moral self-vindication into opposition to
others, and brings them thereby into conflict. The individuals
subject to this pathos are neither what, in the modern use of
the term, we describe as characters, nor are they mere abstractions. They are rather placed in the vital midway sphere
between both, standing there as figures of real stability, which
are simply that which they are, without aught of collision in
themselves, without any fluctuating recognition of some other
pathos, and in so far—in this respect a contrast to our modern
irony—elevated, absolutely determinate characters, whose definition, however, discovers its content and basis in a particular
ethical power. Forasmuch as, then, the tragic situation first
appears in the *antagonism* of individuals who are thus em-
powered to act, the same can only assert itself in the field of
actual human life. It results from the specific character of this
alone that a particular quality so affects the substantive content of a given individual, that the latter identifies himself with
his entire interest and being in such a content, and penetrates
it throughout with the glow of passion. In the blessed gods,
however, it is the divine Nature, in its indifference, which is
what is essential; in contrast to which we have the contradiction, which in the last instance is not treated seriously, rather
is one which, as I have already noticed when discussing the

Homeric Epos, becomes eventually a self-resolving irony. These two modes or aspects—of which the one is as important for the whole as the other—namely, the unsevered consciousness of the godlike, and the combating human action, asserted, however, in godlike power and deed, which determines and executes the ethical purpose—supply the two fundamental elements, the mediation of which is displayed by Greek tragedy in its artistic compositions under the form of *chorus* and *heroic figures* respectively.

In modern times, considerable discussion has been raised over the significance of the Greek chorus, and the question has been raised incidentally whether it can or ought to be introduced into modern tragedy. In fact, the need of some such substantial foundation has been experienced; but critics have found it difficult to prescribe the precise manner in which effect should be given to such a change, because they failed to grasp with sufficient penetration the nature of that in which true tragedy consists and the necessity of the chorus as an essential constituent of all that Greek tragedy implies. Critics have, no doubt, recognized the nature of the chorus to the extent of maintaining that in it we find an attitude of tranquil meditation over the whole, whereas the characters of the action remain within the limits of their particular objects and situations, and, in short, receive in the chorus and its observations a standard of valuation of their characters and actions in much the same way as the public discovers in it, and within the drama itself, an objective representative of its own judgment upon all that is thus represented. In this view we have to this extent the fact rightly conceived, that the chorus is, in truth, there as a substantive and more enlightened intelligence, which warns us from irrelevant oppositions, and reflects upon the genuine issue. But, granting this to be so, it is by no means, like the spectator, a wholly disinterested person, at leisure to entertain such thoughts and ethical judgments as it likes which, uninteresting and tedious on its own account, could only be attached for the sake of such reflections. The chorus is the actual substance of the heroic life and action itself: it is, as contrasted with the particular heroes, the common folk regarded as the fruitful earth, out of which individuals, much as flowers and towering trees from their native soil, grow and whereby they are conditioned in this life. Consequently, the chorus is peculiarly fitted to a view of life in which the obligations of State legislation and settled religious dogmas do not, as yet, act as a restrictive force in ethical and social development, but where morality only exists in its primitive form of directly animated human life, and it is merely the equilibrium of unmoved life which remains assured in its stability against the fearful collisions which the antagonistic energies of individual action produces. We are made aware of the fact that an assured asylum of this kind is also a part of our actual existence by the presence of the chorus. It does not, therefore, practically co-operate with the action; it executes no right, actively, as against the contending heroes; it merely expresses its judgment as a matter of opinion; it warns, commiserates, or appeals to the divine law, and the ideal forces imminent in the soul, which the imagination grasps in external guise as the sphere of the gods that rule. In this self-expression it is, as we have already seen, lyrical; for it does not act and there are no events for it to narrate in epical form. The content, however, retains at the same time the epic character of substantive universality; and its lyric movement is of such a nature that it can, and in this respect in contrast to the form of the genuine ode, approach at times that of the paean and the dithyramb. We must lay emphatic stress upon this position of the chorus in Greek tragedy. Just as the theatre itself possesses its external ground, its scene and environment, so, too, the chorus, that is the general community, is the spiritual scene; and we may compare it to the architectural temple which surrounds the image of the god, which resembles the heroes in the action. Among ourselves, statues are placed under the open sky without such a background, which also modern tragedy does not require, for the reason that its actions do not depend on this substantive basis, but on the personal volition and personality, no less than the apparently external contingency of events and circumstances.

In this respect it is an entirely false view which regards the chorus as an accidental piece of residuary baggage, a mere remnant from the origins of Greek drama. Of course, it is incontestable that its source is to be traced to the circumstance that, in the festivals of Bacchus, so far as the artistic aspect is concerned, the choral song was of most importance until the introduction and interruption of its course by one reciter, whose relation finally was transformed into and exalted by the real figures of dramatic action. In the blossoming season of tragedy, however, the chorus was not by any means merely retained in honour of this particular phase of the festival and ritual of the god Bacchus; rather it became continuously more elaborate in its beauty and harmonious measures by reason of the fact that its association with the dramatic action is essential and, indeed, so indispensable to it that the decline of tragedy is intimately connected with the degeneration of the choruses, which no longer remain an integral member of the whole, but are degraded to a mere embellishment. In contrast to this, in romantic tragedy, the chorus is neither intrinsically appropriate nor does it appear to have originated from choric songs. On the contrary, the content is here of a type which defeats from the first any attempt to introduce choruses as understood by Greek dramatists. For, even if we go back to the most primitive of those so-called mysteries, morality plays, and farces of a similar character, from which the romantic drama issued, we find that these present no action in that original Greek sense of the term, no outbreak, that is, of opposing forces from the undivided consciousness of life and the godlike. To as little extent is the chorus adapted to the conditions of chivalry and the dominion of kings, in so far as, in such cases, the attitude of the folk is one of mere obedience, or it is itself a party, involved together with the interest of its fortune or misfortune in the course of the action. And in general the chorus entirely fails to secure its true position where the main subject-matter consists of particular passions, ends, and characters, or where any considerable opportunity is admitted to intrigue.

In contrast to the chorus, the *second* fundamental feature of dramatic composition is that of the *individuals* who act in *conflict* with each other. In Greek tragedy it is not at all bad will, crime, worthlessness, or mere misfortune, stupidity, and the like, which act as an incentive to such collisions, but rather, as I have frequently urged, the ethical right to a definite course of action. Abstract evil neither possesses truth in itself, nor does it arouse interest. At the same time, when we attribute ethical traits of characterization to the individuals of the action, these ought not to appear merely as a matter of opinion. It is rather implied in their right or claim that they are actually there as essential on their own account. The hazards of crime, such as are present in modern drama, the useless, or quite as much the so-called noble criminal, with his empty talk about fate, we meet with in the tragedy of ancient literature, rarely, if at all, and for the good reason that the decision and deed depends on the wholly personal aspect of interest and character, upon lust for power, love, honour, or other similar passions, whose justification has its roots exclusively in the particular inclination and individuality. A resolve of this character, whose claim is based upon the content of its object, which it carries into execution in one restricted direction of particularization, violates, under certain circumstances, which are already essentially implied in the actual possibility of conflicts, a further and equally ethical sphere of human volition, which the character thus confronted adheres to, and, by his thus stimulated action, enforces, so that in this way the collision of powers and individuals equally entitled to the ethical claim is completely set up in its movement.

The sphere of this content, although capable of great variety of detail, is not in its essential features very extensive. The principal source of opposition, which Sophocles in particular, in this respect following the lead of Aeschylus, has accepted and worked out in the finest way, is that of the *body politic*, the opposition, that is, between ethical life in its social universality and the family as the natural ground of moral relations. These are the purest forces of tragic representation. It is, in short, the harmony of these spheres and the concordant action within the bounds of their realized content, which constitute the perfected reality of the moral life. In this respect I need only recall the "Seven before Thebes" of Aeschylus and, as a yet stronger illustration, the "Antigone" of Sophocles. Antigone reverences the ties of blood-relationship, the gods of the nether world. Creon alone recognizes Zeus, the paramount Power of public life and the commonwealth. We come across a similar conflict in the "Iphigenia in Aulis," as also in the "Agamemnon," the "Choephorae," and "Eumenides" of Aeschylus, and in the "Electra" of Sophocles. Agamemnon, as king and leader of his army, sacrifices his daughter in the interest of the Greek folk and the Trojan expedition. He shatters thereby the bond of love as between himself and his daughter and wife, which Clytemnestra retains in the depths of a mother's heart, and in revenge prepares an ignominious death for her husband on his return. Orestes, their son, respects his mother, but is bound to represent the right of his father, the king, and strikes dead the mother who bore him.

A content of this type retains its force through all times, and its presentation, despite all difference of nationality, vitally arrests our human and artistic sympathies.

Of a more formal type is that second kind of essential collision, an illustration of which in the tragic story of Oedipus the Greek tragedians especially favoured. Of this Sophocles has left us the most complete example in his "Oedipus Rex," and "Oedipus at Colonus." The problem here is concerned with the claim of alertness in our intelligence, with the nature of the obligation implied in that which a man carries out with a volition fully aware of its acts as contrasted with that which he has done in fact, but unconscious of and with no intention of doing what he has done under the directing providence of the gods. Oedipus slays his father, marries his mother, begets children in this incestuous alliance, and nevertheless is involved in these most terrible of crimes without active participation either in will or knowledge. The point of view of our profounder modern consciousness of right and wrong would be to recognize that crimes of this description, inasmuch as they were neither referable to a personal knowledge or volition, were not deeds for which the true personality of the perpetrator was responsible. The plastic nature of the Greek on the contrary adheres to the bare fact which an individual has achieved, and refuses to face the division implied by the purely ideal attitude of the soul in the self-conscious life on the one hand and the objective significance of the fact accomplished on the other.

For ourselves, to conclude this survey, other collisions, which either in general are related to the universally accepted association of personal action to the Greek conception of Destiny, or in some measure to more exceptional conditions, are comparatively speaking less important.

In all these tragic conflicts, however, we must above all place on one side the false notion of *guilt* or *innocence*. The heroes of tragedy are quite as much under one category as the other. If we accept the idea as valid that a man is guilty only in the case that a choice lay open to him, and he deliberately decided on the course of action which he carried out, then these plastic figures of ancient drama are guiltless. They act in accordance with a specific character, a specific pathos, for the simple reason that they are this character, this pathos. In such a case there is no lack of decision and no choice. The strength of great characters consists precisely in this that they do not choose, but are entirely and absolutely just that which they will and achieve. They are simply themselves, and never anything else, and their greatness consists in that fact. Weakness in action, in other words, wholly consists in the division of the personal self as such from its content, so that character, volition and final purpose do not appear as absolutely one unified growth; and inasmuch as no assured end lives in the soul as the very substance of the particular personality, as the pathos and might of the individual's entire will, he is still able to turn with indecision from this course to that, and his final decision is that of caprice. A wavering attitude of this description is alien to these plastic creations. The bond between the psychological state of mind and the content of the will is for them indissoluble. That which stirs them to action is this very pathos which implies an ethical justification and which, even in the pathetic aspects of the dialogue, is not enforced in and through the merely personal rhetoric of the heart and the sophistry of passion, but in the equally masculine and cultivated objective presence, in the profound possibilities, the harmony and vitally plastic beauty of which Sophocles was to a superlative degree master. At the same time, however, such a pathos, with its potential resources of collision, brings them to deeds that are both injurious and wrongful. They have no desire to avoid the blame that results therefrom. On the contrary, it is their fame to have done what they have done. One can in fact urge nothing more intolerable against a hero of this type than by saying that he has acted innocently. It is a point of honour with such great characters that they are guilty. They have no desire to excite pity or our sensibilities. For it is not the substantive, but rather the wholly personal deepening of the personality which stirs our individual pain. His securely strong character, however, coalesces entirely with his essential pathos, and this indivisible accord inspires wonder, not compassion. The drama of Euripides marks the transition to that.

The final result, then, of the development of tragedy conducts us to this issue and only this, namely, that the twofold vindication of the mutually conflicting aspects is no doubt retained, but the *one-sided* mode is cancelled, and the undisturbed ideal harmony brings back again that condition of the chorus, which attributes without reserve equal honour to all the gods. The true course of dramatic development consists in the annulment of *contradictions* viewed as such, in the reconciliation of the forces of human action, which alternately strive to negate each other in their conflict. Only so far is misfortune and suffering not the final issue, but rather the satisfaction of spirit, as for the first time, in virtue of such a conclusion, the necessity of all that particular individuals experience, is able to appear in complete accord with reason, and our emotional attitude is tranquillized on a true ethical basis; rudely shaken by the calamitous result to the heroes, but reconciled in the substantial facts. And it is only in so far as we retain such a view securely that we shall be in a position to understand ancient tragedy. We have to guard ourselves therefore from concluding that a *dénouement* of this type is merely a moral issue conformably to which evil is punished and virtue rewarded, as indicated by the proverb that "when crime turns to vomit, virtue sits down at table." We have nothing to do here with this wholly personal aspect of a self-reflecting personality and its conception of good and evil, but are concerned with the appearance of the affirmative reconciliation and the equal validity of both powers engaged in conflict, if the collision is complete. To as little extent is the necessity of the issue a blind destiny, or in other words a purely irrational, unintelligible fate, identified with the classical world by many; rather it is the rationality of destiny, albeit it does not as yet appear as self-conscious Providence, the divine final end of which in conjunction with the world and individuals appears on its own account and for others, depending as it does on just this fact that the highest Power paramount over particular gods and mankind cannot suffer this, namely, that the forces, which affirm their self-subsistence in modes that are abstract or incomplete, and thereby overstep the boundary of their warrant, no less than the conflicts which result from them, should retain their self-stability. Fate drives personality back upon its limits, and shatters it, when it has grown overweening. An irrational compulsion, however, an innocence of suffering would rather only excite indignation in the soul of the spectator than ethical tranquillity. From a further point of view, therefore, the reconciliation of *tragedy* is equally distinct from that of the *Epos*. If we look at either Achilles or Odysseus in this respect we observe that both attain their object, and it is right that they do so; but it is not a continuous happiness with which they are favoured; they have on the contrary to taste in its bitterness the feeling of finite condition, and are forced to fight wearily through difficulties, losses and sacrifices. It is in fact a universal demand of truth that in the course of life and all that takes place in the objective world the nugatory character of finite conditions should compel attention. So no doubt the anger of Achilles is reconciled; he obtains from Agamemnon that in respect of which he had suffered the sense of insult; he is revenged upon Hector; the funeral rites of Patroclus are consummated, and the character of Achilles is acknowledged in all its glory. But his wrath and its reconciliation have for all that cost him his dearest friend, the noble Patroclus; and, in order to avenge himself upon Hector for this loss, he finds himself compelled to disengage himself from his anger, to enter once more the battle against the Trojans, and in the very moment when his glory is acknowledged receives the prevision of his early death. In a similar way Odysseus reaches Ithaca at last, the goal of his desire; but he does so alone and in his sleep, having lost all his companions, all the war-booty from Ilium, after long years of endurance and fatigue. In this way both heroes have paid their toll to finite conditions and the claim of nemesis is evidenced in the destruction of Troy and the misfortunes of the Greek heroes. But this nemesis is simply justice as conceived of old, which merely humiliates what is everywhere too exalted, in order to establish once more the abstract balance of fortune by the instrumentality of misfortune, and which merely touches and affects finite existence without further ethical signification. And this is the justice of the Epic in the field of objective fact, the universal reconciliation of simple accommodation. The higher conception of reconciliation in tragedy is on the contrary related to the resolution of specific ethical and substantive facts from their contradiction into their true harmony. The way in which such an accord is established is asserted under very different modes; I propose therefore merely to direct attention to the fundamental features of the actual process herein involved.

First, we have particularly to emphasize the fact, that if it is the one-sidedness of the pathos which constitutes the real basis of collisions this merely amounts to the statement that it is asserted in the action of life, and therewith has become the unique pathos of a particular individual. If this one-sidedness is to be abrogated then it is this individual which, to the extent that his action is exclusively identified with this isolated pathos, must perforce be stripped and sacrificed. For the individual here is merely this single life, and, if this unity is not secured in its stability on its own account, the individual is shattered.

The most complete form of this development is possible when the individuals engaged in conflict relatively to their concrete or objective life appear in each case essentially involved in one whole, so that they stand fundamentally under the power of that against which they battle, and consequently infringe that, which, conformably to their own essential life, they ought to respect. Antigone, for example, lives under the political authority of Creon; she is herself the daughter of a king and the affianced of Haemon, so that her obedience to the royal prerogative is an obligation. But Creon also, who is on his part father and husband, is under obligation to respect the sacred ties of relationship, and only by breach of this can give an order that is in conflict with such a sense. In consequence of this we find immanent in the life of both that which each respectively combats, and they are seized and broken by that very bond which is rooted in the compass of their own social existence. Antigone is put to death before she can enjoy what she looks forward to as bride, and Creon too is punished in the fatal end of his son and wife, who commit suicide, the former on account of Antigone's death, and the latter owing to Haemon's. Among all the fine creations of the ancient and the modern world—and I am acquainted with pretty nearly everything in such a class, and one ought to know it, and it is quite possible—the "Antigone" of Sophocles is from this point of view in my judgment the most excellent and satisfying work of art.

The tragic issue does not, however, require in every case, as a means of removing both over-emphasized aspects and the equal honour which they respectively claim, the downfall of the contestant parties. The "Eumenides" ends, as we all know, not with the death of Orestes, or the destruction of the Eumenides, these avenging spirits of matricide and filial affection, as opposed to Apollo, who seeks to protect unimpaired the worth of and reverence for the family chief and king, who prompted Orestes to slay Clytemnestra, but with Orestes released from the punishment and honour bestowed on both divinities. At the same time we cannot fail to see in this adjusted conclusion the nature of the authority which the Greeks attached to their gods when they presented them as mere individuals contending with each other. They appear, in short, to the Athenian of everyday life merely as definite aspects of ethical experience which the principles of morality viewed in their complete and harmonious coherence bind together. The votes of the Areopagus are equal on either side. It is Athene, the goddess, the life of Athens, that is, imagined in its essential unity, who adds the white pebble, who frees Orestes, and at the same time promises altars and a cult to the Eumenides no less than Apollo. As a contrast to this type of objective reconciliation the settlement may be, *secondly*, of a more personal character. In other words, the individual concerned in the action may in the last instance surrender his one-sided point of view. In this betrayal by personality of its essential pathos, however, it cannot fail to appear destitute of character; and this contradicts the masculine integrity of such plastic figures. The individual, therefore, can only submit to a higher Power and its counsel or command, to the effect that while on his own account he adheres to such a pathos, the will is nevertheless broken in its bare obstinacy by a god's authority. In such a case the knot is not loosened, but, as in the case of Philoctetes, it is severed by a *deus ex machina*.

But as a *further* and final class, and one more beautiful than the above rather external mode of resolution, we have the reconciliation more properly of the soul itself, in which respect there is, in virtue of the personal significance, a real approach to our modern point of view. The most perfect example of this in ancient drama is to be found in the ever admirable "Oedipus at Colonos" of Sophocles. The protagonist here has unwittingly slain his father, secured the sceptre of Thebes, and the bridal bed of his own mother. He is not rendered unhappy by these unwitting crimes; but the power of divination he has of old possessed makes him realize, despite himself, the darkness of the experience that confronts him, and he becomes fearfully, if indistinctly, aware of what his position is. In this resolution of the riddle in himself he resembles Adam, losing his happiness when he obtains the knowledge of good and evil. What he then does, the seer, is to blind himself, then abdicate the throne and depart from Thebes, very much as Adam and Eve are driven from Paradise. From henceforward he wanders about a helpless old man. Finally a god calls the terribly afflicted man to himself, the man, that is, who refusing the request of his sons that he should return to Thebes, prefers to associate with the Erinyes; the man, in short, who extinguishes all the disruption in himself and who purifies himself in his own soul. His blind eyes are made clear and bright, his limbs are healed, and become a treasure of the city which received him as a free guest. And this illumination in death is for ourselves no less than for him the more truly visible reconciliation which is worked out both in and for himself as individual man, in and through, that is, his essential character. Critics have endeavoured to discover here the temper of the Christian life; we are told we have here the picture of a sinner, whom God receives into His grace; and the fateful misfortunes which expire in their finite condition are made good with the seal of blessedness in death. The reconciliation of the Christian religion, however, is an illumination of the soul, which, bathed in the everlasting waters of salvation, is raised above mortal life and its deeds. Here it is the heart itself, for in such a view the spiritual life can effect this, which buries that life and its deed in the grave of the heart itself, counting the recriminations of earthly guilt as part and parcel of its own earthly individuality; and which, in the full assuredness of the eternally pure and spiritual condition of blessedness, holds itself in itself calm and steadfast against such impeachment. The illumination of Oedipus, on the contrary, remains throughout, in consonance with ancient ideas, the restoration of conscious life from the strife of ethical powers and violations to the renewed and harmonious unity of this *ethical content itself*.

There is a further feature in this type of reconciliation, however, and that is the *personal* or ideal nature of the satisfaction. We may take this as a point of transition to the otherwise to be contrasted province of *comedy*.

(b) That which is comic is, as we have already seen, in general terms the subjective or personal state, which forces and then dissolves the action which issues from it by its own effect into and in contradiction, remaining throughout and in virtue of this process tranquil in its own self-assurance. Comedy possesses, therefore, for its basis and point of departure that with which it is possible for tragedy to terminate, that is, a soul to the fullest extent and eventually reconciled, a joyous state, which, however much it is instrumental in the marring of its volitional power, and, indeed, in itself comes to grief, by reason of its asserting voluntarily what is in conflict with its aim, does not therefore lose its general equanimity. A personal self-assurance of this character, however, is, from a further point of view, only possible in so far as the ends proposed, and withal the characters include nothing that is on its own account essentially substantive; or, if they do possess such an intrinsic worth, it is adopted and carried out intentionally under a mode which is totally opposed to the genuine truth contained, in a form, therefore, that is destitute of such truth, so that in this respect, as in the previous case, it is merely that which is itself essentially of no intrinsic importance, but a matter of indifference which is marred, and the individual remains just as he was and unaffected.

Such a view is, too, in its general lines the conception of the old classic comedy, in so far as tradition reflects it in the plays of Aristophanes. We should, however, be careful to notice the distinction whether the individuals in the play are aware that they are comic, or are so merely from the specta-tor's point of view. It is only the first class that we can reckon as part of the genuine comedy in which Aristophanes was a master. Conformably to such a type, a character is only placed in a ridiculous situation, when we perceive that he himself is not in earnest about the earnestness of his purpose and volun-tary effort, so that this earnestness is throughout the means of his own undoing, inasmuch as throughout such a character is unable to enter into any more noble and universally valid interest, which necessarily involves it in a situation of conflict; and, even assuming that he does actually partake of it, merely does so in a way that shows a nature, which, in virtue of its practical existence, has already annihilated that which it ap-pears to strive to bring into operation, so that after all one sees such a coalescence has never been really effected. The comic comes, therefore, rather into play among classes of a lower social order in actual conditions of life, among men who re-main much as they are, and neither are able or desire to be anything else; who, while incapable of any genuine pathos, have no doubt whatever as to what they are and do. At the same time the higher nature that is in them is asserted in this that they are not with any seriousness attached to the finite conditions which hem them in, but remain superior to the same and in themselves essentially steadfast and self-reliant against mishap and loss. This absolute freedom of spirit, which brings its own essential comfort from the first in all that a man undertakes, this world of subjective serenity is that to which Aristophanes conducts us. Without a reading of him it is hardly possible to imagine what a wealth of exuberance there is in the human heart.

The interests among which this type of comedy moves are not necessarily taken from spheres opposed to religion, moral-ity, and art. On the contrary the old Greek comedy remains no doubt within the limits of this positive and substantive con-tent of human life; but it is the individual caprice, the vulgar folly and perversity, by reason of which the characters con-cerned bring to nought activities which in their aim have a finer significance. And in this respect an ample and very per-tinent material is supplied Aristophanes partly by Greek gods, and partly by the life of the Athenian people. In other words,

the configuration of the divine in human impersonation itself
possesses, in its mode of presentation and its particularization,
to the extent at least that it is further enforced in opposition
to that which is merely one-sided and human, the contradiction that is opposed to the nobility of its significance; it is thus
permitted to appear as a purely empty extension of this personal life which is inadequate wholly to express it. More particularly, however, Aristophanes revels in the follies of the
common folk, the stupidities of its orators and statesmen, the
blockheadedness of war, and is eager, above all, and with all
the politeness of his satire and the full weight of his ridicule,
but also not without the profoundest meaning, to hand over
the new tendencies of the tragedies of Euripides to the laughter
of his fellow-citizens. The characters he has imported into the
substance of his amazing artistic creations he runs into the
mould of fool from the start with a sportive fancy that seems
inexhaustible, so that the very idea of a rational result is impossible. He treats all alike, whether it be a Strepsiades, who
will join the ranks of philosophers in order to be rid of his
debts, or a Socrates, who offers to instruct the aforesaid
Strepsiades and his son, or Bacchus, whom he makes descend
into the lower world, in order to bring up a genuine tragic
poet, and in just the same way Cleon, the women, and the
Greeks, who would like to pump up the goddess of Peace from
the well. The key-note that we find in all these various creations is the imperturbable self-assurance of such characters one
and all, which becomes all the more emphatic in proportion
as they prove themselves incapable of carrying into effect that
which they project. Our fools here are so entirely unembar-
rassed in their folly, and also the more sensible among them
possess such a tincture of that which runs contrary to the very
course upon which they are set, that they all, the more sensible with the rest, remain fixed to this personal attitude of pro-
digious imperturbability, no matter what comes next or where
it carries them. It is in fact the blessed laughter of the Olympian gods, with their untroubled equanimity, now at home in
the human breast, and prepared for all contingencies. And
withal we never find Aristophanes merely a cold or evil-
disposed mocker. He was a man of the finest education, a most
exemplary citizen, to whom the weal of Athens was of really

deep importance, and who through thick and thin shows himself to be a true patriot. What therefore is in the fullest sense resolved in his comedies is, as already stated, not the divine and what is of ethical import, but the thoroughgoing upside-down-ness which inflates itself into the semblance of these substantive forces, the particular form and distinctive mode of its manifestation, in which the essential thing or matter is already from the first no longer present, so that it can without restriction be simply handed over to the unconcerned play of unqualified personal caprice. But for the very reason that Aristophanes makes explicit the absolute contradiction between the essential nature of the gods, or that of political and social life, and the personal activities of individual persons or citizens, who ought to endow such substantive form with reality, we find in this very triumph of purely personal self-assertion, despite all the profounder insight which the poet displays, one of the greatest symptoms of the degeneracy of Greece. And it is on account of this that these pictures of a wholly unperturbed sense of fundamental well-being are as a matter of fact the last important harvest which we have from the poetry created by the exuberant genius, culture, and wit of the Greek nation.

(2) I shall now direct attention to the dramatic art of the modern world, and here, too, I only propose to emphasize the more general and fundamental features which we find of importance, whether dealing with tragedy or the ordinary drama and comedy.

(a) Tragedy, in the nobility which distinguishes it in its ancient plastic form, is limited to the partial point of view that for its exclusive and essential basis it only enforces as effective the ethically substantive content and its necessary laws; and, on the other hand, leaves the individual and subjective self-penetration of the dramatic characters essentially unevolved; while comedy on its part, to complete what we may regard as the reversed side of such plastic construction, exhibits subjectivity in the unfettered abandonment of its topsy-turvydom and ultimate dissolution.

Modern tragedy accepts in its own province from the first the principle of subjectivity. It makes, therefore, the personal intimacy of character—the character, that is, which is no purely individual and vital embodiment of ethical forces in the classic sense—its peculiar object and content. It, moreover, makes, in a type of concurrence that is adapted to this end, human actions come into collision through the instrumentality of the external accident of circumstances in the way that a contingency of a similar character is also decisive in its effect on the consequence, or appears to be so decisive.

In this connection we would subject to examination the following fundamental points:

First, the nature of the varied *ends* which ought to come into the executive process of the action as the content of the characters therein.

Secondly, the nature of the tragic *characters* themselves, as also of the collisions they are compelled to face.

Thirdly, the nature of the final *issue* and tragic reconciliation, as these differ from those of ancient tragedy.

To start with, we may observe that, however much in romantic tragedy the subjectivity of suffering and passions, in the true meaning of these words, is the focal centre, yet, for all that, it is impossible in human activity that the ground basis of definite ends in the concrete worlds of the family, the State, the Church, and others should be dispensed with, for with activity, man passes wholly into the sphere of true particularity. In so far, however, as in the drama under discussion, it is not the substantive content as such in these spheres of life which constitutes the main interest of individuals, such ends are from a certain point of view particularized in a breadth of extension and variety, as also in exceptional modes of presentment, in which it often happens that what is truly essential is only able to force itself on our attention with attenuated strength. And over and above this fact, these ends receive an entirely altered form. In the province of religion, for example, the content which pre-eminently is asserted is no longer the particular ethical powers exhibited imaginatively under the mode of divine individuals, either in their own person or in the pathos of human heroes. It is the history of Christ, or of saints and the like, which is now set before us. In the political community it is mainly the position of kingship, the power of vassal chiefs, the strife of dynasties, or the particular members of one and the same ruling family which forms the content of the varied picture. Nay, if we take a step further we find as the principal subject-matter questions of civic or private right and other relations of a similar character; and, further, we shall find a similar attention paid to features in the family life which were not yet within the reach of ancient drama. And the reason of this is that, inasmuch as in the spheres of life above-mentioned the principle of the personal life in its independence has asserted its claim, novel phases of existence make their inevitable appearance in each one of them, which the modern man claims to set up as the end and directory of his action.

And, from a further point of view in this drama, it is the right of subjectivity, as above defined, absolutely unqualified, which is retained as the dominating content; and for this reason personal love, honour, and the rest make such an exclusive appeal as ends of human action that, while in one direction other relations cannot fail to appear as the purely external background on which these interests of our modern life are set in motion, in another such relations on their own account actively conflict with the requirements of the more individual state of emotion. Of more profound significance still is wrong and crime, even if a particular character does not deliberately and to start with aim at either, yet does not avoid them to attain his original purpose.

And, furthermore, in contrast to this particularization and individual standpoint, the ends proposed may likewise either in one direction expand to cover the universality and all-inclusive embrace of the content, or they are in another apprehended and carried into execution as themselves intrinsically substantive. In the first respect, I will merely recall to memory that typically philosophical tragedy, the "Faust" of Goethe, in which, on the one hand, a spirit of disillusion in the pursuit of science, and, on the other, the vital resources of a worldly life and earthly enjoyment—in a word, the attempted mediation in the tragic manner of an individual's wisdom and strife with the Absolute in its essential significance and phenomenal manifestation, offers a breadth of content such as no other dramatic poet has hitherto ventured to include in one and the same composition. The "Carl Moor" of Schiller is something of the same fashion. He rebels against the entire order of civic society and the collective condition of the world and the humanity of his time, and fortifies himself as such against the same. Wallenstein in the same way conceives a great and far-reaching purpose, the unity and peace of Germany, an object he fails to carry into effect by the means which, in virtue of the fact that they are welded together in an artificial manner, and one that lacks essential coherence, break in pieces and come to nought precisely in the direction where he is most anxious of their success; and he fails in the same way by reason of his opposition to the imperial authority, upon which he himself and his enterprise are inevitably shattered. Such objects of a world-wide policy, such as a Carl Moor or a Wallenstein pursue, are as a rule not accomplished at the hands of a single individual for whom others become obedient instruments; they carry themselves into effect partly with the will of many, partly against and without their knowledge. As an illustration of a conception of objects viewed in their essential significance, I will merely instance certain tragedies of Calderon, in which love, honour, and similar virtues are respectively to the rights and obligations in which they involve the characters of the action, treated as so many unyielding laws of independent force with all the stringency of a code. We find also frequently much the same thing assumed in Schiller's tragic characters, though the point of view is no doubt wholly different, at least to the extent that such individuals conceive and combat for their ends with the assumption they are universal and absolutely valid human rights. So in the early play of "Kabale und Liebe" Major Ferdinand seeks to defend the rights of Nature against the conveniences of fashionable society, and, above all, claims of the Marquis Posa freedom of thought as an inalienable possession of humanity.

Generally speaking, however, in modern tragedy it is not the substantive content of their object in the interest of which men act, and which is maintained as the stimulus of their passion; rather it is the inner experience of their heart and individual emotion, or the particular qualities of their personality, which insist on satisfaction. For even in the examples already referred to we find that to a real extent in those heroes of Spanish honour and love the content of their ultimate ends is so essentially of a personal character that the rights and obligations deducible from the same are able to fuse in direct concurrence with the individual desires of the heart, and to a large extent, too, in the youthful works of Schiller this continual insistence upon Nature, rights of man, and a converted world somewhat savours of the excess of a wholly personal enthusiasm. And if it came about that Schiller in later years endeavoured to enforce a more mature type of pathos, this was simply due to the fact that it was his main idea to restore once again in modern dramatic art the principle of ancient tragedy.

In order to emphasize still more distinctly the difference which in this respect obtains between ancient and modern tragedy, I will merely refer the reader to Shakespeare's "Hamlet." Here we find fundamentally a collision similar to that which is introduced by Aeschylus into his "Choephorae" and by Sophocles into his "Electra." For Hamlet's father, too, and the King, as in these Greek plays, has been murdered, and his mother has wedded the murderer. That which, however, in the conception of the Greek dramatists possesses a certain ethical justification—I mean the death of Agamemnon—in the contrasted case of Shakespeare's play, can only be viewed as an atrocious crime, of which Hamlet's mother is innocent; so that the son is merely concerned in his vengeance to direct his attention to the fratricidal king, and there is nothing in the latter's character that possesses any real claim to his respect. The real collision, therefore, does not turn on the fact that the son, in giving effect to a rightful sense of vengeance, is himself forced to violate morality, but rather on the particular personality, the inner life of Hamlet, whose noble soul is not steeled to this kind of energetic activity, but, while full of contempt for the world and life, what between making up his mind and attempting to carry into effect or preparing to carry into effect its resolves, is bandied from pillar to post, and finally through his own procrastination and the external course of events meets his own doom.

If we now turn, in close connection with the above conclusions, to our *second* point of fundamental importance in modern tragedy—that is to say, the nature of the characters and their collisions—we may summarily take a point of departure from the following general observations.

The heroes of ancient classic tragedy discover circumstances under which they, so long as they irrefragably adhere to the *one* ethical state of pathos which alone corresponds to their own already formed personality, must infallibly come into conflict with an ethical Power which opposes them and possesses an equal ethical claim to recognition. Romantic characters, on the contrary, are from the first placed within a wide expanse of contingent relations and conditions, within which every sort of action is possible; so that the conflict, to which no doubt the external conditions presupposed supply the occasion, essentially abides within the *character* itself, to which the individuals concerned in their passion give effect, not, however, in the interests of the ethical vindication of the truly substantive claims, but for the simple reason that they are the kind of men they are. Greek heroes also no doubt act in accordance with their particular individuality; but this individuality, as before noted, if we take for our examples the supreme results of ancient tragedy, is itself necessarily identical with an ethical pathos which is substantive. In modern tragedy the peculiar character in its real significance, and to which it as a matter of accident remains constant, whether it happens to grasp after that which on its own account is on moral grounds justifiable, or is carried into wrong and crime, forms its resolves under the dictate of personal wishes and necessities, or among other things purely external considerations. In such a case, therefore, though we may have a coalescence between the moral aspect of the object and the character, yet, for all that, such a concurrence does not constitute, and cannot constitute—owing to the divided character of ends, passions, and the life wholly personal to the individual—the *essential* basis and objective condition of the depth and beauty of the tragic drama.

In view of the great variety of differences which further separates particular characters in this type of poetry, it is impossible to say much in the way of generalization. I will, therefore, restrict myself to a reference to the following fundamental points of view. A primary opposition which at once invites notice is that of an *abstract,* and consequently formal, characterization in its contrast with the actual individuals whom we are accustomed to meet in the concrete living world. As example of this type, we may with exceptional pertinency cite the tragic characters of the French and Italians, which, originating in the imitation of ancient drama, to a greater or less degree merely amount to pure personifications of specific passions, such as love, honour, fame, ambition, tyranny, and so forth, and which, while they present the motives of their actions, as also the gradation and quality of their emotions to the best advantage with a lavish display of declamation, and all the arts of rhetoric, none the less by doing so rather resemble the dramatic failures of Seneca than the dramatic masterpieces of the Greeks. Spanish tragedy also receives the stamp of this abstract style of character-drawing. In this case, however, the pathos of love, in its conflict with honour, friendship, royal prerogative, and the rest is itself of so abstract a subjective character that in the case where the intention is to make this equally subjective substantiality stand out as the genuine object of interest, a more complete particularization of characters is hardly feasible. The characters of Spanish drama, however, often possess a certain kind of solidity, and, if I may use the expression, inflexible personality, however wanting in content it may be, a feature that is absent from French work; and at the same time Spanish writers, here also in contrast to the cold simplicity which the movement of French tragedies exhibits even in their tragic composition, know how to make up with the cleverly invented abundance of interesting situations and developments the deficiency referred to in the matter of characterization.

In contrast to both these schools, and in their mastery of the exposition of fully developed human characters and personality, the English are exceptionally distinguished; and among them, and soaring above the rest at an almost unapproachable height, stands Shakespeare. For even in the cases where a purely formal passion, as for instance ambition in Macbeth, or jealousy in Othello, claims as its field the entire pathos of his tragic hero, such an abstraction impairs by no fraction the full breadth of the personality. Despite this restriction the characters remain throughout entire men. In fact, the more Shakespeare on the infinite embrace of his world-stage, proceeds to develop the extreme limits of evil and folly, to that extent, as I have already observed, on these very boundaries—of course, not without real wealth of poetic embellishment—he concentrates these characters in their limitations. While doing so, however, he confers on them intelligence and imagination; and, by means of the image in which they, by virtue of that intelligence, contemplate themselves objectively as a work of art, he makes them free artists of themselves, and is fully able, through the complete virility and truth of his characterization, to awaken our interest in criminals, no less than in the most vulgar and weak-witted lubbers and fools. Of a similar nature is the style of expression he makes his tragic characters adopt. It is at once individual, realistic, emphatically vital, extraordinarily various, and, moreover, where it seems advisable, it can rise to sublimity and is marked by an overwhelming force of utterance. Its ideal intensity and its qualities of invention are displayed in images and similes that flash from each other with lightning rapidity. Its very rhetoric, here the barren child of no school, but the growth of genuine emotion and penetration into human personality, is such that, if we take into account this extraordinary union of the directness of life itself and ideal greatness of soul, we shall find it hard indeed to point to a single other dramatic poet among the moderns whom we are entitled to rank in his company. No doubt Goethe in his youth made a real effort to achieve some approach to a like natural truth and detailed characterization; but in the ideal force and exaltation of passion his rivalry collapses. Schiller, again, has shown an increasing tendency toward violence, the tempestuous expatiation of which lacks a true core of reality.

Modern characters also differ in the nature of their *constancy* or their spiritual *vacillation* and distraction. We find, no doubt, the weakness of indecision, the fluctuations of reflection, the weighing of reasons, conformably to which a resolve should be directed, here and there in classic drama, and more particularly in the tragedies of Euripides. But Euripides is a writer whose tendency is already to forsake the wholly plastic completeness of characterization and action and to develop exceptional aspects of personal sensibility. In modern tragedy we meet yet more frequently such vacillating characters, more particularly on the ground that they are essentially under the sway of two opposed passions, which make them fluctuate from one resolve or one kind of deed to another. I have already made some observations on this attitude of vacillation in another context, and will now merely supplement this by stating that, although the tragic action must depend on colliding factors, yet where we find such a division in *one* and the same individual such a concurrence is always attended with precarious consequences. And the reason is that this disruption into interests, which are opposed to each other, is due in part to an obscurity and obtuseness of the intelligence, and in some measure, too, to weakness and immaturity. We come across characters of this type in the creations of Goethe's younger days, notably Weislingen, Fernando in "Stella," and above all Clavigo. They are, as we may say, double men, who are unable to secure a ready, and so stable, individuality. It is wholly another matter when two opposed spheres of life or moral obligation are equally sacred to a character which, on its own account, is not deficient in stability, and such a person is under the necessity of ranking himself on *one* side to the exclusion of the other. In a case of that kind, the vacillation is merely a moment of passage, and does not itself constitute, as it were, the nervous system of the character. Again, of a somewhat similar kind, is the tragic case where the spiritual life is seduced, despite its nobler purpose, into objects of passion which are contradictory to the same, as in the case of Schiller's "Holy Maid," and are then forced to seek a recovery from this division of the soul in their own intimate or objective life, or pay the penalty. At the same time, this personal tragedy of inward division, when it is made the pivot on which the tragic action revolves, contains, as a rule, what is merely pitiful and painful, or, from another standpoint, exasperating; and the poet will rather do better to avoid it than go out of his way to find it and develop it. The worst case is that, however, where such a vacillation and veering round of character and the entire personality is—the very dialectic of art being thrown awry for this purpose—made the principle of the entire presentation, as though the truth of all importance was to demonstrate that no character is in itself firmly rooted and self-assured. The one-sided ends of specific passions, it is true, ought not to bring about a realization which is secured without a battle; and also, in everyday life, they cannot fail to experience, through the reactionary power of conditions and individuals which oppose them, their finite character and lack of stability. An issue of this kind, however, before the appearance of which we are unable to get the pertinent conclusion, ought not to be introduced as a dialectical piece of wheel adjustment in the personality itself; if it is, the person concerned, viewed as *this* personal state of the soul, is a wholly empty and undefined form, whose collective living growth is found, no less in respect to its objects than in its character, to be wholly wanting in definition. In much the same way the case, also, is otherwise, where the change in the spiritual condition of the entire man itself appears as a direct consequent of just this, its own kind of self-detachment, so that only that is developed and emphasized which essentially and from the first lay secured in the character. As an example, we find in Shakespeare's Lear that the original folly of the old man is intensified to the point of madness much in the same way that Gloster's spiritual blindness is converted into actual physical blindness, in which for the first time his eyes are opened to the true distinction in the love he entertains for his two sons respectively. It is precisely Shakespeare who, as a contrast to that exposition of vacillating and essentially self-divided characters, supplies us with the finest examples of essentially stable and consequential characters, who go to their doom precisely in virtue of this tenacious hold upon themselves and their ends. Unsupported by the sanction of the moral law, but rather carried onward by the formal necessity of their personality, they suffer themselves to be involved in their acts by the coil of external circumstances, or they plunge blindly therein and maintain themselves there by sheer force of will, even where all that they do is merely done because they are impelled to assert themselves against others, or because they have simply come to the particular point they have reached. The rise of insurgent passion, one essentially consonant with a certain type of character, one which has not as yet fully emerged, but now secures its utmost expansion, this onward movement and process of a great soul, with all the intimate traits of its evolution, this picture of its self-destructive conflict with circumstances, human and objective conditions and results, is the main content of some of Shakespeare's most interesting tragedies.

The last of the subjects which we have still to discuss as proposed is the nature of the *tragic issue* which characters in our present drama have to confront, as also the type of tragic *reconciliation* compatible with such a standpoint. In ancient tragedy it is the eternal justice which, as the absolute might of destiny, delivers and restores the harmony of substantive being in its ethical character by its opposition to the particular forces which, in their strain to assert an independent subsistence, come into collision, and which, in virtue of the rational ideality implied in its operations, satisfies us even where we see the downfall of particular men. In so far as a justice of the same kind is present in modern tragedy, it is necessarily, in part, more abstract on account of the closer differentiation of ends and characters, and, in part, of a colder nature and one that is more akin to that of a criminal court, in virtue of the fact that the wrong and crime into which individuals are necessarily carried, in so far as they are intent upon executing their designs, are of a profounder significance. Macbeth, for instance, the elder daughters of Lear and their husbands, the president in "Kabale und Liebe," Richard III, and many similar examples, on account of their atrocious conduct, only deserve the fate they get. This type of *dénouement* usually is presented under the guise that individuals are crushed by an actual force which they have defied in order to carry out their personal aims. Wallenstein, for example, is shattered on the adamantine wall of the imperial power; but the old Piccolomini, who, in order to maintain the lawful régime, betrays a friend and misuses the rights of friendship, is punished through the death and sacrifice of his son. Götz von Berlichingen, too, attacks a dominant and securely founded political order, and goes to ground, as also Weislingen and Adelheid, who range themselves, no doubt, on the side of this organized power, but, through wrongful deed and disloyalty, prepare the way to disaster. And along with this we have the demand emphasized, in virtue of the personal point of view of such characters, that these should of necessity appear themselves to acknowledge the justice of their fate. Such a state of acceptance may either be of a religious nature, in which case the soul becomes conscious of a more exalted and indestructible condition of blessedness with which to confront the collapse of its mundane personality; or it may be of a more formal, albeit more worldly, type, in so far, that is, as the strength and equanimity of the character persists in its course up to the point of overthrow without breaking asunder; and in this way, despite all circumstances and mischances, preserves with unimpaired energy its personal freedom. Or, as a final alternative, where the substance of such acceptance is of more real value, by the recognition that the lot which the individual receives is the one, however bitter it may be, which his action merits.

From another point of view, however, we may see the tragic issue also merely in the light of the effect of unhappy circumstances and external accidents, which might have brought about, quite as readily, a different result and a happy conclusion. From such a point of view we have merely left us the conception that the modern idea of individuality, with its searching definition of character, circumstances, and developments, is handed over essentially to the contingency of the earthly state, and must carry the fateful issues of such finitude. Pure commiseration of this sort is, however, destitute of meaning; and it is nothing less than a frightful kind of external necessity in the particular case where we see the downfall of essentially noble natures in their conflict thus assumed with the mischance of purely external accidents. Such a course of events can insistently arrest our attention; but in the result it can only be horrible, and the demand is direct and irresistible that the external accidents ought to accord with that which is identical with the spiritual nature of such noble characters. Only as thus regarded can we feel ourselves reconciled with the grievous end of Hamlet and Juliet. From a purely external point of view, the death of Hamlet appears as an accident occasioned by his duel with Laertes and the interchange of the daggers. But in the background of Hamlet's soul, death is already present from the first. The sandbank of finite condition will not content his spirit. As the focus of such mourning and weakness, such melancholy, such a loathing of all the conditions of life, we feel from the first that, hemmed within such an environment of horror, he is a lost man, whom the surfeit of the soul has well-nigh already done to death before death itself approaches him from without. The same thing may be observed in the case of Romeo and Juliet. The ground on which these tender blossoms have been planted is alien to their nature; we have no alternative left us but to lament the pathetic transiency of such a beautiful love, which, as some tender rose in the vale of this world of accident, is broken by rude storms and tempests, and the frangible reckonings of noble and well-meaning devices. This pitiful state of our emotions is, however, simply a feeling of reconciliation that is painful, a kind of *unhappy blessedness* in misfortune.

(b) Much as poets present to us the bare downfall of particular people they are also able to treat the similar contingency of the development of events in such a way, that, though the circumstances in all other respects would appear to give them little enough support, a happy issue of such conditions and characters is secured, in which they elicit our interest. No doubt the favour of such a destiny of events has at least an equal claim upon us as the disfavour. And so far as the question merely concerns the nature of this difference, I must admit that I prefer a happy conclusion. How could it be otherwise? I can myself discover no better ground for the preference of misfortune, simply on its own account as such, to a happy resolution than that of a certain condition of fine sensibility, which is devoted to pain and suffering, and experiences more interest in their presence than in painless situations such as it meets with every day. If therefore the interests are of such a nature, that it is really not worth the trouble to sacrifice the men or women concerned on their altar, it being possible for them either to surrender their objects, without making such surrender as is equivalent to a surrender of their individuality, or to mutually come to an agreement in respect thereof, there is no reason why the conclusion should be tragic. The tragic aspect of the conflicts and their resolution ought in principle merely to be enforced in the cases where it is actually necessary in order to satisfy the claim of a superior point of view. If this necessity is absent there is no sufficient ground for mere suffering and unhappiness. And it is simply due to this fact that social *plays* and *dramas* originate which form, as it were, an intermediate link between tragedies and comedies. I have already in a previous passage explained the poetical standpoint of this class of composition. Among us Germans we find it to some extent appropriating what readily moves us in the world of the citizen and family life; in another direction it is pre-occupied with chivalry, a movement to which the "Götz" of Goethe has given a decided stimulus; mainly, however, we may call it the triumph of *ordinary morality,* which in the large majority of cases is the main thing celebrated. The subject-matter of such plays most in vogue are questions of finance or property, differences of status, unfortunate love affairs, examples of spiritual baseness in the more restricted conditions and affairs of life and so on. In one word, what we have here is that which otherwise is already before our eyes, only with this difference, that in such moral dramas, virtue and duty obtain the victory, and crime is shamed and punished, or betakes itself to repentance, so that in a moral conclusion of this kind the reconciliation ought to centre in this, namely, that whatever happens good is the result. Thereby the fundamental interest is concentrated in the personal or spiritual quality of views held and a good or evil heart. The more, however, the abstractly moral state of mind or heart supplies the pivot on which all turns, so much the less can it be the pathos of a particular matter, or an intrinsically essential object, to which the personality in question is attached. And add to this, from a further point of view, so much the less ultimately is the definite character able to maintain itself and persist in such self-assertion. If all is to be finally focused in the purely moral aspects of the psychological state, or the condition of the heart, from a subjective point of view such as this, with its dominating emphasis on ethical reflection, no standing ground remains for any other definite characteristics, or at least specific ends to be proposed. Let the heart break and change its views. Such seems to be the idea. Pathetic dramas of this type, notably Kotzebue's "Menschenhass und Reue," and also too many moral offences in the dramas of Iffland, strictly speaking, have therefore an issue which we can neither call good or bad. I mean by this that the main thing is as a rule the question of pardon and the promise of moral improvement, and we are therefore confronted with that possibility of spiritual conversion and surrender of the self. No doubt in this fact we discover the exalted nature and greatness of Spirit. When, however, the jolly dog, as the heroes of Kotzebue are for the most part, and not infrequently Iffland's too, after being a scamp and a rascal, suddenly promises to turn over a new leaf, it is frankly impossible with a good-for-nothing chap of this sort that his conversion can be otherwise than mere pretence, or of so superficial a character that it merely affects his skin, and merely supplies a momentary conclusion to the course of events that has no substantial basis, but rather, by all ordinary reckoning, will take the knave to disreputable quarters, if we will only acquaint ourselves with his subsequent history.

(c) As regards our *modern comedy* I must draw particular attention to one point of difference, to which I have already alluded when discussing the old Attic comedy. The point is this—whether the folly and restricted outlook of the characters appears ridiculous to others only, or also to themselves; whether in short the comic figures are an object of laughter only for the audience, or also for themselves. Aristophanes, that creator of genuine comedy, exclusively accepted as the main principle of his plays the latter alternative. Already, however, in Greek comedy of a later date, and subsequently in the hands of Plautus and Terence, the opposite principle came into vogue; and in our modern examples of comedy it has been carried to such a length that we find a large number of comic compositions the inclination of which is more or less the subject-matter which is ridiculous in a purely prosaic sense, or rather we might say matters that leave a sour taste in the mouth of and are repugnant to the comic characters. This is the standpoint of Molière in particular in his best comedies, which have no right to be regarded as farces. The prosaic quality here is justified on the ground that the object aimed at by such characters is a matter of bitter earnest. They are deadly serious in the pursuit of it; they are therefore quite unable to join with satisfaction in the laughter, when they are finally deceived, or themselves are responsible for its failure. They are in short merely the disillusioned objects of a laughter foreign to themselves and generally damaging to themselves. As an example, Molière's "Tartuffe," *le faux dévot*, viewed as the unmasking of a really damned rascal has nothing funny in it, but is a very earnest business, and the deception of the deluded Orgon amounts to a sheer intensity of misfortune, which can only be resolved by the *deus ex machina,* in reference to whom the official of the court of justice utters the following exhortation:

> Remettez-vous, monsieur, d'une alarme si chaude.
> Nous vivons sous un prince, ennemi de la fraude,
> Un prince dont les yeux se font jour dans les cœurs,
> Et que ne peut tromper tout l'art des imposteurs.

We may add, too, that the odious abstract excess of characters so stable as, for example, Molière's "Miser," the absolutely stolid and serious subjection of whom to his idiotic passion renders any emancipation from such fetters impossible, contains in it nothing that is genuinely comic.

It is pre-eminently in this field that for compensation of such defects a fine artistic power in the accurate and exhaustive delineation of character is manifested, or a true mastery of the craft discovers its best opportunity for an admirably thought-out intrigue. As a rule the occasion for such an intrigue is supplied by the circumstance that some character or other endeavours to secure his objects by deluding some one else, such a course appearing to harmonize with these interests and advance them. As a matter of fact, however, it only results in the contradictory situation that it is through this pernicious demand they are self-destructive. In opposition to such a plot we find as a rule a similar plot of dissembled appearances put in motion, which has for its object the like confusion of the original plotter. Such a general scheme admits of an infinite number and degree of ups and downs in the interweaving of its situations which are adapted to every conceivable subtlety. The Spaniards are, in particular, the most consummate masters in the invention of such intrigues and developments, and have composed much that is delightful and excellent in this class of work. The subject-matter generally consists of the attractive incidents of love or affairs of honour and the like. These, which in tragedy bring about the profoundest collisions, in comedy, by contrast—as, for example, pride, love of long standing that doesn't wish to reveal itself, yet directly betrays itself in the end—prove themselves fundamentally without substance and dissolve in the comic. A word in conclusion as to the characters who hatch and carry out such intrigues. Such are usually, following the example of the slaves in the Roman comedy, servants or menials, who have no respect for the objects of their superiors, but rather make them subordinate to their own advantage or bring them to nought, and merely present us with the amusing position, that the real masters are the servants and the masters the slaves, or at least give rise to all kinds of comic situation, which come about accidentally, or are directly the result of intention. We of course, as audience, are in the know of such mysteries, and can fortify ourselves against every sort of cunning and deceit, which often carries the most serious consequences to fathers, uncles, aunts, and the rest, all of the most respectable antecedents; and we may laugh as we please over the contradictory situations that appear before us, or are involved in such ingenious deceptions.

In this kind of way our modern comedy, generally speaking, gives play on the stage to private interests and personalities of the social life I have mentioned in their accidental vagaries, laughable features, abnormal habits and follies, partly by means of character delineation, and partly with the help of comic developments of situations and circumstances. A joviality so frank and genial as that which persists in the Aristophanic comedy as the mediating element of its resolution, does not animate this kind of comedy; or rather cases occur where it can be actually repulsive, that is to say, where that which is essentially evil, the tricks of menials, the treachery of sons and wards towards worthy men, fathers and guardians is triumphant, always assuming that the persons deluded have in no way themselves been influenced by false prejudices or eccentricities of such a kind that there is some reason why they should be made to appear ridiculous in their helpless stupidity and handed over as the sport of the aims of others.

In a converse way, however, and in contrast as such to the above generally prosaic type of treatment, the modern world, too, has elaborated a world of comedy which is both truly comic and poetical in its nature. The fundamental note here again is the cheeriness of disposition, the inexhaustible resources of fun, no matter what may be the nature of miscarriage or bad luck, the exuberance and dash of what is at bottom nothing better than pure tomfoolery, and, in a word, exploited self-assurance. We have here as a result, in yet profounder expatiation, and yet more intense display of humour, whether the sphere of it be more restricted or capacious, and whether the mode of it be more or less important, what runs on parallel lines with that which Aristophanes in the ancient world and in his own field created beyond all rivalry. As the master, who in a similar way outshines all others in his field, or rather the particular portion to which I now refer, I will, though without now further entering into detail, once again emphasize the name of William Shakespeare.

CHAPTER II

DRAMATIC ACTION
AND CHARACTER

[a]The gracious innocence of beatific enjoyment, the inactive repose, the majesty of power in self-reliant tranquillity, as also the concentrated compactness generally of that which is most substantial in a given content—all these are essentially ideal modes of determination. That which is inward, however, and spiritual is in an equal degree active movement and development. One-sidedness and division are inseparable from development. Spirit that is wholly itself and a totality will, expanding into all particularity, step forth out of its repose, in despite of all satisfaction therein, and involve itself in the contradictions of the broken and confused medley of earthly existence, and is by so doing unable in this divided world to withdraw itself from the ill fortune and ill health that cling to finite existence.

Even the immortal gods of polytheism do not dwell in eternal peace, but take sides in mighty conflicts wherein contending passions and interests are roused, being subject themselves to Destiny; nay, more, even the God of Christians is not delivered from a passage of humiliation endured through suffering and shame of death, is not spared the bitterness of soul, which perforce cried aloud, "My God, my God, why hast thou forsaken me?" And the mother of Christ experienced an agony of the same poignant character, and human life in every direction is a life of struggle, battle, and pain. For greatness and force of character is evolved in the greatness and force of con-

[a] *The Philosophy of Fine Art,* vol. I, pp. 240–41.

tending elements, out of which spirit concentrates itself again and again upon its unity. The intensity and depth of subjectivity is only the more emphasized, the more unbroken and unexampled the resistance of circumstances to its unity grows, and the more irreconcilable the contradictions appear under which it has to preserve its own self-centred equilibrium. In this development, and through this alone, the might of the Idea and the Ideal is preserved; for power consists precisely in this self-preservation through a process of self-negation.

Inasmuch as it is the fact, then, that the particularity of the Ideal passes into a relation with the external world through such development, and by so doing is made partaker in a world, which, so far from manifesting the ideally free association of the notion and its external reality, presents an existence which is just that which it ought not to be, in apprehending the true nature of this relation we have to consider how far the determinations which affect the Ideal either in themselves contain immediately the principle of Ideality, or are to a more or less degree susceptible of it.

1. APPROPRIATE WORLD CONDITION

[b]In order to make clear the actual character of the reality which is most adapted to Ideality we will contrast it with that aspect of existence which is not so adapted.

We find the latter pre-eminently where the ethical notion, that is, justice and rational freedom, have already won for themselves and maintain a fixed position in the social *order* regulated by *law*, so that, even in the external world, it appears as a positive and necessary power, which is quite independent of the individuality and subjectivity of specific temperament and characters. This is the case in the life of the *State*, where that life is manifested in a form adequate to the true notion of citizenship. For obviously it is not every chance association of human beings, any more than every patriarchal commu-

[b] *The Philosophy of Fine Art*, vol. I, p. 245.

nity, that will fulfil the requisites of State-life. In the true State, laws, customs, and rights, in so far as they constitute the determinations of freedom applicable to all, are of paramount force even in this *universal* and abstract relation, and are not conditioned in their applicability by the chance requirements of an individual's idiosyncrasy.

(a) ᶜIn regulated States the external environment of man is made secure, and property is protected, and he is only permitted to retain in absolute independence for himself his private views and opinions. But in that condition where the essential features of a State are not found the protection of life and property depends on the isolated energy and courage of each individual by himself, who is compelled to look after his own security and that of everything which belongs to him. Such a condition we are accustomed to identify with the *heroic age*. It is not, of course, our province here either to discuss or decide which of these two contrasted conditions of life is the worthier; suffice it to say that, so far as the Ideal of art is concerned, it is imperatively necessary that this hard and fixed line between the universal as an independent existence and individuality should be removed, however much this distinction may be necessary in other directions for the realization of human existence. The reason of this is that Art and its Ideal is just that universal, in so far as it may be presented to the perception of the senses, and by such presentment is permitted to enter into the variety and living forms of the world of objects.

What we were looking for, therefore, is supplied us by the heroic age, for it is here that virtue, ἀρετὴ in the full sense of that Greek word, creates the root-basis of actions. In this connection it would appear that we must distinguish between ἀρετὴ and *virtus* as understood by the Romans themselves. The Romans had already their State, Fatherland, and legal institutions, and as contrasted with the State, as the controlling object of all, they had surrendered personality. To be simply a citizen of Rome, to have one object for the imagination and for every other personal energy to centre itself upon, namely, the Fatherland and its sovereign majesty, therein lies the earnestness and grit of Roman virtue. Heroes, on the contrary, are individuals who undertake and accomplish a complete enterprise in consistent reliance upon their personal resources and initiative, and with whom it is consequently a purely arbitrary act of their own when they execute anything in accordance with the moral principle. This immediate unity, however, of what we may call the substantive import and individuality of inclination, impulse, and will is the characteristic of Greek virtue. According to this view personality is a law to itself without any further subjection to a law, judgment, and tribunal of independent subsistence. The Greek heroes make their appearance in an epoch anterior to legal enactment, or they are themselves the founders of States, so that right and social order, law and ethical custom, emanate from them, and persist as their own creation in an indefeasible relation to them. In this way Hercules was regarded so highly by the ancients themselves, and represents an Ideal of original and heroic virtue. His free and self-reliant virtue, with which he championed the right and battled against the monstrosities of men and Nature is not a prevailing characteristic of the age, but belongs to him as an exclusive and unique possession. And we may add he was not strictly a moral hero, as his reception of the fifty daughters of Thespius in one night clearly shows us; neither would it appear from the tale about the Augaean stables is he pre-eminent for gentility. He is rather the general type of self-reliant strength and resource in its championship of right and justice, to exemplify which he elected summarily and from a free choice to undergo countless toils and labours. It is true that some of his deeds were carried out at the instigation of Eurystheus, but this submission is, after all, rather a formal association than a real one, no connection at least of legal validity or inevitable necessity through which the strength of his self-reliant personality was diverted from its independent course.

The Homeric heroes are of a similar type. No doubt they have their clan chieftain; but the associating bond is no fixed relation already determined by law, which enforces their submission; of their own free will it is that they follow Agamemnon, who is no monarch in the modern sense of the term. Consequently every hero volunteers his own advice, the enraged

Achilles acts independently for himself in his separation, and, speaking generally, each and all come and go, act, or take their leisure as they please. In much the same independent position, that is to say, united in no fixed organization, to which they are as individuals entirely subordinate, we find the heroes of Arabian poetry portrayed, and even the Shah-Rameh of Ferdusi furnishes us with similar examples. In latter-day Christendom the age of feudalism and knighthood supplies a fertile field for the free growth of heroic enterprise and the type of individuality which belongs to it. Of such are the heroes of the round table, no less than the heroic circle of which Charles the Great is the focus. Charles is, much like Agamemnon, surrounded with independent chieftains of heroic mould, a union which as such is powerless. He is consequently always compelled to take counsel with them, however much each of them may be influenced by private passions; he may bluster like a very Olympian Jupiter, and none the less find himself and his undertakings suddenly left in the lurch while his confederates are off on some adventures of their own. The Cid is perhaps the most complete example of the type. He, too, is the ally of a confederacy, the dependent of a king, and is bound to render duty as vassal; but in opposition to this obligation he is pre-eminently influenced by the principle of honour, the purely personal consideration of his own glory, nobility, and reputation. And so in this case also the king can only determine a fixed line of action and make war after consulting and obtaining the consent of his vassals. If this is not given they do not fight, and, moreover, a mere majority of votes is not sufficient to compel them. Every man is independent of his neighbour, and exercises his will and steers his own course as such. We find in the accounts given us of Saracen heroes an equally brilliant picture of self-reliant and still more inflexible personality. Even the Reinecke Fuchs fable is a fresh example of this state of things. Here, it is true, the lion is master and king, but the wolf and the bear sit in council. Even Reinecke and the rest do just what they like; and when there is a general outcry, the sly fellow either gets out of the mess with his story-telling, or manages to make some particular interest of king and queen work to his own advantage, and in his own cunning way talks over his sovereign somehow.

Moreover, in much the same way that each individual example of this heroic type of *personality* persists in immediate unity with all that he may will, act, and accomplish, a similar unity is further maintained in all the consequences which flow from such initiative. When we ourselves, on the contrary, act or estimate a particular action, we assume that only full responsibility can attach where the individual under consideration is in complete possession of the true nature of his action and its attendant circumstances. If the content of those surrounding conditions is otherwise than that which is present to the agent's consciousness in such a case a man nowadays will not take upon himself the burden of all that is implied in his action. He will thrust on one side that part of it which he would not have done had he known completely or not misconceived the circumstances, and he only accepts that which was fully under his cognizance and carried out with deliberate intention in conformity thereto. The heroic character makes no such distinction. He adheres simply to all the consequences and makes good his personal responsibility for the whole. Oedipus on his way to consult the oracle meets a certain man, quarrels with him and strikes him. In those days such an act was not a crime at all. He only returned a blow after being vigorously attacked. But the stranger was his father. Oedipus further marries a royal lady. His wife is his mother. Without knowing it he commits an act of shame. On learning the truth he acknowledges such enormities to their full extent, inflicts a punishment on himself as murderer of his father and a man of incest, and this although he was entirely ignorant of the true nature of these acts, or had any intention of doing them. The self-reliant stubbornness and entirety of the heroic character refuses to parcel out responsibility and knows nothing of such distinctions as personal intention and the objective act and its consequences. In the evolution and ramification of an action as we moderns regard it these opposed points of view constantly recur, and guilt is thrown into the background as far as possible. No doubt our view of the matter is more in accordance with *ethical principle*, in so far as the condition of a personal knowledge of the particular circumstances, or the consciousness of an object good in itself, in short, generally the intent of an act, is what materially assists us in our judgment.

But in the heroic age, where we find the individual essentially indivisible and the objective act proceeding from himself as entirely his own, each person claims absolutely all that he may do, and refuses to surrender one jot or tittle of responsibility therefor.

To an extent equally minute the heroic figure is separated from the ethical whole, to which he belongs, and his self-consciousness is bound up wholly in substantial unity with that whole. According to the views in vogue now we draw a line of distinction as private individuals between objects which are wholly personal and those which affect the community. The individual acts in all that he does from his own private personality as distinct from others, and views even his actions rather as relative to this than as part of all that is farmed out by the organic whole to which he belongs. We consequently make a distinction between individuals and their families. Such is unknown in the heroic age. The guilt of ancestors adheres to their descendants, and an entire family will suffer for the original defaulter. Men inherit the fatality of guilt and transgression. A condemnation such as this appears to us unjust as an irrational subjection to a blind fate. With us the achievements of ancestors reflect no more honour on children and descendants than the punishments and crimes of such contaminate those that follow after them, and least of all is their private character thus affected; nay, modern opinion is already close to the view that the confiscation of family property is a punishment which violates the profounder conception of liberty. But in the ancient and more plastic totality the individual is not so isolated, but rather a member of his family and race. For this reason the character, action, and fortunes of the family continue to be the private affair of each member of it; and so far from denying the actions of his parents, each man voluntarily accepts them as his own; they live in him, and he is just that which his fathers were, suffered, or transgressed. This appears to us a hardship, but that which we replace it with, this standing alone on our own possessions, and the more subjective self-stability thus acquired is also from another point of view only the abstract self-sufficiency of each. The individuality of heroic times is none the less of a more ideal type, because it does not declare itself as satisfied with the

mere form of freedom and infinity, but remains in unalterable
and immediate unity with all that is most substantial in the
relations of spirit which it of itself endows with living actuality.
In such an individuality the substantial is immediately individual, and the individual thereby himself essentially substantive.

From considerations such as these we conclude that the
ideal figures of art must be sought for in the age of mythos,
that is to say, speaking generally, in past times, where we
shall find the soil most congenial to their growth. If such material is taken from the age we live in, whose most native form,
as we actually find it, is tightly shut off from the imagination,
it matters not how we regard it, then the modifications which
the poet can hardly avoid making in it will not readily escape
the appearance of a purely artificial and intentional composition. The Past entirely belongs to memory, and memory per-
fects the infolding veil of character, events, and actions in the
vesture of universality, through which the particular external
or contingent detail is unable to penetrate. Many trifling circumstances and mediating conditions, many varied and isolated phases of activity, are inseparable from the actual existence of an action or a character: in the mirror of memory
all these insignificant details are obliterated. In this liberation
of his work from what is accidental in the external fact the
artist has a freer hand for his artistic powers of composition,
when dealing with that which is individual and particular in
it, if the actions, histories, and characters are borrowed from
ancient times. He has, it is true, also historical memories, out
of which he must mould a content conformable to the universal; but the picture of the Past possesses, as already observed, an advantage, taken simply as a picture of greater
universality, while the manifold texture of mediating condition and circumstance, interwoven as it is in the entire framework of finite existence which surrounds it, offers him material
ample enough to prevent his hand obliterating the individuality, which is essential to his work of art. The more closely we
consider it, the clearer will be our conclusion that a heroic age
has the advantage over later and more civilized times in that
the isolated character and personality generally in such an age
does not as yet find what is substantive either in the sphere of

ethical custom, or moral obligation opposed to itself in the necessary embodiment of legal institution, and thereby presents
immediately to the poet all that the form of the Ideal requires.
Shakespeare has, for example, selected much material for his
tragedies from chronicles and earlier romances, framed upon
a condition of life which has not as yet received the impression of a fully articulated social order, but in which the energy of individuals, as emphasized in personal resolve and
achievement, is still the prevailing characteristic. His genuine
historical dramas have, on the contrary, a vein of historical
substance running through them in the strictest sense, and for
this reason lean farther away from an ideal exposition, although here, too, both circumstances and actions are made to
fall in with, or are removed to suit, the unyielding self-
sufficiency and wilfulness of particular characters. No doubt
this characteristic remains for the most part in their case a
purely formal self-inclusion, whereas if we contrast it with the
self-subsistency of heroic characters we find that here the essential *content* of all such have proposed to accomplish is
bound up therewith.

It is on account of this contrast that we should find a reason for rejecting the general thesis in connection with the
Ideal, to the effect that the *Idyllic* is exceptionally adapted for
its expression, inasmuch as where that is presented the cleav-
age between what is determined by legal necessity and the
living person is wholly absent. To this we must reply that,
however simple and original idyllic situations may be, however
far removed they may be from the artificial prose-existence of
society, such simplicity, if we consider the nature of its content, has, in fact, too insignificant an interest to satisfy the
most substantial and essential requirements of the Ideal. Material of this sort fails entirely to include the most weighty
motives of heroic character such as Fatherland, moral and
family problems, and their development; it is a kind of treatment which is apt to select as the very core of its subject such
a fact as the loss of a single sheep or the falling in love of a
girl. In this way the Idyllic not infrequently becomes merely
the resource and recreation of our hearts, to which poets such
as Gesner, for example, will add their dose of sickly sweetness
and sentimentalism. The idyllic aspect of the days we live in

have, further, this defect, that this *naïveté*, this domesticated or rural atmosphere in the emotional aspect of love or the enjoyment of a good cup of coffee in the open and things of that sort are not likely to awake much interest, when we find in them nothing but the country parson flavour—find them cut off, that is to say, from all wider relations with the outside world, and not a trace of the profounder web of purposes with which that world is interwoven. It is precisely here that we have reason to admire the genius of Goethe, when he concentrated his poetic talent on material of this kind in his poem of "Hermann and Dorothea." It is true that he selects from the life of the Present a particular theme of very limited extension, but at the same time he unfolds before us as the background and atmosphere of the picture in which his characters are portrayed the great interests of the revolution and his own native country, and, in short, associates with a subject-matter necessarily narrow in its range facts of world-history of the widest and most potent significance.

Generally speaking, we shall find that the ills of life and its evil, war, battles, and revenge, are not excluded from the subject-matter of the Ideal, but are frequently the very source and substance of the heroic age and its myths, whose form grows all the wilder and sterner in proportion to the remoteness of such a period from a fully developed society of law and moral order. In the chivalrous adventures of knight-errantry we find the heroes of such tales themselves often enough sharing the savage and dissolute characteristics of the times, and in much the same way the martyrdom of the heroes of the Church presupposes a condition of ferocious cruelty around them. At bottom, however, the Christian ideal, which is based on the depth and inwardness of man's spiritual nature, stands in a relation of entire indifference to the external world.

We have demonstrated that the condition of particular centuries is more applicable to the Ideal; in the same way Art selects pre-eminently a particular class of society for the form under which the Ideal shall appear, the order, that is to say, of *princes*. And the selection is made not because art is necessarily aristocratic, or has any predilection for gentility, but simply on account of the perfection in which free will and its products may be exemplified imaginatively through the highly placed class. We have in the chorus of ancient tragedy the characteristics and universal background of general maxims, modes of imaginative thought, and emotion, before which the definite movements of the action proceed. In contrast to this appear the more clearly defined individualities of the personages immediately concerned in the action, men and women of authority, and belonging for the most part to royal families. On the other hand, the main impression forced upon us, when seeing representatives of a lower class carrying on pursuits which are of a narrower range, is one of subjection; and, indeed, in an artificial state of society the freedom of action of such a class is fettered in every direction, and is necessarily involved with all its passions and interests in all the medley and despotic forces of external circumstance. It is, in fact, held closely behind the invincible power of the social order, which it is unable to come out of, and is an alien from the authority of the dominant order, even when that is asserted in accordance with just principle. In this limitation of outlook through the hard conditions of life all real independence is wrecked. For this reason both the circumstances and characters which we find in such a sphere of life are more appropriate to the treatment of comedy, everybody being permitted in comedy to rate themselves as they please, and to lay claims to a self-sufficiency in all that they will and think, which is none the less immediately negatived by the spiritual no less than the external dependence of their lives. As a rule, such a false and second-hand self-subsistency must inevitably fall to pieces when confronted with the actual conditions of life and the distorted view which is formed of them. The force of circumstances is presented to the lower orders of society on a totally different level from that in which it acts upon rulers and princes. In Schiller's "Braut von Messina" Don Caesar is able to exclaim, and justly: "there stands no higher judge than myself!" And when he has to be punished he must himself give judgment and execute it. He is, in fact, subject to no external necessity of right and law, and even when punishment is the question is wholly dependent on himself. The characters in the Shakespearean drama do not entirely belong to the princely order and only partially are taken from mythical sources, but they are placed in the era of civil wars, in which the ties of social order and legislative enactment are either weakened or shattered, and they secure from such a condition the exceptional independence and self-sufficiency we are looking for.

(b) If we transfer our attention now from the characteristic conditions of society we have hitherto mainly considered to the actual state of the world around us and its carefully articulated scheme of ethical, judicial, and political institutions, we shall not fail to observe that the material we have here offered us for figures of truly ideal type is of a very restricted character. The province here in which an entirely open field is presented for the display of independent purpose in its fullest individuality is limited both in its range and the measure of opportunity. The qualities that make a man thorough in his relations to his own family and his business, the ideals, in short, of honest citizens and excellent wives, in so far as will and activity are concentrated on the field in which it is still possible for a man to exercise his free personality, to carry out, in short, all that he has a mind to do, this is the prevailing feature of our modern society. Such ideals inevitably lack the depth of a fuller content, and the most significant feature of them is that of the attitude of the individual mind to their realization; for we find here the content is already presented by existing social institutions, and consequently the essential interest we take in it depends on the particular way in which that content is realized and appears in the *personal life*, its moral and inward significance. For this reason it is not possible, as in the case of former times, to create ideals from the positions of judgeship and kingship. If a man carries out his judicial functions nowadays in accordance with duty and the requirements of his office, he merely is acting within the bounds already marked out for him by legislative enactments in the social order as the sphere of his responsibilities. All that may characterize his tenure of office beyond this, as proceeding from personal qualities, such as suavity of demeanour or acuteness of judgment, is not the main point or the substantial content, but rather an aspect of it which it is possible to dispense with as something accidental. In the same way the monarchs of our own day are no longer, as was the case with the heroes of mythical times, in themselves the embodying and culminating unity of society itself, but rather a more or less unsubstantial *centrum* around which all legal and social institutions, however moulded in the course of time, group themselves in independent relations. All the most important functions of the executive have nowadays been separated from the royal prerogative. Kings do not lay down the law, control finance; the preservation of social order is not one of their most characteristic functions. Peace and war are determined through the particular circumstances of international politics, which it is not within their power exclusively either to direct or control; and, if it happens that any important decision with regard to either depends in the last resort on their judgment, such a decision is not generally so much in the nature of its substance the result of any personal preference, as it is the formal seal of monarchical authority on what is already determined on public grounds, the mere imposition of that which is strictly official rather than personal in its character. In the same way, a general or field-marshal of our times has unquestionably great authority; objects and interests of profound importance are under his control and his circumspection; his courage, his determination, and his intelligence are involved in the weightiest decisions; nevertheless, whatever may be definitely traced to the essentially personal characteristics of the man has little opportunity for display in such a result. For, in the first place, the objects upon which his decisions turn are not of his own selection, and arise out of circumstances which lie beyond the sphere of his influence rather than are spontaneously fixed by himself; secondly, the means adopted to carry out such objects are not the sole result of his initiative. On the contrary, they are supplied him from sources which are not immediately under his authority or personal influence, but stand rather quite apart from the sphere of his individual powers as a general.

To sum up, then, though it is true that under the present condition of the civilized world a man may act independently for himself in many directions, the fact remains that in whatever direction he may turn he is still only a member of a fixed order of society and appears as such limited in his range rather than the vital representative and individual embodiment of so-

ciety itself. He acts necessarily under such a condition of restriction, and our interest in such a personality, no less than
in the content of his aims and activity, is entirely devoid of
completeness. In the end we are invariably driven to concentrate our attention on the purely personal interest, how far,
that is to say, he attained success, what was the nature of the
obstacles and complications which, in either, through unto-
ward chance or necessity, confronted or distracted his progress. And if it is, moreover, true that our modern personality
is of infinite significance when we estimate the character thus
manifested as a spiritual product, in its actions, sufferings,
moral opinions, and conduct, that is to say, it is also true that
the moral content which is realized in such an individual is of
a restricted character, rather than, as is the case in the heroic
times, the realization of universal right, custom, and legality.
The individual is no longer the exclusive vehicle and actual
embodiment of these powers as in the previous times.

(c) However, our interest in and need to have presented
us such a completely realized individuality and living self-
dependence will always persist, however strongly we may recognize the worth and reasonable nature of the more developed
condition of an organized and trained civic society. It is this
necessity which makes us regard with astonishment the youthful spirit of Schiller and Goethe when they sought to discover
that lost self-sufficiency in the prevailing conditions of modern
times. How do we find in particular this attempt is made by
Schiller in his earliest works? Simply by a rebellion directed
against the whole organic framework of civil society. Carl
Moor, suffering injury from the existing order at the hands of
those who abuse the power entrusted them, has the courage
to break the bonds which bind him to law and order altogether, cuts himself adrift and creates for himself a heroic
situation, in which he appears as the champion of right, and
the self-constituted avenger of wrong, injustice, and oppression. None the less, how insignificant and isolated must a private revenge of this kind appear, if we estimate it from the
practical point of view, according to the probability of its success; and, in fact, in one aspect of it, it already contains the
germ of wrong which can only lead to the criminal act on
which it will fall to pieces. No doubt, as personal to Carl

Moor himself, this is a misfortune, a fatality, however, which, despite the tragical element in it, can only engraft on mere boys the blight of such a "robber-ideal." In much the same way the characters depicted in "Kabale und Liebe" suffer wrong under prevailing conditions of life, absorbed in the trivial facts and passions wholly personal to themselves. It is not until we come to the dramas of "Fiesco" and "Don Carlos" that we find characters of nobler significance and more substantive content, heroes, for example, resolved to liberate their country, or assert the liberty of religious conviction. With a nobility still more striking Wallenstein places himself at the head of his army that the crisis in the political situation may come to a focus. He is fully cognizant of the nature of the political forces upon which his only means of control, his army, is dependent; consequently he hesitates for long whether to follow his private inclination or his duty. He has barely arrived at a decision when he finds the instrument on which he most depended slip from his grasp; his means of action is gone. For that which in the last instance unites the leading officers and generals is no gratitude for anything that may be due to him on the ground of past services rendered; his fame as a general has nothing to do with it, but rather the duty they owe to the universally recognized seat of government, the oath they have sworn to the head of the State, the emperor of the Austrian monarchy. He finds himself consequently in the end isolated, and is not so much fought with and overcome by an external foe as he is stripped of all means of executing his purpose. He is deserted by his army and from that moment is a lost man. The "Götz" of Goethe starts from a dramatic situation of an analogous though somewhat inverse type. The times of Götz and Franz von Sickingen belong to the interesting epoch in which knight-errantry and the self-reliant individuality of the class of nobility is being superseded by the new creation of an external and legally constituted social order. To have selected precisely this critical time where we find the heroic characteristics of the Middle Ages and the legalized fabric of modern society meet and collide for the subject of his first artistic production shows much penetration on the part of Goethe. For Götz and Sickingen are still heroes in the genuine sense, who are resolved to exercise their influence over circumstances, whether immediately affecting them or of wider range, out of the resources of their own personalities, their courage, and their private sense of right. The new order of things involves Götz in acts of illegality and brings about the catastrophe of his life. It is only in the Middle Ages that knight-errantry and the relations of feudalism will supply a field entirely open to this type of self-reliant manhood. When we find, moreover, the legalized order co-ordinated more completely in its prosaic form, the predominant authority in fact, the adventurous self-dependence of knighthood is left outside it as an unrelated excrescence; and if an attempt is made to assert it as though it were still a valid means of attacking wrong, and assisting the oppressed, it becomes simply an object of ridicule, such as Cervantes illustrates for us in his "Don Quixote."

In this allusion to the opposition which exists between two differently constituted *régimes* of society and the collision which results from action in defiance of their particular character we have already indicated what we have above defined generally as the closer determination and differentiation of the universal state of the world, that is to say, the *situation* as generally expressed.

2. SITUATION AND COLLISION

The ideal world-condition which it is the function of art to present in contrast to prosaic reality we may conclude from our previous discussion to be merely a general background of society of a specific kind; it is merely the *possible* condition necessary for the particular presentation, not the presentation itself. What we have hitherto directed attention to is, in fact, the general background upon which the living figures of art may appear. It is undoubtedly fructified with individuality and is supported by its self-subsistency; but as a *general* condition it is not yet the active movement of particular individuals in the very form of life, just as we may say that the temple which Art erects is not as yet the representation of the personal godhead, but only encloses the germ of the same. [d]Regarded as a stimulating influence of this kind, particular circumstances and conditions create the *situation*, which is specifically presupposed in the actual self-expansion and activity of all that still lies undeveloped in the universal world-condition; it is for this reason we have considered the previous determination of the notion of the situation as necessary to any inquiry into the true constituents of *action*.

[e]The full seriousness and weighty import of a situation can only begin when we find in it the element of disruption, where the determination itself exposes an essential aspect of difference, and by its opposition to something else becomes the source of a collision.

The *collision* arises, as we are now considering it, in an act of *violation*, which is unable to retain its character as such, but is compelled to find a new principle of unity; it is a change in the previously existent condition of harmony, a change which is still in process. The collision is, however, not an *action*, and is to be taken simply as stimulus to action to all that characterizes the situation. And this is true, although the contradiction in which the collision is enclosed may be the result of previous action. As an example of this we may cite the trilogies of the ancients, which carry forward the main theme by presenting at the close of one drama the collision which forms the stimulative impulse of the next, which, in its return, renders necessary the resolution which is carried out by the third. And, moreover, for this very reason that the collision always requires some resolution attendant on this conflict of opposing elements, the more a situation is full of it the more it is peculiarly adapted to the subject-matter of dramatic art, it being the especial claim of that art to present beauty in its completest and profoundest development. Sculpture, on the contrary, is not wholly suited to give embodiment to any action, through which the great spiritual forces are manifested either in their division or reconciliation, and indeed the art of painting, despite its more extended spatial significance, is only able to objectify a single moment of action.

These situations of tragic significance introduce a peculiar

[d] *The Philosophy of Fine Art*, vol. I, p. 266.
[e] *Ibid.*, pp. 272–325.

difficulty in dealing with them which is inherent in their very conception. For inasmuch as they obviously arise from violations of the world-condition they offer to our consideration circumstances which are unable to continue as they are, which render necessary something of a remedial nature to reclothe them. But the beauty of the Ideal consists precisely in its undisturbed unity, repose, and consummation with itself. The collision, on the other hand, disturbs this harmony of what is truly real and ethical, and drives this unity of the Ideal into discord and opposition. Through the representation of such disruption the Ideal itself suffers violation. The function of art will undoubtedly consist partly in preventing the entire destruction of free beauty in this difference, and partly in only carrying this breach of unity and the conflict it occasions to a point in which harmony may again be recovered as the result of such a conflict and its resolution, and in this way become manifest for the first time in its essential perfection. It is, however, impossible to determine on a general principle the precise limit to which such discordance may be carried inasmuch as the several arts in this respect preserve their independent character. The medium of the subjective idea can support a far intenser disruption than that of the plastic arts. In other words, poetry is quite within its right when it breaks up the unity of the world of the imagination even to the point of the extremest form of desperation, and in its delineation of external objects to that of absolute ugliness. In the case of the plastic arts, on the contrary, in painting, that is to say, and even more so in sculpture, the external form remains in unalterable fixity; it can neither be removed nor lightly passed over in such a way that it again disappears. Under such conditions it would be a serious defect to represent once and for all an ugliness, which could not possibly be transmuted. Consequently all that would be quite compatible in dramatic poetry, which is able to represent a momentary appearance that again vanishes, is not within the province of the plastic arts.

In discussing the more obvious types of collision we can only in this portion of our inquiry indicate the most general points of view. We would particularly draw attention to three fundamental aspects under which they may be co-ordinated.

First, there are those collisions which proceed from purely *natural,* that is to say, physical conditions, in so far as these are characterized with qualities which are negative or evil and consequently discordant.

Secondly, we have collisions which are of a *spiritual* nature, but which depend on *natural* conditions, conditions which may in themselves have a positive character yet, for the spirit, contain within themselves the seeds of difference and contradiction.

Thirdly, there are divisions which are caused entirely by disruption in the Spirit alone; to these alone we are justified in attaching the peculiar interest of contradiction which is bound up with genuine *human activity.*

(a) Now with reference to the first type of conflicting forces—for the reason that here it is only external Nature, through the maladies and other evils and infirmities which are incidental to her creating, conditions which destroy the pre-existent harmony of life, replacing such with a state of antagonism—such can at most merely serve as a stimulus for something outside them. Regarded wholly by themselves such collisions are of no interest; they are the subject-matter of art simply for the sake of the disruption which may follow as a *consequence* of some natural misfortune. The "Alcestis" of Euripides, we may add, too, that of Glück, the subject of whose opera is practically the same, are examples of this; in both the sickness of Admetus is necessarily presupposed. That sickness merely by itself could not fitly supply a subject for artistic treatment. It only becomes, even in the handling of Euripides, associated with it by virtue of the individual characters, who, on account of such misfortune, are compelled to face a further collision. It is the word of the oracle that Admetus must die unless another will pass to the underworld for his sake. Alcestis, out of love for her husband, devotes herself to such a sacrifice, resolves to die, in order to restrain Death from touching her beloved, the father of her children, the king. In the "Philoctetes" of Sophocles a physical malady is also the cause of the collision. Here the Greeks during their voyage to Troy place the man who is suffering from a wounded foot, caused by the serpent's bite in Chrysas, on the island of Lemnos. In this case, too, the physical mishap is merely the extreme meeting point and incentive of a further collision. For, according to the prophecy, Troy can only fall when the arrows of Hercules are in the hands of the storming army. Philoctetes refuses to give them up because he has been compelled for nine years to suffer the martyrdom of his banishment. This refusal, no less than the fact of his unrighteous desertion from which it springs, could have been followed by every variety of result other than that which took place; the real interest accordingly does not centre in the malady and its physical necessity, but in the opposition which arises from the refusal of Philoctetes to surrender the arrows. The case of the plague in the Greek camp before Troy is very similar; although this is already represented entirely as the consequence of former transgression, as a punishment, in short, a mode of statement more adapted to epic than dramatic poetry, nevertheless it is closely associated with evils incidental to natural misfortune such as storm, shipwreck, and drought. As a rule, however, art will not represent such mischance as mere accident, but rather as an obstruction and misfortune whose necessity simply consists in assuming precisely this particular form rather than another.

(b) But, to turn now to our second type of the collision, inasmuch as the external powers of Nature are not that which is most essential to the interests and contradictions of human life, in cases where they are found closely associated with such spiritual relations, they will present themselves merely as the ground from which the collision breaks forth in its true character. This is the point of view from which we must regard all situations, where we trace the original source of conflict in the facts of natural *birth*. We will shortly distinguish between three particular cases of this.

In the first place we have the right that is bound up with natural condition, that which constitutes relationship and inheritance for example, which for the very reason that it stands in close connection with Nature carries with it a number of relations that are bound up with her, and this though the right, the fact is one and only one. The most important example of this is the right of succession to the throne. It is important to observe that this right must not as yet, in relation to the collisions which spring from it, be absolutely fixed by rule, otherwise the resultant conflict will be of quite another character. If, that is to say, the right of succession is not as yet entirely controlled by legislation and the social order which it implies, no wrong will necessarily attach to any one of the alternatives, namely, whether it be an older or younger brother, or any other relative of the royal household who obtains the sovereignty. But inasmuch as sovereignty is a qualitative rather than a quantitative possession, which cannot like gold and other material goods be divided up according to a just principle, dispute and contention is inevitably the result of such a form of succession. When Oedipus, for example, leaves the throne of Thebes without a ruler, he leaves his two sons confronting each other with a right and claim of equal strength. The brothers arrange to occupy the throne alternately from year to year. Eteocles, however, breaks the compact and Polynices brings an army against Thebes to enforce his right. The antagonism of brothers has always been in the history of art a fruitful source of collision; it commences indeed with the story of Cain who slew his brother Abel. In the tale of Shah-Rameh, the earliest example we have of a Persian book of heroic legend, it is a contention of throne succession which is the source of the most varied conflicts. In this Feridu divided the Earth among his three brothers. Selm receives as his portion Rum and Chawer; Turan and Osin are given to Thur, and Fredysh becomes lord of the Earth from Iran. All three, however, claim the land which belongs to their brothers, and endless quarrels and wars are the result. In the Middle Ages we find just the same countless examples of family and dynastic broils. Such dissensions, however, appear in themselves to be due to accidental circumstance. It is not necessary that brothers should be at enmity; particular circumstances and more important causes must be attached, such as the in itself tragic birth of the sons of Oedipus, or, as we find in "The Bride of Messina," the author is at pains to shift the quarrel of the brothers on to still more fateful circumstances. In Shakespeare's "Macbeth" a similar collision is the foundation of the tragic *dénouement*. Duncan is king and Macbeth, as his nearest and oldest relation, is consequently heir to the throne with a right precedent even to Duncan's sons. The primary incentive of Macbeth's crime is the wrong which the king has done him in naming his own son as heir to the throne. This justification of Macbeth, which is supported by the chronicles of the time, Shakespeare has entirely passed over, because it was solely his object to bring into startling relief the repulsive aspect of Macbeth's ambitious passion, in order thereby to make his work agreeable to King James, who would be naturally interested in finding the crime of Macbeth depicted without extenuating circumstances. As a consequence we can find no sufficient reason why, under Shakespeare's handling of the subject, Macbeth fails to murder the sons of Duncan no less than their father, lets them escape in fact; nor can we understand why they are wholly overlooked by the nobles. However, the entire collision upon which the drama of Macbeth turns carries us beyond the particular type which we are now mainly considering.

In the *second* of our examples in the type of collision we are now discussing we find the reverse situation to that just discussed, and it consists in this that difference of birth, which carries within itself a *wrong*, is moreover, through ethical *custom* or *law*, held within the chains of an insuperable *barrier*, so that it receives at the same time the appearance of an innate wrong, and consequently is the cause of collisions. Slavery, serfdom, differences of caste, the position of Jews in many states and, with certain qualifications, even the contrast between an aristocratical and citizen class are all of them cases for consideration under this head. The conflict here consists in this, that on the one hand humanity has rights, relations, desires, aims and requirements which belong to it essentially in virtue of its fundamental idea, which nevertheless in each one of the above mentioned examples meet with dangerous restriction and obstruction owing to the compulsive necessity of natural birth. On this type of collision we have the following remarks to offer.

The differences which obtain between classes, such as the ruled and the rulers, are, no doubt, essential to the notion of State-life, and are founded on reason, for they are caused by the inevitable articulation of the organic community, and assert themselves as such through the specific forms of occupation, disposition, modes of life, and general levels of education in all their branches. It is another matter, however, when these differences as they affect individuals are determined absolutely by the accident of birth, so that the individual man from the very start is not on account of any quality in himself, but solely through the accident of Nature, irrevocably relegated to a particular class or caste. In such a case it is obvious these differences appear as innate and are, moreover, though purely external, girt with force in its highest and most aggressive mode. We are not bound to ask ourselves how this fixity and compulsive restraint came originally into existence. For the nation may originally have been united, and the natural distinction between freeman and serf been only evolved at a later time, or the difference between castes, classes, and privileged persons may have grown out of earlier distinctions of nations and races, as many are inclined to think is the explanation of the caste distinctions of India. All this is a matter of no moment to us here. The main point simply consists in this, that vital relations of this kind, which regulate the entire course of human existence, have their source in natural conditions. On general principles, no doubt, distinctions of class can be justified, but at the same time no individual should be wholly robbed of his right to determine as his choice may direct to which particular class he shall belong. Natural capacity, talents, adaptability, and education are the only right means to direct the way and decide in this respect. When, however, the right of choice is debarred from birth onwards and a man is made thereby dependent on Nature and its contingency, there is always the possibility of conflict within the sphere of this necessity between the states thus enforced on the individual by natural conditions and the measure of spiritual education which he may acquire and the higher demand which it may justly make. This is a pathetic and unfortunate type of collision which has its source in an essential *wrong* which the freedom of art is quite unable to respect. In the social condition of our own days distinctions of class, with a few exceptions, are not determined by birth. The ruling dynasty and the peerage are the only exceptions, and these depend on a higher conception of the State altogether. For the rest, the mere fact of birth creates no essential distinction that can ultimately determine the class to which a man may belong if he is otherwise competent to join it. For this reason, however, we must condition the demand for entire liberty of choice with the requirement that in education, knowledge, ability, and general tastes the individual is equal to the particular society with which he may desire to associate. If, on the contrary, the fact of a man's birth presents an insuperable obstacle to such claims, which he would otherwise be quite competent to satisfy by virtue of his own vigorous activity, then such a situation must appear to us not merely a misfortune, but essentially a wrong under which he is compelled to suffer injury. He is thus separated by a purely natural partition wall which is essentially unjust, that is to say, one beyond which his talents, sentiments, and general education have already raised him, from that which he was competent to reach, and a purely natural condition whose legalized fixity has been determined wholly by caprice presumes to oppose insuperable barriers to the freedom rightly demanded by all spiritual life.

To examine more closely the nature of this type of collision we shall do well to look at it from three different points of view, each of which are of essential importance.

In the *first* place, it is necessary that the individual should, in the strength of his own spiritual resources, already really have passed beyond the natural barriers whose opposition is to give way before his aims and desires, otherwise the demand is simply an act of folly. If, for example, a domestic servant, whose education and ability is merely that of a menial, falls in love with a princess or a lady of high society, or, inversely, either of these with him, such a love affair is both absurd and devoid of all taste, and this is so even if the artistic representation of this passion display all the depth and interest of which an ardent heart is capable. In such a case it is not so much the difference of birth which creates the obstacle; this is rather to be found in the entire content of interests, education, aims of life, requirements, and mode of sentiment which distinguish in status, material resources, and social qualifications a lady in high position from a domestic servant. If love is, as in the case assumed, the one and only bond of a union, and is associated with nothing else throughout the entire sphere of all that men and women have to live through in just accordance with that which a particular status requires from their intelligence and experience, it must necessarily remain devoid of content and is simply a union of the senses. Love, to be wholly complete, is nothing less than a real harmony of the entire conscious life, in which the full nobility of sentiment can be shared and appreciated.

The *second* case we wish to examine is that in which the dependence of birth surrounds an essentially free human life and the objects it may rightly set before itself with legalized fetters of obstruction. This collision also presents an element unadapted for artistic treatment, opposed, that is to say, to the notion of the Ideal, despite its love to make use of it and the facility with which it may attempt to do so. If distinctions of birth through positive laws and the powers which support them create a persistent wrong, as doubtless may be the case where a man is born an outcast or a Jew, he obviously, from one point of view, is entirely right in holding with all the strength of his inward life, which rebels before such a barrier, that the same is dissolvable, that he, in fact, recognizes his individuality as apart from it. To oppose such restraint appears to be wholly justifiable. But in so far as it becomes impossible through the force of existing circumstances to overcome such a barrier, which is consequently converted into an irrevocable necessity, a situation of this kind can only be regarded as a misfortune which itself is not without an element of falsity. For the rational man is inevitably forced, in so far as he is unable to subjugate the opposing necessity, to submit to the same: it is not in reason to continue to fight against the inevitable, but rather quietly to let it pass over him. He must, in fact, abandon the sense of interest in and need of that which is, by virtue of this barrier, swept from his reach, and suffer what he fails to overcome with the quiet courage of passive endurance. Where a struggle is of no avail it is the part of wisdom to be quit of it in order at the least to retire into the *formal* independence of personal liberty. By doing so the forces of wrong have no longer power over him; if, on the contrary, he battles against them he must necessarily experience his dependence in its fullest extent. At the same time it remains unquestionable that neither this abstraction of formal independence any more than that content which can lead to no result are truly beautiful when artistically considered.

There is a *third* type of collision which, while being immediately connected with that we have just considered, is equally removed from the genuine Ideal. It is to be found affecting that class of persons who attempt to assert some privilege which the mere fact of birth concedes them and supports with the full weight of a religious title, positive enactments, and the prevailing conditions of society. In such a case, it is true, we have an independent position in harmonious relation with what is externally realized in positive institutions, but when considered as the mere consistency of that which is in itself unjust and irrational it is quite as much as in our former example a purely formal independence, and the notion of the Ideal disappears. We may, no doubt, very possibly persuade ourselves that the Ideal is retained because we have here an appearance as though the personal life is in full union with the universal and its legalized constitution, remaining consistently in such unity; but it will be observed that here the universal does not assert its dominating power in the *particular person,* as we found the heroic Ideal demanded, but only in and through the public authority of positive laws and their administration; moreover, what the individual here asserts is assumed to be essentially wrong, and he loses in consequence the substantive significance which we have seen to be also essential to the Ideal. An affair in which the ideal subject of art is concerned must itself be at bottom true and justifiable. To this type belong the legalized lordship exercised over slaves or serfs, the right to rob a foreigner of his liberty, or to sacrifice the same to the gods. No doubt it is quite possible that such a right may be sustained by individuals with unquestioning belief that they are justified in so doing, as in India, for example, the higher castes make use of their privileges, or as Thoas ordered the sacrifice of Orestes, or in Russia the lords are wont to flout their serfs. In fact, those who are in authority are very likely to execute such rights as legalized rights on account of the interest they may have in preserving them. But in a case of this kind their right will be merely the unrighteous right of the barbarian, and they must themselves appear to us in the category of barbarians, at least, who resolve to carry out and perfect what is essentially injustice. The legalized form, under which the individual shelters himself, is, for the time to which it belongs, and its spirit and the educational standard adapted to it, no doubt to be respected and justified. But if we reflect upon it rationally and apart from that, it is wholly positive, containing no intrinsic claims or authority. Moreover, if the individual makes use of his privileges for purely personal objects, under the mastery of particular passions and the aims of mere selfishness, in addition to our barbarian we get a bad character to boot.

Poets have frequently sought to arouse our pity, and it may be our fear as well, through the presentation of conflicts of this kind, following the rule of Aristotle, who lays it down that fear and compassion are objects of tragedy. Strictly speaking we experience neither fear nor reverence when confronted with rights which only exist among barbarians and are the misfortune of uncivilized times. Any compassion which such situations are likely to arouse is almost immediately converted into a spirit of indignant hostility. The only true artistic *dénouement* of such a conflict is one where we find such illegitimate rights are not carried into execution, as, for example, neither Iphigenia nor Orestes are respectively sacrificed in Aulis and Tauris.

The *third* and last class of that type of collision which is based on purely natural condition is that which is due to personal passion caused by natural peculiarities of temperament and character. The jealousy of Othello is a supreme example of this. Ambition, avarice, nay, even love itself in certain aspects, will furnish other illustrations. Collision of this kind is only properly referred to such passions in so far as individuals, seized and dominated exclusively by the power of such emotions, are thereby forced into antagonism with the truly ethical constitution and inherently justifiable course of human existence, and consequently are plunged into a still more serious conflict.

This carries our inquiry into the consideration of that third subdivision of our original classification of general types of collision, the type of which is based exclusively upon the conflict of spiritual forces, in so far as such opposition is the result of human activity.

(c) We have already observed when dealing with purely natural collisions that they only form the starting-point as it were for further states of contradiction. And the same is more or less true of the second type of conflict already adverted to.

All these, in artistic compositions of really profound significance, are unable to remain in such forms of opposition as we have hitherto discussed. Such disturbances and conflicting elements merely substantiate the opportune moment, out of which the true and essential forces of spiritual life will clash together in opposition and contend for the mastery. That which is spiritual can only be set in activity by virtue of spirit. Consequently the oppositions of Spirit can only win reality in actual human deed, can only thus manifest themselves in their true character.

The position we have arrived at, then, is this. We have on one hand a difficulty, an obstacle, a violation effected through something human life has carried out in action. We have on the other a violation of interests and forces intrinsically just and right. By treating these two forms of determination in close juxtaposition we, for the first time, are able to gauge the full depth of this last type of collision.

We may distinguish between the prominent examples which fall within the consideration of this class of cases as follows:

In passing from the sphere of that type of conflict which we have pointed out rests for its primary basis on what is entirely due to Nature, we observe that the first class of cases which confronts us on crossing the boundary to the consideration of a new type is closely related to that we have just left behind us. If, then, human action is assumed to be responsible for the collision, it will follow that what is carried out as natural through human action, that is to say, in so far as humanity is not entirely *spiritual*, will consist in this that a particular action is performed *unconsciously* and without purpose, which will be found afterwards to be a positive infraction of the forces of self-respecting and civilized society. The consciousness which any man latterly acquires of the injurious nature of an action, of which he was previously unaware, will drive him who still accepts the responsibility of such an action into division and conflict. The ground of such a conflict, in fact, consists in the opposition with which the mind is confronted between that which was actually before it *when the action took place*, and the subsequent discovery of all that was really *implied* in the act itself. The cases of Oedipus and Ajax will at once suggest themselves as examples. The action of Oedipus, if viewed simply with reference to his will and knowledge, amounted merely to the fact that he killed a perfect stranger in a quarrel. The unconscious act was the reality in its full significance, that is to say, the murder of his own father. Ajax, in a fit of frenzy, slaughtered the cattle of the Greeks believing them to be the Greek chieftains. On regaining his senses and discovering what he really did he is seized with a sense of shame which drives him into collision with himself. We must, however, observe that what has been unconsciously violated by a man in the type of collision we are now examining ought to be something which he himself, when fully in a position to judge, would both honour and revere. If such a reverential attitude has its roots merely in personal idiosyncrasy or superstition, such a collision can arouse, to say the least, no really profound interest.

Further, inasmuch as in the cases we are now discussing the conflict arises from a *spiritual* violation of spiritual forces through human action, the collision more generally appropriate to the type will consist in a violation which is perpetrated with full consciousness *proceeding out of such* and the intention it implies. The point of departure here may centre again in passion, violence, folly, and other similar qualities. The Trojan war, for example, originates in the rape of Helen. Agamemnon afterwards sacrifices Iphigenia, and so violates the feelings of her mother, slaying thus the darling of her womb. Clytemnestra, in consequence, murders her spouse. Orestes avenges the murder of his father and king by assassinating his mother. In a similar way in "Hamlet" the father is sent to his grave by a stratagem, and the mother of Hamlet insults the *manes* of the dead man by a precipitate marriage with his murderer.

In the case of these collisions as in those already considered, the main point is this, that humanity is engaged in a self-imposed conflict with what is intrinsically moral, true, and worthy of reverence. If this is not so, then, for all who are really conscious of what is moral and right, such a conflict can only appear without worth or material significance, as is the case, for example, in the famous episode of the Mahâ-Bhârata, with reference to Nalas and Damayanti. King Nalas

marries the princess Damayanti, who is allowed the privilege
of making a free choice among her sisters. All the other suitors
are genii floating in the air; Nalas stands on the Earth alone
as a man, and she has the good sense to select him. The genii
are consequently much enraged, and watch for the moment
when they may find King Nalas tripping. For many years
they can bring to his charge no offence, as he is capable of
none. At last, however, they obtain power over him, for he
commits a great crime; the crime is this, namely, that after
making water, he treads with his foot upon the earth thus
watered. According to Indian ideas this is a severe offence
which cannot escape punishment. From that moment the genii
have him in their power; one renders all his amatory desires
abortive, another excites his brother against him, and finally
poor Nalas, after forfeiting his throne and being reduced to
beggary, is driven forth a wanderer in wretchedness with
Damayanti. At length he is even compelled to part with her,
until, as the tale will have it, after many adventures, he is
once more set on the throne of his original happiness. The
real conflict upon which for the Indians of old days the whole
of this story was supported was an essential desecration of a
sacred thing: according to our notions the tale is absurd from
beginning to end.

Thirdly, it is not necessary that the disruption should
be direct, or, in other words, that the action taken solely by
itself should be an act of collision; the fact of collision may
well appear out of relations and circumstances of opposition
and antagonism which are forced upon the mind during the
process of that action's execution. Juliet and Romeo are in love
with one another. In the mere fact of their love there is nothing to suggest disunion. But they are aware that their families
are living in mutual hate and hostility, that their parents will
never consent to the marriage, and they are carried into collision by virtue of this preassumed situation of antagonistic
forces.

We must content ourselves here with these very general remarks upon the relation which the determinate situation occupies in its opposition to the universal world-condition.
Were we to extend our inquiry into all the divergent aspects,
modifications, and nuances of the subject, attempting thereby

to express an opinion upon every possible form of situation, this chapter would alone present us with sufficient matter for discussions of endless prolixity and diffuseness. The discovery of different situations implies a content of exhaustless possibilities; and in every particular example the essential question involved is how such may be adapted to the treatment of any specific art, in true subordination to the principles and character of such an art. To the fairy story much is permitted which is forbidden to a more stringent mode of artistic representation. And we may say that generally the discovery of the situation is a critical point in the process of art-production which often presents great difficulty to artists. In our own days the difficulty of obtaining a suitable subject-matter as a source for the circumstances and situations which the artist requires is a common complaint. At first sight it may appear to us more in keeping with our notion of poet if he borrow from his own resources, and invent situations himself; but such independence does little to increase his claims as a creative artist. For the situation does not directly constitute the spirituality of his work nor indeed give us its true artistic form: all that it does is to supply the external material in which as its appropriate medium a character or temperament is unfolded before us. It is only after working into this external material in which actions and characters find their starting-point that the true genius of the artist is actively displayed. The poet consequently has little or no claim to our thanks for merely having himself invented this least of all poetical aspects of his production. He is, in fact, fully entitled to draw as much and as frequently as he pleases from anything that comes to his hand, whether it be history, saga, mythos, or chronicle, nay, even from material and situations which have already been artistically treated—just as we find in the art of painting the external matter of the situation is borrowed from legends of saints, and the process has been repeated on similar lines over and over again. To discover the real artistic significance of such artistic work we must penetrate far beyond the mere invention of particular situations. The same remarks will apply in full force to the entire wealth of the circumstances and developments artistically handled. In reference to this it is frequently claimed as a virtue of modern art in contrast with that of the ancients that we find in it an infinitely more exuberant imagination. As a matter of fact, we do find in the artistic creations of the Middle Ages and our modern world the most extraordinary variety and interfusion of situations, events, and occurrences, whether tragic or otherwise. This fullness of detail, however, does not take us far. In spite of it all we have very few dramas or epics of the first excellence. For the main point is not the external course and interchange of a variety of events, when we find such events and histories merely complete the entire content of our work of art; rather it is the ethical and spiritual form which embodies them, and the masterful movements of temperament and character which are exposed and unveiled during the entire process of this artistic embodiment.

Glancing now at the main position we have arrived at, and from which our inquiry will proceed, we have found that circumstances, conditions, and relations, whether determined with a reference to the external world or the subjective consciousness, only create the situation by virtue of the *temperament* or passion which experiences them and derives its nutriment through them. We have further seen that the situation breaks up this determinate form in opposition, obstruction, development, and disruption, so that the *emotional* life feels itself compelled by the force of the affecting circumstances to *react with energy against* this disturbing and restraining influence, which stands in the way of its objects and passions. It is here, in truth, that the action, strictly speaking, commences, when, that is to say, the contradiction has fully asserted itself, which was already implied in the fully defined situation. Inasmuch as, however, the action which is based on this collision disturbs the unity of that which is opposed to it, it calls into being by its antagonism the opposing force of that which it confronts, and consequently the *action* is immediately associated with the *reaction*. With this analysis of the forces rendered necessary by dramatic action, we have at length arrived at the notion of the Ideal as a fully defined process. For we are here presented with two distinct spheres of interest, both of which have been rent, as it were, from the harmony they originally possessed, and confront each other in conflict. Such, by the contradiction which is involved in them, make a *resolution* of the discord necessary. This movement,

regarded as a homogeneous whole, belongs no more to the
province of the mere situation and its conflicts; we are carried
now into that portion of our inquiry to which we have already
given the name of the genuine action.

3. ACTION AND INDIVIDUALITY

In the development of the subject under consideration, the
action immediately follows after the universal *world-condition*
and the particular *situation*. In considering the action in its
external relation to that portion of our inquiry we have just
concluded it will be well to bear in mind the result we arrived
at, that it presupposes circumstances which necessitate collisions, action, and reaction. It is impossible to determine at
what point in the circumstances thus presupposed the action
will *begin*. For that which in one aspect will appear as commencement will very possibly present itself in another as the
result of earlier developments, and to that extent will postpone
the real starting-point. And in like manner this, too, we may
regard as a fact resulting from former collisions. To take an
example; in the house of Agamemnon, Iphigenia in Tauris ex-
piates the guilt and misfortune of her family. The commencement here of this deliverance on the part of Iphigenia is the
fact that Diana carries her to Tauris. This circumstance is,
however, merely the result of earlier stages of the story, such
as the sacrifice in Aulis, which is again conditioned by the
injury done to Menelaus in the rape of Helen by Paris, and
so on, ever backward, until we come to the famous egg of
Leda. In the same way the events which are the subject-
matter of the "Iphigenia in Tauris" presuppose the murder of
Agamemnon, and all the crimes associated with the house of
Tantalus. An analysis of much the same character might be
applied to the Theban circle of mythos. If an action is to be
represented with all the facts that condition it, poetry is the
only real art that can attempt this. Such a complete exposition
of historical fact has already become, as a certain proverb reminds us, rather a wearisome business; it is, in fact, more

within the province of simple prose, and, in contrast with such completeness, poetry will rather consider its true function to be that of taking its audience at once into the heart of the matter. There is a further important reason why it should not be to the interest of art to make its commencement from that point where we find the action under consideration is in the first instance externally conditioned, and it is this: such a point of departure is, after all, only related to the process regarded as natural or historical fact. The association of the action with this commencement merely concerns the empirical unity of its appearance; it may, however, in itself be of no significance at all to the real content of the action. This external unity of historical sequence remains just as it was, however it may chance that one particular person is affected by the involved threads of a varying series of fact. No doubt the entirety of the facts of life, its actions and fatalities, tends to make the individual what he is; but for all that his true nature, the real core of his thoughts and capacities, is manifested in *one* great situation and action independently of them. It is the progress of these which reveals to us really what a character is made of, a character which previously to their occurrence had been known merely in a nominal way, that is the name of one more fact among the external facts of experience.

We must therefore not look for the commencement of the action in that *empirical* source of it; we must rather centre the attention upon those circumstances which have taken a hold upon the particular nature with which we are dealing, and created or satisfied its needs; we must, in fact, reveal the particular collision in whose conflict and resolution the action in question consists. Homer, for example, in the "Iliad," makes a start at once with the particular fact on which his entire epic is founded, that is to say, with the wrath of Achilles. He tells us nothing of earlier history of the life of Achilles, but emphasizes at once the critical collision, and, moreover, does it in a way which unfolds a background of the greatest interest to his picture.

The representation, then, of the action as a process complete in itself, in which action, reaction, and resolution are constituent elements, is, above all, the function of the poetic art; all the other arts can at most only seize upon and secure in their presentation one moment of this process. It is quite true that if we direct our attention to that aspect of the medium they employ which is richest, they may appear to have an advantage over poetry; in painting especially we find a control asserted not merely over the entire external form, but also over the expression of external demeanour and the play of such relatively to other objects grouped around it. Such a means of expression, however, cannot compare as an interpreter of truth with human speech. The action itself is the clearest means of unfolding to us individual character, whether we view it relatively to the entire emotional life or the objects of mind. All that a man is at the very root of his nature is first revealed to us through his acts; and action, for the reason that it is an expression of spirit, finds its ultimate expression as such most clearly and concisely in speech alone. When we speak in general terms of human action we are apt to figure to ourselves an incalculable variety of mode. For Art, however, the sphere of action suitable to artistic representation is, generally speaking, limited. Her province is wholly restricted to the type of action which is conformable to the necessary configuration of the Idea.

There are three points of essential importance necessary to grasp in connection with such action as is capable of artistic representation, and which we may emphasize as follows. The situation and the resulting conflict is that which generally stimulates it; the active movement, however, taken by itself, the element of difference, that is to say, of the Ideal in its activity, is made apparent first by virtue of the reaction. This movement may be resolved into the following component features:

First, we have the *universal forces,* which constitute the essential content and object, for the sake of which the action takes place.

Secondly, we have the *realization* of these forces in the *individuals* who act.

Thirdly, the two aspects above mentioned have to unite themselves in that which, in default of any better generic term, we will here call *character.*

a. Universal Forces of Action

(1) However much we have finally arrived in our consideration of the action at a point where the definition and differentiation of the Ideal is of the first importance, nevertheless
the very notion of art renders it necessary that in the sphere
of true beauty, be the aspect of it whatsoever it may, it must
still have upon it the stamp of the Ideal; it cannot, that is to
say, maintain itself without rationality and the justification it
implies. Interests of an ideal character must inevitably be in
conflict with another, so that might is opposed to might. These
interests are, in fact, the eternal and universal forces of spiritual
existence, the essential cravings of the human heart, the spontaneous and inevitable objects of human action, justifiable and
rational in virtue of their own character, and consequently the
very universal powers to which we have referred. They are
indeed not the absolute Divine itself, but rather the sons of the
one absolute Idea, and consequently dominant and valid. They
are the children of the one universal truth, albeit only determinate, particular moments of the same. Through their very
distinction, it is true, they can fall into contradiction or disunion, yet despite all the element of difference contained, they
must possess the original essentiality within them in order to
appear as the determinate Ideal. Such are the supreme motive forces of art. They are the eternal religious and ethical
modes of relationship, status, personal character, and in the
world of romance, before everything else, honour and love. In
the particular grade of their significance these powers differ,
but all are essentially the product of reason. At the same time
it is these powers in the human heart and mind, which man,
by virtue of his humanity, is bound to recognize, to give free
play to, and to actualize. At the same time they ought not
directly to appear as rights in positive legislation. For, to take
one reason, the form of positive legislation, as we have seen, is
already in partial conflict with the notion and content of the
Ideal; furthermore, it is quite possible that the content of positive rights may contribute to that which is essentially unjust,
albeit entirely clothed in the attributes of law. The relations we

have above referred to, however, are not merely the supreme stable embodiment of the external world, but the essentially substantive powers, which for the very reason that they contain in themselves the actual content of human existence, continue to be the stimulating source of its activity, and ultimately all that ever carried it forward to perfection.

Of this kind are the interests and objects which contend against each other in the "Antigone" of Sophocles. Creon, the king, as ruler of the state, by a decree couched in the severest terms, forbade the right of burial to the son of Oedipus, who had proved himself an enemy of his country by bringing an army against Thebes. This proclamation was so far justifiable that it expressed care for the weal of the entire city. Antigone, however, is animated by an ethical principle of equal authority, in other words by her love for her brother, whom she finds it impossible to leave unburied, the prey of carrion birds. To leave such a duty unfulfilled would be in direct opposition to the sacred instincts of her personal relationship. She consequently violates the decree of Creon.

(2) Collisions of the type with which we are now dealing may be introduced in every possible way; the necessity of the reaction, however, must not be occasioned by means of anything out of place or at cross purposes with the main action, but through that which is in itself reasonable and justifiable. For example, in the well-known German poem of Hartmann von der Aue, "The Poor Henry," the collision is repulsive. The hero in this poem is visited by a fatality, that is to say, an incurable disease. He turns for assistance to the monks of Salerno. They state as the condition of his cure that a human being must willingly surrender his or her life, on the ground that the necessary salve can alone be forthcoming from a human heart. A poor maiden who is in love with the knight offers freely her own life and accompanies him into Italy. This is pure barbarism, and the silent love and pathetic devotion of the maiden are unable, consequently, to produce their full effect. It is true that we find the injustice of human sacrifice presented us by the ancients as the ground of the collision. The famous example is that of the story of Iphigenia, who is first offered as such a sacrifice, and afterwards is on the point of offering up her brother. But, in the first place, it is to be ob-

served that in these examples the conflict is in close connection with other relations which are in themselves justifiable; secondly, the artistic principle is really satisfied, as we have already observed, by the fact that both Iphigenia and Orestes are finally delivered, and the power of a collision which is opposed to our notion of right is thus destroyed. And, indeed, this is also the case in the above-mentioned poem of Hartmann, in so far as we may acknowledge the *dénouement* offered us in which, on Henry refusing to accept the sacrifice, God releases him from his malady, and the maiden is rewarded for her true love.

In apparent association with the positive powers we have enumerated must be added others set over against them, that is to say, the forces of that which is negative and bad, evil in short. That which is purely negative, however, ought not to be taken in the ideal representation of an action as the essential ground-motive for the necessary reaction. The reality of the purely negative case, it is true, corresponds to the negative and its appropriate character, but, if the implied notion and object is already in itself rendered nugatory, it is even less possible that the ugliness which is exposed in the inward life should manifest any genuine beauty upon its external reality. The sophistry of passion can, indeed, by means of the capacity, strength, and energy of a character, make the attempt to graft positive characteristics upon the negative, but we only obtain thereby the vision of a whitewashed grave. For that which is purely negative is generally flat and stale and leaves us consequently either void or drives us back, whether it be used as the motive force of an action or merely as a means to promote a reaction in another. The horrible, unfortunate, the harshness of dominion, and the obduracy of superior power may form part of the content and burden of the imagination when such characteristics are exalted and carried by the abundant greatness of a particular character or object. Evil, however, taken simply for what it is, envy, cowardice, and meanness, is merely repulsive. The devil, if we take him for what he really ought to be, is consequently a bad subject, or rather a figure for which Art has no uses at all. He is just a falsehood and nothing more, and consequently an extremely prosaic personality. In the same way it is perfectly true that the Furies of hate and many other allegorical figures of later times are potencies of a kind, but they are without affirmative subsistency and holdfastness, unfavourable to ideal representation, although in this respect a wide margin of difference is permissible in the several arts respectively, and in the particular mode in which they may immediately visualize such objects. Evil is, to express it in most general terms, essentially cold and devoid of content, because as such it is merely the source of negation, discord, and misfortune. All art, however, which is true to its essential notion, should reflect on us the vision of a harmony. Meanness, above all, is despicable, for it is a quality which arises from the envy and hatred of all that is noble, and does not shrink from distorting even a power that is essentially based upon the good into a means conformable to its own perverse and shameless passion. The great poets and artists of the classical world have in consequence never presented us with the vision of absolute evil and depravity. Shakespeare, on the contrary, in his tragedy of "King Lear," unfolds before us the spectacle of wickedness in all its horrors. The old Lear divides his kingdom among his daughters, and, while doing so, is foolish enough to believe in their false and flattering speeches, and to misinterpret the silent and faithful Cordelia. There is already folly and madness in this, and it is followed by the most outrageous ingratitude and worthlessness of the elder daughters and their husbands to the point of absolute craze. As an antithesis of this the heroes of the French school of tragedy are stretched and puffed out with every sort of grandiose and sublime motive, and make a great parade of their honour and nobility, and yet despite of it all destroy the very meaning of such motives by the mere fact of what they really are and accomplish. But it is in modern times more especially that we find this unstable dissolution of everything spiritual, which forces its way through every dissonance, however repulsive, become quite *à la mode;* moreover, it has even given us what we may describe as the humour of the abominable thing, a kind of burlesque simulation of irony, an atmosphere in which a Theodor Hoffmann, for example, has found himself so much at home.

(3) We may conclude, then, that it is the essentially positive and substantive powers in the spiritual world which sup-

ply the real content of the ideal action. These sources of energy, however, in their artistic embodiment, must not appear in their inherent universality, albeit within the reality of the action they are essential phases of the Idea. Rather they must receive the form of independent individuals. If this were not so they would remain as merely the universals of thought or abstract conceptions which do not properly fall within the province of art. Though in their origin they should be held as intact as it is possible to hold them from mere caprices of the fancy, it is equally necessary that in their development they should acquire determinacy no less than self-consistency, and in this way appear as essentially particularized. Such definition as they possess ought not to be carried to the point of the particularity of external objects, nor should their concentration be carried to that of the subjective self-consciousness. Otherwise the individuality of those universal powers is necessarily involved in all the developments of finite existence. In this respect we may say, then, that the determinacy of their individuality is not to be taken too seriously. The gods of the Greek Pantheon are the most conspicuous example of this manifestation and sway of the universal forces we have just discussed in their self-subsistent form. However they may be brought before us, their blessedness and cheerfulness remains unaffected. Regarded separately as particular gods no doubt they engage in conflict, but in all their battles we shall ultimately find they are not really serious in the sense that they concentrate themselves on any definite object with the entire consequential energy of their character and passion, fully prepared to stake their existence upon the result. They engage in this affair or that wherever it may take place, identify particular interests in concrete examples with their own; they are, however, equally ready to leave the matter at any point and wing their way back happily to Olympus. Such is the view we get of the gods when they engage in warfare on the pages of Homer. The determinacy of their characterization is capable of conflict, but they remain for all that the purely universal determinations which at bottom they are. A battle begins to rage; heroes advance singly one against another; then we lose sight of individuals altogether in the universal storm and crush; it is no longer the specific qualities of individuals which are now set in relief against each other—it is the universal rush of the fight, the daemon of war loosed and roaring, and now it is that the universal powers, the gods themselves, step forth on the scene of battle. From such a temporary display of the contrasts of their characterization they ever withdraw themselves into the solitude of their self-subsistency and repose. For though the individuality of their form carries them perforce into the region of time and contingency, nevertheless inasmuch as the universal they claim as gods is that which ultimately must prevail, the individual characteristic shrinks away into the determination of external form only; they are unable in their personality to penetrate the true arcana of conscious spirit.

Their physical definition is, in fact, either more or less only the accommodating form of their divinity. But this self-subsistency and careless repose is precisely that which gives to them their plastic individuality, and relieves them of any anxiety and constraint in relation to earthly objects and events. For this reason we find in the gods of Homer no final result when actively occupied with the concrete facts of human life, although such activity is displayed for us in many and diverse directions. The material and interest of human events which happen in time is that which gives them something to do and nothing more. And in like manner we may remark other peculiar characteristics attached to the Greek gods, which we can only regard as essentially unrelated to the general notion of divinity which each god respectively connotes. Mercury is, for example, the slayer of Argus; Apollo that of the hydra; of the love affairs of Zeus we have countless tales, and, among other things, he hangs his wife on an anvil. These and many other stories like them are merely supplementary additions, which attach to the gods in their aspect of natural forces by virtue of symbol and allegory, the origin of which we propose to discuss more fully later on. In modern art we shall, it is true, find certain indications which point to a conception of definite and at the same time universal powers. These are, however, for the most part simply cold and frost-like allegories of hate, envy, hope, love, faithfulness, that is to say, generally of virtues and vices in the actual truth of which we can retain no belief. For with us moderns it is the con-

crete subjectivity alone, for which we, in the representations
of art, feel that profounder interest, wherein abstractions such
as these do not appear in their isolation; but are made to appear merely as phases or aspects of human character, whether
we regard it in its particularity or as a concrete whole. In
much the same way the angels possess no essential universality
and self-subsistency such as characterize Mars, Venus, and
Apollo, or even Oceanus and Helios. They are, it is true, objects of imaginative conception, but their specific character is
that of vassals of the one Divine and essential substance,
which is not in this case broken up into self-subsistent individualities, as we find it in the Greek Pantheon. For this reason
we have here no imaginative vision of many objective powers
dwelling in a state of tranquillity, which may be represented
as essentially Divine personalities. We find, on the contrary,
the essential content of such either as subsisting in the Godhead, or realized in a mode which is both particular and subjective in wholly human characters and actions. Nevertheless
it was precisely in the conception of self-subsistency and individualization that the ideal representation of the gods
originated.

b. Individuals in Action

In the cases we have just discussed of the ideal gods it is
not a difficult matter for art to secure the ideality she requires.
But in approaching the concrete action, ideal representation is
confronted with a real difficulty. For though it is here that the
gods and, in general terms, the universal powers may be
identified with a principle which stimulates and compels activity, we are not therefore on the plane of reality entitled to find
in them the source of genuine individual action. Action is
rather essentially the manifestation of human life. Consequently there are in this connection two distinct aspects of the
problem to be considered. On the one hand we have these universal forces in their self-subsistent repose and for that reason
more abstract substantiality; on the other there is the individuality of men, in which we must seek the final spring and determining impulse to action no less than its actual accom-

plishment. It is, of course, only the simple truth that these eternally dominant powers are immanent in the identical nature of mankind, constituting, in fact, the substantive core of its character; but in so far as they are comprehended in their Divine nature themselves as individuals, and thereby in an exclusive way, their relation to the subject of human consciousness must remain an external one. And this fact enables us to see the essential difficulty we noticed above. There is, in truth, a contradiction immediately involved in this relation between the gods and men. It is quite true that the content of the gods is that which belongs to humanity, and announces itself as his passion, resolve, and will. It is, however, equally true that the gods must not only be assumed to be and comprehended as independent from man individually considered in their actual existence, but, furthermore, as the forces at the root of all his activity and determination. And this, too, in such a way that we are forced to consider the same determinations at one time as personified in the self-subsistent and Divine personality, and at another that which appears most essentially to belong to the human heart. And it is for this reason that the free self-subsistency of the gods no less than the freedom of human individuals in their activity is seriously compromised if, to the detriment of human independence, which we have already stated to be of most essential importance to the Ideal of Art, we ascribe an exclusive power of command to the gods. And we may observe this is precisely the same kind of difficulty which confronts us in the form of the religious conceptions of Christianity. It is stated in terms that the spirit of God leads up to God. Taken strictly such a phrase can only imply that the inward life of man is regarded as a purely passive ground, upon which the spirit of God labours. In such a conception the human will disappears as a free will, and at the same time the Divine purpose which motives the "inworking" above mentioned can only appear to man as a kind of Fate, under which he fails to come by his own true personality.

(1) If, however, this question of mutual relation is so understood that man in his action is conceived as standing in a purely external opposition to God, here posited as eternal substance, the relation of both is one of pure matter of fact. God gives a command, and man is obliged to hearken. Even great

poets have found themselves unable to dispense with this conception of external opposition between gods and men. In the "Philoctetes" of Sophocles, for example, we find that Philoctetes, after he has confounded the deceit of Odysseus, persists in his determination not to return to the Grecian camp until Heracles appears at length as *Deus ex machina,* and orders him to yield to the entreaty of Neoptolimus. The content of this apparition is, no doubt, sufficiently motived, and answers to our own expectation; the catastrophe itself, however, is for all that not rightly homogeneous, but rather outside the action; and in his noblest tragedies Sophocles makes no such use of this kind of representation, according to which, if we but carry it one step further, the gods are reduced to lifeless machines, and individual men simply to the instruments of a foreign caprice. In a similar way we constantly in epic poetry meet with the active intervention of the gods represented in a mode which is external to human freedom. Hermes, for example, conducts Priam to Achilles; Apollo gives Patroclus the blow between the shoulders which ends his life. We also frequently find mythological traits treated in such a way that they appear as wholly external to the actual lives of the individuals thus affected. Achilles, for example, is dipped by his mother in the Styx and thereby rendered invulnerable and invincible to the one point of his heels. If we reflect on this rationally it is obvious that all real bravery disappears, and all that is heroic in the character of Achilles is converted from a real trait of his essential manhood to a purely physical advantage. Such a mode of representation is, however, far more permissible to the epic than it is to the dramatic type of poetry, for the good reason that in the epic that aspect of spiritual life which is directly concerned with the intention implied in the execution of objects falls into the background and a larger field is, in general, offered for the play of external characteristics. Such a criticism of the prosaic understanding as the one above, which charges a poet with the absurdity that his heroes are no heroes at all, should only be advanced with the greatest caution, for it is partly in such traits as will appear shortly, that the poetical relation between gods and men is preserved. It is another matter, and we have nothing left us but prose, when in addition the powers, which are posited as substantive individuals, are mere empty shadows, the creations of the caprice of fancy and the arbitrariness of a false originality. They are then for the most part only the adjuncts of superstition or imbecility.

(2) The truly poetic relation of ideality consists, then, in the identity of gods and men; and this must assert itself even though the universal powers are presented as independent and free from the particularity of human beings and passions. In other words, all that we attribute to the gods must at the same time establish itself as that which is essentially cognate with the spiritual life of particular men in this sense, that while the dominating powers appear as essentially personified, yet at the same time all that is thus posited in an external relation to man is none the less clearly that which is immanent in his own spirit and character. The true function of the artist is, therefore, to introduce a mediating link between the difference involved in these two aspects, to bind them, in short, by a finely conceived thread of relation which, while clearly emphasizing their springs in the spiritual life of man, shall make no less visible the universal and essential element which is therein implied and present such to the imagination in individual form. The emotional life of man must reveal itself in the gods, who, in fact, are the self-subsistent and universal embodiments of that which is active and dominant in his own spiritual experience. Then alone are the gods at the same time gods in cognate relation with his own heart and emotions. When, for example, we are told by the ancients that Venus or Amor has put a constraint upon the heart, no doubt in the first place these divinities are apprehended as external powers; but human love is equally a stimulus and a passion, which is implanted in the heart and is part of that it independently contains.

In much the same sense is the frequent reference to the Eumenides. We have to picture in the first instance no doubt these avenging maidens as Furies, who pursue the transgressor in an external form. But this pursuit is but another aspect of the Fury which drives through the soul of the perpetrator of crime; and Sophocles in the "Oedipus at Colonus" (l. 1434) actually refers to them in this sense of inward spiritual forces, as the Eumenides of Oedipus himself, that is to say, who signify the father's curse as the result of the stress of emotion caused by the conduct of his sons. We have, then, and equally have not reason on our side whether we identify the gods with powers external to man, or find in them that which belongs exclusively to his spiritual life. They are in fact both. In Homer, for example, the activity of gods and men is a constantly involved skein. The gods appear to accomplish what is foreign to human activity, and yet for all that execute only that which is in vital co-ordination with his own emotional life. In the "Iliad," for example, when Achilles, in the stress of controversy, is about to raise his sword against Agamemnon, Athene steps forth behind him and takes hold of his head of flaxen hair, visible only to himself. Hera, who is equally anxious over Achilles and Agamemnon, sends for them from Olympus, and their admission there appears to be wholly independent of the desire of Achilles. On the other hand we have no difficulty in seeing that the sudden appearance of Athene, the wisdom which puts constraint upon the hero's wrath, is simply a reflection of internal conflict, that the entire description but states in imaginative form what was experienced in the heart of our hero. In fact Homer himself points this out a few verses previously ("Iliad," I, v. 190), when he relates about the debate that took place in his heart in the following terms:

ἢ ὅγε φάσγανον ὀξὺ ἐρυσσάμενος παρὰ μηροῦ,
τοὺς μὲν ἀναστήσειεν, ὁ δ᾽ Ἀτρείδην ἐναρίξοι,
ἠὲ χόλου παύσειεν, ἐρητεύσείε τε θυμόν.

This inward breaking up of anger into a divided self, this constraint, for it is in opposition to the anger, and Achilles appears at first to be wholly filled with wrath, the epic poet has a perfect right to represent at the same time as an external event. In a similar case in the "Odyssey" we find Minerva acting the part of escort for Telemachus. This attendance is rather more difficult to grasp as a personal experience of the emotional life of Telemachus, although we can readily fix on certain points of contact between the external image and the emotion experienced. And this it is we may generally say which constitutes the cheerful buoyancy of the Homeric gods, and the irony implied in the honour paid to them. Their self-consistency and seriousness are characteristics which tend to dissolve like a cloud, precisely to the extent that they unfold themselves as the very powers which are native to man's emotional life, and thereby, in their manifestation, leave humanity alone with its own possessions.

However, it is not necessary to look so far abroad for a complete example of the conversion of a purely mechanical conception of Divine activity into the atmosphere of the subjective consciousness, the sphere, that is, of freedom and ethical beauty. In his "Iphigenia in Tauris" Goethe has in this connection carried the process through with a beauty that we cannot sufficiently admire. In the drama of Euripides Orestes in complicity with Iphigenia carries off the statue of Diana. This is simply an act of stealing. Then Thoas comes on the scene, and orders their pursuit, and the recovery of the bust of the goddess. Finally, in very prosaic fashion, Athene appears and orders Thoas to stay his hand on the ground that she has independently commended Orestes to the charge of Poseidon, and he, in deference to her wishes, has already carried Orestes far over seas. Thoas submits to her advice and replies to it in the following terms (vv. 1442–43): "Lady Athene, whoever, on hearing the words of the gods, does not obey them is but a fool. For how could it be right and fit to contend with the mighty gods."

In this relation we can only see the bare external command of Athene on the one side, and an equally futile submission of Thoas on the other. In Goethe's treatment of the subject, on the contrary, Iphigenia becomes herself exalted to the rank of a goddess, in reliance upon the truth she feels within herself, the truth of a human heart. In this sense she turns to Thoas and exclaims:

> Is it then man alone who has the right
> To accomplish things none ever heard before!
> Shall he alone impress upon the strength
> Of hearts heroic the impossible?

That which in the drama of Euripides the command of Athene effects, the change in the attitude of Thoas, Goethe's Iphigenia endeavours to bring about, and in fact does bring about, through the depth of the feelings and ideas with which she confronts him.

> With motions strange
> An enterprise audacious soars within me;
> A vast reproach and ills yet graver still
> Will break on me if the event miscarry;
> But, see, I place it on your knees! Be true,
> Be only true and worthy of your fame,
> So your assistance shall declare it truth,
> Truth glorified through me.

And to this reply of Thoas:

> What! you believe
> The Scythian wild and the barbarian
> Hear the wise voice of Truth and hearts humane
> When Atreus of Greece still failed to hear.

she answers with the gentlest, purest trust:

> Nay, all thus hear
> Beneath whatever sky their birth was laid;
> All needs must hear for whom the springs of life
> Flow without let and purely through the soul.

Then it is she makes the final call upon her greatness of soul, and the tenderness of her faith at its highest point of effort; her entreaty touches, then masters and wrings from him, in a way that must appeal to every heart, the permission to return to her own. This alone is necessary. She has no need of the statue of the goddess; she can depart on her journey without deceit or betrayal of trust. And it is with the finest sense of beauty that Goethe refers here to the oracular word of the god:

> Bring but to Greece again the sister who
> All loth at heart in holy temple bides
> On shores of Tauris, and the curse is gone.

The very human reconciliation disclosed in these words is clearly that the pure and holy Iphigenia, the sister, is in fact the divine personification and the protectress of the house.

Noble and beautiful I wot in sooth
All that the goddess counselled seemed to me,

exclaims Orestes to Thoas and Iphigenia:

Like to a holy picture
The fate unalterable which walled our town
By one mysterious word, one word Divine,
Is banished, now that city takes thee back,
Who art the true protectress of our home;
Reserve thyself in holy quietness,
A blessing to thy brother and thine own;
It seemed that all deliverance on Earth
Had passed away, and all comes back with thee.

In the spirit of these healing words of reconciliation Iphigenia has already revealed herself to Orestes by virtue of the purity and ethical beauty of her inner life. It is true that her discernment drives him half mad, who in the convulsion of his spirit has lost all faith in peace; but the pure love of the sister does not fail to heal him from every pang with which he is tortured by the Furies of his soul:

Within thine arms
The evil clawed me with its direst clutch
For the last time, and to the very marrow
I shuddered horribly: and then it vanished,
E'en as a serpent to its lair. Anew,
And all through thee, the day's breadth I enjoy.

Here, as elsewhere throughout it, we can hardly emphasize sufficiently our admiration for the profound beauty of this poem.

The material which has the impress of Christianity upon it is more open to criticism than that which was the subject-matter of antique art. In the sacred legends, and generally speaking where the religious conceptions of Christendom prevail, no doubt we may find the appearance of Christ, the Virgin Mary and other saints the subject of universal belief; but along with them the imagination has clothed itself with fanciful aberrations in every direction, so that witches, ghosts, and every sort of spectral apparition are yet more conspicuous objects. In the face of such conceptions, so far at least as they appear foreign powers to our human nature, and man submits himself unreservedly to the charm, seduction, and influence of their illusions, artistic representation is wholly given up to every kind of folly and caprice of mere contingency. It is of unique importance that in the treatment of such material the artist take care that the freedom and independence of judgment are in no way impaired. Shakespeare has shown us how to do this in most noble fashion. The witches in "Macbeth," for example, appear as external powers, who foretell for Macbeth his future destiny. What they *do* foretell, however, is precisely that which is his own most secret wish, which is reflected back on him and declared in this, merely in appearance, external form. With a still closer regard to beauty, yet profounder insight, is the ghost in Hamlet treated as the purely objective embodiment of Hamlet's own intuitions. We find Hamlet in the first instance overpowered with a vague feeling that something horrible has taken place. His father's ghost then appears and gives definite form to these awful premonitions. We naturally expect that Hamlet, after receiving the facts set forth in his father's warning, will at once proceed with energy and bring the murderer to book, a revenge which appears to have ample excuse. But he delays and delays. Critics have made this inactivity a matter of reproach to Shakespeare, blamed him, in fact, as though for this reason the play to some extent never gets properly off. But we must remember Hamlet is not a strongly practical nature, rather a finely strung one, with emotions held in persistent reserve; a nature which finds it difficult to tear itself from its internal harmony; melancholy too, prone to subtleties, hypochondriacal, with emotions deeply rooted. For this reason it is obvious that he is *prima facie* indisposed to prompt action. And this is fundamentally Goethe's conception of him when he tells us that what Shakespeare sought to represent "was the imposition of some supreme action on a soul whose growth was unadapted to its execution." He in fact interprets the entire drama relatively to this conception of Hamlet. "We have here," he maintains, "an oak tree planted in an exquisite vase, which ought really only to contain and shelter the fair flowers; the roots spread, the vase is shattered." But it should be noticed that Shakespeare, when referring to the apparition of the ghost, contributes a far profounder trait of character in explanation of this debated point. Hamlet delays, because he does not right off wholly believe in the ghost.

> The spirit that I have seen
> May be a devil: and the devil hath power
> To assume a pleasing shape; yea and perhaps,
> Out of my weakness and my melancholy,
> (As he is very potent with such spirits,)
> Abuses me to damn me: I'll have grounds
> More relative than this: the play's the thing,
> Wherein I'll catch the conscience of the king.

In this passage it is obvious that the apparition as such does not leave Hamlet merely devoid of all stability, but that he entertains a reasonable doubt, and is determined to make his conviction a certainty by his own experiments before he proceeds to act upon it.

(3) As a summary description of these universal powers, which appear not merely in their external independence, but are the vital and moving forces in the human heart and all that is implied in its most intimate life, we may borrow an expression in use among the ancients, that is to say Pathos (πάθος). To translate this word adequately is not easy. Passion almost always implies as its concomitant an element of meanness or baseness. We contend in ordinary parlance that a man should not surrender himself to his passions. It must therefore be understood that we use the expression pathos in a nobler and more universal sense than this without the slightest implication of anything blameworthy or egotistic. The devoted love of the sister Antigone is an excellent example of a pathos in the full significance of the Greek use of the term. Pathos in this sense is a power of the emotional life which completely justifies itself, an essential part of the content of rationality and the free will. Orestes, for example, kills his mother not so much on account of any force of his emotional life which we strictly can call passion; rather it is a pathos in itself fully considered upon and essentially sane which carries him on to the awful deed. Thus understood we may add that it is impossible to say that the gods possess pathos. They are

merely the universal content of that which is the stimulating energy in the resolves and actions of human individuality. The gods as such continue in their repose and freedom from passion, and however much they may quarrel or contend among themselves, there is nothing really serious in it all, or their strife possessed merely a symbolical significance in the view we may take of it as a universal war of the gods. We must therefore strictly limit pathos to the actions of mankind, and conceive thereunder the essential or rational content, which is present in the human consciousness identical with itself and throughout suffuses the emotional life.

(a) We may say, then, that pathos constitutes the true mediating link, the veritable domain of art. The representation of it is the most truly effective part of a work of art, as it is its influence upon those who look at it. Pathos sets a string in motion, which vibrates through every human heart. Every one must know the type of worth and reason, which underlies the content of a genuine example of pathos, must recognize it at once when he sees it. And the cause of this is that pathos moves us because it is that which is essentially the vital force of our human existence. And it equally follows that that which is wholly external, the natural environment and particular scene, in its active support of the effect of pathos, need only be treated quite subordinately. Nature must in consequence be drawn upon as a fact essentially symbolical and suffer the pathos to re-echo from her walls, which is the most real subject-matter of artistic representation. Landscape is, for example, a type or genre of painting of less importance than historical painting; but even there we find that the school of landscape most independent should not be without a general harmonic relation to human feeling, and, in fact, possesses a certain type of pathos. In this sense we are told art generally ought to touch the emotions. Before accepting this principle, however, we ought first to inquire through what means this peculiar effect of art must be brought about. "To touch the emotions" is in general the activity of something in union with feeling; and mankind, more particularly the mankind of to-day, are, or a more considerable portion of them are, only too readily open to such experiments. The man who showers tears on us, starts the seeds of tears, which grow up fast enough. In art, however, only that ought to move us which contains in itself the real import of pathos.

(b) For such reasons we may affirm that neither in comedy nor in tragedy ought pathos to be that which is only folly or personal idiosyncrasy. Shakespeare's Timon, for example, is on purely material grounds a misanthrope; his friends have eaten him up, consumed his substance, and when he himself requires their gold desert him. He consequently becomes a passionate enemy of mankind. The situation is both conceivable and consistent with nature, but it contains no pathos that can be justified on principle. Even to a more striking extent is the hate we find in "The Misanthrope," that play of Schiller's apprenticeship, purely a vagary of modern ideas. For in this latter case the misanthrope is in addition a thoughtful, perspicacious, and entirely noble man, great-hearted towards his peasants, whom he has freed from their villeinage, and devoted to his daughter, who is, apart from her beauty, in all respects worthy of his love. In much the same way, in that novel of August Lafontaine, Quintius Heimeran von Flaming is worried with the follies of mankind. It is, however, our most latter-day poetry which, above all, loves to wind itself into every conceivable knot of fantastical falsehood, attempting thereby to secure an effect through mere oddity, but failing to find the slightest response in any sane person for the reason that every vestige of what is really present in human life has vanished from such refinements of mental athletics.

In another direction we may remark that everything which depends solely, that is to say, in so far as scientific apprehension is the main requirement, upon instruction, testimony to the truth, and insight of what is offered as such, is no fit subject-matter for the representation of a genuine pathos. The facts of *scientific knowledge* are a part of this material. And the reason of this is that science demands a particular form of education, an effort towards and a knowledge of the specific forms of science and their relative importance of exceptional variety and extension; an interest in this type of study is by no means a universally moving influence in the hearts of men, but is limited and must ever remain limited to a narrow circle of votaries. The treatment of purely *religious* instruction presents similar difficulty, if we mean by that the development

of the same in its profoundest import. No doubt the universal
content of religion, such as the belief in God and similar theses,
is of the deepest interest to anyone worthy of it. Art is, however, not directly concerned either in the exposition of religious
dogmas, nor, indeed, in any exceptional insight into their
truth; it is consequently of importance that she should be held
aloof from such disquisitions. It is all the more necessary that
we should through art entrust every type of pathos to the human heart, every motive of ethical significance, which are of
practical and vital interest. The influence of religious ideas is
rather upon the subjective world of emotion, the heaven of
the heart, the ever-repeated consolation and uplifting of the
individual life, than upon direct action in the strict sense. For
that which is Divine in religion on its practical side is morality
and the powers which are potent in the ethical life. These
powers, however, in contrast with the heaven of religion in its
purest form, are in definite relation to the world and that which
is entirely human. Among the ancients this worldly content
was fundamentally included in their conception of Deity, and
consequently their gods could be related directly to human
action and its artistic presentation.

From all this it will readily appear that the significant moments of volitional activity which present to us the pathos we
have just endeavoured to define are numerically small and the
range of them restricted. In the opera especially it is inevitable
that the sphere from which such may be selected is a narrow
one; we consequently have for ever dinned in our ears the
plaints and delights, the misfortunes and happiness of love,
fame, honour, friendship, maternal and marital devotion.

(c) Now a pathos of this kind requires for its display not
merely the power of exposition, but also that of perfected
elaboration. And what is more, the soul which entrusts to its
pathos the spiritual wealth it possesses must be one with real
wealth to dispose of, and not one that can rest in a condition
of purely intensive self-concentration. It must, in short, be
ready to give an outward semblance to its self-expression and
rise to the finished perfection of that. The distinction between
this power of self-concentration and that of self-revelation is
of great importance; and we shall find that in this respect the
types of individuality such as generically represent different

races offer essential points of contrast. Nations whose reflective consciousness has been highly trained are more eloquent in the expression of their passions than others who are not so. The ancients, for example, were accustomed to unfold the pathos, which is the animating principle of human personality, in its profoundest significance, without running off into cold generalities or empty tattle. The French also in this respect are naturally gifted, and their eloquence in the expression of passion is not by any means always merely a piling up of words, as we Germans, following the bent of our national reserve, to which the repeated expression of emotion appears to be a kind of wrong inflicted upon it, are only too ready to think it is. In fact, we have gone so far in this direction that we could mention a distinct phase in our poetical history, when the younger spirits, at any rate, sick to death of that which they dubbed "the flush of French rhetorical water-drops," yearned to such an extent after the simplicity of Nature that their artistic energy could only express itself for the most part in interjections. It is hardly necessary to observe, however, that we shall arrive at no "open sesame" with Ahs and Ohs, a damn here and there thrown in, or any other random note of storm and bluster. The inspiration of mere interjections is a feeble one, or rather is simply the way in which the still unrefined nature expresses itself. The spirit which is to reveal to us pathos must be a spirit which is full to running over, which is able to spread itself abroad and give expression to its virtue.

We may add, too, that in this respect Goethe and Schiller present a most marked contrast. Goethe is less pathetic than Schiller, makes use of a mode of artistic expression which is more intensive; more especially in his lyrics we are struck by this characteristic of self-reserve. His songs, and this is the true quality of the pure lyric, go naturally on their way, without entirely giving us all that they contain. Schiller, on the contrary, is clearly anxious to unfold the pathos of his subject to its furthest limit, and with all the clearness and force of expression he can muster. Claudius in "Wandsbecker Boten"[1] has contrasted Voltaire and Shakespeare in much the same fashion, maintaining that the one *is* what the other only *appears*

[1] Vol. i, p. 153.

to be. "Master Arouet tells us: 'I weep'; Shakespeare really weeps!" To this we can only reply that it is precisely with such telling and appearance that art is concerned and not with the mere positive fact. If Shakespeare merely wept while Voltaire made others think he wept, so much the worse for the poet Shakespeare.

To conclude, then, it is necessary that pathos, in order to be in itself concrete, as it should be in ideal art, be presented in its artistic manifestation as the pathos issuing from a spiritual nature, rich and comprehensive. And this result carries us forward to that third aspect of our consideration of "the action" already adverted to, that is to say, an inquiry into what is implied by *character* in this connection.

c. Character

We will summarize the preceding argument. Our point of departure was the *universal* and substantive powers which are the original stimulus to action. Such require as the medium of their active realization human *individuality*, in which they then appear as *affecting* pathos. But, furthermore, the universal inherent in these powers must in particular individuals acquire the concentrated unity and concreteness of a *whole*, and a *single whole*. This totality is man apprehended in his fulfilled spiritual content and the subjectivity therein comprised, in one word the entire self-contained human individuality which we designate as character. The gods are born into the pathos of men, and pathos in its more concrete form of activity is human character.

In character, then, we find the real focus of the ideal exposition of art, that is to say in so far as the embodiment unites in itself the separate aspects of it already developed as consistent phases, in the construction of its own totality. For the Idea as *Ideal*, by which we mean as clothed in a form within the grasp of sensuous imagination and perception, and in its activity as action and accomplishment, is, if we define it strictly, just this self-relation of the *subjective individuality*. The individuality, however, which is truly *free*, and nothing short of this will satisfy the Ideal, has not merely to declare itself as universality, but at the same time to assert its nature as concrete singularity, as the mediating bond which unites and transpierces both sides thus related, which in their *self-related* actuality subsist as unity. And this is precisely what we understand by character, the ideal form of which consists in the wealth of energy with which all the constituent aspects of the subjective life are welded in one whole.

We will now inquire rather more closely into the nature of this conception of character viewed under three distinct aspects.

First, as co-extensive individuality, that is to say, with our attention directed to the wealth of substance contained in it.

Secondly, with direct reference to its particularity, the form in which it is bound to appear, albeit still a totality, as one that is more *defined* or specific.

Thirdly, in our final apprehension of it as a unity which is fully identified with its own determinate form, that is, which is throughout fused with the same by virtue of its own principle of subjective self-identity, and thereby attaches to the whole the significance of an essentially *assured* character.

We will now develop and elucidate more fully what we conceive to be implied in the above general propositions.

(1) And first we would draw attention to the fact that this pathos, though an essential feature in the development of completed individuality, is not, in the specific form of its appearance, the *sole* or exclusive interest of the individuality portrayed. It is, in fact, merely one aspect of the efficient character, if one of paramount importance. To put it in rather a strong way, the human soul does not merely carry within it *one* god as the original of its pathos; on the contrary, the spiritual scope of humanity has wider borders, and we may affirm that many gods make their dwelling in one true man, or, rather, all the powers which are scattered throughout the heaven of the gods are enclosed within that one breast. It is co-extensive with the entire field of Olympus. In this sense one of old has said: "Out of thine own passions, O man, hast thou created the gods." And, as a matter of fact, in proportion as the intelligence of the Hellenic folk quickened, the number of their gods increased; and, furthermore, the gods of their earliest days were less intelligent, that is to say, they were godlike

figures deficient both in individuality and determinate character.

In this wealth of content, accordingly, it is necessary that the character adequate to ideal art should display itself. And this is just that which creates the interest we feel in a character, namely, that a totality such as that we have above described emerges from it, and the character, while reposing on its abundance, nevertheless persists in perfect equality with itself, as one secure and self-excluding subject. If the character, however, be not conceived and depicted as this rounded and subjective unity, is abstract in the sense that it is entirely the sport of one passion, such must then appear as self-destructive, or at least cracked, weak, and without real fibre. For the weakness and inertness of individuals is just this very thing, that the eternal forces of which we have spoken never assert themselves in them as a real part of their most essential substance, as, to put it logically, predicates which adhere to them as the subjects of such.

In Homer, for example, every hero is the living focus of a whole congeries of qualities and traits. Achilles is the most youthful hero in the host, but his youthful exuberance is represented as quite compatible with all other entirely human qualities, and Homer unfolds before us this variety through situations which offer the finest contrast. He loves his mother, Thetis, he weeps for Briseis, when she is snatched from him, and his violated sense of honour drives him into the conflict with Agamemnon, which is the original fount of all the events that follow after it in the "Iliad." Add to this he is the truest friend of Patroclus and Antilochus; moreover, he is the most blooming, fiery youth, swift of foot, brave, yet full of reverence for gray hairs; the faithful Phoenix and trusty servant are at his feet, and at the funeral of Patroclus the hoary Nestor is treated with the highest deference and honour. And, in contrast to all this, Achilles is represented as inflammable to a degree, effervescent, revengeful, and full of the most brutal austerity when face to face with the foe. He binds the slain Hector to his chariot, trails the corpse in fell hunter's fashion three times round the walls of Troy; yet stays his anger when the old Priam comes to his tent, and, as he thinks within his heart of his own old father, reaches to the weeping king the hand

which has done to death his son. Of Achilles we may well exclaim: "here is a man indeed, and human nature, ay, noble
human too, in all the length and breadth of its riches, is unveiled before us in this one man!" It is just the same with all
the other Homeric characters—Odysseus, Diomedes, Ajax, Agamemnon, Hector, Andromache—every one of them is a whole,
a world in itself, a complete and living member of humanity,
something very different at least from your allegorical abstract
of some one particular trait. What frosty, faded personalities,
despite all their vigour and rigour, are the horned Siegfried,
Hagen of Troy, nay, even Volker, the musician, in comparison.

It is this variety of characterization, and this alone, which
can give to a character the interest of life. At the same time
this fullness of detail must really appear as included in the
personality itself, that is, it must not strike us as the mere di-
version, passing freak, or suggestion of an excited fancy, such
as we see in the case of children who will take up everything
in turn, and even make something out of it, yet, for all that, are
without essential character. Character in this latter sense will
penetrate and make itself a home in the most diverse phases
of the emotional life of man, will steep itself to overflowing
with that abundance, and, at the same time, not remain thus
immersed, but throughout all the congeries of interest, objects,
qualities, all the traits that distinguish or arrest it, maintain
the form of its self-exclusive and alert subjectivity intact.

For the representation of such exhaustive types of character
epic poetry is, above all others, adapted, dramatic and lyrical
poetry are less so.

(2) Art, however, will not be content to remain at the point
which the course of our inquiry has reached, namely, the notion of character as a mere congeries of traits. For the object
we have before us now is the Ideal in its specific determination, and singularity, or, rather, concrete *individuality,* are both
of them prominent and necessary features. Action, more than
anything else, in its conflict and reaction is impossible without
some restriction and clear definition of form. For this reason
the heroes of dramatic poetry are for the most part of simpler
definition than those of epic poetry. And the way we get at a
clear definition is through some pathos out of the ordinary
which is so portrayed as to make some essential trait of char-

acter stand out in bold relief, and itself to be the stimulus to particular objects, resolves, and actions. If, however, this simplification is carried so far that any character appears as though it were pared down to a mere shadow-like semblance of any form of pathos, such as love or honour, all real vitality and spiritual depth must necessarily vanish, and the representation, as is not infrequently the case in the French school of drama for this very reason, can only offer us a cold and jejune result. We may therefore conclude that in this aspect of particularity the prominent feature which asserts itself pre-eminently will be this, that within the borders of this very limitation the fullness of life is completely preserved, so that the personality in question has free scope allowed it for further expansion in many directions, a power to adapt itself to every variety of situation, and, in short, is able to unfold and express in every possible way the wealth of a truly complete spiritual life. Despite the supreme simplicity of their pathos the characters in the Sophoclean drama possess this intrinsic vitality. We may indeed compare them in their plastic self-seclusion to the figures of sculpture. For it is also quite possible that sculpture express very various delineations of character despite all the tenacity of its definition. In contrast to the bluster of overpowering passion, which concentrates all its forces upon one single point, it exhibits out of its tranquillity and speechlessness that predominant neutrality, which peacefully envelops all powers within itself; but this unperturbed unity does not, however, persist in any indissoluble union with mere formal definition, but, rather, in virtue of its beauty, suffers at the same time the birth-throes of all that pertains to it to disrobe itself as through a cloud of immediate possibility into fresh relations of every variety. In the finest figures of sculpture we behold a tranquil depth, which unfolds, as it were, the pregnant womb, from which all other potencies may be born. In contrast with sculpture it is yet of more vital importance to the arts of painting, music, and poetry, that they should display the inmost complexity of character, and real artists of every age have recognized this. In Shakespeare's "Romeo and Juliet," for example, the most pathetic characteristic of Romeo is his love: but he is also placed before us under relations of the greatest contrast, whether it be in reference to his parents, his friends, his love troubles, or his affair of honour in which he fights with Tybalt, his attitude of deference and trust to the monk, nay, even on the verge of the grave his conversation with the apothecary, from whom he purchases the poison. Throughout he is the same worthy and noble man of deep emotions. In the same way the character of Juliet is unfolded throughout the range of her relations to father, mother, nurse, the Count Paris, and father Lawrence. And, despite this, she is as deeply immersed in her one preoccupation as she is in every one of these situations, and her entire character is transpierced with and carried away by the one single emotion, her passionate love for her lover, which is as deep and broad as the unbounded sea, so that it is but the simple truth when she exclaims, "The more I give, the more I possess, both are infinite."

From all this it appears that even when there is but one pathos visible, it must unfold itself as the wealth of all it possesses. And this is what really happens even in lyrical poetry, where we find the pathos is not attached to actions determined by positive circumstances and conditions. For in this latter case the pathos can only assert itself as the spiritual state of an emotional nature otherwise complete in itself, which is, that is to say, free to express itself in any other conceivable circumstance and situation which may confront it. The use of words of vital significance, an imagination which can associate itself with all the world, can restore the Past to the Present, can transform the entire external environment of man's life to a symbolical expression of his spirit, can bravely adventure into the depths of comprehensive thought, and, while doing so, reveal an exuberant, capacious, clear, exalted, and noble nature —a wealth of character such as this, freely expressing such a world, is a prize indeed for the Lyric Muse. No doubt a purely logical reflection may find it impossible that such variety of character should co-exist with a masterful clearness of type. We may be asked, for instance, in reference to the heroic character of Achilles, whose strength of youth is the pre-eminent trait of his beauty, how it is possible to reconcile the tender heart so manifest in his relations to his father and his friend with the cruel act of revenge wherewith he drags Hector round the walls. Precisely the same kind of inconsequence is to be met with in Shakespeare's clowns. They are, with scarcely an exception, bubbling over with wit and the humour of genius. And, no doubt, there will always be fools enough to ask us how men thus spiritually gifted could ever betake themselves to such tomfooleries. The truth is that the reflection of the formal logic is sure to emphasize one aspect of a character, and conclude that the entire man is minted under its impression to the exclusion of all others. To such everything that asserts itself as alien to the hallmark of its beggarly mintage can only appear as an inconsequence. In the truly rational contemplation of the whole as distinct from the parts, and thereby of the living thing, that which appears as inconsequent will be precisely that which brings all into fit co-ordination. For our humanity is just this very paradox. We have not merely to carry the contradictions of our complex nature, but to suffer the load with patience, and throughout prove staunch to our burden.

(3) We may conclude, then, that character must fuse together its particularity in the element of its spiritual substance; it should possess a definite type, and at the same time retain in this distinction the force and stability of a *single* fully self-consistent pathos. Where we find our humanity represented without such a centre of unity, the different aspects of such variety it may possess will lose all relative meaning or significance and fall away from each other. In art we shall find that what we distinguish in our conception of personality as infinite or the Divine is just this self-consistency in unity. If this view be a just one it is obvious that such characterizations as stability and determination are of great importance in the ideal representation of character. And we shall only obtain such a result, as already observed, in so far as the universality of the powers inherent in our humanity are permitted to transpierce the mere particularity of the individual character and, by virtue of the unity thus set up, create a subjective and at the same time individual life which supplies its own principle of unity and self-identity.

Such a condition is all important, and we must now advert to a number of artistic compositions, more particularly of later times, in express relation to it.

In the "Cid" of Corneille, for example, the collision between the opposing principles of love and honour is a match, no doubt, of brilliant effects. A pathos of this kind, involved as it is in the opposition of distinct forces may, no doubt, be the operative ground of conflicts; but when we find such portrayed as the spiritual struggle of one and the same character, though such antagonism may very readily supply us with the material for brilliant rhetoric and effective monologue, the cataclysm which is here presented in the emotional life of one person driven thus by turns from its abstract subjection to honour into the equally abstract one of love, and forthwith hounded back again, is not favourable to the portrayal of a character of genuine stability and homogeneousness.

It is equally inconsistent with the delineation of resolute personality when a leading character, already under the predominant influence of some specific pathos, is portrayed as one overmastered by the direction or persuasion of a subordinate character, and is thus enabled to shift the responsibility upon other shoulders. This is what actually takes place in the "Phedra" of Racine when the mind of Phedra is depicted as entirely motived by the words of Oenone. A character of real distinction acts out of its own initiative, and will not suffer the views of a mere stranger to be that which determines its own resolution. Only when action is the direct result of its own reflections do we get that clear relation between personal initiative and the consequent result which carries with it the full weight of guilt or responsibility.

We find yet another type of this instability of character as quite a peculiar possession of the more recent literary output of Germany. It is a type of character in which a kind of flatulence in emotion is the rule no less than the source. The classic example is the Werther of Goethe's romance, a thoroughly morbid type of character, without any vestige of real manliness such as might carry him beyond the egotism of his love-passion. What makes him interesting is the passion and beauty of his emotional life, the intimate fellowship between himself and Nature which the course of his spiritual experience and the pliability of his temperament accentuate. This effeminacy has yet more recently embodied itself in many other forms of expression which descend with increasing rapidity to the lowest circle of jejune and tasteless egotism. We must not even

omit, for instance, to include in our list that illustration of the
lovely soul which we find in Jacobi's "Woldemar." In this romance we are made a present of the glory of emotional volu-
bility in all its pretensions. It would be difficult, indeed, to cite
a better example of the self-deceptive illusion of personal virtue and excellence. Here we have all that sublimity and divinity of soul, which relates itself crookedly to every possible aspect of the actual world; that type of feebleness which is
wholly unable to share in or tolerate any portion of the labours
or interests of practical life as it really is. So rooted is it in its
own consciousness of superiority it passes everything as unworthy of it on the other side. It is, in fact, a peculiar feature
of this type of "lovely soul" that, even when face to face with
the truly ethical interests and wholly sane objects of life, instead of meeting them frankly, it retires into the seclusion of
itself, where it weaves its own threads of finery and passes its
time in hatching out its exquisite brood of religious and moral
reflections. And connected closely with this personal enthusiasm for our superabundant excellence, which we set forth in
front of ourselves with such a brave show, there will always
be an intense sensitiveness for all other beings who may appear at any moment to sympathize with, comprehend, and
appreciate this beauty of the solitary life. If such fellow-feeling
is not forthcoming we find the very heart of us troubled to its
depths and infinitely bruised. We have lost at one stroke all
humanity, friendship, and love. We are unable to put away
with whatever act of pedantry or rudeness may be in question,
some trivial circumstance or stupidity over which the vision
of any character of breadth or strength would pass without a
tremor. It whirls away the thought of everything else, and that
which is by itself of least significance proves to be that which
finally most reduces us to despair. Such is the source of all that
endless train of melancholy, trouble, heartache, peevishness,
sickness, dejection, and poverty of spirit which follows, such
the spring of all those self-torturing reflections one on the top
of another, that cramp and obstinacy, nay, finally, that cruelty
of soul, through which the wretchedness and weakness of the
spiritual content of such a type of "loveliness" consummates
and declares itself. No heart that is truly sound can wish to
unite itself with such an emotional hermitage. For it is a fun-

damental characteristic of all genuine character that it carries within itself both the courage and the strength to do and to will some actual thing. The interest, therefore, that such natures which are for ever revolving round themselves may arouse in us is after all an empty interest, and necessarily so despite all the conviction with which such natures may assure us that they belong to a higher and purer sphere than our own, a sphere which has revealed to our vision that peculiar type of the Divine they have uncovered from their secret parts and finally present to us, to borrow an apt figure, *en negligée*.

This want of genuine solidity of character appears in yet another form where we find the particular manifestations of this world of "fine feelings" turned as it were upside down and hypostatized as independent forces. Much that passes for magic, magnetism, spiritualism, the apparitions of *clairvoyance*, the morbid condition of sleep-walking, is attributable to this source. The living person in question is placed in a relation to these abstruse powers, which from one point of view identifies him with them, and in another makes them appear as something foreign to his spiritual life, which determines and controls it. It is assumed that underlying these undefined forces there is some inexplicable truth which borders on the marvellous, or at any rate passes comprehension. From the world of art, however, all such powers of darkness should be banished. In art there is no darkness at all, but all is lucid and transparent, and in adventuring after such types of myopy, speech merely flounders into spiritual disease, or plays loose as poetry with the nebulous, empty, and trivial, a good example of which is the verse of Hoffmann, and that piece by Heinrich von Kleist entitled the "Prince of Homburg." The truly ideal character has nothing in his composition, or the pathos which expresses it, of another world and its ghosts, but only actual interests, in which he finds himself at home. More particularly is this feature of *clairvoyance* become a trivial and vulgar recipe of our more modern poets. In Schiller's "Tell," on the contrary, when the old Attinghausen on the brink of the grave foretells the destiny of his country, the prophetic instinct is quite in its right place. It is always, however, a misfortune for an artist to find himself forced to exchange the sanity of a character with some malady of the soul whether it be to motive the collision or excite interest. For this reason he should only avail himself of the condition of insanity in quite exceptional cases.

In conclusion we may connect with these distortions of a sane vision, which are so much opposed to all real unity and consistency of character, the principle of our latter-day irony. This false theory has betrayed the poet into grafting upon his characters qualities so essentially diverse that they are incapable of all homogeneous relation; the essential unity of every character is thus confounded. According to this theory a character is first presented as characterized in a certain way, and immediately after we have that very determination converted into its opposite, and the character itself is propounded to us as nothing more than the negation of what it was and is. Moreover this very futility is accepted by this irony as the supreme discovery of art. An audience should not, in short, be carried away by an essentially positive interest, but should be pulled up at the critical moment, much as the irony itself is no sooner launched upon anything than it is off again. They would even explain the characters of Shakespeare according to such a principle. We are informed that Lady Macbeth was an irreproachable wife of the tenderest feeling, despite the fact that she not only falls in with the suggestion of the murder, but actually eggs her husband on to its execution. But if the signet mark of Shakespeare is conspicuous on any one quality it is on the firm and decisive delineation of his characters, even when it is only the formal greatness and consistency of evil that is in question. Hamlet, it is true, is a case of mental indecision, but even he is only in doubt as to the way he shall carry out his purpose, not at all as to what has to be done. Yet nowadays they would assimilate even Shakespeare's characters to a world of ghosts, and appear to think that this futility and indecision of ups and downs, this general squeamishness in short can by itself contribute to our interest. The Ideal, however, is centred in this, that Idea is made *actual*, and our humanity is associated with such actuality as subject and consequently as a unity which is essentially firm-rooted.

We may here, so far at least as this portion of our inquiry is concerned, bring our observations upon the individuality which is consistent with real character to a close. That which we have mainly sought to emphasize is a pathos which is at once self-determined and essential, the possession of a rich and complete nature, the spiritual world of which such a pathos transfuses under such a form that this process of transfusion no less than the pathos itself receives its artistic presentment. At the same time this pathos must not be allowed to come into conflict with itself in the hearts of men so as to stultify its very nature and consistency as pathos.

CHAPTER III

DRAMATIC MOTIVATION
AND LANGUAGE

[a]Classical beauty, with its infinite range of content, material and form, is the gift bestowed on the Greek people; and this folk is entitled to our respect on the ground that it has produced art in its highest form of vitality. The Greeks, if we regard the form of their realized life immediately presented us, lived in that happy middle sphere of self-conscious and subjective freedom and substantive ethical life. They did not persist, on the one hand, in the unfree Oriental unity, which is necessarily bound up with a religious and political despotism for the reason that the individuality of the subject is overwhelmed in a universal substance, or, in some particular aspect of the same, because it has essentially as personality no right, and consequently no ground to stand on; neither, on the other, did they pass beyond to that subjective penetration, in which the particular subject separates itself from the whole and the universal, in order to make itself more explicit in its ideality; and only through a higher return to the ideal totality of a purely spiritual world, succeeds in its final purification of the substantive and essential. On the contrary, in the ethical life of Greece, the individual was self-substantive and essentially free, without disengaging himself from the general interests of the realized State immediately visible to him and the positive immanence of spiritual freedom in the temporal condition. The universal of morality and the abstract freedom of personality, both in its ideal and external aspect, remains in

a *The Philosophy of Fine Art*, vol. II, pp. 181–84.

accordance with the principle of Greek life in undisturbed harmony, and during the time in which, even in real existence,
this principle asserted itself in still unimpaired purity, the self-
substantiality of the citizen did not stand forth in relief in
contrast to a morality which was to be distinguished from it:
the substance of political life was so far merged in the individual, as he on his part sought his own liberty absolutely in the
universal ends of the entire civic life. The feeling for beauty,
the significance and spirit of this joyous harmony interpene-
trates all productions, in which the freedom of Greece is self-
conscious, and in which she has made visible to herself her
being. Consequently her view of the world is just the midway
ground on which beauty commences its true life and breaks
open its serene dominion; the intermediate realm, that is, of
free vitality, which is not merely a fact at once immediate and
natural, but one which is the creation of a spiritual point of
view revealed by art; the realm, that is, of a culture of reflection, and at the same time of an absence of reflection, which
neither isolates the individual nor on the other hand is competent to bring back again its negativity, pain, and unhappiness
to a positive unity and reconciliation; a realm, however, which,
just as in the case of Life itself, is at the same time only a
point of passage, however true it be that it scales at this point
the summit of beauty, and in the form of its plastic individuality is so spiritually concrete and rich, that all tones have their
interplay within it, and also, too, that which is for its own
standpoint what lies behind it, albeit it is no longer present as
an absolute and unqualified principle, is nevertheless felt as
that which accompanies it—a kind of background to it. In this
sense the Greek nation has also, in the representation of its
gods, made its spirit visible to the perceptions and the imaginative consciousness, and bestowed on them by means of art
a determinate existence, which is entirely conformable with
their true content. By virtue of this homogeneous form, which
is alike consistent with the fundamental notion of Greek art
and Greek mythology, art became in Greece the highest expression for the Absolute, and Greek religion is the religion of
art itself, whereas romantic art, which appeared later, although it is undoubtedly art, suggests a more exalted form of
consciousness than art is in a position to supply.

In establishing the position, as we have just done, on the one hand, that essentially free individuality is the content of classical art, and, on the other, that a like freedom is the equally requisite determinant of the form, we have already assumed that the entire blending of both together, however much it may be presented in the immediate form, is nevertheless no original unity such as Nature's, but is necessarily an *artificial* association made possible by the subjective spirit. Classical art, in so far as its content and its form is spontaneity, originates in the freedom of the Spirit that is clear to itself. And for this reason also we may say that in the *third* place the artist occupies a position different from that of his predecessors. That is to say his production declares itself as the spontaneous *product* of a man in the full possession of his senses, who as truly *knows* what he wills as he is *able* to accomplish such a purpose; who is consequently obscure to himself neither in respect to the significance and substantive content of that which he has resolved to make visible in the form of art, nor finds himself hindered by any defects of technique from executing the result aimed after.

If we look more closely at this change in the position of the artist we shall in the first place find this freedom announced to us relatively to the *content* in this way, that he does not feel compelled to seek for it with the restless process of symbolical fermentation. Symbolic art remains the captive of its travail to bring to birth and make clear its form to its own vision, and this embodiment is itself only the original form, that is, on the one side Being in the immediate guise of Nature, and on the other the ideal abstraction of the universal, unity, conversion, change, becoming, origination, and passing away. In this original form of the artistic process, however, art does not come to its rightful possessions. Consequently, these representations of symbolic art, which should be expositions of content, remain still themselves riddles and problems, and merely testify to the struggle after clarity and the effort of Spirit, which on and on seeks to discover without obtaining the rest and repose of discovery. In contrast to this troublous search the content must for the classic artist be presented him as something *already there* in the sense that as a thing essentially positive, as belief, popular opinion, or as an actual event either of myth or tradition, it is determined for his imagination in all its essential character. Relatively to this objectively determined material the artist is placed in the freer relation that he does not himself undertake the process of production and fermentation, and pass no further than the impulse after the real significances of his art, but rather that for him a completely explicit and unfolded content lies before him which he accepts and freely reproduces from himself. The Greek artists received their material from the popular religion in which already that which had been brought over to Greece from the Orient had begun to receive a form of its own. Pheidias borrowed his Zeus from Homer, and other tragedians also did not create the fundamental groundwork of that they represented. [b]It is true that Herodotus says, in a passage already cited, of Homer and Hesiod, that they had created their gods for the Greeks, but he also speaks expressly of particular gods, how this or that one was Egyptian or some other form: the poetic activity does not therefore exclude the reception of material from other sources, but merely suggests an essential transformation. For the Greeks possessed mythological conceptions before the time in which Herodotus places those original poets. The main fact of Greek theology is this, that it creates itself and constitutes itself from that which has gone before, which takes its place in the origins and process of its own generic history.

1. MYTH AND MOTIVATION IN CLASSICAL DRAMA

[c]In proceeding further to examine this fundamental aspect of our present subject I must at once give utterance to the preliminary caution that the historic investigation of the varied and multifold conceptions of Greek mythology lies outside our present task. All we are concerned to inquire into here are the essential phasal steps of this process of reconstruction, in so far as the same notify themselves as phases of universal im-

[b] *The Philosophy of Fine Art,* vol. II, p. 190.
[c] *Ibid.,* p. 204.

port in the new artistic configuration and its content. As for that infinite mass of particular myths, narrations, histories, things referable to a local origin and symbolism, which collectively still assert their predominance in the world of later gods, and incidentally appear in artistic production, but for all that do not belong to the vital point of interest to which our own effort is directed—we must necessarily leave all this broad field of material on one side, and can merely refer to an example or two by way of illustration.

a. Conflict between the Old and New Gods

(1) [d]To take, then, first the *oracles*, it will not be necessary for us now to dilate on them to any considerable extent. The essential point which concerns us here is merely due to this fact, that in classical art the phenomena of Nature are no longer revered as such—in the way that the Parsees, for example, pray to naphthetic regions or fire, or as among the Egyptians, gods remain inscrutable, mysterious, and mute riddles—but that the gods, being themselves subjects of knowledge and volition, do verily give to man by means of natural phenomena indications of their wisdom. In this sense the ancient Hellenes made inquiry at the oracle of Dodona,[1] whether they should accept the names of gods, which have come to them from barbarians, and the oracle replied: "Use them."

(a) The signs by means of which the gods thus made their revelations are for the most part of the simplest description. At Dodona such were the rustle and whisper of the sacred oak, the murmur of the spring, the tones of the brazen vessel, which the wind made thus to reverberate. In like manner at Delos it was the laurel which rustled and at Delphi, too, the sound of the wind on the brazen tripod was full of significance. Over and above, however, such immediately natural sounds man is also the voice-piece of the oracle in so far as he is rendered deaf to and whirled away from the alert common sense of his ordinary mind to a natural condition of enthusiasm; as, for example, the Pythia at Delphi was wont, stupefied

[d] *Ibid.*, pp. 205–25.
[1] Herod. ii, 52.

by exhalations, to deliver the oracular words, or in the cave of Trophonius the inquirer of the oracle met with faces, from the interpretation of which an answer was delivered him.

(b) There is, however, another aspect which we should set alongside of the purely external sign. For in the oracles God is, it is true, accepted as He who *knows,* and the oracle of most famed repute is dedicated to Apollo, the god of wisdom. The form, however, in which he reveals his will, remains the wholly indefinite voice of Nature, either a natural sound, that is, or the unconnected tones of words. In this obscurity of form the spiritual content is itself equally obscure and requires *interpretation* and explanation.

(c) This explanation, albeit it brings under a mode of spiritual life the deliverance of the god which in the first instance is presented purely in the form of Nature's own voice, remains despite this fact obscure and equivocal. For the god is in his knowledge and volition concrete universality. And of the same type also must the advice or command unavoidably be which the oracle declares. The universal, however, is not one-sided and abstract, but as concrete universal contains the one side no less than the other. Inasmuch, then, as man stands over against the knowing god as one unknowing he accepts the oracular word itself in ignorance. In other words, the concrete universality of the same is not open to his intelligence, and he can merely select from the equivocal word of the god, assuming that he decides to act upon it, *one* aspect thereof, for the reason that every action under particular circumstances is unavoidably *definite,* only, that is to say, giving a decisive impulse in *one* direction and shutting off another. His action is barely accomplished, and the deed—which consequently has become his own and for which he must now be answerable—really carried through when he finds a collision confronting him. All in a moment he is aware that the other side, which lay already folded in the oracular sentence, is turned against himself and the fatality of his deed, his knowledge and will notwithstanding, has him in the toils; a fatality which he may not know, but of which we must suppose the gods are aware. Conversely again the gods are determinate potencies and their expressed will, when it carries this character of essential determinacy, as, for example, the bidding of Apollo, which drives Orestes forward to his revenge, brings about a collision of forces in the selfsame way. For the reason, then, that in one aspect of it the form, which the spiritual knowledge of the god assumes in the oracle, is the wholly undefined external expression or the abstract ideality of the word, and the form itself through the equivocal sense it contains includes the possibility of discord, we find that in classical art it is not sculpture, but poetry, and pre-eminently dramatic poetry, in which oracles contribute their share of the content and are of importance. In *classical* art, however, they do essentially maintain a place, because in it human individuality has not forced its way to the full height of spiritual attainment, where the subject draws the determination of his actions without infringement from his own resources. What we in our modern sense of the term call conscience, has not here secured its rightful place. The Greek acts often, it is true, at the beck of his passion, bad no less than good; the genuine pathos, however, which is here held to quicken him, and does in fact so quicken him, proceeds from the gods, whose content and might is the universal of such a pathos; and the heroes are either immediately instinct with the same, or they interrogate oracles for advice, when the gods do not present themselves openly to their vision, by way of quickening the deed to be done.

(2) Moreover, as in the oracle the *content* is to be found in the gods that *know* and *will*, while the form of the external phenomenon is the external which is abstract and a part of *Nature*, from the other point of view that which is *natural*, if we look at it relatively to its universal forces and the activities which belong to these, becomes the *content*, from out of which the independent individuality has first to force its way up, and receives as its original form merely the formal and superficial personification. The thrusting back of these purely natural forces, the opposition and contention through which they are overcome is just the significant centre, for which we are indebted primarily to classical art, and which we must consequently submit to a closer examination.

(a) The first thing we would remark in this connection is attributable to the circumstance that we are not here concerned—as in that view of the world which belongs to the Sublime, or in part even that appropriate to Hindoo doctrines—

with God already essentially devoid of any relation to sense, when regarded as the starting point of all creation, but rather with that in which Nature's gods, and we may add in the first instance the more universal forces of Nature such as Chaos, Tartarus, Erebus, the entire savage and subterranean substance, and, furthermore, Uranos, Gaia, the Titan Eros, Kronos, and the rest, supply the beginning. It is from out of these, then, that the better defined powers, such as Helios, Oceanos, and others like them first have their being; while they, in their turn, become the natural cradle for the later spiritual and individualized divinities. We find, therefore, again here another theogony and cosmogony which is the work of the imagination, whose earliest gods, however, still remain for the observer under one aspect of an undefined character, or vaguely extend beyond all reasonable limit; and, if viewed from another standpoint, still carry with them much that is essentially symbolical.

(b) The more detailed distinctions among these Titan potencies may be thus indicated:

(i) First, we have those powers of the Earth and the stars, without spiritual and ethical content, consequently dissolute, a raw, savage race, gigantic and formless, as though they were scions of Hindoo or Egyptian imagination. They are to be classed with other individualities of Nature such as Brontes, Steropes, and again with the hundred-handed Kottos, Briareus, and Gyges, the giants and the rest standing in the first instance beneath the lordship of Uranos, then of Kronos, that chief of the Titans, who obviously is a kind of personified *Time*, devouring all his children, just as Time eventually annihilates everything that it has brought to birth. This myth is not without a symbolical significance. For the life of Nature is, in fact, subjugate to Time, and brings only the Past into existence, just as in the same way the prehistoric times of some people, which is only one nation, one stock, yet constitutes no genuine State, and pursues no definite objects essentially made clear to itself, becomes the sport of the power of a Time, which is destitute of history. We touch solid ground for the first time when we come to law, morality, and the State, something permanent which remains though races pass away, as it is said that the Muses give permanence and a defence to everything, which, as the life of Nature and present action, had only vanished swept away with Time.

(ii) But, further, it is not only that the forces of Nature belong to this sphere of the old gods, but also the forces noted as earliest over the elements. In particular the first active agency upon metal through the force of what is still raw, and elementary Nature, that is air, water, fire, is of importance. We may mention in illustration the Corybantes, the Telchines, demons of both beneficent and evil influence, the Pataeci, pygmies, dwarfs, cunning in the woodman's craft, small, with big paunches.

More prominent notice should be taken of Prometheus, as illustrating in the chief place a fundamental point of new departure. Prometheus is a Titan of exceptional type and deserves exceptional attention. Together with his brother Epimetheus he appears in the first instance as favourable to the young gods; then he stands out as the benefactor of men, who in other respects have no defined relation with the new gods or the Titans. He brings fire to man, and thereby supplies them with the means of satisfying their needs and working the technical arts, which are no longer, however, regarded as natural products, and consequently it would appear do not stand in any closer association with Titan workmanship. For this interference Zeus punishes Prometheus until Hercules finally releases him from suffering. At the first glance there would appear to be nothing strictly Titanesque in these main features of the story; nay, it would not be difficult to point out an inconsequence in the fact that Prometheus, just as Ceres, is a benefactor of mankind, and is none the less numbered among the old Titanic potencies. If we look at the matter more closely, however, this inconsequence will at once disappear. In this connection several passages from Plato's works will help us sufficiently to clear the difficulty. There is the myth in which the guest-friend recites to the younger Socrates that in the time of Kronos men originated from the Earth, while the god, on his part, devoted his attention to the whole. After this step a movement of opposite tendency sprang up, and the Earth was left to itself, so that now the beasts became savage, and mankind, whose means of nourishment and all their other needs had hitherto passed immediately into their hands, were left alone without advice or assistance. Well, according to this myth, it was in such a condition[2] that fire was brought to mankind by Prometheus, all other accessories of craftsmanship being communicated by Hephaestos and his companion in craftsmanship, Athene.

Here we have notified expressly a distinction between fire and the thing which artistic ability produces by working on the raw material; and only the gift of fire is ascribed to Prometheus. Plato narrates the myth of Prometheus at greater length in the "Protagoras." There we read:[3] "There was once a time when gods indeed existed, but mortal beings had not appeared. When the foreordained time of their birth also had come, the gods created them in the inward parts of the Earth, composing their substance of Earth and fire and that which is the union of both these elements. When the gods were desirous of bringing them into the light, they handed them over to Prometheus and Epimetheus to apportion and arrange the energies of each singly as was right. Epimetheus, however, requested of Prometheus that the apportionment might be left to him. After I have done this, quoth he, you may mark and express an opinion. Epimetheus, however, by a blunder apportioned everything worth having to the animal world, so that there was nothing left over for mankind; and when Prometheus made his inspection he found that though all other living things were wisely provided with all their needs mankind remained naked, unprotected, without covering or weapons. But already the appointed day had appeared in which it was necessary that man should pass from the bowels of the Earth into the light. In the embarrassment in which he was placed to procure some assistance for mankind Prometheus stole the wisdom that is shared by Hephaestos and Athene by taking fire— for without fire it would be impossible to possess it or make it of use—and made a present of this to men. Man now, it is true, possessed the wisdom necessary for the support of his life, but he was still *without political wisdom,* for this was still lodged with Zeus. Entry, however, to the stronghold of Zeus was no longer permitted Prometheus, and apart from this the awful watchers of Zeus barred the way. He passed, how-

[2] "Politicus" ex rec. Bekk. ii, 2, p. 283; Steph. 274.
[3] "Protag." I, 1, pp. 170–74; Steph. 320–23.

ever, secretly into the chamber which Hephaestos and Athene shared in the practice of their art, and having secured the forging-art of Hephaestos he pilfered that other art (the art of weaving) which was possessed by Athene and presented this to mankind. Out of these possessions the means of satisfying the needs of Life is provided for man (ἐυπορία τοῦ βίου). Prometheus receives, however, as already narrated, punishment for the thefts he commits owing to the blunders of Epimetheus."

Plato further tells us in a passage which immediately follows the above that mankind was still destitute of the art of war for their protection against the animal world, which was merely a part of the art of politics, and consequently were collected into cities, and would have so outraged each other and finally broken up such asylums for the reason that they were without all political organization, that Zeus found it necessary to send down to them, under the escort of Hermes, Shame and Right.

In these passages the distinction between the immediate objects of life, which are related to physical comfort, that is, the provision for the satisfaction of the most primary necessaries and political organization, such as sets before itself as its object what is spiritual, custom, law, right of property, freedom, and communal existence is expressly emphasized. This principle of ethical life and right, Prometheus did not give to men; he merely taught them the cunning by means of which they might overcome natural objects and make them serviceable to their needs. Fire and the craftsmanship which makes use of fire have nothing ethical about them in themselves; and it is just the same with the art of weaving; in the first instance they are devoted to the exclusive service of private individuals, without coming into any relation with that which is shared in human existence or with Life in its public character. For the reason, then, that Prometheus was unable to furnish mankind with anything more spiritual or ethical, he also does not belong to the race of new gods, but to the Titans. Hephaestos, it is true, also possessed fire and the particular crafts to which it is essential as an instrument for his field of activity, and is none the less accredited as a new god: but Zeus cast him from Olympus, and he continued to limp ever after. Just as little is it, therefore, an inconsequence when we find Ceres placed among the younger gods, who proved herself a benefactor of mankind just as Prometheus did. For that which Ceres taught was agriculture, with which at the same time property, and yet more, marriage, social custom, and law stand in close association.

(iii) A third class of the ancient gods contains, it is true, neither personified potencies of Nature, as such, nor the might which next follows as lord over the particular elements of Nature in the service of the more subordinate human necessities, but is already contestant with that which is essentially in itself ideal, universal, and spiritual. What, however, is none the less lacking in the powers we have here to reckon with is spiritual individuality and its appropriate form and manifestation, so that they also more or less relatively to their operations keep a position which is more nearly akin to the necessity and essential being of Nature. In illustration of this type we may recall the conception of Nemesis, Dike, the Erinyes, Eumenides, and Moirai. No doubt we find associated with these figures the determinate notions of right and justice; but this inevitable right, instead of being conceived and clothed in the essentially spiritual and substantive medium of social morality, remains either persistent in the universal abstract notion, or is related to the obscure right of that which is natural within the circle of spiritual connections, the love of kindred, for example, and its paramount claim, which does not appertain to Spirit in the open freedom of itself self-recognized; and consequently also does not appear as lawful right, but in opposition to this as the irreconcilable right of revenge.

To bring the view of the above nearer I will merely draw attention to one or two ideas bound up with it. Nemesis, for example, is the might to humiliate the exalted, and to cast down the man all too fortunate from his lofty seat, and consequently to restore equilibrium. The claim or right of equilibrium is the purely abstract and external right, which, it is true, certifies itself as operative in the range of spiritual circumstances and conditions, without, however, making the ethical organization of the same the content of justice. Another aspect of importance attaches to this circumstance, that the right of the family-condition is apportioned by the ancient gods, in so far as these repose on a condition of Nature, and thereby are in antagonism with the public right and law of the community. We may adduce the "Eumenides" of Aeschylus as the clearest illustration of this point. The direful maidens pursue Orestes on account of the murder of his mother, a murder which Apollo, the younger god, had directed, in order that Agamemnon, the slaughtered spouse and king, should not remain unavenged. The entire drama consequently is concentrated in a conflict between these divine Powers, which confront each other in person. On the one side we have the goddesses of revenge, the Eumenides; but they are called here the beneficent, and our ordinary conception of the Furies, into which we convert them, is set before us as rude and uncouth. For they possess an essential right thus to persecute, and are therefore not merely hateful, wild, and ferocious in the torments which they impose. The right, however, which they enforce as against Orestes is only the family-right in so far as this is rooted in the blood relation. The profoundest association of son and mother is the substantive fact which they represent. Apollo opposes to this natural ethical relation, rooted as it is already both on the physical side and in feeling, the right of the spouse and the chieftain who has been violated in respect to the highest right he can claim. This distinction is in the first instance brought to our notice in an external way since both parties are champions for morality within one and the same sphere, namely the family. The sterling imagination of Aeschylus has, however, here—and we cannot sufficiently value it on this score—discovered for us a contradiction, which is not by any means a superficial one, but of fundamental significance. That is to say, the relation of children to parents reposes on the unity of the natural nexus; the association of man and wife on the contrary must be accepted as marriage, which does not merely proceed from purely natural love, that is from the blood or natural affinity, but originates out of a conscious inclination, and for this reason belongs to the free ethical sphere of the self-conscious will. However much, therefore, marriage is bound up with love and feeling it is none the less to be distinguished from the purely natural emotion of love, because it also freely recognizes definite obligations quite independent of the same, which persist when that feeling of love may have ceased. The notion, in short, and the knowledge of the substantiality of marital life is something later and more profound than the purely natural connection between mother and son, and constitutes the beginning of the State as the realization of the free and rational will. In like manner we shall find resident in the relation of prince to citizen the association of a similar political right, law, and the self-conscious freedom and spirituality of similar social aims. This is the reason why the Eumenides, the ancient goddesses, pursue Orestes with punishment, whereas Apollo—the clear, knowing and self-consciously knowing ethical sense—defends the right of the spouse and the chief, justly opposing the Eumenides: "If the crime of Clytemnestra were not scented out I should be in verity without honour and despised as nought by the consummator Hera and the Councils of Zeus."[4]

Of still greater interest, albeit wholly involved in human feeling and action, is the contradiction which we have set before us in the "Antigone," one of the most sublime, and in every respect most consummate work of art human effort ever produced. Not a detail in this tragedy but is of consequence. The public law of the State and the instinctive family-love and duty towards a brother are here set in conflict. Antigone, the woman, is pathetically possessed by the interest of family; Creon, the man, by the welfare of the community. Polynices, in war with his own father-city, had fallen before the gates of Thebes, and Creon, the lord thereof, had by means of a public proclamation threatened everyone with death who should give this enemy of the city the right of burial. Antigone, however, refused to accept this command, which merely concerned the public weal, and, constrained by her pious devotion for her brother, carried out as sister the sacred duty of interment. In doing this she relied on the law of the gods. The gods, however, whom she thus revered, are the *Dei inferi* of Hades,[5] the instinctive Powers of feeling, Love and kinship, not the daylight gods of free and self-conscious, social, and political life.

(c) The *third* point, which we would advert to in connection with the theogony of the outlook of artists in the classic period, has reference to the difference between individuals of

---

[4] "Eum." vv. 206–9.
[5] Soph., "Ant." v. 451: ἡ ξύνοικος τῶν κάτω θεω   ι κη.

the older gods relatively to their powers and the duration of their authority.

(i) In the first place, the origin of these gods is a succession. From Chaos, according to Hesiod, proceeds Gaia, Uranos, and others, after that Kronos and his race, finally Zeus and his subjects. This succession appears in one aspect of it as a rise from the more abstract and formless to the more concrete and already fairly defined powers of Nature; in another as the beginnings of the superiority of the spiritual over the natural. Thus in his "Eumenides" Aeschylus makes the Pythia in the temple of Delphi begin with the words: "First of all I revere in my prayer her who first gave us oracles, Gaia, and after her Themis, who as second after her mother had her prophetic seat in this place." Pausanias, on the other hand, who also names the Earth first as giver of oracles, says that Daphne was ordained by her afterwards in the prophetic office. In another series again Pindar places Night in the first place, after her he makes Themis follow, then comes Phoebe, and finally he closes the succession with Phoebus. It would be of interest to analyse more closely these particular differences; such an inquiry, however, lies outside our present purpose.

(ii) This succession further, in addition to its aspect of being an extension into essentially profounder conceptions of godhead, possessing, that is, a fuller content, also appears as the degradation of the earlier and more abstract type within the range of the older race of gods itself. The primary and most ancient powers are robbed of their masterdom, just as we find Kronos dethroned Uranos, and the later representatives are set up in their place.

(iii) In this way the negative relation of the reformation, which we settled at once to be the essence of this first stage of the classic type of art, becomes the proper centre of the same. And it is so for the reason that personification is here the universal form, in which the gods are presented to the imagination, and the progressive movement comes into opposition with human and spiritual individuality. And although this appears in the first instance still in a form indeterminate and formless, we necessarily find that the imagination presents this negative attitude of the younger gods against the more ancient under the image of conflict and war. The essential advance is,

however, from Nature to Spirit, implying by the latter the true
content and the real form appropriate to classical art. This
progress and the conflicts by means of which we perceive that
it is carried forward, belong no longer exclusively to the sphere
of the old gods, but centre in the war through which the new
gods lay the foundation of their enduring mastery over the
ancient.

(3) The opposition between Nature and Spirit is in the nature of the case inevitable. For the notion of Spirit, as in very
truth totality, is, as we have already seen, *essentially* simply
this, to split itself in twain, that is into its intrinsic constituents
as objectivity and as subject, in order that by means of this
opposition it may emerge from Nature and confront the same
forthwith free and jubilant as vanquisher and superior might.
This fundamental phase, rooted in the very essence of Spirit,
is consequently a material aspect in the conception which it
supplies to itself of that nature. Regarded historically, that is
on the plane of ordinary reality, this passage asserts itself as
the reconstruction through progressive steps of the natural man
into the condition where right, property, laws, constitution and
political life are paramount. Regarded under a mode which
relates this process to gods and *sub specie eternitatis* it becomes the conception of the victory over the natural Powers
by means of the spiritual and individual Divinities.

(a) This contest exposes an absolute catastrophe, and is the
essential deed of the gods, by virtue of which the fundamental
distinction between the old and new gods is first made visible.
Consequently we ought not to point to the war, which exposes this distinction as a mythical story in the same way we
should point to any other myth; rather we should regard it as
the mythos, which in fact punctuates a great moment of transition, and expresses the creation of the later theogony.

(b) The result of this violent strife among the gods is the
ruin of the Titans, the unique victory of the new gods, who
forthwith receive in their assured dominion a plenitude of gifts
in every direction from the imagination. The Titans, on the
other hand, are banished, and compelled to huddle in the hol-
lows of the Earth, or, like Oceanos, dally on the dark skirts of
the clear, joyful world, or still endure many grievous punishments. Prometheus, for example, is fettered on the Scythian

mountains, where an eagle insatiable devours the liver that ever renews itself. In like manner an infinite and inexhaustible thirst torments Tantalus in the lower world, and Sisyphus is for ever constrained to roll up hill in vain the rock that for ever rolls back again. These punishments are, in truth, the false type of infinity, the yearning of the indefinite aspiration or the unsatisfied craving of natural desires, which in their eternal repetition fail to discover rest or final satisfaction. For the truly godlike intuition of the Greeks regarded the mere extension into space and the region of the indefinite, not, as some modern votaries of such longings do, as the highest attainment of mankind, but as a damnation which it relegates to Tartarus.

(c) If we ask ourselves in a general way, what from this point must for classical art fall into the background, failing, that is, to have any right to figure as its final form and adequate content, we shall find at the earliest point of departure the elements of Nature. With them disappear from the world of the new gods all that is gloomy, fantastical, void of clarity, every wild confusion between Nature and Spirit, between significances essentially substantive and the accidental incidents of externality. In a world such as this the creations of an unrestricted imagination, which has not yet for its principle the measure of spiritual proportion, have no place, and are compelled and justly so to vanish before the clear light of day. We may furbish up the monstrous Cabeiri, the Corybantes, these representatives of procreative force as much as we choose, yet for all that such presentations in every trait of them —to say nothing of the ancient Baubo, whom Goethe sets careering over the Blocksberg on an old sow—belong to a greater or less degree to the twilight of consciousness. Only that which is spiritual imperatively demands the light; and that which does not reveal itself and in itself expound its own interpretation is the unspiritual, which fades again once more into Night and obscurity. That which is of Spirit on the contrary reveals itself, and purifies itself, by itself defining its external form, from the caprice of the imagination, the flood of obstructing shapes, and the otherwise perturbed accessories of symbolical sense.

For the same reasons we now find that human activity, in so far as it is limited merely to Nature's wants and their satisfaction, falls into the background. That old right, Themis, Dike and the rest, as one not determinate through laws which originate in self-conscious Spirit, loses its unimpaired validity, and in the same way, if conversely, that which is purely local, albeit there is still room left for its play, passes by incorporation into the universal figures of the gods; in which we may still trace the lingering vestiges that remain of it. For as in the Trojan war the Greeks fought and conquered as *one* people, so, too, the Homeric gods, who already have their conflict with the Titans behind them in the past, are one essentially secure and defined god-world, a world which is yet further with ever-increasing fullness made definite and unassailable by later poetry and the plastic arts. This invincible consistency is in its relation to the content of the Greek world of gods Spirit and only Spirit; but not Spirit in its abstract ideality, but as identified with its external and adequate existence, just as with Plato soul and body, as in union brought into one nature and in this consolidation from one piece, is at once the Divine and Eternal.

b. Survival of the Natural Divinities in the Humanized Gods

Despite, then, the victory of the new gods that which came before them still remains in the classical type of art partly preserved and revered in the original form in which we have already recognized it, partly under a transmuted mode. It is only the limited Jewish national god which is unable to tolerate other gods in its company for the reason that it purports as *the* one god to include everything, although in regard to the definition of its form it fails to pass beyond its exclusiveness wherein the god is merely the God of His own people. Such a god manifests his universality in fact only through his creation of Nature and as Lord of the heavens and the earth. For the rest he remains the god of Abraham, who led his people Israel out of Egypt, gave them laws on Sinai, and divided the land of Canaan among the Jews. And through this narrow identification of him with the Jewish nation he is in a quite peculiar way the god of this folk; and consequently, speaking generally, neither stands in positive consonance with

Nature, nor appears truly as absolute Spirit referable back from his determinate character and objectivity to his universality. Consequently this austere, national god is so jealous, and ordains in his jealousy that men shall see elsewhere merely false idols. The Greeks, on the contrary, discovered their gods among other nations and accepted what was foreign among themselves. For the god of classical art has spiritual and bodily individuality and is for this reason not the one and only one, but merely a *particular* godhead, which, as everything else that shares particularity, has a circle of particularity which surrounds it or in opposition to it as its Other, from which it is the result, and which is qualified to preserve its validity and worth. The process here is analogous to that of the particular divisions of Nature. Although the world of vegetation is the truth of the geological image of Nature, the animal again the higher truth of the vegetable, yet the mountains and the flooded land persist as the solid basis of trees, shrubs, and flowers, which in their turn do not lose their existence alongside the world of animals.

(1) The earliest form under which among the Greeks we come upon this ancient residue, are the *Mysteries*. The Greek Mysteries were nothing secret in the sense that the Greek nation was not in a general way aware of their content. On the contrary, the majority of the Athenians and a large number of foreigners were among the initiated in the Eleusinian mysteries; but they were not permitted to speak of that in which they had been instructed through initiation. In our own times people have been at great pains to discover more nearly the type of conceptions which prevailed in these mysteries, and to investigate the kind of religious services which were used in their celebration. It appears, however, that on the whole there was no extensive wisdom or profound knowledge concealed in the Mysteries. They merely preserved the old traditions, the basis, that is, of what was latterly reconstructed by the genuine type of art, and consequently, so far from containing the true, higher, and more valuable content, rather unfolded that which was of less significance and of inferior rank. Whatever it was, this holiness was not clearly expressed in the mysteries, but merely handed down in its symbolical features. And in fact this character of secrecy and reticence is bound

up with the old telluric, sidereal, and Titanic deposit; Spirit alone is the revealed and the self-revealer. Consonant, too, with this it is the symbolical mode of expression which constitutes the other aspect of secrecy in the mysteries, because in symbolism the interpretation remains obscure, and contains a something other than the external image, which it purports to display, in fact offers to the view. In this sense, for example, the mysteries of Demeter and Bacchus were, it is true, spiritually interpreted, and contained a profounder sense. The form of the same remained quite externally isolated from this content, so that it was impossible clearly to disengage it from it. Consequently the Mysteries had very little influence over art; for though we are told of Aeschylus, that he wilfully betrayed something which attached to the Demeter mysteries, this merely amounts to an assertion on his part that Artemis had been the daughter of Ceres, which is not very profound wisdom after all.

(2) But, *secondly*, we find that the reverence and preservation of the old *régime* is yet more clearly indicated in actual artistic representation. We have already referred to Prometheus as the chastised Titan who appears in the stage immediately prior to that of genuine art. We meet with him however again as delivered. For as the Earth and as the Sun, so also the fire, which Prometheus brought down to men, that is, the eating of flesh, which he taught them, is an essential feature of human life, a necessary condition for the satisfaction of their needs; and consequently Prometheus is honoured with an enduring recognition. In the "Oedipus at Colonus" of Sophocles we have the words:

χῶρος μὲν ἱερὸς πᾶς ὅδ ἔστ· ἔχει δέ νιν
σεμνὸς Ποσειδῶν· ἐν δ᾽ ὁ πορφόρος θεὸς
Τιτὰν Προμηθέυς [6]

and the scholiast adds that Prometheus was revered in the Academy along with Athenę, as Hephaestos was, and a temple was shown in a grove of the goddess, and an ancient pedestal near the entrance, where there was not only an image of Hephaestos, but also one of Prometheus. Prometheus, how-

---

[6] Vv. 54–56. "This entire spot is sacred; awful Poseidon holds it, and therein is the firebringing god, the Titan Prometheus."

ever, according to the statement of Lysimachides, was represented as primary and more ancient, and he held in his hand a sceptre; Hephaestos as the younger and in the second place, and the altar on the pedestal was shared by both. Prometheus, then, according to the tale, was not obliged to endure his chastisement for ever, but was released from his fetters by Hercules. In this story of his liberation we come across certain remarkable traits. In other words, Prometheus is delivered from his agony because he informs Zeus of the danger which threatens his empire at the hands of the thirteenth descendant. This descendant is Hercules, to whom, we may add in illustration, Poseidon exclaims in the "Birds" of Aristophanes,[7] "he will do himself an injury, if he strike a bargain with reference to the transference of the divine headship, for all that Zeus leaves behind him on his decease will most assuredly take place." And, in fact, Hercules is the only man who passed over into Olympus, became a god after being a man, and stands higher than Prometheus, who remained a Titan. Moreover, the overturning of the old race of tyrants is intimately connected with the name of Hercules and the Heraklidae. The Heraklidae break up the power of the old dynasties and royal houses, in which we may remark the selfish desire of personal aggrandizement and lawlessness no less than disregard for their subjects admitted no judicial restraint, and consequently was responsible for the grossest cruelties. Hercules, though himself in the service of a superior lord, overcame the savagery of this despotism.

In a similar way we may, to linger once more for a moment by the illustrations we adduced on a former page, recall again to our readers the "Eumenides" of Aeschylus. The conflict between Apollo and the Eumenides is to be settled by the intervention of the Areopagus. In other words, a human tribunal, as a whole, at whose head stands Athene, stands forth as the concrete spirit of the folk, and is as such to terminate the collision. The judges, however, give an equal number of votes for condemnation and acquittal, having an equal reverence both for the Eumenides and Apollo; the white pebble of Athene, however, decides the conflict in favour of Apollo. The

[7] Vv. 1645–48.

Eumenides break out in indignation against this decision of Athene; she, however, allays their wrath by promising them worship and altars in the famous grove of Colonus. What the Eumenides have to give in return to her people is a protection against the evils[8] which result from the elements of *Nature*, the earth, the heavens, the sea, and the winds; they have further to ward off unfruitfulness in the fields, the failure of living seed, and misbirths in all else that is procreated. Pallas, on her part, takes beneath her protection the strife of wars and sacred contests. In a similar way Sophocles, in his "Antigone," not only makes Antigone suffer and die, but to a like extent we find that Creon is punished by the loss of his wife and the death of Haemon, both of whom perish through the death of Antigone.

(3) *Thirdly*, the ancient gods do not merely preserve their place in juxtaposition to the new, but, what is of more importance, the natural basis itself is maintained by the new gods, and receives, continuing to make its echo sound in them, if in conformity with the spiritual individuality of classical art, a reverential acceptance.

And for this reason people are not infrequently led into the error of conceiving the Greek gods, in respect to their human character and form, as mere *allegories* of such natural elements. This is not so. In this sense we frequently hear it stated that Helios is the god of the sun, Diana the goddess of the moon, or Neptune the god of the sea. Such a separation, however, between the natural element, as content, and the humanly shaped personification, as form, no less than the external association of both, regarded merely as the masterdom of the god over the natural fact, as we are accustomed to it in the Old Testament, is quite inapplicable to Greek conceptions. We never find among the Greeks such an expression as ὁ θεὸς τοῦ ἡλίου, τῆς θαλάσσης, and so forth, though it is quite certain they would have used with others such an expression for the relation in question, had it been compatible with their point of view. Helios is the sun as god.

We must, however, at once insist on the further fact that the Greeks never regarded mere Nature as itself divine. On

8 Vv. 901 *et seq.*

the contrary, they retained the definite conception that what was purely natural was not divine. This is partly contained, if unexpressed, in what their gods actually are, in part also it is expressly stated so by themselves. Plutarch, for example, in his essay upon Isis and Osiris, refers incidentally to the modes of interpretation current of myths and divinities. Osiris and Isis belong to the Egyptian theogony, and had yet more of the natural element for their content than the Greek gods, who correspond to them; they merely express the longing and conflict to escape out of the circle of Nature to that of Spirit. In later times they were very highly honoured in Rome, and the mysteries allied with them were of great importance. Yet for all that it is Plutarch's view that it would be an interpretation beneath the level of the subject to think of explaining them as sun, earth, or water. Only that which in the sun, earth, and so forth, is without measure or co-ordination, defective or superfluous, can strictly be referred to the natural elements, and all that is good and conformable to order is as exclusively a work of Isis, and the rational principle, the λόγος, a work of Osiris. It is not, therefore, the natural as such which is adduced as the substantive content of these gods, but the spiritual principle, the universal, λόγος, reason, conformity to law.

c. The Classical Ideal and Its Dissolution

[e]Despite this substantive foundation we have seen the general elaboration of the gods of classical art manifest itself out of the repose of the Ideal within the variety of the individual and external embodiment, in all the detail of events, occurrences, and actions, which become ever and ever more human. By this means classical art finally, if we consider its content, carries yet further the process of *articulating* the accidental individualization, when we consider it as a mode of making the same *pleasurable* and attractive. In other words that which pleases is the elaboration of the particular aspect of the external phenomenon at every point of the same; by this means

[e] *The Philosophy of Fine Art,* vol. II, pp. 259–60.

the work of art no longer arrests the spectator merely in its connection with his own concrete soul-life, but also contains many affiliating links with the finite aspect of his subjectivity. For it is precisely in the finiteness of the art-creation that the closer association subsists with that aspect of the individual which is itself finite, and which rediscovers itself once more with satisfaction in every respect as mobile and stable existence in the art-product. The seriousness of the gods becomes a grace, which does not agitate with violence or lift a man over his ordinary existence, but suffers him to persist there tranquil, and simply claims to bring him content. Just as we generally find that the imagination when it masters religious conceptions, and endows them with a form appropriate to its notions of beauty, has a tendency to make the earnest character of devotion disappear, and in this respect destroys religion strictly as religion; so, too, this very process moves forward at the stage we are discussing for the most part by the addition of that which is agreeable and pleases. For it is not by any means the substantial aspect, the significance of the gods, or their universal character, which is evolved by virtue of what delights. Rather it is the finite side, their sensuous existence and subjective inward life, which purports to awake interest and provide satisfaction. The more, therefore, the charm of the existence reproduced is the dominant factor in its beauty to that extent the gracefulness is disentwined from the embrace of the universal and removed from the content, through which alone the profounder penetration could rest satisfied.

The transition to another province of the forms of art is closely united with this externality and articulate definition. For under the mode of externality reposes the manifold of the finite condition; a manifold which, so soon as it secures a free field, asserts itself finally in opposition to the spiritual Idea, its universality and truth, and begins to rouse up the dissatisfaction of thought in a reality which is no longer adequate to express it.

(1) ᶠThe gods of classical art contain in themselves the germ of their overthrow; consequently, when this fatal defect which they include is brought to consciousness through the elabora-

ᶠ *The Philosophy of Fine Art,* vol. II, p. 261.

tion of art itself, they bring about the dissolution of the classical Ideal at the same time. We established as the principle of this, so far as we have here to deal with it, that kind of spiritual individuality which secures in every respect an adequate expression in bodily or external existence immediate to our senses. This individuality was enclosed within a complex of divine personalities, whose definition is not essentially and withal from the first given up to the contingent condition in which the everlasting gods receive the appearance of dissolution for man's conscious life no less than for his artistic creation.

(2) ᵍIf we look more closely at the concrete conditions which correspond to the principle indicated, we shall see, we have already done so, that the Greek gods possess as their content the substantive *materiae* of real human life and action. Over and above the vision of the gods we have now the highest mode of determination, the universal interest and the end in determinate life, that is to say, presented at the same time as an existing fact. Just as it was essential to the spiritual configuration of Greek art to appear both as external and real, so, too, the spiritual growth of mankind in its absolute significance has elaborated itself in a reality that both externally appears and is real, with whose substance and universality the individual has put forward a claim to be in accordant fusion. This highest end was in Greece the life of the State, the collective body of citizens and their morality and living patriotism. Outside this supreme interest there was no other more lofty or true. The life of the State, however, as an external phenomenon of the world, fades into the Past, as do the conditions of the entire reality of the outside world. It is not difficult to demonstrate that a State under the type of such a freedom, so immediately identical with all its citizens, which as such already possess in their grasp the highest activity in all public transactions, is inevitably small and weak, and in part must prove suicidal to itself, in part fall into ruins in the natural course of the history of nations. In other words, by reason of this immediate coalescence of individual life with the universality of State-life, on the one hand we find that the peculiar idiosyncrasies of spiritual experience and its particular

ᵍ *The Philosophy of Fine Art*, vol. II, pp. 270–73.

aspects as private life do not receive their full dues, nor do they receive sufficient opportunity for a development innocuous to society at large. Rather, as distinct from the concrete substance, into which it has not been accepted, such a nature remains simply the limited and natural egoism, which goes on its own way independently, pursues its interests however much they are alien to the true interest of the whole, and, consequently, is an instrument to the ruin of the State, against which, in the last resort, it strains to oppose its individual forces. On the other hand within the circle of this freedom itself the need of a higher personal liberty is roused, which not merely in the State, as the substantive totality, nor merely in the accepted code of morals and law, but in the very soul of the man himself asserts its claim to exist, in so far as he is ready to give life to goodness and rectitude out of the wealth of his own nature and in the light of his own personal knowledge, and to recognize the same at its real worth. The individual subject demands of consciousness that it should be, in virtue of its claim as self-identity, a substantive whole. Consequently there arises in this freedom a new breach between the end of the State and that of the man's own personal welfare as essentially free himself. Such a conflict as this had already begun in the time of Socrates, while on the other side the vanity, self-seeking and unbridled character of democracy and demagogy corrupted the true State to such a degree that men like Plato and Xenophon experienced a loathing for the internal condition of their mother-city, where the direction of all public transactions lay in the hands of those who were either frivolous, or those who sought nothing but personal aims.

(3) The spirit of this transition, therefore, depends in the first instance on the general line of severation between Spirit in its unfolded self-subsistency and external existence. The spiritual in this separation from its reality, in which it no longer finds itself reflected, is then the abstract mode of Spirit; it is not, however, the one Oriental god, but on the contrary the actual self-knowing conscious subject, which brings to the fore and retains within the clasp of its ideal subjectivity all that is universal in thought, truth, goodness, and morality, and possesses therein not so much the knowledge of a pre-existing

reality as simply the content of its thoughts and convictions. This relation, in so far as it persists in this opposition, and sets up the two aspects of the same as purely opposites to one another, would be of an entirely prosaic character. We do not, however, at this stage as yet arrive at this point of bare prose. In other words it is true that on the one hand we have a consciousness present, which as self-secure, wills the Good, the fulfilment of its desires, conceives the reality of its notion in the virtue of its emotional life, much as we find it thus imaged in the ancient gods, morals, and laws. At the same time, however, this consciousness is split up in opposition to its existence as part of existing Life, in other words the actual political life of the time, the dissolution of the old modes of conception, the former type of patriotism and political wisdom, and adheres thereby unquestionably to that opposition between the inward life of soul and the real environment outside it. And the reason of this hesitancy is this that the bare conceptions of genuine ethical truth which it derives from its own inner world are unable to fully satisfy it; it consequently faces that which is exterior to this, to which it relates itself in a negative and hostile spirit with the object of changing it. This consciousness is, as already stated, on the one hand no doubt an inward and present content, which, self-determined and at the same time deliberately articulate, is concerned with a world that confronts it, to which this content is opposed, and which receives the task to depict this same reality in the semblance of the very traits of the corruption peculiar to that world, and which form such a contrast with its own ideas of goodness and truth. From another point of view this very contrast is cancelled by art itself. In other words, another type of art arises, in which the conflict of this opposition is not emphasized through the medium of mere thoughts, remaining thus in its disunion; but this reality in the very folly of its corruption is itself submitted to a mode of artistic presentation, which exposes it as self-destructive, and exposes it in such a way that it is precisely in and through this self-destructive process of what is of no weight that truth is enabled to assert itself upon this mirror as the secure and endurable power, and thereby all the force of a direct opposition to what is essentially true is removed from that side represented by folly and unreasonableness. This art is comedy, of the type Aristophanes dramatized for his fellow-citizens, connecting it closely with all that was essential in the world around him, and doing so with equanimity, in a mood of pure and hearty joviality.

2. SUBJECTIVE MOTIVES OF ROMANTIC DRAMA

[h]We have already defined classical art the Ideal of humanity certified as true in its objective self-subsistence. Its imaginative vitality requires as its core a content which is substantive in type and excludes an ethical pathos. The Homeric poems, the tragedies of Sophocles and Aeschylus, are in the main concerned with interests of an absolutely factual content, an austere treatment of the passions reflected therein, a solid style of speech and execution in conformity with the nature of the ideas expressed, and above this domain of heroes and other figures which alone are in their individual self-concentration at home in such an atmosphere of pathos we have the realm of the gods at a still more advanced stage of objective presentment. Even in the case where art, in more introspective fashion, is occupied with the infinite experiments of sculpture, bas-reliefs and similar forms, or the later elegies, epigrams, and other diversions of lyrical poetry, we still have the same type before us, that is to say, the type which portrays the object more or less as it finds it, and obedient to the claim that it already has secured its constructive presentment. We have, in short, represented figures of the imagination already established and defined in their characterization such as Venus, Bacchus, or the Muses. It is just the same with the later epigrams, where we get the description of a material already to hand or, as in the case of Meleager, a posy of well-known flowers, bound together with the cords of exquisite feeling and taste. It is, in short, an exhilarating mode of activity carried on in a wealthily furnished house overflowing in its stores with every kind of bounty, image and provision for

[h] *The Philosophy of Fine Art,* vol. II, pp. 329–31.

every conceivable object. The poet and the artist is simply the magician, who wafts them into use, collects and groups them.

It is wholly different in romantic poetry. In so far as it is of the world worldly, and is not directly associated with the story of our Lord, the virtues and objects of its heroism are not those of the Greek heroes, whose type of morality Christendom in its early days simply regarded as a brilliant enormity. Greek morality presupposes the presence of humanity in its complete configuration, in which the volition then and there as it ought to act comfortably to its essential notion of independence has received a definite content and the actual conditions of freedom imperatively valid such as belong to that content. Such are the relations of parents and children, married persons, or of citizens of city or State in the realized liberty of such. Now inasmuch as this objective content of human affairs belongs to the *evolution* of man's spirit on the basis of Nature cognized and insured as actual fact, it is unable any longer to satisfy that self-absorbed introspection of the religious life, which seeks to destroy the natural aspect of human life, and must deviate considerably from the virtue of humility which opposes it, and the surrender of human freedom and its staunch self-dependence. The virtues of Christian piety simply prove the death of such a world-attitude if held in their extreme of abstraction, and only make the individual free, when he absolutely denies the human part of him. The individual freedom of our present sphere is no doubt no longer conditioned by mere endurance and self-sacrifice but essentially positive in the world arena; that infinite self-relation of the individual has, however, as we have already discovered, the inward realm of the soul as its content and only that, the subjective soul, that is, whose movement is in its own peculiar medium, as the secular ground of its own domain. In this connection poetry does not draw from any objective material already presented it, no mythology, for instance, no imaginative pictures and embodiments, which already lie ready waiting for its expression. It stands there wholly free, without any extraneous matter, purely creative and productive. It is free as a bird that sings straight from its breast. It follows, then, if this subjective activity proceeds also from a noble will and a profound soul, we shall merely have in its workings and relations and existence the evidence of caprice and contingency, for the reason that freedom and its aims proceed, relatively to a content which is throughout immaterial, from internal self-reflection. And, consequently, we do not find so much in individuals a particular pathos in the Greek conception of the term and a vital self-subsistency of character associated with it by the closest bonds, as that which is simply a grade of heroic conception in its connection with love, honour, bravery, and fidelity; a grade into which it is mainly the nobility or depravity of soul which imports the distinguishing features. The characteristic trait, however, which the heroes of the Middle Ages possess in common with those of antiquity is that of *bravery*. Yet even this receives a totally different complexion. It is not so much a natural courage, which reposes on the character that is sane and sound, and flows forth from the growth of an unimpaired robustness of body and will, assisting the execution of objective interests. Rather it is the outcome of the secret wealth of the soul, its honour and chivalry, and is in the main a creation of the phantasy, which undertakes adventures that have their origin in individual caprice and the chance intricacies of external circumstance or the impulses of mystical piety, and we may add generally the personal attitude of the individual.

a. Honour

[1]The motive of honour was unknown to ancient classic art. In the "Iliad" it is quite true that the wrath of Achilles constitutes both the content and the motive principle, so that the entire series of events is dependent upon it; but what we moderns understand by the term honour is not grasped here at all. Achilles believes himself to be insulted to all intents and purposes only in the fact that the share in the booty which he considers justly to belong to him and the reward of his personal merits, his γέρας, has been taken away by Agamemnon. The insult here has a direct reference to something actual,

[1] *The Philosophy of Fine Art,* vol. II, pp. 332–33.

a bounty, in which no doubt a privilege, a recognition of fame and bravery was reposed, and Achilles is enraged because Agamemnon meets him unworthily and lets the Greeks know that they are not to pay any attention to him. An insult of this kind is not driven home to the real centre of personality in its abstract purity; in fact Achilles expresses himself satisfied with the restitution of the abducted slave and the addition of other goods and bounties, and Agamemnon finally makes this reparation although from our point of view they have both insulted one another in the grossest fashion. Maledictions of this kind, however, have only made them angry; and, after all, the particular insult, which has reference to a matter of fact, is done away with in the same matter-of-fact fashion.

The honour of romance is, on the contrary, of another kind. Insult has no reference here to the factual values of real things, property, status, obligation, etc., but to personality simply, and its idea of its own importance, the work which the individual claims as his right. This worth is in the cases we are now discussing of an infinite significance equal to that of personality itself. In honour, therefore, man possesses the earliest positive consciousness of his infinite spiritual medium, independent of the content. What the individual has, what in him something peculiar creates, after the loss of which it may yet subsist precisely as it did before—in this elusive something the absolute validity of the entire subjective life is reposed and apprehended in it both for itself and others. The determining measure of honour therefore does not depend on what the individual really is, but on what is contained in this personal self-regard. This regard, however, raises all particularity to the level of the universal conception that the personal core in its full significance resides in this particularity which it claims as its own. Honour is merely an outward show it is sometimes said. No doubt this is so: but from our present point of view we must, if we look at it more narrowly, accept it as the appearance and reappearance of the personal medium self-reflected, which as the semblance of an entity essentially infinite is itself infinite. And through this infinitude it is just this show or semblance of honour which is the real existence of the individual, its highest actuality; and every particular quality, into which honour is reflected and appropriates as its own is by virtue of this show exalted itself to an infinite worth. This type of honour constitutes a fundamental determinant in the romantic world, and presupposes that man has not merely passed beyond the limits of purely religious conception and inward life, but actually entered the arena of the great world and makes itself vital in the material of the same simply by virtue of the pure medium of its personal self-subsistence and absolute intension.

ʲInasmuch, then, as honour is not only a semblance in me myself, but must also exist in the mind and recognition of *another*, which again on its part makes a claim to a similar honourable recognition, honour is the extreme embodiment of *vulnerability*. For it is purely a matter of personal caprice how far I choose to extend the claim and to what material I care to relate it. The smallest offence may be in this respect of significance; and inasmuch as man is placed relatively to concrete reality in the most manifold relations with a thousand things, and is able to extend practically without limit the sphere of that which he conceives to affect him, and to which he is placed in the relation of honour it follows that when we come to deal with the independence of mankind and the obstinate isolation of their units, aspects for which the principle of honour is in the main responsible, there is no end to the strife and contention to which they give rise. Moreover, in the case of insult also no less than in that of honour generally, the important matter is not the content, in which I necessarily feel myself insulted; for that which is negated has reference to the personality which has appropriated such a content as its own, and now conceives itself as this ideal centrum of infinity attacked.

b. Love

ᵏThe second emotional source which plays a predominant part in the productions of romantic art is *love*.

(1) We have found in honour that the individual conscious life, as it prefigures itself in its absolute *independence*, forms

ʲ *The Philosophy of Fine Art,* vol. II, pp. 335–36.
ᵏ *Ibid.,* pp. 337–38.

the fundamental determinant; in a similar way the highest attitude of love is the *surrender* of the personal life to some object of the opposed sex, a sacrifice of its independent consciousness and its personal isolation, which for the first time in the consciousness of another, is aware emotionally that it has thoroughly brought home to itself its own self-knowledge. In this respect we may contrast love and honour. Conversely, however, we are entitled to regard love as the *realization* of that which was already inherent in honour, in so far as honour claims recognition that it should be received in another as the infinite significance of personality. This recognition is only true and complete when it is not merely my personality in the abstract, or in a concrete and consequently restricted case, is respected by another, but when I, in the entire significance of my personal resources, with everything this either emphasizes or includes, as this particular person in all my past, present, and future relations, both penetrate the conscious life of another, and, in fact, constitute the object of his real volition and knowledge, his effort and his property. In this respect it is this same inward infinitude of the individual which makes love of such importance to romantic art, an importance which is materially enhanced by the exalted character of the wealth which the notion of love itself carries.

[1]The lofty tragedy of the ancients does not recognize the passion of love in its romantic significance. Pre-eminently in the case of both Aeschylus and Sophocles we find that it makes no pretension to contribute to the main interest of the drama. For although Antigone is the accepted lover of Haemon, and Haemon claims her before his father, nay, goes to the length of committing suicide because he is unable to deliver her, yet it is the external aspects of the case rather than the power of his own personal passion, which, we may also note, is not that of a modern lover, which he emphasizes before Creon. As a more essential type of pathos love is treated by Euripides in the "Phaedra." But here, too, it rather makes itself felt as a criminal aberration of the blood, as a passion of the senses, initiated by Aphrodite, who is desirous of slaying Hippolytus, because he refuses to sacrifice to her. In the same way we

[1] *Ibid.*, pp. 339–48.

have, no doubt, in the Medicean Aphrodite a plastic figure of love, whose exquisite pose and lovely elaboration of bodily form is quite consummate; but any profound expression of soul-life such as romantic art demands is wholly absent. On the other hand, the immortality of Petrarca, although he himself treated his sonnets in the light of recreation, and it was rather through his Latin poems and other works that he appealed to posterity, is due to this very love of the fancy which, under an Italian sky, joined sisterly hands with religion in the medium of a somewhat artificial outpouring of the heart. Dante's exaltation, too, originated in his love for Beatrice, which was transfigured in his soul to the white fervour of religious ecstasy, while the courage and boldness of his genius created energetically a religious outlook on the world, in which he dared, an attempt impossible without such gifts, to constitute himself the judge of mankind, and to apportion to individuals hell, purgatory, or paradise. In contrast to an exaltation of this kind, love is placed before us by Boccaccio in those romances of his, in which he brings before our eyes the morals and life of his country, partly in all its impetuosity of passion, partly, too, in the spirit of frivolity without any ethical aim whatever. In the songs of the German Minnesingers we find a type of love, sensitive, tender, without much generosity of imagination, sportive, melancholy, and monotonous. Among the Spaniards it is copious in imaginative expression, chivalrous, somewhat casuistical in its discovery and defence of rights and duties, so far as they relate to private affairs of honour; and in this respect also possesses all the richest splendour of enthusiasm. In contrast to this, among Frenchmen of more modern times love is more an affair of gallantry with a distinct bias toward vanity, an artificial state of feeling converted to the uses of poetry with a kind of sophistry of the senses often marked with the finest wit, at one time expressing a kind of sensuous enjoyment which is devoid of passion, at another a passion that brings with it no enjoyment, a sublimated condition of feeling and sensibility which feeds upon the maxims of reflection. But I must here break off these general indications which our subject does not permit me now to carry further.

(2) More closely looked at the secular interest may be

treated under two general divisions. We have on the one side secularity as actually organized, such as family life, the tie of citizenship and politics, law, justice, morality, and the rest; and in opposition to this independent and assured existence love springs up in noble and impetuous spirits; this world-religion of hearts, which at one time we find joining hands with religion in every respect, while at another it supersedes it, forgets it, and by constituting itself the single essential, or rather the unique and supreme condition of life, is not only prepared to renounce all else, and to fly for refuge to a desert with the beloved, but proceeds in this extremity of its passion, which we can only exclude from the domain of beauty, to sacrifice all the worth of humanity in a manner at once servile, degrading, and despicable. An example of this we have in "Kätchen von Heilbronn." On account of this cataclysm of life's essential interests the objects of love cannot be realized without *collisions* in the theatre of the world. For despite of love the general conditions of life make their demand and assert their claims and the despotism of love's passion is unable to maintain itself against them with impunity.

(a) The first and most frequently exemplified type of collision we may draw attention to is that between *honour* and *love*. In other words, honour possesses just as love possesses in its own right this infinitude of claim, and may accept a content, which may confront love as a positive obstacle in its path. The obligations of honour may require the sacrifice of love. From a certain point of view it would be, for example, dishonourable for a man of high rank to wed one of the lower classes. The distinction between class and class is a necessary fact of natural condition as ordinarily presented. And so long as our secular life has not been emancipated through the infinite notion of true freedom, whatever may be the class or profession from which that life in the particular individual and his free choice takes its rise, to that extent it will always be Nature, that is, the birth condition, which to a greater or less degree will, on the one hand, determine the social position; and, on the other, these distinctions of status, as they thus originate, and quite independently of general grounds of honour, in so far as social position is made an affair of honour, will maintain themselves as of absolute and infinite stability.

(b) Quite apart, however, from questions of honour we must add as a further example of collision that the eternal and *substantive* powers themselves, the interests of the State, love of country, family obligations, and the rest, come into conflict with love and preclude its realization. Particularly in modern representations, in which the objective conditions of life have been already elaborated in all their available stringency, this is a favourite type of collision. Love is in such cases, as itself an important right of the personal soul, either set forth in opposition to other rights and duties, or despite of its own recognition of such it enters upon a conflict with them reliant upon itself and with the power of its private passion. The "Maid of Orleans"[9] is an example of a drama which rests upon a collision of this kind.

(c) And in the *third* case we may find that merely *external* conditions and impediments obstruct the path of love. Such are the ordinary course of events, the prose of ordinary existence, misfortunes, passion, prejudice, follies, the selfishness of others, occurrences of every conceivable complexity and kind. Much will here present itself that is hateful, terrible, and mean, for it is mainly the evil, ruthless, and savage aspects of other forms of human passion which work contrary to the tender spiritual beauty of love. More particularly in later times we frequently come across external collisions of this sort in dramas, narratives, and romances, works whose main interest centres in a sympathy for the sufferings, expectations, and ruined prospects of unhappy lovers and affect or satisfy us by means of their bad or happy endings, or merely provide entertainment. This type of conflict, however, on the ground that it merely depends upon accidental matters, is a subordinate one.

(3) No doubt love, from whatever of these points of view you choose to regard it, possesses a lofty quality, in so far as it does not merely remain an impulse of sex-attraction, but emphasizes the bounty of a really rich, beautiful, and noble soul, and is a living, active, courageous, and disinterested bond of union between one person and another. But romantic love is also not without its *limitation*. That which disappears from its

[9] Schiller's drama.

content is the essentially realized *universality*. It is merely the *personal* feeling of one particular individual, which does not attest itself as fulfilled with interest of eternal import and the actual content of organic human life, as made up of family, political aims, one's own country, obligations of profession, status, freedom, and religion, but merely with the personal consideration which is intent upon receiving again such private feeling as reflected back from some one else. Such a content of what is itself still but a formal mode of spiritual life does not correspond in full truth to the totality, which the essentially complete personality ought to be. In the family, marriage, duty, and the State the personal feeling simply as such and the unity which issues from it with some particular person and no other is not the main point of interest. In the love of romance, however, all centres in the fact that this man or woman loves that woman or man and *no one else*. Yet it is precisely this fact that it is only this or that person, which is solely based upon personal idiosyncrasy, in other words, the contingency of caprice. There is no lover who does not think his beloved, no maiden who does not fancy her lover, as the fairest and most supreme, to the exclusion of all others, although they may appear very ordinary mortals in the eyes of other folk. But in just this fact that all the world or, let us say, a large number, act thus exclusively, and will not make an exception in favour of the unique Aphrodite herself, but rather possess an Aphrodite of their own, and very easily somewhat more than Aphrodite, we can only very obviously conclude that there are many who pass for the same fairy Princess, as no doubt every one knows well enough, that there are a whole bevy of pretty or good and excellent girls in the world, all of whom, or let us hope the majority, will secure their own lovers, adorers, and husbands, to whom they doubtless appear as gifted in like manner with all the beauty and virtue of Christendom. To bestow in every case our preference on one, and only one, is obviously a wholly private affair of the heart and of the separate individuality of each person, and the incommensurable obstinacy in discovering as though by a law of necessity one's life and supremest sense of such in just that one individual is proof that it is a caprice no less infinite in its significance than it is inevitable. We have with-

out question in this attitude the loftier freedom of the personal
life and its absolute power of choice recognized, the power to
be, not merely as we find in the "Phaedra" of Euripides, under
the constraint of a pathos, a divinity; but in regard to the absolutely individual volition, from which such a liberty proceeds,
such a choice appears at the same time to be a mere idiosyncrasy, an inflexibility of that which is wholly self-exclusive.

For this reason the collisions of love, more particularly when
it is set in hostile opposition to substantive interests, retain an
aspect of contingency and lack of authorization, because it is
the personal life as such which confronts in opposition with a
demand not independently justifiable that which for its own
essential sake has a claim to recognition. The personalities
in the lofty tragedy of the ancients such as Agamemnon,
Clytemnestra, Orestes, Oedipus, Antigone, and Creon have, it
is true, among other things a personal object; but the substantive thing, the pathos, which as the content of their action
is the compelling force behind them, is of absolute authority,
and for this very reason, is also itself essentially of universal
interest. The destiny which affects them on account of their
action does not therefore move us on the ground that it is a
fate of misfortune, but because it is a misfortune which affects
or redounds to their honour. In other words the pathos, which
will not rest until it is satisfied, possesses an essentially necessary content. When the guilt of Clytemnestra, in this concrete
case of it, receives no punishment, when the insult which
Antigone receives as sister is not removed, in both cases we
have a substantial wrong. These sufferings of love, however,
these shattered hopes, this being in love generally, these infinite pains experienced by lovers, this measureless happiness
and bliss which such imagine, are no such essential interest
but rather something that merely affects themselves. All men,
it is true, should be sensitive to love and may claim satisfaction
in this respect. But when a man fails to secure that object in
some particular place, in precisely this or that association,
under just these circumstances and in respect to one unique
maiden we can admit no absolute wrong. There is nothing essentially inevitable in the fact that a man should capriciously
select any particular young woman, and that we should interest ourselves consequently for that which is in the highest

degree accidental, a caprice of his own conscious life, which carries with it no impersonal expansion or universal significance. We have here the source of that tendency to cool which we cannot help feeling in the representation of the passion of romantic love however that passion may be emphasized.

c. Fidelity

The third type of soul-life which is of importance to the romantic consciousness on the field of its activity in the world is *fidelity*. By fidelity in the sense we are now using it we do not mean either the permanent adherence to the avowal of love once given, nor yet the stability of friendship in the beautiful image of the same such as we have left us by the ancients in that of Achilles and Patroclus, or with yet more intimacy, that of Orestes and Pylades. Youth is pre-eminently both the soil and the occasion from which friendship of this latter type originates. Every man has to construct his path of life independently, to work out and sustain a given mode of realization. The time of youth, when individuals still live in an undefined atmosphere of external relations which they share, is the one in which they associate closely, and are bound together so nearly in *one* mode of thought, volition, and activity, that everything that any one of them undertakes becomes at the same time the undertaking of another. When men attain maturity this is no longer the case. The circumstantial life of the grown man pursues its independent course and will not admit of so close an affiliation with that of another that we can affirm of it that one cannot accomplish it without the other. Men make acquaintances and then separate; their interests and business are at one time disjoined, at another they coalesce; friendship, intimacy of mutual opinions, of principles, and the general trend of their life may remain; but this is not the friendship of youth, in which no individual unit either makes a decision or carries it into effect without inevitably making it a matter in which another is concerned. It is an essential principle at the very root of our life that in general every man must look after himself, must, in other words, prove by himself his capacity to confront the reality which affects him.

(1) Fidelity in friendship and love, then, subsists solely between equals. The fidelity which we have now to consider is relative to a superior, one more highly placed, a *master*. A fidelity of this type is to be found even among the ancients in that of servants to the family, the house of their lord. The most beautiful example of such a relation is supplied us by the swine-herd of Odysseus, who sweats by night and through tempest in order that he may look after his swine; who is full of anxiety on his master's account, to whom he finally gives loyal assistance against the suitors. Shakespeare offers us a picture of fidelity no less moving, though it is here shown entirely on the side of the feelings, in his "King Lear."[10] Lear asks Kent, "Dost thou know me, fellow?" And Kent replies: "No, sir; but you have that in your countenance which I would fain call master." This borders as close as possible on that which we would make clear as romantic fidelity. Fidelity at this stage is not the loyalty of slaves and churls, however true and pathetic such unquestionably may be, which is none the less devoid of the free independence of individuality and its unrestricted aims and actions, and is consequently of subordinate rank. What we, in short, have before us is the liege-service of chivalry, in which each vassal preserves intact his own free self-dependence as an essential element in the attitude of subordination to one of higher rank, whether lord, king, or emperor. This type of fidelity, however, is a principle of supreme importance in chivalry for the reason that it forms the fundamental bond of union in a common society and its social co-ordination at least in the original form of its appearance.

(2) The object which thus receives a fuller content and is made apparent in this new type of association between individuals is not, however, by any means patriotism regarding that as an objective and universal interest, but a bond merely with one person, the lord, and for this reason conditioned by private honour, personal advantage and opinion. In its fullest brilliancy we find fidelity of this kind in a surrounding world

10 Act I, sc. 4.

that is unregulated and uncouth, beyond the control of right and law. Within a lawless reality of this kind the most powerful and commanding spirits stand out as fixed points of attraction, as leaders and nobles, and the rest rally round them of their own free will. Such a condition is later on elaborated into a legalized co-ordination of fealty, in which every vassal has his own claim to rights and privilege. The fundamental principle, however, upon which the entire system reposes is in its primary origins free choice, no less in relation to the dependent vassal than to the conditions under which he remains faithful to his vassalage. For this reason the fidelity of chivalry is quite prepared to maintain property, right, and personal independence and honour, and is on this account not simply recognized as an *obligation* which may be enforced to the entire disregard of the private inclinations of the vassal however they may arise. Quite the contrary. Every subordinate unit only continues there and helps to establish the general social order so long as the same falls in with his own wishes, inclinations, and opinions.

(3) On this account fidelity and obedience to the feudal lord can very readily clash with private feelings, an exasperated sense of honour, sensitiveness to insult, love, and many other chance incidents of the personal or external life. It is consequently of a highly precarious character. A knight, for example, is loyal to his lord, but a friend of his happens to quarrel with him. He has now to choose between the two objects of his fidelity, and, chief of all, he has to consider himself, the claims of his personal honour and advantage. The most beautiful example of such a conflict we have in the "Cid." He remains as true to himself as he is to his king. If the king acts wisely he assists him with his arm's strength; if his feudal lord acts wrongly or the Cid feels touched on the point of honour this powerful support is withdrawn. The paladins of Charles the Great exhibit much the same attitude. It is a tie of chieftainship and obedience not unlike that which we have already observed between Zeus and the other gods. The superior lord commands, blusters, and scolds, but the independent and powerful individualities resist him precisely when and as they please. We find the most consistent and charming picture of the conditional and easy terms under which this

bond is maintained in the "Reinecke Fuchs." Just as the mag-
nates in this kingdom are most really true to their own aims
and independence, we find that the German barons and
knights in the Middle Ages were not at home when called
upon to act for the sake of the general weal and their emperor;
and it really looks as though our chief praise of the Middle
Ages must consist in this that no man is in such a period justified in his own eyes or a man of honour, except in so far as
he runs after his own inclinations, in other words, does precisely that which he is not suffered to do in a State which is
organized on a rational basis.

In all these three stages of honour, love, and fidelity, we
shall find the soil on which the self-subsistency of personality,
the soul, is supported, an independence which, however, constantly unfolds in a wider and more affluent content, remaining in the same self-reconciled. Here stretches before us in romantic art the fairest strip of country which we can find
anywhere outside the enclosure of religion in its strict sense.

d. The Self-Subsistency of Romantic Character

[m]A self-subsistency of character of this kind is only able to
appear, where the secular or natural man, in other words, humanity in its particularity has secured its fullest claim.

(1) Pre-eminently the characters of Shakespeare are of this
type. It is just this iron steadfastness and exclusiveness which
constitutes the aspect of them which most excites our wonder.
We have no word here of religion for religion's sake, or action
as the embodiment of human reconciliation, in the unqualified
religious sense, or of morality pure and simple. On the contrary we are presented with individuals, conceived as dependent solely on themselves, possessed with aims that are their
own exclusively, exclusively deducible from their individuality,
and which they carry through as best satisfies them with the

[m] *The Philosophy of Fine Art*, vol. II, pp. 356–67.

unmitigated consequences of passion, and with no incidental reflection on the principles involved.

(a) In particular the tragedies, such as "Macbeth," "Othello," "Richard III" and others contain one character of this type for their main interest surrounded by others less pre-eminent for such elemental energy. Macbeth is forced by his character, for example, into the fetters of his ambitious passion. At first he hesitates, then he stretches his hand to seize the crown; he commits a murder in order to secure it, and in order to maintain it storms on through the tale of horror. This re-gardless tenacity, this identity of the man with himself, and the object which his own personality brings to birth is the source to him of an abiding interest. Nothing makes him budge, neither the respect for the sacredness of kingship, nor the madness of his wife, nor the rout of his vassals, nor de-struction as it rushes upon him, neither divine nor human claims—he withdraws from them all into himself and persists. Lady Macbeth is a character of the same mould, and it is merely the chatter of our latter-day tasteless criticism which can find in her the least flavour of affection. At her very first entrance, on reading Macbeth's letter reporting his meeting with the witches and their prophecy in the words:[11] "Hail to thee, thane of Cawdor! Hail to thee king that shall be!" she exclaims, "Glamis thou art and Cawdor; and shall be what thou art promised. Yet do I fear thy nature; it is too full o' the milk of human kindness, to catch the nearest way." She shows no affectionate trait, no joy over the happiness of her husband, no moral emotion, no sympathy, no pity of a noble soul; she simply fears lest the character of her husband will stand in the path of his ambition. She regards him simply as a means. With her there is no recoil, no uncertainty, no con-sideration, no retreating, as we find is at first the case with Macbeth, no repentance, but the pure abstraction and rigour of character, which perpetrates that which falls in with it, un-til it finally breaks. This collapse which comes in a tempest on Macbeth from the outside as he executes his object, be-comes madness of the mind in Lady Macbeth. Of the same type is Richard III, Othello, the old Margaret and many an-

[11] Act I, sc. 5.

other also. We have its opposite in the wretched coherence of
modern characters, such as those of Kotzebue, which are outwardly noble in the highest degree, great and excellent, yet in
their soul-force are all rags and tatters. Later writers have done
no better in other relations, despite their supreme contempt
for Kotzebue. Heinrich von Kleist is an example with his
Kätchen and Prince von Homburg, characters in which, in
contrast to the alert condition of real causal effect, magnetism,
somnambulism, and sleep-walking are depicted as that which
is of highest and most effective moment. This Prince von Homburg is a most pitiable exhibition of a general; he is distracted
when he makes his military dispositions, writes out his orders
in a way none can decipher them, is engaged in the night
previous to the battle with morbid forebodings, and acts on
the day of battle like a fool. And despite such duality, rag-
gedness, and lack of harmony in their characters these writers
imagine that they tread in the footsteps of Shakespeare. Wide
indeed is the distance which separates them, for the characters
of Shakespeare are essentially consequent in what they do; they
remain staunch to their master passion; in what they are and
in what confronts them, nothing makes them veer round
but what is in strict accord with their rigidly determinate
character.

(b) The more particular, then, the character is, which relies purely on itself, and consequently readily approaches evil,
to that extent it is forced in the concrete world of reality to
maintain itself, not merely against the obstacles which lie in
its path and prevent the realization of life's aims, but so much
more by this very realization such is driven headlong to its
downfall. In other words, on account of the fact that it
achieves its object, the fate that has its origin in the specific
nature of its character itself, deals it a blow in a mode of destruction it has itself prepared. The development of this fatality
is, however, not merely a development from the *action* of the
particular personality, but quite as much a growth of the
soul, a development of the *character* itself in its headlong
movement, its running wild, its shattering in pieces or exhaus-
tion. Among the Greeks, for whom pathos, the substantive
content of action, rather than the personal character, is the
important feature, a destiny affects the character that is thus

sharply defined to a less degree for this reason, that it is not further evolved within the sphere of its activities, but remains at their conclusion what it was at the start. In the compass of our present subject-matter, however, by the carrying through of the action itself, the inner life of the personality is evolved quite as much as the progress of the action; the advance is not simply on the outside. The action of Macbeth appears at the same time a descent of the soul into savagery, accompanied by a result which, when all irresolution is thrown to the winds, and the dice is cast, leaves nothing further able to restrain it. His wife is from the very first decided: development is shown here merely as the anxiety of the soul, which is carried to the point of physical and spiritual ruin, the madness, in short, which strikes her down. And this is the kind of process which we can follow in the majority of Shakespeare's characters, whether important or unimportant. The characters of ancient drama assert themselves, no doubt, also on fixed lines, and we find them even face to face with opposed forces, relief from which is no longer possible except through the advent of a *deus ex machina*. Yet this stability, as in the case of Philoctetes, is united to a content, and, on the whole, penetrated with a pathos which may be vindicated on ethical grounds.

(c) In the sphere of presentation we are now considering, owing to the contingent nature of all that the characters which belong to it seize upon as their aim and the independence of their individuality, no *objective reconciliation* is possible. The environment of all that they are, and what opposes their progress, is in part without defined lines, but also in part we see that there is neither a "Whence" nor a "Whither" unriddled for themselves. Here we have once more presented to us that Fate which is the most abstract form of Necessity. The only reconciliation of the individual issues from the infinite mode of his soul-life, his own steadfastness, in which he stands supreme over his passion and his destiny. "Thus it came to pass," whatever falls in his way, whether it be due to a controlling destiny, necessity or accident, there is his "Wherefore"; he accepts it at once without further reflection. It is fact, and man adjusts himself thereto, and tries to make himself as stone toward its authority.

(2) In absolute contrast to the above, however, there is a further or *second* mode in which the formal aspect of character may find its seat within the *innermost* of soul-life, and in which the individual may remain fixed without being able to extend its range or execute its effects.

(a) Such are those spiritual natures of intrinsic substance, who, while self-absorbed in a complex whole, are only able in the simplicity of their compactness to perfect that profound activity within the shrine of the soul without further development or explication in the world around them. The formalism which we have hitherto been examining was relative to the defined character of the content, the entire self-concentration of the individual upon one object, which it makes to appear in all its unrelieved severity, a concentration which expressed itself, was carried out, and in which, just as circumstances fell out, either collapsed or held on to the end. This further mode of formalism is emphasized in a converse way by its undisclosed and formless character, and by its defect of expression and expository power. A soul of this type is like some precious jewel, which is only visible at certain points, a manifestation which is that of a lightning flash.

(b) And the reason that such state of self-seclusion should still be of worth and interest to us is due to the fact that it presupposes a secret wealth of the soul, which, however, only permits its infinite depth and fullness, and precisely, by means of this silence, to show itself in a few and so to speak half-muted ways of expression. Such simple natures, unconscious of what they possess, and without speech, may exercise an extraordinary fascination. But that this may be so their silence must be like the unruffled stillness of the sea upon its surface, over its unsounded depths, not the silence of all that is shallow, hollow, and stupid. It is quite possible sometimes for the dullest fellow to succeed by means of an external demeanour that manages very little to expose itself, and merely presents now and again something that is but half intelligible, to awake in others the opinion that it is the veil of a profound wisdom and spiritual depth, so that people wonder what in the world lies hidden in such a heart and soul, where we find in the end there is just nothing. The infinite content and profundity of *silent* souls of the genuine type is made clear to us—and to declare it makes the greatest demand on the intuitive powers and executive ability of the artist—by means of isolated, unrelated, naïve, and involuntary expressions of soul-life, which quite unintentionally make it plain to all who can grasp their significance that such a soul has seized upon the substantial import of all that confronts it with the richest quality of spiritual insight, that its reflective capacity, however, is not carried further by positive expansion into the general environment of particular interests, motives, and finite aims, but rather preserves its original purity that the fact it refuses to have its powers dissipated by the commonplace excitements of the heart and the serious quests and modes of sympathy which are thus inevitable, may remain unknown to the world.

(c) A time must, however, arrive for a soul of this type in which it becomes uniquely affected at one definite point of attachment in that inward world; it concentrates the whole of its undivided powers in one supreme form of emotion that dominates its life-current; it adheres to this with a force that refuses to be diverted, and secures happiness therein, or goes to ground from lack of support. To retain a hold on life a man requires a constantly expanding breadth of ethical sustenance, which alone supplies an objective stability. To this type of character belong some of the most fascinating figures in romantic art, whose full perfection of beauty we shall find among the creations of Shakespeare. As an illustration we may take the Juliet in his "Romeo and Juliet." It is possible at this moment to see a reproduction of this play in this city.[12] It is well worth going to. The picture we have given us there of this character is a moving, lifelike, passionate, talented, highly finished and noble one. But for all that it is possible to entertain a somewhat different conception of the part. In other words, we may figure for ourselves a maiden in the first instance simple as a child, of only fourteen or fifteen years of age, who, it is quite clear, has as yet no self-knowledge or world wisdom, no emotional activity, no strong inclination or wishes of the heart, but has rather glanced into the motley show of the world as into some *laterna magica* without learn-

[12] This was the representation which took place in Berlin in 1820, with Mademoiselle Erelinger as Juliet.

ing anything from it, or reflecting upon what is seen there. All in a twinkling we behold the development of the entire strength of this soul, of its artfulness, its circumspection, its force; it is prepared to sacrifice everything and to submit itself to the severest ordeals, so that in its entirety it now suddenly appears to be the first breaking forth of the full rose in all its petals and folds, an infinite outburst of the innermost purity which gushes from the spring source of the soul, in which it had held itself back previously as yet undiscerned, unmoulded and undeveloped; which moreover, as the now existing creation of *one* awakened interest, betrays itself unpremeditated in the fullness and strength of its beauty from the previous seclusion of spirit. It is a brand which one spark has kindled, a bud which at the first bare touch of love breaks unawares before us in full bloom. And yet the faster it unfolds the more rapidly it also sinks, and its petals fall from it. An impetuous progress is still more conspicuous in the case of Miranda. Brought up in seclusion we have her portrayed for us by Shakespeare at the critical moment when she first makes the acquaintance of manhood. He depicts her in a few scenes, but in those we get a picture that is complete and unforgettable. We may also include Schiller's Thecla under the same type, despite the fact that it is rather the creation of a reflective kind of poetry. Though placed in the midst of a life of such amplitude and richness she remains unaffected by it; she remains within it without vanity, without reflection, purely absorbed by the one interest which alone dominates her soul. And as a general rule it is chiefly the beautiful and noble natures of women, in which the world and their own heart-life blossoms for the first time in love, so that it is as though their spiritual birth here takes its rise.

Under the same type of spiritual intensity, which is unable fully to unfold itself, we may for the most part classify those folksongs, more particularly our German ones, which, in the copious compactness of the soul-life therein reflected, and however much such is displayed to us as carried away by any one absorbing interest, are yet unable to express the same except in broken flashes, and thereby fully reveal just this very depth. It is a mode of artistic presentment, which in its reserve is apt to fall back on the effects of symbolism. What it offers us is not so much the open, transparent display of the entire inward life as it is purely a *sign* and indication of that life. But we do not get, however, from it a symbol, the significance of which, as was the case previously, remains a general abstraction, but an expression the inward content of which is nothing more nor less than this personal, living, and actual soul. In times like our own, dominated by a critical reflectiveness, which lies so far removed from a self-absorbed *naïveté* of this kind, such presentations are of the greatest difficulty, and if successful, are a sure proof of an original creative genius. We have already seen that Goethe, more particularly in his lyrics, has shown himself a master in this respect, namely, that he can depict and unfold to us in a symbolical way, in other words with a few simple, apparently external and insignificant traits, the entire truth and infinite wealth of a soul. His poem, "The King of Thule," one of his most lovely bits of poetical work, is of this class. The king here makes us aware of his love by just one thing only, namely, the drinking cup which the old man preserved as a gift of his beloved. The old carouser stands up there on the point of death in his lofty palace hall; his knights, his kingdom, his possessions are around him; and he bequeaths them all to his heir, but the goblet he flings into the waves; no one shall have that.

> Er sah ihn stürzen, trinken,
> Und sinken tief in's Meer,
> Die Augen thäten ihm sinken,
> Trank nie ein Tropfen mehr.[13]

A soul, however profound and still of this kind, which retains its energy of spirit pent up like the spark in the flint, unopened to form, which does not elaborate its existence and reflection beyond its own boundaries, has also failed to free itself by such expansion. It remains exposed to the remorseless contradiction that, if the false note of unhappiness ring through its life, it possesses no remedial aptitude, no bridge as a way of passage between the heart and reality; it is equally unable

---

13 "He saw it plunge, drink boldly,
Then sink in sea-depths lost;
And what his eyes saw loosed him,
No drop the king drank more."

to ward off external conditions from itself, and by so doing to preserve an independent ground of vantage in its own self-reliance. When the collision comes therefore it is helpless; it acts hastily and without circumspection, or bows passively to the movement of events. So, for example, we have in Hamlet a beautiful and noble soul; one not so much spiritually weak, but one that wanders astray without a strong grasp of life's realities, moving in an atmosphere of dejection, a sombre and half articulate melancholy. Gifted with a finely intuitive sense he feels that all is not well with him, that things are not as they should be though he has no external sign, no single ground for suspicion; nevertheless he surmises the atrocious deed that has been perpetrated. The ghost of his father gives yet closer embodiment to his feelings. He is at once ready in spirit to revenge, his sense of duty is always before him reflecting the innermost craving of his heart, but he is not carried away with the flood, as Macbeth; he cannot either kill, rage, or strike with the directness of a Laertes; he persists in the inactivity of a beautiful, introspective soul, which can neither realize its aims nor make itself at home in the conditions of actual life. He dallies, seeks for more positive certainty buoyed up by the fair integrity of his soul; he can, however, come to no firm decision, much as he has sought it, and permits himself to follow the course of external events. In this atmosphere of unreality he goes yet further astray in matters that lie directly in his path; he kills the old Polonius instead of the king; he acts in a hurry where he should have been more circumspect, yet persists in his self-absorption, where decided action is essential; until at length, without any action on his part, the fated *dénouement* of the entire drama, including that of his own persistently self-retiring personality, has unravelled itself on the broad highway of Life's external incidents and accidents.

We are particularly presented with this attitude in modern times among men of the lower levels of life, who are without an education which extends to aims of universal significance, or are devoid of the variety of objective interests. Consequently when some *particular* aim of their life fails they are unable to secure any further stay of their spiritual forces and a centre of control for their activities. This lack of education tends to make reserved natures, in proportion as it is undeveloped, adhere with the more rigidness and obstinacy to that which, through its appeal to their entire individuality, makes a claim upon them however limited in its range it may be. We find pre-eminently such a monotonous attitude incidental to this class of self-absorbed and speechless men among German characters, who for this reason appear in their seclusion inclined to stubbornness, ready to bristle up, crabbed, inaccessible, and in their dealings and expressions wholly unreliable and contradictory. As a master in the delineation and exposition of such obtuse characters of the poorer classes we will mention but one example, Hippel, the author of "Life's Careers in the Line of Ascent," one of our few German works stamped with original humour. He keeps himself wholly removed from Jean Paul's sentimentality and want of taste in plot construction, and possesses moreover an astonishing individuality, freshness, and vitality. He understands, in quite an exceptional way, and one that seizes on our interest at once, how to depict the thickset type of people who are unable to breathe freely and who consequently, when they do give themselves the rein, do so with a violence that is simply fearful. They put an end of their own accord to the infinite contradiction of their spiritual life and the unhappy circumstances in which they are involved in an appalling manner; and bring about by such means that which is otherwise the result of an external fate, as we find, for instance, in "Romeo and Juliet," where external accidents mar all the wise and able offices of the holy father's intervention and cause the death of the lovers.

(3) We find, then, that characters of this formal quality generally either expose merely the infinite volitional force of the individual's personality, which asserts itself frankly just as it is and storms ahead in the bare impulse of the will; or, to take the further aspect, present to us an essential self-contained, if not wholly articulate soul, which, affected as it becomes by one specific aspect of its spiritual experience, concentrates the entire breadth and depth of its personality on this point, yet, owing to the fact of its possessing no development externally, is unable to find its proper place or to act with practical sense when it comes into collision with that world. We have yet a *third* point to mention, which consists

in this, that when characters of this type, wholly one-sided and restricted as they are in respect to their aims if at the same time fully developed in mental power, awake in us not merely a *formal*, but also a *substantial* interest, we cannot fail to receive the impression that this limitation of their personal life is itself only a condition that is inevitable; in other words it is a result which grows out of the particular way in which their character is defined along with the profounder content of their personal life. Shakespeare in fact enables us to see this depth and wealth in such characters. He presents them to us as men of imaginative power and genius by showing how their reflective faculty commands them and lifts them above that which their condition and definite purpose would make them, so that they are all the while as it were forced by the misfortune of circumstances and the obstacles of their position into doing that which they accomplish. At the same time we do not mean this to the extent of asserting, for example, that the bad witches were to blame for all that Macbeth dared after consulting them. These witches are rather to be looked at as the reflex of his own obstinate will. All that the characters of Shakespeare execute, that is the particular purpose they propose, originates and finds the taproot of its force in their own personality. But along with this they maintain in one and the same individuality a loftiness, which brushes aside that which they actually are, so far as their aims, interests, and actions are concerned, and which amplifies them and exalts them above themselves. In like manner Shakespeare's more vulgar characters, such as Stephano, Trinculo, Pistol, and that hero among them all, Falstaff, though saturated with their own debasement, assert themselves as fellows of intelligence, whose genial quality is able to take in everything, to possess a large and open atmosphere of its own, and in short makes them all that great men are. In the tragedies of the French on the contrary even the greatest and most worthy characters only too frequently, if viewed critically, assert themselves as so many evil offshoots of the brute creation, whose only intelligence consists in this that it can furnish dialectical arguments in its vindication. In Shakespeare we find neither vindication nor damnation, but merely a review of the general condition of destiny, which inevitably places such characters uncomplaining and unrepentant where they are, and from the starting-point of which they see everything, themselves included; and yet as independent spectators of themselves decline and fall.

In all these respects the realm which is peopled by such individual characters is an infinitely rich one, a kingdom, however, which very easily collapses in hollowness and dulness, so that only quite a few masters have received the gifts of poetical and intuitional power sufficient to enable them to reveal its truth.

3. NOTES ON LANGUAGE

[n]Language and the sounds of words are neither a symbol of spiritual conceptions, nor an adequate mode of projecting ideality under the condition of spatial objectivity in the sense applicable to the corporeal forms of sculpture and painting, nor yet an intonation in musical sound of the entire soul. They are an abstract *sign* simply. As the vehicle of the poetic image or conception, however, it is necessary that this side also, in theory no less than deliberate elaboration, appear as distinct from the kind of expression appropriate to prose.

We may for this purpose emphasize with more detail three main points of distinction.

Our *first* point is this, that although poetic expression is throughout exclusively embodied in articulate words, and apparently as such is simply related to human speech, yet in so far as the words themselves are merely abstract signs representative of *ideas,* the true source of poetic speech is not to be discovered in the selection of particular words, and in the manner they are associated in sentences and elaborated phrases, nor in harmonious rhythm, rhyme and so forth, but in the type of *conception* employed. We have, in short, to look for our point of departure for the constructive use of expression in the choice of the idea or image, and our first and fore-

[n] *The Philosophy of Fine Art,* vol. IV, pp. 56–60.

most question will be what kind of conception will give us an expression suitable to poetry.

What in the plastic arts the sensuous visible *form* expressed by means of stone and colour is, or what in the realm of music animating strains of harmony and melody are, this—we must repeatedly insist on the fact—can only be, in respect to poetic expression, the idea or image itself. The force of the poet's creation centres consequently in the fact that the art moulds a content in an ideal medium, and without bringing before us the actual forms of external Nature and the progressions of musical sound; by doing so, therefore, it translates the objective presence accepted by the other arts into an ideal form, which Spirit or intelligence expresses for the imagination under the mode which is and must remain that of our conscious life.

Imaginative poetry in its *origin* is not as yet a consciously distinct form from those extremes of ordinary conscious life, one of which brings everything to vision under the mode of immediate and therewith contingent singularity, without grasping the ideal essence implied therein, and the manifestation of the same; while the other, in one direction, differentiates concrete existence into its various characteristics, making use of abstract generalization, and in another avails itself of the scientific faculty as the correlating and connecting focus of such abstractions. The idea is only poetical in so far as it holds these extremes in unviolable mediation, and thereby is able to maintain a position of genuine stability midway between the vision of ordinary consciousness and that of abstract thought.

In general terms we may define the poetic imagination as *plastic* in so far as it brings before our vision concrete reality rather than the abstract generalization, and in the place of contingent existence an appearance of such a kind that we recognize what is substantive immediately in it by virtue of its embodiment itself and its individuality, and as inseparable from it, and by virtue of this are able to grasp the concrete conception of the fact in question no less than its determinate existence as one and the same vital whole reposing in the ideal medium of the imagination. In this respect we find a fundamental distinction between that whereof the plastic or constructive idea is the source and all that is otherwise made vivid to us through other means of expression. The same truth will appear to us, if we analyse what we mean by mere reading. We understand what the letters mean, which are indicative points for articulate utterance, by the mere act of sight, and without being further obliged to listen to their sound. Only the illiterate reader will find it necessary to speak aloud the separate words that he may understand their sense. But in the case of poetry just what seems to be here the mark of stupidity is an indication of beauty and excellence. Poetry is not satisfied with an abstract effort of apprehension, nor does it bring objects before us as we find them in the form of reflection and in the unimaginative generalization of our memory. It helps us to approach the essential notion in its positive existence, the generic as clothed in its specific individuality. In the view of ordinary common sense I understand by language, both in its impression on my hearing or sight, the meaning in its immediacy, in other words, without receiving its image before the mind. The phrases, for instance, "the sun," or "in the morning," possess each of them no doubt a distinct sense; but neither the Dawn or the Sun are themselves made present to our vision. When, however, the poet says: "When now the dawning Eos soared heavenwards with rosy fingers," here without question we have the concrete fact brought home to us. The poetical expression adds, however, yet more, for it associates with the object recognized a vision of the same, or we should rather say the purely abstract relation of knowledge vanishes, and the real definition takes its place. In the same way take the phrase, "Alexander conquered the Persian empire." Here, no doubt, so far as content is concerned, we have a concrete conception; the many-sided definition of it, however, expressed here in the word "victory," is concentrated in a featureless and pure abstraction, which fails to image before us anything of the appearance and reality of the exploit accomplished by Alexander. This truth applies to every kind of similar expression. We recognize the bare fact; but it remains pale and dun, and from the point of view of individual existence undetermined and abstract. The poetic conception consequently embraces the fullness of the objective phenomenon

as it essentially exists, and is able to elaborate the same united
with the essential ideality of the fact in a creative totality.

What follows as a primary result of this is that it is of interest to the imagination to *linger* near the external characteristics of the fact, to the extent at least that it seeks to express
the same in its positive reality, deems this as essentially worthy
of contemplation and insists on this very attitude.

Poetry is consequently in its manner of expression *descriptive*. Description is, however, not the right word for it. We
are, in fact, accustomed to accept as descriptive, and in contrast to the abstract definition, in which a content is otherwise
brought home to our intelligence, much that the poet passes
by, so that from the point of view of ordinary speech poetic
composition can only appear as a roundabout way and a useless superfluity. The poet must, however, manage to bring his
imagination to bear upon the explication of the actual phenomenon he is attempting to depict with a vital interest. In
this way, for instance, Homer adds a descriptive epithet to every hero. So Achilles is the swift-footed, the Achaeans bright-
greaved, Hector as of the glancing helm, Agamemnon the lord
of peoples, and so forth. The name is no doubt descriptive of a
personality, but the name alone brings nothing further to our
vision. To have some distinct idea of this we require further
attributes. We have in fact similar epithets attached by
Homer to other objects, which are essential to our vision of
the epic, such as sea, ships, sword and others, epithets which
seize and place before us an essential quality of the particular
object, depicting it more precisely, and which enable us to
apprehend the fact in its concrete appearance.

Secondly, we must distinguish such reconstruction of actual
facts from definition *wholly imagined*. This offers a further
point of view for discussion. The real image merely places before us the fact in the reality it possesses. The expression of
the poet's imagination, on the contrary, does not restrict itself
to the object in its immediate appearance; it proceeds to depict something over and above this, by means of which the
significance of the former picture is made clear to our mind.
Metaphors, illustrations, similes become in this way an essential feature of poetic creation. We have thereby a kind of veil
attached to the content, which concerns us, and which, by its

difference from it, serves in part as an embellishment, and in part as a further unfolding of it, though it necessarily fails to be complete, for the reason that it only applies to a specific aspect of this content.

a. The Metaphor

[o]If we look at the aim and interest of that which is metaphorical, the first thing which strikes us is that a word in the strict sense is an independently intelligible expression, the metaphor otherwise. The question consequently presents itself, what is the reason of this twofold means of expression, or, to put it another way, why is it that we have the metaphorical which essentially implies this division? The common explanation is that metaphors are used to give vivacity to poetical composition, and this animating effect is the ground in virtue of which Heyne, in particular, insists on their value. The vivacity consists in the support they offer to imaginative vision in the direction of clear definition, divesting the word, which is always something generalized, of its purely indefinite character, and bringing it home to sense by means of an image. No doubt a greater degree of vivacity is to be found in metaphors than in the strict expressions of ordinary speech; genuine vitality, however, is not to be sought for in metaphors, whether in isolation or combination, whose figurative plasticity, it is true, may frequently include a relation, which by good chance attaches at the same time to the expression an increased perspicuity and a higher definition, but quite as often, if every detail of the process of thought is thus figuratively emphasized in isolation, makes the whole unwieldy, overloading it thus with its emphasis on singular aspects.

The genius of metaphorical diction is consequently, as we shall have to elucidate more closely in our consideration of simile, to be regarded as responding to a need and potency of mind and the emotional life, which will not rest satisfied with that which is entirely simple, ordinary, and homely, but make an effort beyond this and over into something more rec-

[o] *The Philosophy of Fine Art*, vol. II, pp. 141–44.

ondite under the attraction which distinction offers and the impulse to co-ordinate contrasted effects. This binding together has itself again various causes, which may be notified as follows:

(1) *First,* we have it for the sake of *reinforcing* an effect. The emotional life, under the pressure and movement of its passions, gives visible utterance to these forces by means of the piling up of sensuous image. More than this, it strives to express its own whirl and tumble, or persistence in the ideas which crowd upon it by means of a similar letting itself go into phenomena cognate with such a condition, and its own free movement among images of the greatest variety. In Calderon's supplication to the Cross, Julia utters the following words when she looks upon the dead body of her only just deceased brother, and her lover, Eusebio, the man who has killed Lisardo, stands before her:

> O that I might close for ever
> Eyes before this blood here guiltless,
> Blood which cries for vengeance with its
> Flooding stream of purple flowers!
> Would that I could deem thee pardoned
> In the rush of tears that blind thee:
> Wounds and eyes are mouths which swallow
> Lies which seek admittance never, etc.

With a still more vehement burst of passion Eusebio starts back from the sight of her, when Julia finally is for surrendering herself to him, as he exclaims:

> Flaming sparks thine eyeballs scatter;
> Every sigh is breath that scorches;
> Every word is a volcano,
> Every hair a scribbled lightning,
> Every word is Death, and every
> Soft caress is Hell's own anguish;
> Such the horror stirs within me
> As I see—O awful symbol,
> Crucifix thy bosom carries.

The human soul on the swell of its emotion keeps adding image on image to that immediately confronting it, and with all this impetuous seeking to and fro for new means of expression barely lays to rest its own tumult.

(2) A *second* rationale of the metaphorical consists in this that the human soul, after adding to its own depth by this the motion of its own life into the varied survey of objects cognate with it, is stirred at the same time to cast itself free of the externality of such objects, to the extent that it seeks to rediscover itself in what is external; it transmutes that external in its own free activity, and by clothing both itself and its passions in the forms of beauty, proclaims furthermore its power to present in visible semblance its own exaltation above the bare fact.

(3) A *third* ground of figurative expression, and one of at least equal force, may be found in the purely ribald exuberance of the phantasy, which is unable to set before us an object in its own outlines for what they are worth, or a significance in its unadorned simplicity, but on all occasions hankers after some concrete embodiment cognate with it, or is overmastered by the ingenuity of a personal caprice, which, in order to escape the commonplace, abandons itself to the charms of the piquant novelty, a caprice that is never satisfied until it has discovered for us points of affinity in material the most remote apparently from that before us, and has thereby related the same to the most distant objects.

And we may here observe that it is not so much the *prosaic* and *poetic* style generally as the style of the *classic* world in contrast with that of later periods which presents such a marked difference in the pre-eminent importance they attach to genuine or metaphorical expression respectively. It is not merely the Greek philosophers, such as Plato and Aristotle, or the great historians and orators, such as Thucydides and Demosthenes, but also the great poets, Homer and Sophocles, who, albeit we find examples of the simile in all them, remain on the whole, and without exception, constant in the use of their direct form of expression. Their plastic severity and sterling substance will not permit them such a multifarious product, as is bound up with the use of metaphor, nor will it suffer them, even for the sake of gathering the so-called flowers of expression, to waver fitfully in devious ways from their ideal mintage of the completely simple and co-ordinate result as of one metal cast in one mould. The metaphor, in fact, is always an interruption to the logical course of conception and invariably to that extent a distraction, because it starts images and brings them together, which are not immediately connected with the subject and its significance, and for this reason tend to a like extent to divert the attention from the same to matter cognate with themselves, but strange to both. The prose of ancient writers in the extraordinary clarity and flexibility of its utterance and their poetry in the repose of its completely unfolded content, are equally removed from the frequent use of metaphor by modern writers.

On the other hand it is particularly the East, and above all the later literature of Mohammedan poetry, which makes use of the indirect or figurative modes of expression, and, indeed, finds them essential. The same thing may be said, if less emphatically, of modern European literature. The diction of Shakespeare, for instance, is full of metaphor. The Spaniards, too, are very fond of this flowery region, and, indeed, have wandered off into it to the point of the most tasteless exaggeration and superfluity. Jean Paul falls under the same charge. Goethe by virtue of the equal strength and clarity of his vision to a less extent. Schiller, however, is even in his prose exceedingly rich both in image and metaphor; in his case this is rather due to his effort to bring really profound ideas within the range of the imaginative vision without being forced to expound all they imply for the mind in the technical language of philosophy. We behold and find there the essential unity of the speculative reason reflected on the mirror of Life as it stands before us.

b. The Simile

ᵖWe must conceive the object of the simile to consist in this, that the subjective imagination of the poet, however much it has brought home to the artist's consciousness the content, which it seeks to express, with distinctive emphasis according to its more abstract generality and expresses it in this universal

ᵖ *The Philosophy of Fine Art,* vol. II, pp. 148–49.

aspect, yet it finds itself equally under a constraint to seek out a concrete form for it, and to envisualize for itself in the phenomena of sense that which already is clearly before the mind as its significance. Looked at in this way we shall find that the simile is, no less than the image and the metaphor, indicative of the bravery which invariably distinguishes imaginative power when it faces its object, it matters not what, it may be a single object of sense-perception, a definite condition, or a general significance—the enterprise, that is, to bind together with its own activity that which lies remote from it in its external environment, and by so doing to carry away by force objects of the greatest variety, and unite them to the interest which its unified content possesses, and generally to annex to the matter in hand a whole world of diversified phenomena. And this power of the imagination continually to find out the new plastic shape, and cement together heterogeneous material by means of the relations and associations of sense is, in general terms, also the rational basis of the simile.

ªWe have now to emphasize a motive cause of similes with particular reference to dramatic poetry. The content of the drama is made up of the conflict of passions, activities, pathos, actions, and the accomplishment of the thing willed by the soul, a content which does not, as in the case of the epic, take the form of a narrative of past events, but the dramatic poet places the individuals themselves before our eyes and makes them unfold their emotions personally in an objective form, and their actions as taking place in the present: his mediate position between ourselves and the objects represented therefore ceases. Looked at from this point of view it would appear as though in order to make this presence in Nature clear to us a primary requirement of drama would be that the expression of passions and the vehemence of their grief, consternation, and delight should be painted as naturally as it was possible to paint it, and consequently the simile would be here out of place. To let individuals, on the very plane of their action, in the full storm of emotion, and in the continuous strain of the busy world, speak much in the language of metaphor or image is obviously, from the common

ª *Ibid.*, pp. 155–61.

sense point of view, an unnatural proceeding and injurious to the directness aimed at. We are by the simile diverted from the immediate situation, and the characters, whose actions and emotions are involved in it, to something external and strange to it, which in short does not strictly belong to it, as part of its own present; consequently the general course of the dialogue must unavoidably appear to lag under the interruption thus imposed. And for this reason it came about also in Germany when at last our young bloods were all for freeing themselves from the fetters of French rhetorical taste, that the Spaniards, Italians, and French were regarded as artists who did nothing more than place their own personal flights of fancy or witticism, their own conventional attitude to society and elegance of speech in the mouth of their dramatic characters in situations, too, when the very tempest of emotion cried out for Nature's most direct expression to the exclusion of all other. We find as a result of such an insistence on the principle of realism that in many dramas, which hail from this time, the outcry of emotion, with all the exclamatory signs and hyphens which may render its nudity more visible, takes the place of a noble and dignified diction, rich in image and simile. In much the same sense even English critics have often charged Shakespeare with a superabundant and too varied recourse to the simile, some of which he not infrequently will attach to characters in the full strain of personal bereavement, where the stress of emotion least of all admits of the tranquillity necessary to reflection, the attitude of mind which is indispensable to this type of comparison. We may no doubt admit that now and again we meet with in Shakespeare an exaggerated tendency to pile up image upon image, and that his diction is thereby overweighted. At the same time we shall see, if we examine the matter in all its bearings, that even in drama the simile is entitled to a position essential to this form of poetry and vital to its action.

In other words if the emotion makes a pause in similes for the reason that it is absorbed in its object and is unable to free itself therefrom, there is also on the plane of *active life* a distinct purpose subserved by it, namely, to indicate that the individual is not thus so exclusively preoccupied with the particular situation or state of the emotions then uppermost, but possesses a fine and noble nature superior to such conditions and able to assert its independence. In passion, soul-life is restricted and fettered to its own seclusion, narrowed down to the point of concentrated heat, either thereby a mute, an ejaculation of monosyllables, or the rage that vents itself at random. Greatness of soul and intellectual power alike refuse to submit to such limitations: they are wings which carry the soul in a fine tranquillity over and above the storm of pathos that moves it. It is this deliverance of the soul, which the simile primarily expresses by the very mode under which it is asserted. In other words it is only a really profound composure and strength which is able to make itself the object of its pain and suffering, to compare itself with something else, and by doing so to view itself impartially in a strange material; or it may be in a mood of the most terrible scorn to set forth in the external thing the confronting image of its own annihilation, and still persist in the repose of its own obdurate forces. In epical poetry, as we before observed, it was the poet's undoubted function to transmit to his audience, by means of those halts by the way which his picturesque similitudes offered, that sense of tranquillity which is essential to fine art. In dramatic art, on the contrary, the *dramatis personae* appear as themselves the *poets* and *artists*. Here it is the characters who objectify their own soul-life in that which they are powerful enough to imagine and inform, thereby further manifesting to us the nobility of their receptive faculties and the inherent force of their emotional resources. For this absorption into something else that is external is now the deliverance of the world within from a purely practical interest, or at least is that which lifts the immediacy of emotion to the level of forms the soul may contemplate in freedom; and for this reason every comparison instituted simply for the comparison's sake in the way we have already observed it under the first aspect of the simile discussed, is vindicated now in a much profounder sense than was then possible; it can now only appear as a victory over the exclusive obsession of passion and the release from its masterdom. In following up the course of this liberating process we will now emphasize several important distinctions to illustrate which we shall borrow exclusively from Shakespeare.

(1) Now in the first place we would observe that when we have a soul set before us about to meet with a grave misfortune, by which it will be shaken to its depths, and the pain of this inevitable cataclysm is at length actually entered upon, it would be nothing less than an indication of a nature essentially commonplace if it were there and then to break out into the cry of horror, pain, and desperation, and so make a clean breast of it. A strong and noble spirit on the contrary holds its lamentation as such in reserve, keeps a hand of iron upon its pain, and by this means preserves a free power to embody in far-distant material imaginatively presented the profound sense of its anguish, and to express its own tragic state under the image of that which is remote. Thus man rises superior to his suffering; he is not utterly with all that is in him bondman to it; rather he is as wholly distinct from it as he is one with it; and consequently he can still pause before that which is outside and beyond him, which he relates to his emotion as an independent force cognate with his own. This will explain to us those words of the old Northumberland in Shakespeare's "Henry IV," when he inquires of the messenger who comes to inform him of the death of Percy, what news he brings him of his son and his brother, and, on receiving no reply, gives utterance to the composure of the most poignant grief as follows:

> Thou tremblest; and the whiteness of thy cheek
> Is apter than thy tongue to tell thy errand.
> Even such a man, so faint, so spiritless,
> So dull, so dead in look, so woe-begone,
> Drew Priam's curtain in the dead of night,
> And would have told him half his Troy was burnt;
> But Priam found the fire ere he his tongue,
> And I my Percy's death ere thou report'st it.[14]

This attitude of the soul, which spins about itself as it were the garments of its pain, and yet retains the power throughout to image itself under new modes of comparison, receives a particularly striking illustration in the character of Richard II, where we find him repentant over the youthful frivol-

[14] "Henry IV, Part II," Act I, sc. 1.

ity of his days of prosperity. In fact there is no trait in this royal grief that is more touching or suggestive of a child's simplicity than the fact that he always expresses himself under the objective form of most pertinent images, and in the play of this type of self-expression preserves his suffering all the more profoundly. When, for example, Henry demands of him the crown, he replies:

> Give me the crown. Here, cousin, seize the crown;
> Here cousin;
> On this side my hand, and on that side yours.
> Now is this golden crown like a deep well
> That owes two buckets, filling one another,
> The emptier ever dancing in the air,
> The other down, unseen and full of water.
> That bucket down and full of tears am I,
> Drinking my griefs while you mount up on high.[15]

(2) The other aspect to which we would now draw attention is this, namely, that a character which is already made one with its interests, its sorrow, and its destiny, endeavours by means of the simile to release itself from this immediate union, and makes this deliverance obvious to us by the very fact that it shows itself still able to deduce such similitudes. In "Henry VIII,"[16] for instance, the Queen Katherine, on being forsaken by her royal consort, expresses the depth of her desolation in the words:

> I am the most unhappy woman living!
> Alas, poor wenches, where are now your fortunes?
> Shipwreck'd upon a kingdom, where no pity,
> No friends, no hope; no kindred weep for me;
> Almost no grave allow'd me: like the lily,
> That once was mistress of the field and flourish'd,
> I'll hang my head and perish.

In a still more admirable manner in "Julius Caesar"[17] Brutus exclaims to Cassius, to whose want of spirit he has vainly striven to give the spur:

[15] "King Richard II," Act IV, sc. 1.
[16] "King Henry VIII," Act III, sc. 1.
[17] "Julius Caesar," Act IV, sc. 3.

> O Cassius, you are yoked with a lamb
> That carries anger as the flint bears fire;
> Who, much enforced, shows a hasty spark,
> And straight is cool again.

That Brutus in such a situation can find room for a simile is already an excellent proof that he himself has thrust his scorn into the background, and has begun to assert himself as master of it.

For the most part Shakespeare, by endowing his criminal characters with greatness of soul in crime no less than in misfortune, exalts them before he leaves them above their own evil passions; he will not let them rest in the purely abstract assertion of crimes they are for ever going to do, but never really commit, as is the French style, but actually infuses them with the imaginative power, by means of which they stand out before us as distinctly as any other personification that is new to us. Macbeth, for instance, when his last hour has struck,[18] exclaims in the well-known words:

> Out, out, brief candle!
> Life's but a walking shadow, a poor player
> That struts and frets his hour upon the stage
> And then is heard no more: it is a tale
> Told by an idiot, full of sound and fury
> Signifying nothing.

The same thing may be said of those last words of Cardinal Wolsey in "Henry VIII,"[19] uttered at the close of his career when struck down from the summit of his greatness:

> Farewell! a long farewell to all my greatness!
> This is the state of man: to-day he puts forth
> The tender leaves of hopes: to-morrow blossoms,
> And bears his blushing honours thick upon him;
> The third day comes a frost, a killing frost;
> And when he thinks, good easy man, full surely
> His greatness is a-ripening, nips his root,
> And then he falls, as I do.

[18] "Macbeth," Act V, sc. 5.
[19] "Henry VIII," Act III, sc. 2.

(3) In this impersonal relation of objective fact and its expression of the comparative mode, the repose and substantial
self-command of character returns to itself; it is the means
whereby the pain of a great downfall is softened. So Cleopatra
exclaims[20] to Charmian, after she has already put the mortal
aspic to her breast:

> Peace, peace!
> Dost thou not see my baby at my breast,
> That sucks the nurse asleep?
> As sweet as balm, as soft as air, as gentle——

The bite of the serpent relaxes her members so gently that
Death is himself deceived and holds himself to be Sleep. And
this image may well pass as itself a counterfeit of the mild
and allaying influence of such similitudes.

c. Verbal Expression

[r]Inasmuch as the poetic imagination is distinct in its operation from that of all other artists in virtue of the fact that it
necessarily clothes its images in words, and communicates the
same through human *speech,* it becomes imperative that
throughout this process it should endeavour to co-ordinate all
its ideas, in the form which with most completeness will disclose them, through the means articulate speech thus places at
its disposal. And, in short, we may affirm that the poetic content only assumes the form of poetry in its restricted sense
after it has been actually embodied and rounded off in the
vehicle of words.

This literary aspect of the art of poetry would readily supply
us with a boundless field of discursive observation and logical
argument, which I must, however, pass over in order that I
may reserve space for more weighty problems which lie before
us. I merely propose, therefore, to touch very briefly on a few
fundamental points.

(1) Human art should in all its associations place us on a
ground quite other than that we confront in ordinary life, or

[20] "Antony and Cleopatra," Act V, sc. 2.
[r] *The Philosophy of Fine Art,* vol. IV, pp. 64–70.

indeed in our religious consciousness, active life, or the specula-
tions of philosophy. This is possible on the side of literary or
verbal expression only in so far as another mode of speech is
adopted than that obtaining in those other spheres. Art has
therefore not only, from one point of view, to avoid that in
its instrument of expression which will fail to rise above the
trivialities of ordinary speech and ordinary prose, but it must,
furthermore, avoid falling into the tone and manner of religious edification and philosophical research. Above all it must
keep aloof from the precise analyses and *methods* of the scientific faculty, the categories of pure thinking as we find these
illustrated in the logical forms of judgment and deduction.
These at once remove art from the imaginative realm to another region altogether. But in all these respects it still remains
a difficult matter to determine the lines of boundary on which
we may actually affirm that poetry ends and prose begins. And
in fact we may admit absolute precision and confidence of
statement to be impossible from the nature of the case.

(2) If we pass now to a discussion of the particular *means*
which poetic-speech can appropriate as instrumental to its task
the following points appear to me pregnant and suggestive.

(a) *First,* we find particular *words* and exclamations that
are obviously peculiar to poetry, whether they be used to en-
noble it, or to introduce the vulgarity and excess of comedy.
We find a similar novelty in the specific collocation of various
words or turns of expression. In such a field poetry is no doubt
entitled on the one hand to borrow from an obsolete nomen-
clature, obsolete at least in everyday speech, and on the other
to declare itself as pre-eminently an innovator, moulding novel
modes of speech. Such a field, provided only the vital genius
of the language is preserved, supplies material for astonishing
boldness of invention.

(b) *Secondly,* we have the problem of verbal order. It is
here that we meet with those so-called figures of speech, in
so far as, we should add, the same have reference to verbal
embodiment as such. The use of these, however, easily de-
generates into rhetoric and declamation in the bad sense of
these terms; the vitality of individual character is destroyed
where we find that such forms substitute a fixed and artificial
mode of expression for the genuine impulse of feeling or pas-

sion, and thereby offer the very opposite to the personal, laconic and broken utterance required, the utterance whose emotional depth is incapable of saying much, and for this reason, in romantic poetry especially, is of great effect as a presentment of suppressed states of soul. But generally speaking we may admit that the relative order of words is an instrument of the external form of poetry of quite extraordinary resource.

(c) *Thirdly*, we have still to draw attention to the construction of *periods*, which essentially embrace all the other aspects of composition and which, by means of either their simple or more involved course, their restless dislocations and distortions, or their quick onward motion, their acceleration and their flood contribute so materially to the reflection of such soul experience. And, in short, it is essential that the external presentment in speech should mirror and assume a character similar to the ideality of such experience in all its variety.

(3) In the *application* of the means of speech above considered it will be useful to distinguish once more the several stages of poetic thought to which they correspond and to which we drew attention when we considered the nature of poetic conception or composition.

(a) Poetic diction can, in the first instance, appear with real vitality among a people and at an epoch when the general speech is not as yet perfected, but in fact only by virtue of its poetry receives its real development. At such a time the utterance of the poet, as generally expressive of soul-life, is from the first a real novelty, which stirs admiration on its own account by revealing in its speech what remained previously unveiled. This new creation appears as the marvel of a gift and personal power. The weight of custom has not as yet fallen upon it. It enables that which is buried in the depths of the human heart for the first time to freely unfold itself before the amazement of men. Under such conditions it is the native force of the expression, the creation of the fact of speech, not so much the varied and craftful elaboration of the same, which is the main point. Diction here remains exceedingly simple. In such early times it is indeed impossible that we should have either much fluency of idea or any varied versatility of expression. The subject-matter of such poetry is depicted with an artless directness, which has not yet attained the delicate nuances, transitions, mediatory matter and other advantages of a later artistic culture. In such an age the poet is in fact the first person to give an utterance to the national voice, to express ideas in speech, and thereby to encourage the imagination itself. Speech is, if we may so express it, not yet inseparable from ordinary life, and poetry can still freely, with an effect of freshness, avail itself of all that in later times, as the speech of common life, gradually is severed from art. In this respect, for example, Homer's type of expression is to the modern man barely distinguishable from ordinary speech. For every idea we have the direct word; metaphorical expressions are comparatively rare; and although the poem is composed with a close attention to detail, the speech itself remains very simple indeed. In a similar way Dante was able to create for his own nation a vital form of poetic expression, and asserted in this, as in other respects, the dauntless energy of his creative genius.

(b) When, however—this is a *further* point—the circle of ideas enlarges with the appearance of methodical modes of thought the ways in which idea is associated with idea increase, and in this very process the ability to use it increases also, and the expression of speech is elaborated in all the fluency of which it is capable. When this is so the position of poetry on the side of verbal expression is wholly changed. In other words, we have now a nation possessing the fully developed prose speech of everyday life, and poetic expression must now, in order to retain its interest, swerve aside from ordinary parlance, and receive a resurrection under the remoulding energy of genius. In our daily life the contingency of the moment is the motive of speech. In the creation of a work of art, however, we must have deliberate circumspection in the place of instantaneous feeling; even the spirit of enthusiasm must be judiciously restrained. The creation of genius should be permitted to unfold itself from the artistic repose, and become informed under the prevailing temper of an intelligence that surveys the whole with clarity. In former times this spirit of concentration and tranquillity is to be inferred from the fact and utterance of poetry itself. In a more recent age, on the contrary, the nature of the composition and execution has itself to enforce the distinction which obtains between the expression of poetry and prose. In this respect poems which belong to epochs in which we find already an elaborated prose diction differ essentially from those of times and peoples in which the art originates.

The executive talent of a poet can be carried so far in this direction that the elaboration of formal expression becomes the main thing, and the aim is less directed to ideal truth than to formal construction, a polished elegance and mere effect of the composition under its literary aspect. We have then a situation, in which, as already observed, rhetoric and declamation are elaborated in a manner destructive to the ideal vitality of the poetic spirit. The formative intelligence asserts itself under the principle of *purposiveness*, and a self-consciously regulated art disturbs that more genuine effect, which ought to present the appearance of ingenuous openness and simplicity. Entire nations have, with the rarest exceptions, failed to produce any type of poetic creation other than this rhetorical one. The Latin language, even in Cicero, still preserves a genuine ring of naïveté and naturalness. With the Latin poets, however, such as Virgil, Horace and the rest, we already feel that Art is to a real extent nothing but artifice, elaboration of effect on its own account. We recognize a prosaic content, which is merely set off with an external embellishment. We find a poet who, in the absence of original genius, endeavours to discover, in the sphere of literary versatility and rhetoric effects, some compensation for that which in genuine power and effect of creation and composition he fails to possess. France too, in the so-called classical period of its literature, has produced poetry very similar, a poetical style to which didactic poems and satires are singularly appropriate. Rhetorical figures of speech in all their variety are here in their rightful place. The exposition remains for all that, as a whole, prosaic; and the literary expression is at its best rich in image and embellishment, much in the style of Herder's or Schiller's diction. These last-mentioned writers, however, availed themselves of this style of literary expression mainly in the interests of prose composition; and by the weightiness of their reflections and the happy use of such a style knew how to win both a critical assent and a hearty approval. The Spanish poets also are not wholly free from the ostentation inseparable from the too self-conscious diction of art. And, as a general rule, Southern nations, such as the Spaniards and the Italians, and previously to them the Mohammedan Arabs and Persians, are conspicuous for a wealth and tedious prolixity of image and simile. With the ancients, more especially in the case of Homer, the flow of expression is characterized by smoothness and tranquillity. With the nations above mentioned, on the contrary, we have a vision of life gushing forth in a flood which, even where the emotions are in other respects at rest, is ever intent upon expatiation, and owing to this expressly volitional effort of the will is dominated by an intelligence which at one time is visible in abrupt parentheses, at another in subtle generalization, at another in the playful conjunction of its sallies of wit and humour.

(c) Genuine poetic expression in short is as far removed from all rhetorical declamation as above described as it is from all ostentation and witty conceits of diction, in so far at least as such defects do injury to the ideal truth of Nature, and the claims of the content are forgotten in the verbal form and expression of the composition. It is, however, possible, despite this, that the author's free enjoyment in his work declare itself with real beauty. In a word that aspect of the composition we define as formal diction ought not to be treated on its own and independent account alone, or as an aspect of first and even exclusive importance. And, generally speaking, in this analysis of the composition of poetry under its formative aspect, we repeat that what is the product of careful thought must not lose the appearance of genuine spontaneity: everything should impress us as though it had of itself blossomed from the ideal germ or heart of the subject-matter.

CHAPTER IV

ETHICS AND TRAGEDY

[a]The *tragic* destruction of figures whose ethical life is on the highest plane can interest and elevate us and reconcile us to its occurrence only in so far as they come on the scene in opposition to one another together with equally justified but different ethical powers which have come into collision through misfortune, because the result is that then these figures acquire guilt through their opposition to an ethical law. Out of this situation there arises the right and wrong of both parties and therefore the true ethical Idea, which, purified and in triumph over this one-sidedness, is thereby reconciled in *us*. Accordingly, it is not the highest in us which perishes; we are elevated not by the destruction of the best but by the triumph of the true. This it is which constitutes the true, purely ethical, interest of ancient tragedy (in romantic tragedy the character of the interest undergoes a certain modification). All this I have worked out in detail in my *Phenomenology of Mind*.

1. SELF-CONSCIOUSNESS AND THE SOCIAL ORDER

[b]The Social Order, the Ethical World (*Sittlichkeit*) is nothing else than the absolute spiritual unity of the essential sub-

[a] *Hegel's Philosophy of Right*, tr. T. M. Knox. Oxford, 1942, p. 102 ftn.
[b] *The Phenomenology of Mind*, tr. J. B. Baillie. London, 1910, pp. 375–82.

stance (*Wesen*) of individuals in their independent reality; it
is an inherently universal self-consciousness, which is aware of
being so concrete and real in an other consciousness, that this
latter has complete independence, is looked on as a "thing",
and the universal self-consciousness is aware precisely therein
of its unity with that "thing," and is only then self-consciousness, when thus in unity with this objective being (*Wesen*).
This ethical substance when taken in its abstract universality
is only the conception of law, thought-constituted law; but
just as much it is immediately actual self-consciousness, it is
Custom (*Sitte*). The single individual conversely, is only a
"this," a given existent unit, in so far as he is aware of the
universal consciousness as his own being in his own particular
individuality, seeing that his action and existence are the universal custom.

In point of fact the notion of the realization of self-conscious
reason—of directly apprehending complete unity with another
in his independence: of having for my object an other in the
fashion of a "thing" found detached and apart from me, and
the negative of myself, and of taking this as my own self-
existence (*Fürmichseyn*)—finds its complete reality in fulfilment in the life of a nation.

The purely particular activity and business of the individual
refer to needs which he has as a part of nature, i.e. as a mere
existent particular. That even these, its commonest functions,
do not come to nothing, but have reality, is brought about
by the universal sustaining medium, the might of the entire
nation.

It is not merely, however, this *form* of subsistence for his
activity in general that the individual gets in the universal substance, but likewise also his *content;* what he does is what all
are capable of doing, is the custom all follow. This content,
in so far as it is completely particularized, is, in its concrete
reality, confined within the limits of the activity of all. The
labour of the individual for his own wants is just as much a
satisfaction of those of others as of himself, and the satisfaction of his own he attains only by the labour of others.

As the individual in his own particular work *ipso facto* accomplishes unconsciously a universal work, so again he also
performs the universal task as his *conscious* object. The whole

becomes *in its entirety* his work, for which he sacrifices himself, and precisely by that means receives back his own self from it.

There is nothing here which may not be reciprocal, nothing in regard to which the independence of the individual may not, in dissipating its existence on its own account (*Fürsichseyn*), in negating itself, give itself its positive significance of existing for itself. This unity of existing for another, or making self a "thing", and of existence for self, this universal substance, utters its universal language in the *customs* and *laws* of a nation. But this existent unchangeable nature (*Wesen*) is nothing else than the expression of the particular individuality which seems opposed to it: the laws give expression to that which each individual is and does; the individual knows them not merely to be what constitutes his universal objective nature as a "thing," but knows himself, too, in that form, or knows it to be particularized in his own individuality and in each of his fellow-citizens. In the universal mind, therefore, each has the certainty only of himself, the certainty of finding in the actual reality nothing but himself; he is as certain of the others as of himself. I apprehend and see in all of them that they are in their own eyes (*für sich selbst*) only these independent beings just as I am. I see in their case the free unity with others in such wise that just as this unity exists through me, so it exists through the others too—I see them as myself, myself as them.

In a free nation, therefore, reason is in truth realized. It is a present living spirit, where the individual not only finds his destiny (*Bestimmung*), i.e. his universal and particular nature (*Wesen*), expressed and given to him in the fashion of a thing, but himself is this essential being, and has also attained his destiny. The wisest men of antiquity for that reason declared that wisdom and virtue consist in living in accordance with the customs of one's own nation.

From this happy state, however, of having attained its destiny, and of living in it, the self-consciousness, which in the first instance is only immediately and in principle spirit, has broken away; or perhaps it has not yet attained it: for both can be said with equal truth.

Reason must pass out of and leave this happy condition.

For only implicitly or immediately is the life of a free nation the real objective ethical order (*Sittlichkeit*). In other words, the latter is an existent social order, and in consequence this universal mind is also an individualized mind. It is the totality of customs and laws of a particular people, a specifically determinate ethical substance, which casts off this limitation only when it reaches the higher moment, namely, when it becomes conscious regarding its own nature; only with this knowledge does it get its absolute truth, and not as it is immediately in its bare existence. In this latter form it is, on the one hand, a restricted ethical substance, on the other, absolute limitation consists just in this that mind is in the form of existence.

Hence, further, the individual, as he immediately finds his existence in the actual objective social order, in the life of his nation, has a solid imperturbable confidence; the universal mind has not for him resolved itself into its abstract moments, and thus, too, he does not think of himself as existing in singleness and independence. When however he has once arrived at this knowledge, as indeed he must, this immediate unity with mind, this undifferentiated existence in the substance of mind, his naïve confidence, is lost. Isolated by himself he is himself now the central essential reality—no longer universal mind. The element of this singleness of self-consciousness is no doubt in universal mind itself, but merely as a vanishing quantity, which, as it appears with an existence of its own, is straightway resolved within the universal, and only becomes consciously felt in the form of that confidence. When the individual gets fixity in the form of singleness (and every moment, being a moment of the essential reality, must manage to reveal itself as essential), the individual has thereby set himself over against the laws and customs. These latter are looked on as merely a thought without absolutely essential significance, an abstract theory without reality; while he *qua* this particular ego is in his own view the living truth.

If, then, we for our part find the truth of this rational self-consciousness to be ethical substance, that self-consciousness on its part finds here the beginning of its ethical experience of the world. From the point of view that it has not yet attained to its ethical substance, this movement presses onwards to that end, and what is cancelled in the process are the particular moments which self-consciousness takes as valid in isolation. They have the form of an immediate will-process, or impulse of nature, which attains its satisfaction, this satisfaction itself being the content of a new impulse. Looking at self-consciousness, however, as having lost the happiness of being in the substance, these natural impulses are bound up with a consciousness that their purpose is the true destiny and essential nature of self-consciousness. Ethical substance has sunk to the level of a floating selfless adjective, whose living subjects are individuals, which have to fill up their universality through themselves, and to provide for their destiny out of the same source.

Taken in the former sense, then, those forms and modes are the process by which the ethical substance comes to be, and precede this substance: in the latter they succeed it, and disclose for self-consciousness what its destined nature is. In the former aspect the immediacy or raw brute impulses get lost in the process of finding out what their truth is, and their content passes over to a higher. In the latter aspect, however, the false idea of consciousness, which puts its characteristic nature in those impulses, passes to a higher idea. In the former case the goal which they attain is the immediate ethical substance; while, in the latter, the end is the consciousness of that substance, such a consciousness as knows the substance to be its own essential being; and to that extent this process would be the development of morality (*Moralität*), a higher state or attitude than the former (*Sittlichkeit*). But these modes at the same time constitute only one side of the development of morality, that, namely, which belongs to self-existence, or in which consciousness cancels *its* purposes; they do not constitute the side where morality arises out of the substance itself. Since these moments cannot yet have the signification of being made into purposes in opposition to the lost social order (*Sittlichkeit*), they hold here no doubt in their simple uncriticized content, and the end towards which they work is the ethical substance: but since with our time is more directly associated that form of these moments in which they appear after consciousness has lost its ethical custom-constituted (*sittliches*) life, and in the search for it repeats those forms, they may be represented more after this latter manner of expression.

Self-consciousness, which is as yet merely the notion of mind, takes this path with the specific characteristic of being to itself the essential reality *qua* individual mind, and its purpose, therefore, is to give itself actualization as individual, and to enjoy itself, *qua* individual, in so doing.

a. Pleasure and Necessity

[c]In so far as it has risen from out of the substance of ethical life and the quiescent state of thought, and attained its conscious independence, self-consciousness has left behind the law of custom and of substantial existence, the kinds of knowledge acquired through observation, and the sphere of theory; these lie behind it as a grey shadow that is just vanishing. For this latter is rather a knowledge of something, the independent existence (*Fürsichseyn*) and actuality of which are other than those of self-consciousness. It is not the seemingly divine spirit of universality in knowledge and action, wherein (all individual) feeling and enjoyment are stilled, that has passed into and fills this new level of self-consciousness; but the spirit of the earth, a spirit which holds that being alone as true reality which is the reality of individual consciousness.

> It repudiates sense and science
> The highest gifts possessed by men—
> It has gone over to the devil,
> And must be o'erthrown.[1]

It plunges thus into life, and carries to its completion the pure individuality in which it appears. It does not so much make its own happiness as take it directly and enjoy it. The grey shades of science, laws and principles, which alone stand between it and its own reality, vanish like a lifeless mist that cannot contend against the living certainty of its reality. It takes to itself

[c] *Phenomenology*, pp. 384–89.
[1] *Faust* (adapted).

life much as a ripe fruit is plucked, which comes to meet the hand that takes it.[2]

Its action is only in one respect an act of Desire; it does not aim at abolishing the objective fact in its entirety, but only the form of its otherness or objectivity, which is an unreal appearance; for it holds this to be inherently and implicitly the same reality as its own self. The sphere in which desire and its object subsist independently and indifferent towards each other is that of living existence; the enjoyment of desire cancels this existence, so far as it belongs to the object of desire. But here this element, which gives to both separate and distinct actuality, is rather the category, a form of being which has essentially the character of a presented being. It (i.e. the element) is therefore the *consciousness* of independence—it may be natural consciousness, or the consciousness developed into a system of laws—which preserves the individuals each for himself. This separation does not *per se* hold for self-consciousness, which knows the other as its own proper self-hood. It attains therefore to the enjoyment of *Pleasure,* to the consciousness of its actualization in a consciousness which appears as independent, or to the intuition of the unity of both independent self-consciousnesses. It succeeds in its purpose, but only to learn there what the truth of that purpose is. It conceives itself as this individual self-existent (*Fürsichseinde*) being; but the actualization of this purpose is just the cancelling of the purpose. For it comes consciously to be, not object in the sense of a given particular individual, but rather as unity of its self and the other self-consciousness, consequently as cancelled and transcended individual, i.e. as universal.

The pleasure enjoyed has, indeed, the positive significance that the self has become aware of itself as objective self-consciousness: but the negative import is there as well—that of having cancelled itself. And since it took its realization in the former sense only, its experience comes consciously before it as contradiction, in which the acquired reality of its individual existence finds itself destroyed by the negative element, which stands without reality and without content over against the former, and yet is the force which consumes it. This nega-

[2] Cp. Spenser's "Faerie Queene," Bk. 2: Canto 12, 54.

tive element is nothing else than the notion of what this individuality inherently is. This individuality is, however, as yet the poorest form of self-realizing mind; for it is to itself still simply the abstraction of reason, or is the merely immediate unity of being-for-self and being-in-self (*Für-sich und Ansichseyns*), of explicit and implicit self. Its essential nature therefore is only the abstract category. Still it has no longer the form of immediate simple *being* as in the case of Observation, where it is abstract being, or, when affirmed as something alien, is thinghood in general. Here in the case before us there has entered into this thinghood self-existence (*Fürsichseyn*) and mediation. It comes on the scene here, therefore, in the form of a circular process, whose content is the developed pure relation of the simple essential elements. The actualization attained in the case of this individuality consists, therefore, in nothing else than its having turned out this cycle of abstractions from the restricted confines of simple self-consciousness, and put them into the sphere and condition of "being for consciousness" existence, where they appear spread out in detail as distinct objects.

The sort of object, then, that self-consciousness in its pleasurable enjoyment takes to be its true reality, is the detailed expansion of those bare essential elements—of pure unity, of pure difference, and of their relation. Further than this the object, which individuality experiences as its true nature, has no content. It is what is called *Necessity*. For Necessity, Fate, or the like, is just that about which we are unable to say what it is doing, what its definite laws and its positive content actually are, because it is the absolute pure notion itself, viewed as *being*, relation bare and simple, but imperturbable, irresistible, and immovable, whose work is merely the nothingness of individual existence. It is this firm unbending connection, because that which is connected consists in pure essentialities or empty abstractions. Unity, Difference, and Relation are categories, each of which is nothing as it stands by itself, but only in its relation to its opposite, and they therefore cannot come apart from one another. They are by their own notion related to each other, for they are the pure notions themselves; and this absolute relation and abstract process constitute Necessity. The merely particular individuality, which has in the first instance only the pure notion of reason for its content, instead of having escaped from dead theory and plunged into actual life, has thus only precipitated itself into consciousness of its own lifelessness, and enjoys itself merely as naked and alien necessity, *lifeless* actuality.

The transition takes the place from the form of oneness to that of universality, from one absolute abstraction into the other; it proceeds from that purpose of pure explicit existence-for-self, which has cast off fellowship and communion with others, into the sheer opposite—i.e. into equally abstract implicit immanent existence—into mere being-in-itself. This appears consequently in such form that the individual is simply reduced to naught, and the utter atomicity of separate individual existence is pulverized on the equally hard but continuous actuality.

Since it is *qua* consciousness the unity of itself and its opposite, this transition is still a fact *for* it. Its purpose, and its realization as well as the contradiction of what constituted for it its essential nature, and what *inherently* that nature is—all this it is consciously aware of. It learns the double meaning which lies in what it did, when it sought to "take" and possess its life: it "took" life, but thereby rather laid hold on death.

This transition of its living being into lifeless necessity appears to it therefore a perversion which is mediated by no agency at all. The mediating factor would have to be that in which both sides would be one, where consciousness thus knew the one moment in the other, found its purpose and action in Fate, and its fate in its purpose and action, saw its own true nature in this Necessity. But, for consciousness the meaning of this unity here is just pleasure itself, or simple particular feeling; and the transition from the moment of this its purpose into the moment of its true nature is for it a mere leap into the opposite. For these moments are not contained and combined in feeling, but only in the bare pure self, which is a universal or thought. Consciousness, therefore, through the experience in which its truth ought to have come to light, has instead become to itself a dark riddle; the consequences of its deeds are to it not really its own deeds. What happens to it is found to be not the experience of what it inherently is; the transition is not a mere alteration in form of the same con-

tent and essential nature, presented now as content and true
reality of consciousness, thereafter as object or intuitively perceived essence of itself. The abstract necessity thus gets the significance of the merely negative uncomprehended power of
universality, on which individuality is broken in pieces.

The appearance of this mode of self-consciousness goes as
far as this stage. The last moment of the existence of this
mode is the thought of its loss and annihilation in necessity,
or the thought of itself as a being (*Wesen*) entirely alien to
itself. Self-consciousness in itself, however, has survived this
loss; for this necessity or pure universality is its own proper
nature (*Wesen*). This reflection of consciousness into self, the
knowledge that necessity is itself, is a new mode or attitude
of consciousness.

b. The Law of the Heart, and the Frenzy of Self-Conceit

[d]Necessity is for this new mode of consciousness what in
truth self-consciousness finds necessity in its own case to be.
In its new attitude self-consciousness regards itself as the
necessary element. It knows that it has the universal, the law,
immediately within itself, a law which, because of this characteristic of being immediately within consciousness as it is for
itself, is called the Law of the *Heart*. This mode or attitude
of consciousness is for itself, *qua* individual, essential reality
as the former mode similarly was; but in the present case it
is richer by the characteristic that this self-existence is taken
as necessary or universal.

The law, therefore, which is primarily the law proper of
self-consciousness, or a "heart" which however has in it a law,
is the purpose which the self proceeds to realize. It remains
to be seen whether its realization corresponds to its notion, and
whether it will therein come to find this its law to be the essential ultimate fact.

Opposed to this "heart" stands a reality. For in the "heart"
the law is in the first place merely for itself; it is not yet
actualized, and thus, too, is something other than what the

[d] *Phenomenology*, pp. 391–400.

notion is. This other is thereby characterized as a reality which is the antithesis of what is to be realized, and consequently is the contradiction of the law and the individual. This reality is thus on the one hand a law by which the particular individuality is crushed and oppressed, a violent ordinance of the world which contradicts the law of the heart, and, on the other hand, a humanity suffering under that ordinance—a humanity which does not follow the law of the heart, but is subjected to an alien necessity.

This reality, appearing in opposition to the present mode of consciousness, is, as is evident, nothing but the foregoing diremption of individuality and its truth, a relation of gruesome necessity, under which the former is crushed. We, who trace the process, see the preceding movement, therefore, as in opposition to the new form, because the latter has essentially arisen from it, and the moment whence the new form comes is necessary for it. The new mode, however, looks on that moment as something simply met with, since it has no consciousness of its origin, and takes its real essence to consist rather in being independent, in being for itself, or negatively disposed toward this positive, implicit, immanent content.

The aim and object of this individuality is thus to cancel and transcend this necessity which contradicts the law of the heart, as also to do away with the suffering thereby arising. There is in consequence no longer here the frivolity of the former mode, which merely wanted private and particular pleasure; it is the earnestness of a high purpose, which seeks its pleasure in displaying the excellence of its own true nature, and in bringing about the welfare of mankind. What it realizes is itself the law, and its pleasure is at the same time universal, a pleasure which all hearts feel. To it both are inseparable; its pleasure is what conforms to the law and the realization of the law of all mankind affords it its particular pleasure. For within its own self individuality and necessity are immediately and directly one; the law is a law of the heart. Individuality is not yet removed from its place; and the unity of both has not been brought about by means of the development of individuality, has not yet been established by discipline. The realization of the immediate undisciplined nature passes for a display of excellence and for bringing about the well-being of mankind.

The law, again, which is opposed to the law of the heart is divided from the heart, and exists on its own account. Mankind, which is bound to it, does not live in the blissful unity of the law with the heart, but either lives in dismal separation and suffering, or at least in deprivation of the enjoyment of itself in obeying the law, and without the consciousness of its own excellence in overstepping it. Because that all-dominating divine and human ordinance is divided from the heart it is regarded by the latter as a delusion, which ought to lose what it still possesses, namely, power and actuality. It may, indeed, in its content agree by chance with the law of the heart, and then the latter can acquiesce in it. But, for the heart, it is not the bare conformity to law as such which constitutes the essential fact (*Wesen*), but the consciousness of itself which the "heart" thereby obtains, the fact that it has therein found self-satisfaction. Where the content of universal necessity, however, does not agree with the heart, necessity is, as regards its content also, nothing in itself, and must give way before the law of the heart.

The individual, then, fulfils, carries out the law of his heart. This law becomes a universal ordinance, and pleasure becomes a reality which, as it stands, conforms to law. But in this realization, the law has, in point of fact, escaped the individual; and thus there arises immediately only that relation which ought to be cancelled. The law of the heart ceases through its very realization to be a law of the heart. For it thereby takes on the form of actually "being," and is now universal power, which holds this particular "heart" to be a matter of indifference; so that the individual, in establishing his own ordinance, no longer finds it to be his own. By realizing his law he consequently brings about, not *his* law, but—since the realization is inherently and implicitly his own, but explicitly alien and external—merely this: he gets involved and entangled in the actual ordinance, and, indeed, entangled in it, not merely as something alien to himself but as a hostile, overpowering dominion.

By his act he takes his place in, or rather as, the general element of existent actuality; and his act is, even in his own regard, intended to have the value of a universal ordinance. But thereby he has let himself get detached from his own self; *qua* universality he lives, grows on his own account, and purifies himself of individuality. The individual who will only recognize universality in the form of his own immediate self-subsistence (*Fürsichseyn*) does not, therefore, recognize himself in this liberated and independent universality, while all the same he belongs to it, because the latter is his doing. This doing thus has the reverse significance; it contradicts the universal ordinance. For the individual's act is intended to be that of his individual heart, and not independent universal reality; and at the same time he has, in fact, recognized and acknowledged this latter, for the act has the import of setting up his essential nature as free and independent reality, that is to say, of recognizing reality to be his own essential being.

The individual has, by the very principle of his action, determined the more special manner in which actual universality, to which he has leagued himself, gets turned against him. His act, *qua* actuality, belongs to the universal; its content, however, is his own individuality, which wants to preserve itself as this particular individuality in opposition to universality. It is not any specific law whose establishment is in question; on the contrary, the immediate unity of the individual heart with universality is the idea—raised to the dignity of a law and claiming to be valid—that every heart must recognize its own self in what is universal law. But only the heart of this individual has established its reality in his act, which, in his view, expresses his self-existence (*Fürsichseyn*) or his pleasure. The act is intended to stand immediately for what is universal; that is to say, it is in truth something particular, and has merely the form of universality: his particular content is, as such, to pass for universal. Hence others find in this content not the law of their heart fulfilled, but rather that of some one else; and precisely in accordance with the universal law, that each is to find *his own* heart in what is law, they turn against that reality which he set up, just as he on his side turned against theirs. The individual therefore finds, as at first merely the rigid law, so now the hearts of men themselves opposed to his excellent intentions, and to be detested and detestable.

Because this type of consciousness finds universality in the first place merely as immediate, and knows necessity as necessity of the heart, the nature of actualization and effective activity is to it unknown. This consciousness is unaware that effective realization involves objective existence, and is in its truth the inherently universal in which the particular life of consciousness, which commits itself to it in order to have being in the sense of this immediate individual life, is really submerged. Instead of obtaining this particular life of its own in that objective existence, it thus becomes estranged from itself. But that in which it does not know itself is no longer dead necessity, but necessity animated by universal individuality. It took this divine and human ordinance, which it found authoritative, to be a dead reality, wherein not only its own self—which claims the position of a particular individual, insists on being a particular "heart" with a life of its own and opposed to the universal—but those as well who were subject to this reality had no consciousness of themselves. Now, however, it finds that reality animated by the consciousness of all, and a law for all hearts. It learns through experience that the reality in question is an ordinance infused and endowed with life, and learns this, indeed, just by the fact that it actualizes the law of its own heart. For this means nothing else than that individuality becomes its own object in the form of universality, without however recognizing itself therein.

Thus, then, what the experience of this mode of self-consciousness reveals as the truth, contradicts what this mode takes itself to be. What, however, it takes itself to be has for it the form of absolute universality; and what is immediately one with consciousness of self is the law of the heart. At the same time the stable living ordinance is likewise its own true nature and work; it produces nothing else but that; the latter is in equally immediate union with self-consciousness. In this way self-consciousness here has the characteristic of belonging to a twofold antithetic essence; it is inherently contradictory and torn to distraction in its inmost being. The law of "this individual heart" is alone that wherein self-consciousness recognizes itself; but the universal and accepted ordinance has by actualizing that law become for self-consciousness likewise its own essential nature and its own reality. What thus contradicts itself within its consciousness has for it in both cases the character of essence, and of being its own reality.

In that it gives expression to this moment of its own conscious destruction, and thereby expresses the result of its experience, it shows itself to be this inner perversion of itself, to be consciousness gone crazy, its own essence being immediately not essence, its reality immediately unreality.

The madness here cannot be taken to mean that in general something unessential is regarded as essential, something unreal as real, so that what for one is essential or actual might not be so for another, and thus the consciousness of real and of unreal, or of essential and unessential, would fall apart. If something in point of fact is real and essential for consciousness in general, but for me is not so, then, in being conscious of its nothingness, I have, since I am consciousness in general, at the same time the consciousness of its reality; and since they both are fixed and rooted within me, this is a union which is madness in general. In this state, however, there is only an *object* deranged for consciousness—not consciousness as such within itself and for itself. But in the result of the process of experience, which has here come about, consciousness is in its law aware of its self as this individual reality; and at the same time, since precisely this same essential fact, this same reality, is estranged from it, it is—*qua* self-consciousness, *qua* absolute reality—aware of its unreality. In other words, both aspects are held by it in their contradiction to be directly its essence, which is thus in its utmost being distracted.

The heart-throb for the welfare of mankind passes therefore into the rage of frantic self-conceit, into the fury of consciousness to preserve itself from destruction; and to do so by casting out of its life the perversion which it really is, and by straining to regard and to express that perversion as something else. The universal ordinance and law it, therefore, now speaks of as an utter distortion of the law of its heart and of its happiness, a perversion invented by fanatical priests, by riotous, revelling despots and their minions, who seek to indemnify themselves for their own degradation by degrading and oppressing in their turn—a distortion practised to the nameless misery of deluded mankind.

Consciousness in this its frenzy proclaims individuality to

be deranging, mad, and perverted, but this is an alien and accidental individuality. It is the heart, however, or the particular consciousness immediately seeking to be universal, that is thus raving and perverted, and the outcome of its action is merely that this contradiction comes to its consciousness. For the truth in its view is the law of its heart, something merely *intended*, which has not stood the test of time as the permanent ordinance has done, but rather is overthrown, as time indeed discloses. This its law ought to have reality: herein the law *qua* reality, *qua* valid ordinance, is for it purpose and essential nature; but that reality, that very law as valid ordinance, is at once and at the same time for it nothingness and void.

Similarly its *own* reality, itself as individual consciousness, is in its view the essential truth. Its purpose, however, is to establish that particularity as existent. It thus in the first instance rather takes its self *qua not*-individual to be the truly real; or its self is purpose in the sense of law, and hence precisely a universality, which its self is held to be as object for its consciousness. This its notion comes by its own act to be its object. Its (individual) self is thus discovered to be unreal, and unreality it finds out to be *its* reality. It is thus not an accidental and alien individuality, but just this particular "heart," which is in every respect inherently perverted and perverting.

Since, however, the directly universal individuality is that which is perverted and perverting, this universal ordinance, being the law of all hearts, and so of the perverted consciousness, is no less itself in its very nature the perverted element, as indeed raging frenzy declared. On the one hand this ordinance proves itself to be a law for all hearts, by the resistance which the law of one heart meets with from other individuals. The accepted and established laws are defended against the law of a single individual because they are not empty necessity, unconscious and dead, but are spiritual substance and universality, in which those in whom this spiritual substance is realized live as individuals, and are conscious of their own selves. Hence, even when they complain of this ordinance, as if it went contrary to their own inmost law, and maintain in opposition to it the claims of the "heart," in point of fact they inwardly cling to it as being their essential nature; and if they are deprived of this ordinance, or put themselves outside the range of its influence, they lose everything. Since, then, it is precisely in this that the reality and power of public ordinance consist, the latter appears as the essence, self-identical and everywhere alive, and individuality appears as its form.

On the other hand, however, this ordinance is the sphere of perversion. For in that this ordinance is the law of all hearts, in that all individuals are immediately this universal, it is a reality which is only that of self-existing individuality, i.e. of the heart. When consciousness therefore sets up the law of its heart, it finds itself resisted by others because it conflicts with the equally individual laws of their heart; and the latter in opposing it are doing nothing else but setting up in their turn and making valid their own law. The universal here presented, therefore, is only a universal resistance and struggle of all against one another, in which each makes good his own individuality, but at the same time does not come off successfully, because each individuality meets with the same opposition, and each is reciprocally dissipated by the others. What appears as public ordinance is thus this state of war of each against all, in which every one for himself wrests what he can, executes even-handed justice upon the individual lives of others, and establishes his own individual existence, which in its turn vanishes at the hands of others. We have here the *Course of the World*, the mere semblance of a constant regular trend, which is only a pretence of universality, and whose content is rather the meaningless insubstantial sport of setting up individual beings as fixed and stable, and then dissipating them.

If we put both sides of the universal ordinance over against one another and consider them, we see that this later universality has for its content restless individuality, which regards opinion or mere individualism as law, the real as unreal, and the unreal as real. That universality is, however, at the same time the side of realization of the ordinance, for to it belongs the independent self-existence (*Fürsichseyn*) of individuality. The other side is the universal in the sense of stable passive essence; but, for that very reason, the universal is only something inner, which is not indeed absolutely non-existent, but still not an actual reality, and can itself only become actual by cancelling the individuality, that has presumed to claim actuality. This type of consciousness, which becomes aware of itself in the law; which finds itself in what is inherently true and good not as mere individual, but only as essentially real; and which knows individuality to be what is perverted and perverting, and hence feels bound to surrender and sacrifice individualism of consciousness—this type of consciousness is *Virtue*.

c. Virtue and the Course of the World

[e]It is from virtue that the universal is now to receive its true reality, by cancelling individuality, the principle of perversion. Virtue's purpose is by this means to transmute again the perverted world's process, and bring out its true inner nature. This true being is in the world-process merely in the form of its implicit inherent nature; it is not yet actual; and hence virtue merely *believes* it. Virtue proceeds to raise this faith to sight, without, however, enjoying the fruit of its labour and sacrifice. For so far as it is individuality, it is the active carrying-on of the contest which it wages with the world's process. Its purpose and true nature, however, lie in conquering the reality of the world's process; and the existence of the good thereby effectuated carries with it the cessation of its action, i.e., of the consciousness of individuality.

How this struggle itself will come off, what virtue finds out in the course of it, whether, by the sacrifice which virtue takes upon itself to undergo, the world's process succumbs while virtue triumphs—all this must be decided from the nature of the living weapons the combatants carry. For the weapons are nothing else than the essential being of the combatants themselves, a being which only makes its appearance for them both reciprocally. What their weapons are is in this way already evident from what is inherently implied in this struggle.

[f]The virtuous consciousness enters into conflict with the way of the world as if this were a factor opposed to the good. What the conflict brings to light is the universal, not merely

[e] *Phenomenology*, p. 404.
[f] *Ibid.*, pp. 406–12.

as an abstract universal, but as one animated by individuality, and existing for an other, in other words the universal in the sense of the actually real good. Wherever virtue comes to grips with the world's process, it always hits upon places where goodness is found to exist; the good, as the inherent nature of the world's process, is inseparably interwoven with all the manifestations of it, with all the ways in which the world's process makes its appearance, and where it is real the good has its own existence too. Virtue thus finds the world's process invulnerable. All the moments which virtue was to jeopardize in itself when dealing with the world's process, all the moments which it was to sacrifice—these are just so many ways in which goodness exists, and consequently are inviolable relations. The conflict can, therefore, only be an oscillation between conserving and sacrificing; or rather there can be no place for either sacrificing one's own or doing harm to what comes from elsewhere. Virtue is not merely like the combatant whose sole concern in the fight is to keep his sword polished; but it has even started the fight simply to preserve its weapons. And not merely is it unable to use its own weapons, but it must also preserve intact those of its enemy, and protect them against its own attack, seeing they are all noble parts of the good, on behalf of which it entered the field of battle.

This enemy, on the other hand, has as its essential element not the inherent universal, but individuality. Its force is thus the negative principle before which nothing stands, nothing is absolutely sacred, but which can risk and endure the loss of everything and anything. In so doing it feels victory to be assured, as much from its very nature as by the contradiction in which its opponent gets entangled. What is to virtue implicit and inherent is taken merely as an explicit objective fact in the case of the world's process. The latter is detached from every moment which virtue finds fixed and to which it is fast secured. The world process has such a moment under its power and has consequently in its control the tethered knight of virtue bound thereto, by the fact that this moment is held to be merely one which the world's process can as readily cancel as let be. This knight of valour cannot work himself loose from it as he might from a cloak thrown round him, and get free by leaving it behind; for it is to him the essential element which he cannot give up.

Finally, as to the ambush out of which the inherent good is cunningly and craftily to fall on the rear of the world process, this hope is vain and foolish from its very nature. The world process is the mind sure of itself and ever on the alert, that can never be got at from behind, but fronts breast-forward every quarter; for it consists in this that everything is an objective element *for* it, everything stands *before* it. But when the inherent goodness is for its enemy, then it finds itself in the struggle we have seen; so far, however, as it is *not* for its enemy, but subsists in itself, it is the passive instrument of gifts and capacities, material without reality. If represented as object, it would be a dormant consciousness, remaining in the background, no one knows where.

Virtue is thus overpowered by the world process, because the abstract unreal essence is in fact virtue's own purpose, and because its action as regards reality rests on distinctions that are solely a matter of words. Virtue wanted to consist in the fact of bringing about the realization of goodness through sacrificing individuality; but the aspect of reality is itself nothing else than the aspect of individuality. The good was meant to be what is implicit and inherent, and opposed to what *is;* but the implicit and inherent, taken in its real truth, is simply *being* itself. The implicitly inherent element is primarily the abstraction of essence as against actual reality: but the abstraction is just what is not true, but a distinction merely for consciousness; this means, however, it is itself what is called actual, for the actual is what essentially is for an other—or it is being. But the consciousness of virtue rests on this distinction of implicitness and explicit being, a distinction without any true validity.

The world process was supposed to be the perversion of the good, because it took individuality for its principle. But this latter is the principle of actual reality, for it is just that mode of consciousness by which what is implicit and inherent is for an other as well. The world process transmutes and perverts the unchangeable, but does so in fact by transforming it out of the nothingness of abstraction into the being of reality.

The course of the world is, then, victorious over what, in

opposition to it, constitutes virtue; it is victorious over that which took an unreal abstraction to be the essential reality. But it is not victorious over something real, but over the production of distinctions that are no distinctions, over this pompous talk about the best for mankind and the oppression of humanity, about sacrifice for goodness' sake and the misuse of gifts. Imaginary idealities and purposes of that sort fall on the ear as idle phrases, which exalt the heart and leave the reason a blank, which edify but build up nothing that endures: declamations whose only definite announcement is that the individual who professes to act for such noble ends and indulges in such fine phrases holds himself for a fine creature: a swollen enlargement which gives itself and others a mighty size of a head, but big from inflation with emptiness.

Virtue in the olden time had its secure and determinate significance, for it found the fullness of its content and its solid basis in the substantial life of the nation, and had for its purpose and end a concrete good that existed and lay at its hand: it was also for that reason not directed against actual reality as a general perversity, and not turned against a world process. The virtue above considered, however, is removed from that substantial life, and is outside it, a virtue with no essential being, a virtue merely in idea and in words, and one that is deprived of all that content.

The vacuousness of this rhetorical eloquence in conflict with the world's process would be at once discovered if it were to be stated what all its eloquent phrases amount to. They are therefore assumed to be familiar and well-understood. The request to say what, then, this "well-known" is would be either met by a new swell of phrases, or in reply there would be an appeal to the "heart" which "inwardly" tells what they mean —which is tantamount to an admission of inability to say what the meaning is.

The fatuousness of that style of eloquence seems, too, in a quasi-unconscious manner to have got the length of being an acknowledged certainty for the cultivated minds of our time, since all interest in the whole mass of those rhetorical spread-eagle phrases has disappeared—a loss of interest which is betrayed in the sheer wearisomeness they produce.

The result, then, arising from this opposition, consists in the fact that consciousness lets the idea of an inherent good, which yet has no actual reality, slip from it like a mere cloak. Consciousness has learned in the course of its struggle that the world's process is not so bad as it looked; for the reality of the world's process is that of the universal. With the discovery of this it is seen that there is no way of producing the good through the sacrifice of individuality, the means for doing so have gone; for individuality is precisely the explicit actualization of what is implicitly and inherently real (i.e. the universal); and the perversion ceases to be looked at as a perversion of goodness, for it is just the transmuting of the good, *qua* bare purpose, into actual reality. The movement of individuality is the reality of the universal.

In point of fact, however, what as world process stood opposed to the consciousness of the inherently and implicitly real, has likewise been vanquished and has disappeared with the attainment of the above result. The self-existence of individuality was there in opposition to the inner essential nature, the universal, and made its appearance as a reality cut off from the inherent implicit nature. Since, however, it has come out that reality is in undivided unity with the universal, the self-existence of the world's process proves not to be more than an aspect, just as the inherent nature (*Ansich*) of virtue is merely an aspect too (*Ansicht*). The individuality of the world's process may doubtless think it acts merely for itself or selfishly; it is better than it thinks; its action is at the same time one that is universal and with an inherent being of its own. If it acts selfishly, it does not know what it is doing; and if it insists that all men act selfishly, it merely asserts that all men are unaware as to what action is. If it acts for itself, this is just the explicit bringing into reality of what is at first implicit and inherent. The purpose of its self-existence, of its "being for itself," which it fancies opposed to the inherent nature—its futile ingenuity and cunning, as also its fine-spun explanations which so knowingly demonstrate the existence of selfishness everywhere—all these have as much vanished as the purpose of the inherent element and its rhetoric.

Thus, then, the effort, the struggle, the activity of individuality is inherently an end in itself; the use of powers, the play of their outward manifestations—that is what gives them life:

otherwise they would be lifeless, potential, and merely implicit (*Ansich*). The inherent implicit nature is not an abstract universal without existence and never carried into effect; it is itself immediately this actual present and this living actuality of the process of individuality.

2. OBJECTIVE SPIRIT: THE ETHICAL ORDER

[g]Spirit, in its ultimate simple truth, is consciousness, and breaks asunder its moments from one another. An act divides spirit into spiritual substance on the one side, and consciousness of the substance on the other; and divides the substance as well as consciousness. The substance appears in the shape of a universal inner nature and purpose standing in contrast to itself *qua* individualized reality. The middle or mediating term, infinite in character, is self-consciousness, which, being *implicitly* the unity of itself and that substance, becomes so, now, explicitly (*für sich*), unites the universal inner nature and its particular realization, raises the latter to the former and acts *ethically:* and, on the other hand, brings the former down to the latter and carries out the purpose, the substance presented merely in thought. In this way it brings to light the unity of its self and the substance, and produces this unity in the form of its "work," and thus as actual concrete fact (*Wirklichkeit*).

When consciousness breaks up into these elements, the simple substance has in part acquired the attitude of opposition to self-consciousness; in part it thereby manifests in itself the very nature of consciousness, which consists in distinguishing its own content within itself—manifests it as a world articulated into its spheres. The substance is thus an ethical being split up into distinct elemental forms, a human and a divine law. In the same way, the self-consciousness appearing over against the substance assigns itself, in virtue of its inner nature, to one of these powers, and, *qua* involving knowledge, gets broken

[g] *Phenomenology*, pp. 462–63.

up into ignorance of what it is doing, on the one hand, and knowledge of this, on the other—a knowledge which for that reason proves a deception. It learns, therefore, through its own act, at once, the contradictory nature of those powers into which the inner substance divided itself, and their mutual overthrow, as well as the contradiction between its knowledge of the ethical character of its act and what is truly and essentially ethical, and so finds *its own* destruction. In point of fact, however, the ethical substance has by this process become actual concrete self-consciousness: in other words *this* particular self has become self-sufficient and self-dependent—(*Anund Fürsichseyenden*), but precisely thereby the ethical order has been overthrown and destroyed.

a. The Ethical World: Law Human and Divine: Man and Woman

[h]The simple substance of spirit, being consciousness, divides itself into parts. In other words, just as consciousness of abstract sensuous existence passes over into perception, so does immediate certainty of real ethical existence; and just as for sense-perception bare "being" becomes a "thing" with many properties, so for ethical perception a given act becomes a reality involving many ethical relations. For the former, again, the unnecessary plurality of properties concentrates itself into the form of an essential opposition between individual and universal; and still more for the latter, which is consciousness purified and substantial, the plurality of ethical moments is reduced to and assumes a twofold form, that of a law of individuality and a law of universality. Each of these areas or "masses" of the substance remains, however, spirit in its entirety. If in sense-perception "things" have no other substantial reality than the two determinations of individual and universal, these determinations express, in the present instance, merely the superficial opposition of both sides to one another.

Individuality, in the case of the subject (*Wesen*) we are here considering, has the significance of self-consciousness in

[h] *Phenomenology*, pp. 466–82.

general, not of any particular consciousness we care to take. The ethical substance is, thus, in this determination actual concrete substance, Absolute Spirit realized in the plurality of distinct consciousnesses definitely existing. It [this spirit] is the community (*Gemeinwesen*) which, as we entered the stage of the practical embodiment of reason in general, came before us as the absolute and ultimate reality, and which here comes objectively before itself in its true nature as a conscious ethical reality (*Wesen*), and as the essential reality for that mode of consciousness we are now dealing with. It is spirit which is *for itself*, since it maintains itself by being reflected in the minds of the component individuals; and which is *in itself* or substance, since it preserves them within itself. *Qua* actual substance, that spirit is a Nation (*Volk*); *qua* concrete consciousness, it is the Citizens of the nation. This consciousness has its essential being in simple spirit, and is certain of itself in the actual realization of this spirit, in the entire nation; it has its truth there directly, not therefore in something unreal, but in a spirit which exists and makes itself felt.

This spirit can be named Human Law, because it has its being essentially in the form of self-conscious actuality. In the form of universality, that spirit is the law known to everybody, familiar and recognized, and is the everyday Customary Convention (*Sitte*); in the form of particularity it is the concrete certainty of itself in any and every individual; and the certainty of itself as a single individuality is that spirit in the form of Government. Its true and complete nature is seen in its authoritative validity openly and unmistakably manifested, an existence which takes the form of unconstrained independent objective fact, and is immediately apprehended with conscious certainty in this form.

Over against this power and publicity of the ethical secular human order there appears, however, another power, the Divine Law. For the ethical power of the state, being the movement of self-conscious action, finds its opposition in the simple immediate essential being of the ethical order; *qua* actual concrete universality, it is a force exerted against the independence of the individual; and, *qua* actuality in general, it finds inherent in that essential being something other than the power of the state.

We mentioned before that each of the opposite ways in which the ethical substance exists contains that substance in its entirety, and contains all moments of its contents. If, then, the community is that substance in the form of self-consciously realized action, the other side has the form of immediate or directly existent substance. The latter is thus, on the one hand, the inner principle (*Begriff*) or universal possibility of the ethical order in general, but, on the other hand, contains within it also the moment of self-consciousness. This moment which expresses the ethical order in this element of immediacy or mere being, which, in other words, is an immediate consciousness of self (both as regards its essence and its particular this-ness) in an "other"—and hence, is a *natural* ethical community —this is the *Family*. The family, as the inner indwelling principle of sociality operating in an unconscious way, stands opposed to its own actuality when explicitly conscious; as the basis of the actuality of a nation, it stands in contrast to the nation itself; as the *immediate* ethical existence, it stands over against the ethical order which shapes and preserves itself by work for universal ends; the Penates of the family stand in contrast to the universal spirit.

Although the ethical existence of the family has the character of immediacy, it is within itself an *ethical* entity, but not so far as it is the natural relation of its component members, or so far as their connection is one immediately holding between individual concrete beings. For the *ethical* element is intrinsically universal and this relation established by nature is essentially just as much a spiritual fact, and is only ethical by being spiritual. Let us see wherein its peculiar ethical character consists.

In the first place, because the ethical element is the intrinsically universal element, the *ethical* relation between the members of the family is not that of sentiment or the relationship of love. The ethical element in this case seems bound to be placed in the relation of the individual member of the family to the *entire* family as the real substance, so that the purpose of his action and the content of his actuality are taken from this substance, are derived solely from the family life. But the conscious purpose which dominates the action of this whole, so far as that purpose concerns that whole, is itself the individual member. The procuring and maintaining of power and wealth turn, in part, merely on needs and wants, and are a matter that has to do with desire; in part, they become in their higher object something which is merely of mediate significance. This object does not fall within the family itself, but concerns what is truly universal, the community; it acts rather in a negative way on the family, and consists in setting the individual outside the family, in subduing his merely natural existence and his mere particularity and so drawing him on towards virtue, towards living in and for the universal. The positive purpose peculiar to the family is the individual as such. Now in order that this relationship may be ethical, neither the individual who does an act nor he to whom the act refers must show any trace of contingency such as obtains in rendering some particular help or service. The content of the ethical act must be substantial in character, or must be entire and universal; hence it can only stand in relation to the entire individual, to the individual *qua* universal. And this, again, must not be taken as if it were merely in idea that an act of service furthered his entire happiness, whereas the service, taken as an immediate or concrete act, only does something particular in regard to him. Nor must we think that the ethical act, like a process of education, really takes him as its object, and, dealing with him as a whole, in a series of efforts, produces him as a kind of work; for there, apart from the purpose, which operates in a negative way on the family, the real act has merely a limited content. Finally, just as little should we take it that the service rendered is a help in time of need, by which in truth the entire individual is saved; for such help is itself an entirely casual act, the occasion of which is an ordinary actuality which can as well be as not be. The act, then, which embraces the entire existence of the blood relation does not concern the citizen, for he does not belong to the family, nor does it deal with one who is going to be a citizen and so will cease to have the significance of a mere particular individual: it has as its object and content this specific individual belonging to the family, takes him as a universal being, divested of his sensuous, or particular reality. The act no longer concerns the living but the dead, one who has passed through the long sequence of his broken and diversified existence and gathered up his being into its one completed embodiment, who has lifted himself out of the unrest of a life of chance and change into the peace of simple universality. Because it is only as citizen that he is real and substantial, the individual, when not a citizen, and belonging to the family, is merely unreal insubstantial shadow.

This condition of universality, which the individual *as such* reaches, is mere being, death; it is the immediate issue of the process of nature, and is not the action of a conscious mind. The duty of the member of a family is on that account to attach this aspect too, in order that this last phase of being also (this universal being), may not belong to nature alone, and remain something irrational, but may be something actually *done*, and the right of consciousness be asserted in it. Or rather the significance of the act is that, because in truth the peace and universality of a self-conscious being does not belong to nature, the apparent claim which nature has made to act in this way may be given up and the truth reinstated.

What nature did in the individual's case concerns the aspect in which his process of becoming universal is manifested as the movement of an existent. It takes effect no doubt within the ethical community, and has this in view as its purpose: death is the fulfilment and highest task which the individual as such undertakes on its behalf. But so far as he is essentially a particular individual, it is an accident that his death was connected directly with his labour for the universal whole, and was the outcome of his toil; partly because, if it was so, it is the *natural* course of the negativity of the individual *qua* existent, in which consciousness does not return into itself and become self-conscious; or, again, because, since the process of the existent consists in becoming cancelled and transcended and attaining the stage of independent self-existence, death is the aspect of diremption, where the self-existence, which is obtained, is something other than that being which entered on the process.

Because the ethical order is spirit in its immediate truth, those aspects into which its conscious life breaks up fall also into this form of immediacy; and the individual's particularity passes over into this abstract negativity, which, being in itself without consolation or reconcilement, must receive them essentially through a concrete and external act.

Blood-relationship therefore supplements the abstract natural process by adding to it the process of consciousness, by interrupting the work of nature, and rescuing the blood-relation from destruction; or better, because destruction, the passing into mere being, is necessary, it takes upon itself the act of destruction.

Through this it comes about that the universal being, the sphere of death, is also something which has returned into itself, something self-existent; the powerless bare particular unity is raised to universal individuality. The dead individual, by his having detached and liberated his being from his action or his negative unity, is an empty particular, merely existing passively for some other, at the mercy of every lower irrational organic agency, and the [chemical, physical] forces of abstract material elements, both of which are now stronger than himself, the former on account of the life which they have, the latter on account of their negative nature.[3] The family keeps away from the dead this dishonouring of him by the desires of unconscious organic agencies and by abstract elements, puts its own action in place of theirs, and weds the relative to the bosom of the earth, the elemental individuality that passes not away. Thereby the family makes the dead a member of a community[4] which prevails over and holds under control the powers of the particular material elements and the lower living creatures, which sought to have their way with the dead and destroy him.

This last duty thus accomplishes the complete divine law, or constitutes the positive ethical act towards the given individual. Every other relation towards him which does not remain at the level of love, but is ethical, belongs to human law, and has the negative significance of lifting the individual above the confinement within the natural community to which he belongs as a concrete individual. But, now, though human right has for its content and power the actual ethical substance consciously aware of itself, the entire nation, while divine right and law derive theirs from the particular individual who is

[3] The description here refers to the process of bodily corruption.
[4] I.e., the earth?

beyond the actual, yet he is still not without power. His power lies in the abstract pure universal, the elemental individual, which seizes upon the individuality that cuts itself loose from the element and constitutes the self-conscious reality of the nation, and draws it back into the pure abstraction which is its essential nature: draws it back just as that essence is its ultimate ground and source. How this power is made explicit in the nation itself will come out more fully as we proceed.

Now in the one law as in the other there are differences and stages. For since these laws involve the element of consciousness in both cases, distinction is developed within themselves: and this is just what constitutes the peculiar process of their life. The consideration of these differences brings out the way they operate, and the kind of self-consciousness at work in both the universal essential principles (*Wesen*) of the ethical world, as also their connection and transition into one another.

The community, the upper law whose validity is open to the light of day, has its concrete vitality in government; for in government it is an individual whole. Government is concrete actual spirit reflected into itself, the self pure and simple of the entire ethical substance. This simple force allows, indeed, the community to unfold and expand into its component members, and to give each part subsistence and self-existence of its own (*Fürsichseyn*). Spirit finds in this way its realization or its objective existence, and the family is the medium in which this realization takes effect. But spirit is at the same time the force of the whole, combining these parts again within the unity which negates them, giving them the feeling of their want of independence, and keeping them aware that their life only lies in the whole. The community may thus, on the one hand, organize itself into the systems of property and of personal independence, of personal right and right in things; and, on the other hand, articulate the various ways of working for what in the first instance are particular ends— those of gain and enjoyment—into their own special guilds and associations, and may thus make them independent. The spirit of universal assemblage and association is the single and simple principle, and the negative essential factor at work in the segregation and isolation of these systems. In order not to let them get rooted and settled in this isolation and thus break up the whole into fragments and let the common spirit evaporate, government has from time to time to shake them to the very centre by War. By this means it confounds the order that has been established and arranged, and violates their right to independence, while the individuals (who, being absorbed therein, get adrift from the whole, striving after inviolable self-existence [*Fürsichseyn*] and personal security), are made, by the task thus imposed on them by government, to feel the power of their lord and master, death. By thus breaking up the form of fixed stability, spirit guards the ethical order from sinking into merely natural existence, preserves the self of which it is conscious, and raises that self to the level of freedom and its own powers. The negative essential being shows itself to be the might proper of the community and the force it has for self-maintenance. The community therefore finds the true principle and corroboration of its power in the inner nature of divine law, and in the kingdom of the nether world.

The divine law which holds sway in the family has also on its side distinctions within itself, the relations among which make up the living process of its realization. Amongst the three relationships, however, of husband and wife, parents and children, brothers and sisters, the relationship of husband and wife is to begin with the primary and immediate form in which one consciousness recognizes itself in another, and in which each knows that reciprocal recognition. Being natural self-knowledge, knowledge of self on the basis of nature and not on that of ethical life, it merely represents and typifies in a figure the life of spirit, and is not spirit itself actually realized. Figurative representation, however, has its reality in an other than it is. This relationship, therefore, finds itself realized not in itself as such, but in the child—an other, in whose coming into being that relationship consists, and with which it passes away. And this change from one generation onwards to another is permanent in and as the life of a nation.

The reverent devotion (*Pietät*) of husband and wife towards one another is thus mixed up with a natural relation and with feeling, and their relationship is not inherently self-complete; similarly, too, the second relationship, the reverent devotion of parents and children to one another. The devotion of parents towards their children is affected with emotion just by their being consciously realized in what is external to themselves (viz. the children), and by their seeing them become something on their own account without this returning to the parents; independent existence on the part of the children remains a foreign reality, a reality all their own. The devotion of children, again, towards their parents is conversely affected by their coming into being from, or having their essential nature in, what is external to themselves (viz., the parents) and passes away; and by their attaining independent existence and a self-consciousness of their own solely through separation from the source whence they came—a separation in which the spring gets exhausted.

Both these relationships are constituted by and hold within the transience and the dissimilarity of the two sides, which are assigned to them.

An unmixed intransitive form of relationship, however, holds between brother and sister. They are the same blood, which, however, in them has entered into a condition of stable equilibrium. They therefore stand in no such natural relation as husband and wife, they do not desire one another; nor have they given to one another, nor received from one another, this independence of individual being; they are free individualities with respect to each other. The feminine element, therefore, in the form of the sister, premonizes and foreshadows most completely the nature of ethical life (*sittliches Wesen*). She does not become conscious of it, and does not actualize it, because the law of the family is her inherent implicit inward nature, which does not lie open to the daylight of consciousness, but remains inner feeling and the divine element exempt from actuality. The feminine life is attached to these household divinities (*Penates*), and sees in them both her universal substance, and her particular individuality, yet so views them that this relation of her individuality to them is at the same time not the natural one of pleasure.

As a daughter, the woman must now see her parents pass away with natural emotion and yet with ethical resignation, for it is only at the cost of this condition that she can come to that individual existence of which she is capable. She thus cannot see her independent existence positively attained in her relation to her parents. The relationships of mother and wife, however, are individualized partly in the form of something natural, which brings pleasure; partly in the form of something negative, which finds simply its own evanescence in those relationships; partly again the individualization is just on that account something contingent which can be replaced by an other particular individuality. In a household of the ethical kind, a woman's relationships are not based on a reference to this particular husband, this particular child, but to *a* husband, to children *in general*,—not to feeling, but to the universal. The distinction between her ethical life (*Sittlichkeit*) (while it determines her particular existence and brings her pleasure) and that of her husband consists just in this, that it has always a directly universal significance for her, and is quite alien to the impulsive condition of mere particular desire. On the other hand, in the husband these two aspects get separated; and since he possesses, as a citizen, the self-conscious power belonging to the universal life, the life of the social whole, he acquires thereby the rights of desire, and keeps himself at the same time in detachment from it. So far, then, as particularity is implicated in this relationship in the case of the wife, her ethical life is not purely ethical; so far, however, as it is ethical, the particularity is a matter of indifference, and the wife is without the moment of knowing herself as *this* particular self in and through an other.

The brother, however, is in the eyes of the sister a being whose nature is unperturbed by desire and is ethically like her own; her recognition in him is pure and unmixed with any sexual relation. The indifference characteristic of particular existence and the ethical contingency thence arising are, therefore, not present in this relationship; instead, the moment of individual self-hood, recognizing and being recognized, can here assert its right, because it is bound up with the balance and equilibrium resulting from their being of the same blood, and from their being related in a way that involves no mutual desire. The loss of a brother is thus irreparable to the sister, and her duty towards him is the highest.[5]

This relationship at the same time is the limit at which the circumscribed life of the family is broken up and passes be-

[5] Cp. "Antigone," l. 910.

yond itself. The brother is the member of the family in whom its spirit becomes individualized, and enabled thereby to turn towards another sphere, towards what is other than and external to itself, and pass over into consciousness of universality. The brother leaves this immediate, rudimentary, and, therefore, strictly speaking, negative ethical life of the family, in order to acquire and produce the concrete ethical order which is conscious of itself.

He passes from the divine law, within whose realm he lived, over to the human law. The sister, however, becomes, or the wife remains, director of the home and the preserver of the divine law. In this way both the sexes overcome their merely natural being, and become ethically significant, as diverse forms dividing between them the different aspects which the ethical substance assumes. Both these universal factors of the ethical world have their specific individuality in naturally distinct self-consciousnesses, for the reason that the spirit at work in the ethical order is the immediate unity of the substance [of ethical life] with self-consciousness—an immediacy which thus appears as the existence of a natural difference, at once as regards its aspect of reality and of difference. It is that aspect which, in the notion of spiritual reality, came to light as "original determinate nature," when we were dealing with the stage of "Individuality which is real to itself." This moment loses the indeterminateness which it still has there, and the contingent diversity of "constitution" and "capacities." It is now the specific opposition of the two sexes, whose natural character acquires at the same time the significance of their respective ethical determinations.

The distinction of the sexes and of their ethical content remains all the same within the unity of the ethical substance, and its process is just the constant development of that substance. The husband is sent forth by the spirit of the family into the life of the community, and finds there his self-conscious reality. Just as the family thereby finds in the community its universal substance and subsistence, conversely the community finds in the family the formal element of its own realization, and in the divine law its power and confirmation. Neither of the two is alone self-complete. Human law as a living and active principle proceeds from the divine, the law holding on earth from that of the nether world, the conscious from the unconscious, mediation from immediacy; and returns too whence it came. The power of the nether world, on the other hand, finds its realization upon earth; it comes through consciousness to have existence and efficacy.

The universal elements of the ethical life are thus the (ethical) substance *qua* universal, and that substance *qua* particular consciousness. Their universal actuality is the nation and the family; while they get their natural self, and their operative individuality, in man and woman. Here in this content of the ethical world we see attained those purposes which the previous insubstantial modes of conscious life set before them. What Reason apprehended only as an object has become Self-consciousness, and what self-consciousness merely contained within it is here explicit true reality. What Observation knew —an object given externally and picked up, and one in the constitution of which the subject knowing had no share—is here a given ethical condition, a custom found lying ready at hand, but a reality which is at the same time the deed and product of the subject finding it. The individual who seeks the "pleasure" of enjoying his particular individuality finds it in the family life, and the "necessity" in which that pleasure passes away is his own self-consciousness as a citizen of his nation. Or, again, it is knowing the "law of his own heart" as the law of all hearts, knowing the consciousness of self to be the recognized and universal ordinance of society: it is "virtue," which enjoys the fruits of its own sacrifice, which brings about what it sets out to do, viz. to bring the essential nature into the light of the actual present,—and its enjoyment is this universal life. Finally, consciousness of "fact as such" (*der Sache selbst*) gets satisfaction in the real substance, which contains and maintains in positive form the abstract aspects of that empty category. That substance finds a genuine content in the powers of the ethical order, a content that takes the place of those insubstantial commands which the "healthy human reason" wanted to give and to know: and in consequence thus gets a concrete inherently determinate standard for "testing," not the laws, but what is done.

The whole is a stable equilibrium of all the parts, and each part a spirit in its native element, a spirit which does not seek

its satisfaction beyond itself, but has the satisfaction within itself for the reason that itself is in this balanced equipoise with
the whole. This condition of stable equilibrium can, doubtless,
only be living by inequality arising within it, and being
brought back again to equipoise by Righteousness and Justice.
Justice, however, is neither an alien principle (*Wesen*) holding somewhere remote from the present, nor the realization
(unworthy of the name of justice) of mutual malice, treachery, ingratitude, etc., which, in the unintelligent way of chance
and accident, would fulfil the law by a kind of irrational connection without any controlling idea, action by commission
and omission, without any consciousness of what was involved.
On the contrary, being justice in human law, it brings back to
the whole, to the universal life of society, what has broken
away separately from the harmony and equilibrium of the
whole:—the independent classes and individuals. In this way
justice is the government of the nation, and is its all-pervading
essential life in a consciously present individual form, and is
the personal self-conscious will of all.

That justice, however, which restores to equilibrium the universal when getting the mastery over the particular individual,
is similarly the simple single spirit of the individual who has
suffered wrong; it is not broken up into the two elements, one
who has suffered wrong and a far-away remote reality (*Wesen*). The individual himself is the power of the "nether"
world, and that reality is *his* "fury," wreaking vengeance upon
him.[6] For his individuality, his blood still lives in the house,
his substance has a lasting actuality. The wrong, which can be
brought upon the individual in the realm of the ethical world,
consists merely in this, that a bare something by chance happens to him. The power which perpetrates on the conscious
individual this wrong of making him into a mere thing is "nature"; it is the universality not of the community, but the
abstract universality of mere existence. And the particular individual, in wiping out the wrong suffered, turns not against
the community—for he has not suffered at its hands—but
against the latter. As we saw,[7] the consciousness of those who
share the blood of the individual removes this wrong in such a

[6] The reference here is to Orestes.
[7] P. 264 above.

way that what has happened becomes rather a work of their own doing, and hence bare existence, the last state, gets also to be something willed, and thus an object of gratification.

The ethical realm remains in this way permanently a world without blot or stain, a world untainted by any internal dissension. So, too, its process is an untroubled transition from one of its powers to the other, in such a way that each preserves and produces the other. We see it no doubt divided into two ultimate elements and their realization: but their opposition is rather the confirming and substantiation of one through the other; and where they directly come in contact with each other as actual factors, their mediating common element is the immediate permeation of the one with the other. The one extreme, universal spirit conscious of itself, becomes, through the individuality of man, linked together with its other extreme, its force and its element, with *unconscious* spirit. On the other hand, divine law is individualized, the unconscious spirit of the particular individual finds its existence in woman, through the mediation of whom the unconscious spirit comes out of its unrealizedness into actuality, and rises out of the state of unknowing and unknown, into the conscious realm of universal spirit. The union of man with woman constitutes the operative mediating agency for the whole, and constitutes the element which, while separated into the extremes of divine and human law, is, at the same time, their immediate union. This union, again, turns both those first mediate connections (*Schlusse*) into one and the same synthesis, and unites into one process the twofold movement in opposite directions—one from reality to unreality, the downward movement of human law, organized into independent members, to the danger and trial of death,—the other, from unreality to reality, the upward movement of the law of the nether world to the daylight of conscious existence. Of these movements the former falls to man, the latter to woman.

b. Ethical Action. Knowledge, Human and Divine. Guilt and Destiny

[1]In the form presented by the opposition of elements in the realm just dealt with, self-consciousness has not yet come to its rights as a single individuality. Individuality there has, on one side, the sense of merely universal will, on the other, of consanguinity of the family. *This* particular individual has merely the significance of shadowy unreality. There is as yet no performance of an act. The act, however, is the realized self. It breaks in upon the untroubled stable organization and movement of the ethical world. What there appears as ordinance and harmony between both its constituent elements, each of which confirms and complements the other, becomes through the performing of an act a transition of opposites into one another, by which each proves to be the annihilation rather than the confirmation of its self and its opposite. It becomes the process of negation or destruction, the eternal necessity of awful destiny, which engulfs in the abyss of its bare identity divine and human law alike, as well as both the self-conscious factors in which these powers subsist; and, to our view, passes over into the absolute self-existence of mere single self-consciousness.

The basis from which this movement proceeds, and on which it takes effect, is the kingdom of the ethical order. But the activity at work in this process is self-consciousness. Being ethical consciousness, it is the pure and simple direction of activity towards the essential principle of the ethical life—it is *Duty*. There is no caprice, and likewise no struggle, no indecision in it, since it has given up legislating and testing laws: the essential ethical principle is, for it, something immediate, unwavering, without contradiction. There is therefore neither the painful spectacle of finding itself in a collision between passion and duty, nor the comic spectacle of a collision between duty and duty—a collision, which so far as content goes is the same as that between passion and duty; for passion can

[1] *Phenomenology*, pp. 484–99.

also be presented as a duty, because duty, when consciousness withdraws into itself and leaves its immediate essential substance (*Wesenheit*), comes to be the formal universal, into which one content fits equally well with another, as we found before. The collision of duties is, however, comical, because it brings out the contradiction inherent in the idea of an absolute standing opposed to another absolute, expresses something absolute and then directly the annihilation of this so-called absolute or duty. The ethical consciousness, however, knows what it has to do; and is decided, whether it is to belong to divine or human law. This directness which characterizes its decision is something immanent and inherent (*Ansichseyn*), and hence has at the same time the significance of a natural condition of being, as we saw. Nature, not the accident of circumstances or choice, assigns one sex to one law, the other to the other law; or conversely both the ethical powers themselves establish their individual existence and actualization in the two sexes.

Thus, then, because on the one side the ethical order consists essentially in this immediate directness of decision, and therefore only the one law is *for consciousness* the essential reality; while, on the other side, the powers of the ethical order are actual in the self of conscious life—in this way these forces acquire the significance of excluding one another and of being opposed to one another. They are explicit in self-consciousness just as they were merely implicit in the realm of the ethical order. The ethical consciousness, because it is decisively on the side of one of them, is essentially *Character*. There is not for it equal essentiality in both. The opposition therefore appears as an unfortunate collision of duty merely with reality, on which right has no hold. The ethical consciousness is *qua* self-consciousness in this opposition, and being so, it at once proceeds either to subdue by force this reality opposed to the law which it accepts, or to get round this reality by craft. Since it sees right only on its own side, and wrong on the other, so, of these two, that which belongs to divine law detects, on the other side, mere arbitrary fortuitous human violence, while what appertains to human law finds in the other the obstinacy and disobedience of subjective self-sufficiency. For the commands of government have a universal sense and meaning open to the light of day; the will of the other law, however, is the inner concealed meaning of the realm of darkness (*unterirdisch*), a meaning which appears expressed as the will of a particular being, and in contradicting the first is malicious offence.

There arises in this way in consciousness the opposition between what is known and what is not known, just as, in the case of substance, there was an opposition between the conscious and the unconscious; and the absolute right of ethical self-consciousness comes into conflict with the divine right of the essential reality. Self-consciousness, *qua* consciousness, takes the objective actuality, as such, to have essential being. Looking at its substance, however, it is the unity of itself and this opposite, and the ethical self-consciousness is consciousness of that substance: the object, *qua* opposed to self-consciousness, has, therefore, entirely lost the characteristic of having essential being by itself. Just as the spheres [of conscious life] where the object is merely a "thing" are long past and gone, so, too, are these spheres, where consciousness sets up and establishes something from out itself, and turns a particular moment into the essential reality (*Wesen*). Against such one-sidedness actual concrete reality has a power of its own; it takes the side of truth against consciousness and shows consciousness itself what the truth is. The ethical consciousness, however, has drunk from the cup of the absolute substance, forgotten all the one-sidedness of isolating self-existence, all its purposes and peculiar notions, and has, therefore, at the same time drowned in this Stygian stream all essentiality of nature and all the independence claimed by the objective reality. Its absolute right, therefore, when it acts in accordance with ethical law, is to find in this actualization nothing else than the fulfilment and performance of this law itself: and that the deed should manifest nothing but ethical action.

The ethical, being absolute essence and absolute power at once, cannot endure any perversion of its content. If it were merely absolute essence without power, it might undergo perversion at the hands of individuality. But this latter, being ethical consciousness, has renounced all perverting when it gave up its one-sided subjectivity (*Fürsichseyn*). Conversely, again, mere power might be perverted by the essential reality, if power were still a subjectivity of that kind. On account of this unity, individuality is a pure form of the substance which is the content, and action consists in transition from thought over into reality, merely as the process of an unreal opposition, whose moments have no special and particular content distinct from one another, and no essential nature of their own. The absolute right of ethical consciousness is, therefore, that the deed, the mode and form of its realization, should be nothing else than it *knows*.

But the essential ethical reality has split asunder into two laws, and consciousness, taking up an undivided single attitude towards law, is assigned only to one. Just as this simple consciousness takes its stand on the absolute right that the essential reality has appeared to it *qua* ethical as that reality inherently is, so, too, this essence insists on the right belonging to its reality, i.e., the right of having a double form.[8] This right of the essential reality does not, however, at the same time stand over against and opposed to self-consciousness, as if it were to be found anywhere else; rather it is the essential nature of self-consciousness. Only there has it its existence and its power; and its opposition is the act of self-consciousness itself. For the latter, just in that it is a self to itself, and proceeds to act, lifts itself out of the state of simple immediacy, and itself sets up the division into two. By the act it gives up the specific character of the ethical life, that of being pure and simple certainty of immediate truth, and sets up the division of itself into self as active and reality over against it, and for it, therefore, negative. By the act it thus becomes *Guilt*. For the deed is its doing, and doing is its inmost nature. And the guilt acquires also the meaning of Crime; for as simple ethical consciousness it has turned to and conformed itself to the one law, but turned away from the other and thus violates the latter by its deed.

Guilt is not an external indifferent entity (*Wesen*) with the double meaning, that the deed, as actually manifested to the light of day, may be an action of the guilty self, or may not be so, as if with the doing of it there could be connected something external and accidental that did not belong to it, from

[8] Viz., divine and human law.

which point of view, therefore, the action would be innocent. Rather the act is itself this diremption, this affirming itself for itself, and establishing over against this an alien external reality. That such a reality exists is due to the deed itself, and is the outcome of it. Hence, innocence is an attribute merely of the want of action (*Nicht-thun*), a state like the mere being of a stone, and one which is not even true of a child.

Looking at the content, however, the ethical act contains the element of wrongdoing, because it does not cancel and transcend the natural allotment of the two laws to the two sexes; but rather, being an undivided attitude towards the law, keeps within the sphere of natural immediacy, and, *qua* acting, turns this one-sidedness into guilt, by merely laying hold of one side of the essential reality and taking up a negative relation towards the other, i.e. violating it. Where, in the general ethical life, guilt and crime, deeds and actions, come in, will be more definitely brought out later. Meantime, so much is at once clear, that it is not *this* particular individual who acts and becomes guilty. For he, *qua* this particular self, is merely a shadowy unreality; he *is* merely *qua* universal self, and individuality is purely the formal aspect of doing anything at all, while its content is the laws and customs, which, for the individual, are, specifically, the laws and customs of his class or station. He is the substance *qua* genus, which by its determinateness becomes, no doubt, a species, but the specific form remains at the same time the generic universal. Self-consciousness within the life of a nation descends from the universal only down as far as specific particularity, but not as far as the single individuality, which sets up an exclusive self, establishes in its action a reality negative to itself. On the contrary, the action of that self-consciousness rests on secure confidence in the whole, into which there enters nothing alien or foreign, neither fear nor hostility.

Ethical self-consciousness now comes to find in its deed the full explicit meaning of concrete real action as much when it followed divine law as when it followed human. The law manifest to it is, in the essential reality, bound up with its opposite; the essential reality is the unity of both; but the deed has merely carried out one as against the other. But being bound up with this other in the inner reality, the fulfilment of the one calls forth the other, in the shape of something which, having been violated and now become hostile, demands revenge—an attitude which the deed has made it take up. In the case of action, only one phase of the decision is in general in evidence. The decision, however, is inherently something negative, which plants an "other" in opposition to it, something foreign to the decision, which is clear knowledge. Actual reality, therefore, keeps concealed within itself this other aspect alien to clear knowledge, and does not show itself to consciousness as it fully and truly is (*an und für sich*). In the story of Oedipus the son does not see his own father in the person of the man who has insulted him and whom he strikes to death, nor his mother in the queen whom he makes his wife. In this way a hidden power shunning the light of day, waylays the ethical self-consciousness, a power which bursts forth only after the deed is done, and seizes the doer in the act. For the completed deed is the removal of the opposition between the knowing self and the reality over against it. The ethical consciousness cannot disclaim the crime and its guilt. The deed consists in setting in motion what was unmoved, and in bringing out what in the first instance lay shut up as a mere possibility, and thereby linking on the unconscious to the conscious, the non-existent to the existent. In this truth, therefore, the deed comes to the light;—it is something in which a conscious element is bound up with what is unconscious, what is peculiarly one's own with what is alien and external:—it is an essential reality divided in sunder, whose other aspect consciousness experiences and also finds to be its own aspect, but as a power violated by its doing, and roused to hostility against it.

It may well be that the right, which kept itself in reserve, is not in its peculiar form present to the consciousness of the doer, but is merely implicit, present in the subjective inward guilt of the decision and the action. But the ethical consciousness is more complete, its guilt purer, if it knows beforehand the law and the power which it opposes, if it takes them to be sheer violence and wrong, to be a contingency in the ethical life, and wittingly, like Antigone, commits the crime. The deed when accomplished transforms its point of view; the very performance of it *eo ipso* expresses that what is ethical has to be actual; for the realization of the purpose is the very purpose of acting. Acting expresses precisely the unity of reality and the substance; it expresses the fact that actuality is not an accident for the essential element, but that, in union with that element, it is given to no right which is not true right. On account of this actuality and on account of its deed ethical consciousness must acknowledge its opposite as its own actuality; it must acknowledge its guilt.

Because of our sufferings we acknowledge we have erred.[9]

To acknowledge this is expressly to indicate that the severance between ethical purpose and actuality has been done away; it means the return to the ethical frame of mind, which knows that nothing counts but right. Thereby, however, the agent surrenders his character and the reality of his self, and has utterly collapsed. His being lies in belonging to his ethical law, as his substance; in acknowledging the opposite law, however, he has ceased to find his substance in this law; and instead of reality this has become an unreality, a mere *sentiment*, a frame of mind. The substance no doubt appears as the "pathic" element[10] in the individuality, and the individuality appears as the factor which animates the substance, and hence stands above it. But the substance is a "pathic" element which is at the same time his character; the ethical individuality is directly and inherently one with this its universal, exists in it alone, and is incapable of surviving the destruction which this ethical power suffers at the hands of its opposite.

This individuality, however, has all the same the certainty that that individuality, whose "pathic" element is this opposite power [the opposed law], suffers no more harm than it has inflicted. The opposition of the ethical powers to one another, and the process of the individualities setting up these powers in life and action, have reached their true end only in so far as both sides undergo the same destruction. For neither of the powers has any advantage over the other that it should be a more essential moment of the substance common to both. The

[9] An adaptation from "Antigone," 926.
[10] The element that so permeates his being as to constitute his controlling necessity and destiny.

fact of their being equally and to the same degree essential, and subsisting independently beside each other, means their having no separate self; in the act they have a self-nature, but a different self,—which contradicts the unity of the self and cancels their claim to independent right, and thus brings about their necessary destruction. Character too, in part, looking at its "pathic" element, the substance, belongs to one alone; in part, when we look at the aspect of knowledge, the one character like the other is divided into a conscious element and an unconscious: and since each itself calls forth this opposition, and the want of knowledge is by the act also its doing, each falls into the guilt which consumes it. The victory of one power and its character, and the defeat of the other side, would thus be merely the part and the incomplete work, which steadily advances till the equilibrium between the two is attained. It is in the equal subjection of both sides that absolute right is first accomplished, and the ethical substance, as the negative force devouring both sides, in other words omnipotent and righteous Destiny, makes its appearance.

If both powers are taken according to their specific content and its individualization, we have the scene presented of a contest between them as individuated. On its formal side, this is the struggle of the ethical order and of self-consciousness with unconscious nature and a contingency due to this nature. The latter has a right as against the former, because this is only objective spirit, merely in immediate unity with its substance. On the side of content, the struggle is the rupture of divine and human law. The youth goes forth from the unconscious life of the family and becomes the individuality of the community [i.e. Ruler]. But that he still shares the natural life from which he has torn himself away is seen in the fact that he emerges therefrom only to find his claim affected by the contingency that there are *two* brothers[11] who with equal right take possession of the community;[12] the inequality due to the one having been born earlier and the other later, an inequality which is a natural difference, has no importance for them when they enter the ethical life of society. But government, as the single soul, the self of the national spirit, does

[11] Eteocles and Polynices: *v.* "Oedipus at Colonus."
[12] Viz., the throne of their Father Oedipus.

not admit of a duality of individuality; and in contrast to the ethical necessity of this unity, nature appears as by accident providing more than one. These two [brothers], therefore, become disunited; and their equal right in regard to the power of the state is destructive to both, for they are equally wrong. Humanly considered, he has committed the crime who, not being in actual possession, attacks the community, at the head of which the other stood. While again he has right on his side who knew how to seize the other merely *qua* particular individual, detached from the community, and who banished him, while thus powerless, out of the community; he has merely laid hands on the individual as such, not the community, not the essential nature of human right. The community, attacked and defended from a point of view which is merely particular, maintains itself; and both brothers find their destruction reciprocally through one another. For individuality, which involves peril to the whole in the maintenance of its own self-existence (*Fürsichseyn*), has thrust its own self out of the community, and is disintegrated in its own nature. The community, however, will do honour to the one who is found on its side; the government, the re-established singleness of the self of the community, will punish by depriving of the last honour him who already proclaimed its devastation on the walls of the city. He who came to affront the highest spiritual form of conscious life, the spirit of the community, must be stripped of the honour of his entire and complete nature, the honour due to the spirit of the departed.[13]

But if the universal thus lightly knocks off the highest point of its pyramid, and doubtless triumphs victoriously over the family, the rebellious principle of individuation, it has thereby merely put itself into conflict with divine law, the self-conscious with the unconscious spirit. For the latter, this unconscious spirit, is the other essential power, and therefore the power undestroyed, and only insulted by the former. It finds, however, only a bloodless shade to lend it help towards actually carrying itself out in the face of that masterful and openly enunciated law. Being the law of weakness and of darkness, it therefore gives way, to begin with, before law which

[13] V. "Antigone."

has force and publicity; for the strength of the former is effective in the nether realm, not on earth and in the light of day. But the actual and concrete, which has taken away from what is inward its honour and its power, has thereby consumed its own real nature. The spirit which is manifest to the light of day has the roots of its power in the lower world: the certainty felt by a nation, a certainty which is sure of itself and which makes itself assured, finds the truth of its oath binding all its members into one, solely in the mute unconscious substance of all, in the waters of forgetfulness. In consequence, the fulfilment of the public spirit turns round into its opposite, and learns that its supreme right is supreme wrong, its victory rather its own defeat. The slain, whose right is injured, knows, therefore, how to find means of vengeance which are equally as real and strong as the power at whose hands it has suffered. These powers are other communities,[14] whose altars the dogs or birds defiled with the corpse of the dead, which is not raised into unconscious universality by being restored, as is its due, to the ultimate individuum, the elemental earth, but instead has remained above ground in the sphere of reality, and has now received, as the force of divine law, a self-conscious actual universality. They rise up in hostility, and destroy the community which has dishonoured and destroyed its own power, the sacred claims, the "piety" of the family.

Represented in this way, the movement of human and divine law finds the expression of its necessity in individuals, in whom the universal appears as a "pathic" element, and the activity of the movement as action of individuals, which gives the appearance of contingency to the necessity of the process. But individuality and action constitute the principle of individuation in general, a principle which in its pure universality was called inner divine law. As a moment of the visible community it does not merely exhibit that unconscious activity of the nether world, its operation is not simply external in its existence; it has an equally manifest visible existence and process, actual in the actual nation. Taken in this form, what was represented as a simple process of the "pathic" element as embodied in individuals, assumes another look, and crime and

[14] Refers to the attack of Argos against Thebes: *v.* "Antigone."

the resulting ruin of the community assume the proper form of their existence.

Human law, then, in its universal mode of existence is the community, in its efficient operation in general is the manhood of the community, in its actual efficient operation is the government. It has its being, its process, and its subsistence by consuming and absorbing into itself the separatist action of the household gods (*Penates*), the individualization into insular independent families which are under the management of womankind, and by keeping them dissolved in the fluent continuum of its own nature. The family at the same time, however, is in general its element, the individual consciousness its universal operative basis. Since the community gets itself subsistence only by breaking in upon family happiness, and dissolving [individual] self-consciousness into the universal, it creates its enemy for itself within its own gates, creates it in what it suppresses, and what is at the same time essential to it—womankind in general. Womankind—the everlasting irony in the life of the community—changes by intrigue the universal purpose of government into a private end, transforms its universal activity into a work of this or that specific individual, and perverts the universal property of the state into a possession and ornament for the family. Woman in this way turns to ridicule the grave wisdom of maturity, which, being dead to all particular aims, to private pleasure, personal satisfaction, and actual activity as well, thinks of, and is concerned for, merely what is universal; she makes this wisdom the laughing-stock of raw and wanton youth, an object of derision and scorn, unworthy of their enthusiasm. She asserts that it is everywhere the force of youth that really counts; she upholds this as of primary significance; extols a son as one who is the lord and master of the mother who has borne him; a brother as one in whom the sister finds man on a level with herself; a youth as one through whom the daughter, freed from her dependence (on the family unity), acquires the satisfaction and the dignity of wifehood.

The community, however, can preserve itself only by suppressing this spirit of individualism; and because the latter is an essential element, the community likewise creates it as well, and creates it, too, by taking up the attitude of seeking to suppress it as a hostile principle. Nevertheless, since, by cutting itself off from the universal purpose, this hostile element is merely evil, and in itself of no account, it would be quite ineffective if the community itself did not recognize the force of youth, (manhood, which, while immature, still remains in the condition of particularity), as the force of the whole. For the community, the whole, is a nation, it is itself individuality, and really only is something for itself by other individualities being for *it*, by its excluding these from itself and knowing itself independent of them. The negative side of the community, suppressing the isolation of individuals within its own bounds, but originating activity directed beyond those bounds, finds the weapons of its warfare in individuals. War is the spirit and form in which the essential moment of ethical substance, the absolute freedom of ethical self-consciousness from all and every kind of existence, is manifestly confirmed and realized. While, on the one hand, war makes the particular spheres of property and personal independence, as well as the personality of the individual himself, feel the force of negation and destruction, on the other hand this engine of negation and destruction stands out as that which preserves the whole in security. The individual who provides pleasure to woman, the brave youth, the suppressed principle of ruin and destruction, comes now into prominence, and is the factor of primary significance and worth. It is now physical strength and what seems like the chance of fortune, that decide as to the existence of ethical life and spiritual necessity. Because the existence of the ethical life thus rests on physical strength and the chances of fortune, it is *eo ipso* settled that its overthrow has come. While only household gods, in the former case, gave way before and were absorbed in the national spirit, here the living individual embodiments of the national spirit fall by their own individuality and disappear in one universal community, whose bare universality is soulless and dead, and whose living activity is found in the particular individual *qua* particular. The ethical form and embodiment of the life of spirit has passed away, and another mode appears in its place.

This disappearance of the ethical substance, and its transition into another mode are thus determined by the ethical consciousness being directed upon the law essentially in an immediate way. It lies in this character of immediacy that nature at all enters into the acts which constitute the ethical life. Its realization simply reveals the contradiction and the germ of destruction, which lie hid within that very peace and beauty belonging to the gracious harmony and peaceful equilibrium of the ethical spirit. For the essence and meaning of this immediacy contains a contradiction: it is at once the unconscious peace of nature and the self-conscious unresting peace of spirit. On account of this "naturalness," this ethical nation is, in general, an individuality determined by nature, and therefore limited, and thus finds its dissolution in, and gives place to, another individuality. This determinateness, being given a positive existence, is a limitation, but at the same time is the negative element in general and the self of individuality. In so far, however, as this determinateness passes away, the life of spirit and this substance, conscious of itself in all its component individuals, are lost. The substance comes forth and stands apart as a formal universality of all the component individuals, and no longer dwells within them as a living spirit; instead, the uniform solidarity of their individuality has burst into a plurality of separate points.

3. THE SPIRITUAL WORK OF ART

[j]Since then its trust is broken, and the substance of the nation cracked, spirit, which was the connecting medium of unstable extremes, has now come forward as an extreme—that of self-consciousness grasping itself as essential and ultimate. This is spirit certain within itself, which mourns over the loss of its world, and now out of the purity of self produces its own essential being, raised above actual reality.

At such an epoch art in absolute form comes on the scene. At the earlier stage it is instinctive in its operation; its operation is steeped in existence, works its way out of existence and works right into the existent; it does not find its substance in

[j] *Phenomenology*, pp. 711–12.

the free life of an ethical order, and hence, too, as regards the self operating does not exercise free spiritual activity.

Later on, spirit goes beyond art in order to gain its higher manifestation, viz. that of being not merely the substance born and produced out of the self, but of being, in its manifestation as object, this very self; it seeks at that higher level not merely to bring forth itself out of its own notion, but to have its very notion as its shape, so that the notion and the work of art produced may know each other reciprocally as one and the same.

Since, then, the ethical substance has withdrawn from its objective existence into its pure self-consciousness, this is the aspect of the notion, or the activity with which spirit brings itself forth as object. It is pure form, because the individual in ethical obedience and service has so worked off every unconscious existence and every fixed determination, as the substance has itself become this fluid and undifferentiated essence. This form is the night in which the substance was betrayed, and made itself subject. It is out of this night of pure certainty of self that the ethical spirit rises again in a shape freed from nature and its own immediate existence.

The existence of the pure notion into which spirit has fled from its bodily shape, is an individual, which spirit selects as the vessel for its sorrow. Spirit acts in this individual as his universal and his power, from which he suffers violence, as his element of "Pathos," by having given himself over to which his self-consciousness loses freedom. But that positive power belonging to the universal is overcome by the pure self of the individual, the negative power. This pure activity, conscious of its inalienable force, wrestles with the unembodied essential being. Becoming its master, this negative activity has turned the element of pathos into its own material, and given itself its content; and this unity comes out as a work, universal spirit individualized and consciously presented.

a. The Earliest Language of Spirit: Epic

kOn the highest level, this work consists first in the earliest language, the Epic as such, which contains the universal content, at any rate universal in the sense of completeness of the world presented, though not in the sense of universality of thought. The Minstrel is the individual and actual spirit from whom, as a subject of this world, it is produced, and by whom it is borne. His "pathos" is not the deafening power of nature, but Mnemosyne, Recollection, a gradually evolved inwardness, the memory of an essential mode of being once directly present. He is the organ and instrument whose content is passing away; it is not his own self which is of any account, but his muse, his universal song. What, however, is present in fact, has the form of an inferential process, where the one extreme of universality, the world of gods, is connected with individuality, the minstrel, through the middle term of particularity. The middle term is the nation in its heroes, who are individual men like the minstrel, but only ideally presented, and thereby at the same time universal like the free extreme of universality, the gods.

In this Epic, then, what is inherently established in the cult, the relation of the divine to the human, is set forth and displayed as a whole to consciousness. The content is an "act" of the essential Being conscious of itself. Acting disturbs the peace of the substance, and awakens the essential Being; and by so doing its simple unity is divided into parts, and opened up into the manifold world of natural powers and ethical forces. The act is the violation of the peaceful earth; it is the trench which, vivified by the blood of the living, calls forth the spirits of the departed, who are thirsting for life, and who receive it in the action of self-consciousness. There are two sides to the business the universal activity is concerned to accomplish: the side of the self—in virtue of which it is brought about by a collection of actual nations with the prominent individualities at the head of them; and the side of the universal

k Phenomenology, pp. 732–49.

—in virtue of which it is brought about by their substantial forces. The relation of the two, however, took, as we saw just now, the character of being the synthetic connection of universal and individual, i.e. of being a process of ideal presentation. On this specific character depends the judgment regarding this world.

The relation of the two is, by this means, a commingling of both, which illogically divides the unity of the action, and in a needless fashion throws the act from one side over to the other. The universal powers have the form of individual beings, and thus have in them the principle from which action comes; when they effect anything, therefore, this seems to proceed as entirely from them and to be as free as in the case of men. Hence both gods and men have done one and the same thing. The seriousness with which those divine powers go to work is ridiculously unnecessary, since they are in point of fact the moving force of the individualities engaged in the acts; while the strain and toil of the latter again is an equally useless effort, since the former direct and manage everything. Overzealous mortal creatures, who are as nothing, are at the same time the mighty self that brings into subjection the universal beings, offends the gods, and procures for them actual reality and an interest in acting. Just as, conversely, these powerless gods, these impotent universal beings, who procure their sustenance from the gifts of men and through men first get something to do, are the natural inner principle and the substance of all events, as also the ethical material, and the "pathos" of action. If their cosmic natures first get reality and a sphere of effectual operation through the free self of individuality, it is also the case that they are the universal, which withdraws from and avoids this connection, remains unrestricted and unconstrained in its own character, and, by the unconquerable elasticity of its unity, extinguishes the atomic singleness of the individual acting and his various features, preserves itself in its purity, and dissolves all that is individual in the current of its own continuity.

Just as the gods fall into this contradictory relation with the antithetic nature having the form of self, in the same way their universality comes into conflict with their own specific character and the relation in which it stands to others. They are the eternal and resplendent individuals, who exist in their own calm, and are removed from the changes of time and the influence of alien forces. But they are at the same time determinate elements, particular gods, and thus stand in relation to others. But that relation to others, which, in virtue of the opposition it involves, is one of strife, is a comic self-forgetfulness of their eternal nature. The determinateness they possess is rooted in the divine subsistence, and in its specific limitation has the independence of the whole individuality; owing to this whole, their characters at once lose the sharpness of their distinctive peculiarity, and in their ambiguity blend together.

One purpose of their activity and their activity itself, being directed against an "other" and so against an invincible divine force, are a contingent and futile piece of bravado, which passes away at once, and transforms the pretence of seriousness in the act into a harmless, self-confident piece of sport with no result and no issue. If, however, in the nature of their divinity, the negative element, the specific determinateness of that nature, appears merely as the inconsistency of their activity, and as the contradiction between the purpose and result, and if that independent self-confidence outweighs and overbalances the element of determinateness, then, by that very fact, the pure force of negativity confronts and opposes their nature, and moreover with a power to which it must finally submit, and over which it can in no way prevail. They are the universal, and the positive, as against the individual self of mortals, which cannot hold out against their power and might. But the universal self, for that reason, hovers over them [the gods in Homer] and over this whole world of imagination to which the entire content belongs; and is for them the unintelligible void of Necessity,—a mere happening to which they stand related selfless and sorrowing, for these determinate natures do not find themselves in this purely formal necessity.

This necessity, however, is the unity of the notion, a unity dominating and controlling the contradictory independent subsistence of the individual moments, a unity in which the inconsistency and fortuitousness of their action is coherently regulated, and the sportive character of their acts receives its serious value in those acts themselves. The content of the world of imagination carries on its process in the middle element [term] detached by itself, gathering round the individuality of some hero, who, however, feels the strength and splendour of his life broken, and mourns the early death he sees ahead of him. For individuality, firmly established and real in itself, is isolated and excluded to the utmost extreme, and severed into its moments, which have not yet found each other and united. The one individual element, the abstract unreal moment, is necessity which shares in the life of the mediating term just as little as does the other, the concrete real individual element, the minstrel, who keeps himself outside it, and disappears in what he imaginatively presents. Both extremes must get nearer the content; the one, necessity, has to get filled with it, the other, the language of the minstrel, must have a share in it. And the content formerly left to itself must acquire in itself the certainty and the fixed character of the negative.

b. The Higher Language: Tragedy

This higher language, that of *Tragedy*, gathers and keeps more closely together the dispersed and scattered moments of the inner essential world and the world of action. The substance of the divine falls apart, in accordance with the nature of the notion, into its shapes and forms, and their movement is likewise in conformity with that notion. In regard to form, the language here ceases to be narrative, in virtue of the fact that it enters into the content, just as the content ceases to be merely one that is ideally imagined. The hero is himself the spokesman, and the representation given brings before the audience—who are also spectators—*self-conscious* human beings, who know their own rights and purposes, the power and the will belonging to their specific nature, and who know how to state them. They are artists who do not express with unconscious naïveté and naturalness the merely external aspect of what they begin and what they decide upon, as is the case in the language accompanying ordinary action in actual life; they make the very inner being external, they prove the righteousness of their action, and the "pathos" controlling them is soberly asserted and definitely expressed in its universal individuality, free from all accident of circumstance and the particular peculiarities of personalities. Lastly, it is in actual human beings that these characters get existence, human beings who impersonate the heroes, and represent them in actual speech, not in the form of a narrative, but speaking in their own person. Just as it is essential for a statue to be made by human hands, so is the actor essential to his mask—not as an external condition, from which, artistically considered, we have to abstract; or so far as abstraction must certainly be made, we thereby state just that art does not yet contain in it the true and proper self.

The general ground, on which the movement of these shapes produced from the notion takes place, is the consciousness expressed in the imaginative language of the Epic, where the detail of the content is loosely spread out with no unifying self. It is the commonalty in general, whose wisdom finds utterance in the Chorus of the Elders; in the powerlessness of this chorus the generality finds its representative, because the common people itself compose merely the positive and passive material for the individuality of the government confronting it. Lacking the power to negate and oppose, it is unable to hold together and keep within bounds the riches and varied fullness of divine life; it allows each individual moment to go off its own way, and in its hymns of honour and reverence praises each individual moment as an independent god, now this god and now again another. Where, however, it detects the seriousness of the notion, and perceives how the notion marches onward shattering these forms as it goes along; and where it comes to see how badly its praised and honoured gods come off when they venture on the ground where the notion holds sway;—there it is not itself the negative power interfering by action, but keeps itself within the abstract selfless thought of such power, confines itself to the consciousness of alien and external destiny, and produces the empty wish to tranquillize, and feeble ineffective talk intended to appease. In its terror before the higher powers, which are the immediate arms of the substance; in its terror before their struggle with one another, and before the simple self of that necessity, which crushes them as well as the living beings bound up with them; in its compassion for these living beings, whom it knows at once to be the same with itself—it is conscious of nothing but ineffective horror of this whole process, conscious of equally helpless pity, and, as the end of all, the mere empty peace of resignation to necessity, whose work is apprehended neither as the necessary act of the character, nor as the action of the absolute Being within itself.

Spirit does not appear in its dissociated multiplicity on the plane of this onlooking consciousness [the chorus], the indifferent ground, as it were, on which the presentation takes place; it comes on the scene in the simple diremption of the notion. Its substance manifests itself, therefore, merely torn asunder into its two extreme powers. These elementary universal beings are, at the same time, self-conscious individualities—heroes who put their conscious life into one of these powers, find therein determinateness of character, and constitute the effective activity and reality of these powers. This universal individualization descends again, as will be remembered, to the immediate reality of existence proper, and is presented before a crowd of spectators, who find in the chorus their image and counterpart, or rather their own thought giving itself expression.

The content and movement of the spirit, which is object to itself here, have been already considered as the nature and realization of the substance of ethical life. In its form of religion spirit attains to consciousness about itself, or reveals itself to its consciousness in its purer form and its simpler mode of embodiment. If, then, the ethical substance by its very principle broke up, as regards its content, into two powers—which were defined as divine and human law, law of the nether world and law of the upper world, the one the family, the other state sovereignty, the first bearing the impress and character of woman, the other that of man—in the same way, the previously multiform circle of gods, with its wavering and unsteady characteristics, confines itself to these powers, which owing to this feature are brought closer to individuality proper. For the previous dispersion of the whole into manifold abstract forces, which appear hypostatized, is the dissolution of the subject which comprehends them merely as moments in its self; and individuality is therefore only the superficial form of these entities. Conversely, a further distinction of characters than that just named is to be reckoned as contingent and inherently external personality.

At the same time, the essential nature [in the case of ethical substance] gets divided in its form, i.e. with respect to knowledge. Spirit when acting, appears, *qua* consciousness, over against the object on which its activity is directed, and which, in consequence, is determined as the negative of the knowing agent. The agent finds himself thereby in the opposition of knowing and not knowing. He takes his purpose from his own character, and knows it to be essential ethical fact; but owing to the determinateness of his character, he knows merely the one power of substance; the other remains for him concealed and out of sight. The present reality, therefore, is one thing in itself, and another for consciousness. The higher and lower right come to signify in this connection the power that knows and reveals itself to consciousness, and the power concealing itself and lurking in the background. The one is the aspect of light, the god of the Oracle, who as regards its natural aspect [Light] has sprung from the all-illuminating Sun, knows all and reveals all, Phoebus and Zeus, who is his Father. But the commands of this truth-speaking god, and his proclamations of what *is*, are really deceptive and fallacious. For this knowledge is, in its very principle, directly *not* knowledge, because consciousness in acting is inherently this opposition. He,[15] who had the power to unlock the riddle of the sphinx, and he too who trusted with childlike confidence,[16] are, therefore, both sent to destruction through what the god reveals to them. The priestess, through whose mouth the beautiful god speaks,[17] is in nothing different from the equivocal sisters of fate,[18] who drive their victim to crime by their promises, and who, by the double-tongued, equivocal character of what they gave out as a certainty, deceive the King when he relies upon the manifest and obvious meaning of what they say. There is a type of consciousness that is purer than the latter[19] which believes in witches, and more sober, more thorough, and more solid

[15] Oedipus.
[16] Orestes.
[17] In the Delphic Oracle.
[18] The witches in "Macbeth."
[19] Macbeth.

than the former which puts its trust in the priestess and the beautiful god. This type of consciousness,[20] therefore, lets his revenge tarry for the revelation which the spirit of his father makes regarding the crime that did him to death, and institutes other proofs in addition—for the reason that the spirit giving the revelation might possibly be the devil.

This mistrust has good grounds, because the knowing consciousness takes its stand on the opposition between certainty of itself on the one hand, and the objective essential reality on the other. Ethical rightness, which insists that actuality is nothing *per se* in opposition to absolute law, finds out that its knowledge is one-sided, its law merely a law of its own character, and that it has laid hold of merely one of the powers of the substance. The act itself is this inversion of what is known into its opposite, into objective existence, turns round what is right from the point of view of character and knowledge into the right of the very opposite with which the former is bound up in the essential nature of the substance—turns it into the "Furies" who embody the right of the other power and character awakened into hostility. The lower right sits *with* Zeus enthroned, and enjoys equal respect and homage with the god revealed and knowing.

To these three supernatural Beings the world of the gods of the chorus is limited and restricted by the acting individuality. The one is the substance, the power presiding over the hearth and home and the spirit worshipped by the family, as well as the universal power pervading state and government. Since this distinction belongs to the substance as such, it is, when dramatically presented, not individualized in two distinct shapes [of the substance], but has in actual reality the two persons of its characters. On the other hand, the distinction between knowing and not knowing falls within each of the actual self-consciousnesses; and only in abstraction, in the element of universality, does it get divided into two individual shapes. For the self of the hero only exists as a whole consciousness, and hence includes essentially the whole of the distinction belonging to the form; but its substance is determinate, and only one side of the content distinguished belongs

[20] Hamlet.

to him. Hence the two sides of consciousness, which have in concrete reality no separate individuality peculiarly their own, receive, when ideally represented, each its own particular form: the one that of the god revealed, the other that of the Furies keeping themselves concealed. In part both enjoy equal honour, while again, the form assumed by the substance, Zeus, is the necessity of the relation of the two to one another. The substance is the relation [1] that knowledge is for itself, but finds its truth in what is simple; [2] that the distinction, through and in which actual consciousness exists, has its basis in that inner being which destroys it; [3] that the clear conscious assurance of certainty has its confirmation in forgetfulness.

Consciousness disclosed this opposition by action, through doing something. Acting in accordance with the knowledge revealed, it finds out the deceptiveness of that knowledge, and being committed, as regards its inner nature, to one of the attributes of substance, it did violence to the other and thereby gave the latter right as against itself. When following that god who knows and reveals himself, it really seized hold of what is not revealed, and pays the penalty for having trusted the knowledge, whose equivocal character (since this is its very nature) it also had to discover, and an admonition thereanent to be given. The frenzy of the priestess, the inhuman shape of the witches, the voices of trees and birds, dreams, and so on, are not ways in which truth appears; they are admonitory signs of deception, of want of judgment, of the individual and accidental character of knowledge. Or, what comes to the same thing, the opposite power, which consciousness has violated, is present as express law and authentic right, whether law of the family or law of the state; while consciousness, on the other hand, pursued its own proper knowledge, and hid from itself what was revealed. The truth, however, of the opposing powers of content and consciousness is the final result, that both are equally right, and, hence, in their opposition (which comes about through action) are equally wrong. The process of action proves their unity in the mutual overthrow of both powers and both self-conscious characters. The reconciliation of the opposition with itself is the Lethe of the nether world in the form of Death—or the Lethe of the upper

world in the form of absolution, not from guilt (for consciousness cannot deny its guilt, because the act was done), but
from the crime, and in the form of the peace of soul which
atones for the crime. Both are forgetfulness, the disappearance
of the reality and action of the powers of the substance, of
their component individualities, and of the powers of the abstract thought of good and evil. For none of them by itself
is the real essence: this consists in the undisturbed calm of the
whole within itself, the immovable unity of Fate, the quiescent
existence (and hence want of activity and vitality) of the family and government, and the equal honour and consequent indifferent unreality of Apollo and the Furies, and the return of
their spiritual life and activity into Zeus solely and simply.

This destiny completes the depopulation of Heaven—of that
unthinking blending of individuality and ultimate Being—a
blending whereby the action of this absolute Being appears
as something incoherent, contingent, unworthy of itself; for
individuality, when attaching in a merely superficial way to
absolute Being, is unessential. The expulsion of such unreal insubstantial ideas, which was demanded by the philosophers of
antiquity, thus already has its beginning in tragedy in general,
through the fact that the division of the substance is controlled
by the notion, and hence individuality is the essential individuality, and the specific determinations are absolute characters.
The self-consciousness represented in tragedy knows and acknowledges on that account only one highest power, Zeus.
This Zeus is known and acknowledged only as the power of
the state or of the hearth and home, and, in the opposition belonging to knowledge, merely as the Father of the knowledge
of the particular,—a knowledge assuming a figure in the
drama:—and again as the Zeus of the oath and of the Furies,
the Zeus of what is universal, of the inner being dwelling in
concealment. The further moments taken from the notion
(*Begriff*) and dispersed in the form of ideal presentation
(*Vorstellung*), moments which the chorus permits to hold
good one after the other, are, on the other hand, not the "pathos" of the hero; they sink to the level of passions in the hero
—to the level of accidental, insubstantial moments, which the
impersonal chorus no doubt praises, but which are not capa-

ble of constituting the character of heroes, nor of being expressed and revered by them as their real nature.

But, further, the persons of the divine Being itself, as well as the characters of its substance, coalesce into the simplicity of what is devoid of consciousness. This necessity has, in contrast to self-consciousness, the characteristic of being the negative power of all the shapes that appear, a power in which they do not recognize themselves, but perish therein. The self appears as merely allotted amongst the different characters, and not as the mediating factor of the process. But self-consciousness, the simple certainty of self, is in point of fact the negative power, the unity of Zeus, the unity of the substantial essence and abstract necessity; it is the spiritual unity into which everything returns. Because actual self-consciousness is still distinguished from the substance and fate, it is partly the chorus, or rather the crowd looking on, whom this movement of the divine life fills with fear as being something alien and strange, or in whom this movement, as something closely touching themselves, produces merely the emotion of passive pity. Partly again, so far as consciousness co-operates and belongs to the various characters, this alliance is of an external kind, is a hypocrisy—because the true union, that of self, fate, and substance, is not yet present. The hero, who appears before the onlookers, breaks up into his mask and the actor, into the person of the play and the actual self.

The self-consciousness of the heroes must step forth from its mask and be represented as knowing itself to be the fate both of the gods of the chorus and of the absolute powers themselves, and as being no longer separated from the chorus, the universal consciousness.

c. The Self-Conscious Language: Comedy

Comedy has, then, first of all, the aspect that actual self-consciousness represents itself as the fate of the gods. These elemental Beings are, *qua* universal moments, no definite self, and are not actual. They are, indeed, endowed with the form of individuality, but this is in their case merely put on, and does not really and truly belong to them. The actual self has no such abstract moment as its substance and content. The subject, therefore, is raised above such a moment, as it would be above a particular quality, and when clothed with this mask gives utterance to the irony of such a property trying to be something on its own account. The pretentious claims of the universal abstract nature are shown up and discovered in the actual self; it is seen to be caught and held in a concrete reality, and lets the mask drop, just when it wants to be something genuine. The self, appearing here in its significance as something actual, plays with the mask which it once puts on, in order to be its own person; but it breaks away from this seeming and pretence just as quickly again, and comes out in its own nakedness and commonness, which it shows not to be distinct from the proper self, the actor, nor again from the onlooker.

This general dissolution, which the formally embodied essential nature as a whole undergoes when it assumes individuality, becomes in its content more serious, and hence more petulant and bitter, in so far as the content possesses its more serious and necessary meaning. The divine substance combines the meaning of natural and ethical essentiality.

As regards the natural element, actual self-consciousness shows in the very fact of applying elements of nature for its adornment, for its abode and so on, and again in feasting on its own offering, that *itself* is the Fate to which the secret is betrayed, no matter what may be the truth as regards the independent substantiality of nature. In the mystery of the bread and wine it makes its very own this self-subsistence of nature together with the significance of the inner reality; and in Comedy it is conscious of the irony lurking in this meaning.

So far, again, as this meaning contains the essence of ethical reality, it is partly the nation in its two aspects of the state, or Demos proper, and individual family life; partly, however, it is self-conscious pure knowledge, or rational thought of the universal. Demos, the general mass, which knows itself as master and governor, and is also aware of being the insight and intelligence which demand respect, exerts compulsion and is befooled through the particularity of its actual life, and exhibits the ludicrous contrast between its own opinion of itself and its immediate existence, between its necessity and contingency, its universality and its vulgarity. If the principle of its individual existence, cut off from the universal, breaks out in the proper figure of an actual man and openly usurps and administers the commonwealth, to which it is a secret harm and detriment, then there is more immediately disclosed the contrast between the universal in the sense of a theory, and that with which practice is concerned; there stand exposed the entire emancipation of the ends and aims of the mere individual from the universal order, and the scorn the mere individual shows for such order.[21]

Rational thinking removes contingency of form and shape from the divine Being; and, in opposition to the uncritical wisdom of the chorus—a wisdom, giving utterance to all sorts of ethical maxims and stamping with validity and authority a multitude of laws and specific conceptions of duty and of right —rational thought lifts these into the simple Ideas of the Beautiful and the Good. The process of this abstraction is the consciousness of the dialectic involved in these maxims and laws themselves, and hence the consciousness of the disappearance of that absolute validity with which they previously appeared. Since the contingent character and superficial individuality which imagination lent to the divine Beings vanish, they are left, as regards their natural aspect, with merely the nakedness of their immediate existence; they are Clouds,[22] a passing vapour, like those imaginative ideas. Having passed in accordance with their essential character, as determined by thought, into the simple thoughts of the Beautiful and the Good, these latter submit to being filled with every kind of content. The force of dialectic knowledge[23] puts determinate laws and maxims of action at the mercy of the pleasure and levity of youth, led astray therewith, and gives weapons of deception into the hands of solicitous and apprehensive old age, restricted in its interests to the individual details of life. The pure thoughts of the Beautiful and the Good thus display a comic spectacle:—through their being set free from the opinion, which contains both their determinateness in the sense of content and also their absolute determinateness, the firm hold of

[21] Cp. Cleon in Aristophanes, "Knights."
[22] Cp. Aristophanes, "Clouds."
[23] Cp. the arguments in the "Clouds."

consciousness upon them, they become empty, and, on that very account, the sport of the private opinion and caprice of any chance individuality.

Here, then, the Fate, formerly without consciousness, consisting in empty rest and forgetfulness, and separated from self-consciousness, is united with self-consciousness. The individual self is the negative force through which and in which the gods, as also their moments, (nature as existent fact and the thoughts of their determinate characters), pass away and disappear. At the same time, the individual self is not the mere vacuity of disappearance, but preserves itself in this very nothingness, holds to itself and is the sole and only reality. The religion of art is fulfilled and consummated in it, and is come full circle. Through the fact that it is the individual consciousness in its certainty of self which manifests itself as this absolute power, this latter has lost the form of something ideally presented (*vorgestellt*), separated from and alien to consciousness in general—as were the statue and also the living embodiment of beauty or the content of the Epic and the powers and persons of Tragedy. Nor again is the unity the unconscious unity of the cult and the mysteries; rather the self proper of the actor coincides with the part he impersonates, just as the onlooker is perfectly at home in what is represented before him, and sees himself playing in the drama before him. What this self-consciousness beholds is that whatever assumes the form of essentiality as against self-consciousness is instead dissolved within it—within its thought, its existence and action,—and is quite at its mercy. It is the return of everything universal into certainty of self, a certainty which, in consequence, is this complete loss of fear of everything strange and alien, and complete loss of substantial reality on the part of what is alien and external. Such certainty is a state of spiritual good health and of self-abandonment thereto, on the part of consciousness, in a way that, outside this kind of comedy, is not to be found anywhere.

CHAPTER V

HISTORICAL, RELIGIOUS, AND PHILOSOPHICAL SUBSTANCE OF TRAGEDY

[a]It has been long a much vexed question whether the arts and the religion of the Greeks were developed independently or through foreign suggestion. Under the conduct of a one-sided understanding the controversy is interminable; for it is no less a fact of history that the Greeks derived conceptions from India, Syria, and Egypt, than that the Greek conceptions are peculiar to themselves, and those others alien. Herodotus (II. 53) asserts, with equal decision, that *"Homer and Hesiod invented a Theogony for the Greeks,* and assigned to the gods their appropriate epithets" (a most weighty sentence, which has been the subject of deep investigation, especially by Creuzer)—and, in another place, that Greece took the names of its divinities from Egypt, and that the Greeks made inquiry at Dodona, whether they ought to adopt these names or not. This appears self-contradictory: it is, however, quite consistent; for the fact is that the Greeks evolved the Spiritual from the materials which they had received. The Natural, as *explained* by man—i.e. its internal essential element—is, as a universal principle, the beginning of the Divine. Just as in Art the Greeks may have acquired a mastery of technical matters from others—from the Egyptians especially—so in their religion the commencement might have been from without; but by their independent spirit they transformed the one as well as the other.

[a] *The Philosophy of History,* tr. J. Sibree. New York, 1899, pp. 237–39.

Traces of such foreign rudiments may be generally discovered (Creuzer, in his "Symbolik," dwells especially on this point). The amours of Zeus appear indeed as something isolated, extraneous, adventitious, but it may be shown that foreign theogonic representations form their basis. Hercules is, among the Hellenes, that Spiritual Humanity which by native energy attains Olympus through the twelve far-famed labours: but the foreign idea that lies at the basis is the Sun, completing its revolution through the twelve signs of the Zodiac. The Mysteries were only such ancient rudiments, and certainly contained no greater wisdom than already existed in the consciousness of the Greeks. All Athenians were initiated in the mysteries—Socrates excepted, who refused initiation, because he knew well that science and art are not the product of mysteries, and that Wisdom never lies among arcana. True science has its place much rather in the open field of consciousness.

1. NECESSITY AND FREEDOM IN THE PANTHEON OF GODS

In summing up the constituents of the *Greek Spirit*, we find its fundamental characteristic to be, that the freedom of Spirit is conditioned by and has an essential relation to some stimulus supplied by Nature. Greek freedom of thought is excited by an alien existence; but it is free because it transforms and virtually reproduces the stimulus by its own operation. This phase of Spirit is the medium between the loss of individuality on the part of man (such as we observe in the Asiatic principle, in which the Spiritual and Divine exists only under a Natural form), and Infinite Subjectivity as pure certainty of itself—the position that the Ego is the ground of all that can lay claim to substantial existence. The Greek Spirit, as the medium between these two, begins with Nature, but transforms it into a mere objective form of its (Spirit's) own existence; Spirituality is therefore not yet absolutely free; not yet absolutely *self*-produced—is not self-stimulation. Setting out from surmise and wonder, the Greek Spirit advances to definite conceptions of the hidden meanings of Nature. In the subject itself too, the same

harmony is produced. In Man, the side of his subjective existence which he owes to Nature is the Heart, the Disposition,
Passion, and Variety of Temperament: this side is then developed in a spiritual direction to free Individuality; so that the
character is not placed in a relation to universally valid moral
authorities, assuming the form of duties, but the Moral appears as a nature peculiar to the individual—an exertion of will,
the result of disposition and individual constitution. This
stamps the Greek character as that of *Individuality conditioned
by Beauty*, which is produced by Spirit, transforming the
merely Natural into an expression of its own being. The activity of Spirit does not yet possess in itself the material and
organ of expression, but needs the excitement of Nature and
the matter which Nature supplies: it is not free, self-deter-
mining Spirituality, but mere naturalness formed to Spirituality—Spiritual Individuality. The Greek Spirit is the plastic artist,
forming the stone into a work of art. In this formative process
the stone does not remain mere stone—the form being only
superinduced from without; but it is made an expression of the
Spiritual, even contrary to its nature, and thus *trans*formed.
Conversely, the artist *needs* for his spiritual conceptions, stone,
colours, sensuous forms to express his idea. Without such an
element he can no more be conscious of the idea himself, than
give it an objective form for the contemplation of others; since
it cannot in Thought alone become an object to him. The
Egyptian Spirit also was a similar labourer in Matter, but the
Natural had not yet been subjected to the Spiritual. No advance was made beyond a struggle and contest with it; the
Natural still took an independent position, and formed one side
of the image, as in the body of the Sphinx. In Greek Beauty
the Sensuous is only a sign, an expression, an envelope, in
which Spirit manifests itself.

It must be added, that while the Greek Spirit is a transforming artist of this kind, it knows itself free in its productions;
for it is their creator, and they are what is called the "work of
man." They are, however, not merely this, but Eternal Truth
—the energizing of Spirit in its innate essence, and quite as
really not created as created by man. He has a respect and
veneration for these conceptions and images—this Olympian
Zeus—this Pallas of the Acropolis—and in the same way for the

laws, political and ethical, that guide his actions. But He, the human being, is the womb that conceived them, he the breast that suckled them, he the Spiritual to which their grandeur and purity are owing. Thus he feels himself calm in contemplating them, and not only free in himself, but possessing the consciousness of his freedom; thus the honour of the Human is swallowed up in the worship of the Divine. Men honour the Divine in and for itself, but at the same time as their deed, their production, their phenomenal existence; thus the Divine receives its honour through the respect paid to the Human, and the Human in virtue of the honour paid to the Divine.

ᵇIn the Idea of the Greek Spirit we found the two elements, Nature and Spirit, in such a relation to each other, that Nature forms merely the point of departure. This degradation of Nature is in the Greek mythology the turning point of the whole —expressed as the War of the Gods, the overthrow of the Titans by the race of Zeus. The transition from the Oriental to the Occidental Spirit is therein represented, for the Titans are the merely Physical—natural existences, from whose grasp sovereignty is wrested. It is true that they continue to be venerated, but not as governing powers; for they are relegated to the verge [the limbus] of the world. The Titans are powers of Nature, Uranus, Gaea, Oceanus, Selene, Helios, etc. Chronos expresses the dominion of abstract Time, which devours its children. The unlimited power of reproduction is restrained, and Zeus appears as the head of the new divinities, who embody a spiritual import, and are themselves Spirit. It is not possible to express this transition more distinctly and naïvely than in this myth; the new dynasty of divinities proclaim their peculiar nature to be of a Spiritual order.

The second point is, that the new divinities retain natural elements, and consequently in themselves a determinate relation to the powers of Nature, as was previously shown. Zeus has his lightnings and clouds, and Hera is the creatress of the *Natural*, the producer of crescent vitality. Zeus is also the political god, the protector of morals and of hospitality. Oceanus, as such, is only the element of Nature which his name denotes. Poseidon has still the wildness of that element in his character;

ᵇ *The Philosophy of History*, pp. 244–46.

but he is also an ethical personage; to him is ascribed the building of walls and the production of the Horse. Helios is the sun as a natural element. This Light, according to the analogy of Spirit, has been transformed to self-consciousness, and Apollo has proceeded from Helios. The name Λύκειος points to the connection with light; Apollo was a herdsman in the employ of Admetus, but oxen not subjected to the yoke were sacred to Helios: his rays, 'represented as arrows, kill the Python. The idea of Light as the natural power constituting the basis of the representation, cannot be dissociated from this divinity; especially as the other predicates attached to it are easily united with it, and the explanations of Müller and others, who deny that basis, are much more arbitrary and far-fetched. For Apollo is the prophesying and discerning god—Light, that makes everything clear. He is, moreover, the healer and strengthener; as also the destroyer, for he kills men. He is the propitiating and purifying god, e.g., in contravention of the Eumenides—the ancient subterrene divinities—who exact hard, stern justice. He himself is pure; he has no wife, but only a sister, and is not involved in various disgusting adventures, like Zeus; moreover, he is the discerner and declarer, the singer and leader of the dances—as the sun leads the harmonious dance of stars.—In like manner the Naiads became the Muses. The mother of the gods, Cybele—continuing to be worshipped at Ephesus as Artemis—is scarcely to be recognized as the Artemis of the Greeks—the chaste huntress and destroyer of wild beasts. Should it be said that this change of the Natural into the Spiritual is owing to our allegorizing, or that of the later Greeks, we may reply, that this transformation of the Natural to the Spiritual is the Greek Spirit itself. The epigrams of the Greeks exhibit such advances from the Sensuous to the Spiritual. But the abstract Understanding cannot comprehend this blending of the Natural with the Spiritual.

It must be further observed, that the Greek gods are to be regarded as individualities—not abstractions, like "Knowledge," "Unity," "Time," "Heaven," "Necessity." Such abstractions do not form the substance of these divinities; they are no allegories, no abstract beings, to which various attributes are attached, like the Horatian "Necessitas clavis trabalibus." As little are the divinities symbols, for a symbol is only a sign, an adumbration of something else. The Greek gods express of themselves what they are. The eternal repose and clear intelligence that dignifies the head of Apollo, is not a symbol, but the expression in which Spirit manifests itself, and shows itself present. The gods are personalities, concrete individualities: an allegorical being has no qualities, but is itself one quality and no more. The gods are, moreover, special characters, since in each of them one peculiarity predominates as the characteristic one; but it would be vain to try to bring this circle of characters into a system. Zeus, perhaps, may be regarded as ruling the other gods, but not with substantial power; so that they are left free to their own idiosyncrasy.

cZeus rules them in fatherly, patriarchal fashion, which implies that the ruler does in the end what the others on the whole wish, while these give their assent to all that occurs. But this sovereignty is not serious. The higher absolute unity, in the form of absolute Power, stands over them as their pure and absolute power. This power is Fate or Destiny, simple necessity.

a. Formless Necessity

This unity, as being absolute necessity, has universal determinateness within it. It is the fullness of all determinations; but it is not developed in itself, the fact rather being that the content is divided in a particular way among the many gods who issue forth from this unity. It is itself empty and without content, despises all fellowship and outward embodiment, and rules in dread fashion over everything as blind, irrational, unintelligible power. It is unintelligible because it is the concrete alone of which we can form an intelligent conception; but this necessity is still abstract, and has not yet developed so as to have the conception of an end, has not yet reached definite determinations.

Necessity, accordingly, essentially relates itself to the world. For determinateness is a moment in necessity itself, and the concrete world is developed determinateness, the kingdom of

c *Lectures on the Philosophy of Religion,* tr. E. B. Speirs and J. Burdon Sanderson. London, 1895, vol. II, pp. 239–43.

finitude, of definite existence generally. Necessity has at first a merely abstract relation to the concrete world, and this relation is the external unity of the world, equality or uniformity simply, which is without any further determination in itself, and is incomprehensible—Nemesis, in short. It brings down what is high and exalted, and thus establishes equality. But this equalizing is not to be understood as meaning that when what pushes itself forward or is too high is brought down, what is low is, in its turn, raised up. On the contrary, that which is low is as it was meant to be; it is the finite which has no particular claims, and no kind of infinite value in itself to which it could appeal. It is thus not *too* low. It has in it power, however, to rise above the common lot and the ordinary limit of finitude, and when it thus acts in opposition to uniformity it is again thrust down by Nemesis.

If we now directly consider the relation of the finite self-consciousness to this necessity, we see that under the pressure of its iron power it is to have only an obedience without inward freedom. But *one* form of freedom is at least present when we look at the matter from the side of feeling. The Greek who has within him the feeling of the necessity calms his soul with that. *It is so;* there is nothing to be done against it; with this I must content myself; just in this feeling that I must be content with it, that this even pleases me, we have the freedom which is implied in the fact that it is mine.

This mental attitude implies that man has this simple necessity before him. In that he occupies the standpoint, "It is so," he has set all that is particular on one side, has made a renunciation of and abstracts from all particular ends and interests. The vexation, the discontent which men feel consists just in this, that they stick to a definite end, and will not give this up; and then if things do not fit in with this end, or, as may happen, go quite contrary to it, they are dissatisfied. There is then no harmony between what is actually present and what men wish to have, because they have the "ought to be" within themselves—"That ought to be."

Thus discontent, division, are inherently present; but those who occupy the standpoint referred to cling to no aim, no interest, as against actually existing circumstances. Misfortune, discontent, is nothing but the contradiction implied in the fact that something is contrary to my will. If the particular interest is given up, then by this act I have retreated into this pure rest, into this pure Being, into this "is."

There is here no consolation for man, but then it is not necessary. He requires consolation when he desires compensation for some loss; but here he has renounced the inner root of worry and discontent, and has wholly given up what is lost, because he has the power which enables him to look into necessity. It is, accordingly, nothing but a false illusion to imagine that consciousness is annihilated when brought into relation to necessity—that it relates itself to something which is absolutely beyond its own world, and finds in it nothing having a relationship with itself. Necessity is not one person, and accordingly consciousness does not exist in it on its own account, for itself, or in other words, it is not an individual or selfish oneness in its immediacy. In relation to that which is one person it is independent, wishes to be independent, to be for itself, and to stand on its own basis. The servant or vassal, in performing his service, in his condition of subjection, has fear, and in doing any base act against his master he has a self-seeking design. But in relation to necessity the subject appears as something which does not exist independently, or as determined for itself; it has, on the contrary, surrendered itself, retains no end for itself, and the revering of necessity is just this indeterminate attitude of self-consciousness, this attitude which is wholly devoid of the element of opposition. What we now-a-days call fate is just the opposite of this attitude of self-consciousness. We speak of just, unjust, merited fate. We use the word fate by way of explanation, that is, as suggesting the reason of any condition in which individuals are, or of the fate of individuals. Here there is an external union of cause and effect by which an inherited evil, an ancient curse that rests on his house, breaks out in the individual. In such cases fate implies that there exists some sort of reason, but a reason that is at the same time away beyond the present, and fate is here nothing but a connection of causes and effects, of causes, which, so far as the person is concerned upon whom the fate falls, should be finite causes, and where there is nevertheless a hidden connection between that which the sufferer is in himself and that which befalls him as something unmerited.

The perception of and reverent regard for necessity is, on the other hand, the direct opposite of the foregoing. In it that mediation and the superficial reasoning about cause and effect are done away with. We cannot speak of a belief in necessity as if necessity were something essentially existing, or were a connection of relations, such as that of cause and effect, and as if it thus stood opposed to consciousness in some objective outward form. On the contrary, the expression "it is necessary" directly presupposes the abandonment of all argumentative reasoning, and the shutting up of the spirit within simple abstraction. Noble and beautiful characters are produced by this attitude on the part of the human spirit, which has thus given up that which, as the saying goes, fate wrests from us. It produces a certain grandeur and repose and that free nobility of soul which is also found amongst the ancients. This freedom is, however, only of the abstract kind, which merely stands above the concrete and particular, but does not actually come to be in harmony with what is definite, i.e., it is pure thought, Being, Being-within-self, the relinquishment of the particular. In the higher forms of religion, on the contrary, there exists the consolation that the absolute end and aim will be reached even in misfortune, so that the negative changes round into the affirmative. "The sufferings of the present are the path to bliss."

Abstract necessity, as this abstraction of thought and of the return into self, is the one extreme; the other extreme is the singularity or individual existence of the particular divine powers.

b. Posited Necessity or the Particular Gods

The divine particular powers belong to what is implicitly universal, to necessity, but they come out from it because it is not yet posited for itself as the Notion and determined as freedom. ^dIt is necessity that has to appear in a divine fashion, i.e., in definite existence as necessity in immediate unity with this concrete existence. This is posited necessity, i.e., definitely

^d *Lectures on the Philosophy of Religion*, vol. II, pp. 248–88.

existing necessity, which exists as simple reflection into itself.

Imagination is now the organ with which self-consciousness gives outward form to the inwardly abstract or to the external, which is at first something having immediate Being, and posits it as concrete. In this process the natural loses its independence and is reduced to being the outward sign of the indwelling spirit, in such a way that this latter alone is essentially allowed to appear.

The freedom of Spirit here is not yet the infinite freedom of thought; the spiritual essences are not yet in the element of Thought. Did man exercise thought in such a way that pure thought constituted the basis, there would be for him only one God. Just as little, however, does man come upon his essential beings as present immediate natural forms; on the contrary, he brings them forward into existence for idea or figurative thought, and this bringing of them forward as representing the middle stage between pure thought and the immediate perception of Nature, is imagination or fancy.

In this way the gods are formed by human imagination, and they originate in a finite fashion, being produced by the poet, by the muse. They have this finitude essentially in themselves, because so far as the content is concerned they are finite, and in virtue of their individuality have no connection with each other. They are not discovered by the human mind as they are in their essentially existent rational content, but in so far as they are *gods*. They are made, invented, but are not fictitious. They certainly come forth out of the human imagination in contrast to what actually exists, but they do this as *essential* forms, and this product of the mind is at the same time recognized as being what is essential.

It is in this sense we are to understand the remark of Herodotus that Homer and Hesiod made their gods for the Greeks. The same might be said of every priest and wise "ancient" who was capable of understanding and explaining the presence in the natural of the divine and of the essentially existing powers.

When the Greeks heard the roaring of the sea at the funeral of Achilles, Nestor came forward and explained it as meaning that Thetis was taking part in the mourning. Thus, too, in the case of the pestilence, Calchas says that Apollo had brought

it about because he was angry with the Greeks. This interpretation just means that an embodiment is given to natural phenomena, that they get the form of a divine act. What takes
place within the mind is similarly explained. According to
Homer, for instance, Achilles would like to draw his sword, but
he calms himself and restrains his anger. This inward prudence
is Pallas, who represses anger. In this interpretation originated
those innumerable charming tales and the endless number of
Greek myths which we possess.

From whatever side we consider the Greek principle, the
sensuous and natural element is seen to force its way into it.
The gods as they issue out of necessity are limited, and they
have also still traces of the natural element in them, just because they reveal the fact that they have sprung from the
struggle with the forces of Nature. The manifestation by which
they announce themselves to self-consciousness is still external,
and the imagination which gives shape and form to this manifestation does not yet elevate their starting-point into the region
of pure thought. We have now to see how this natural moment is wholly transfigured into a beautiful form.

c. The Beautiful Form of the Divine Powers

In absolute necessity determinateness is reduced to the unity
of immediacy, "it is so." But this means that the determinateness, the content, is rejected, and the stability and freedom of
the feeling which keeps to this sensuous perception consists
only in the fact that it abides firmly by the empty "is." But
definitely existing necessity is for immediate perception, and
indeed exists for it in its character as natural determinate existence which in its determinateness takes itself back into its
simplicity, and actually exhibits in itself this act of withdrawal
or taking of itself back. Determinate existence, which is only
this process, is in the state of freedom, or, to put it otherwise,
determinateness exists as negativity, as reflected into itself, and
as sinking itself into simple necessity. This determinateness
which relates itself to itself is subjectivity.

For this process of concretely existing necessity the reality
is accordingly the spiritual, the human form. This is a sensuous

and natural object and thus exists for immediate perception, and it is at the same time simple necessity, simple reference to self, in virtue of being which it plainly announces the presence of thought. In every instance of its contact with reality, of its externalization, it is directly decomposed, dissolved, and merged in simple identity; it is an externalization, a manifestation, which is really the externalization of Spirit.

This relationship is not easily grasped, namely, that the fundamental determination and the one side of the Notion is absolute necessity, while the side of reality in virtue of which the Notion is Idea, is the human form. The Notion must, above all, have actual reality. This determination accordingly is more directly involved in necessity itself, for it is not abstract Being, but what is actual and determinate, determinate in and for itself. Thus the determinateness, just because it is at the same time natural, external, reality, is further directly taken back into simple necessity, so that it is this necessity which exhibits itself in this variegated sensuous element. It is only when it is no longer necessity but Spirit, which constitutes the Divine, that the latter comes to be regarded as existing wholly in the element of thought. Here, however, the moment of external perceptibility still remains, in which, in spite of its material character, simple necessity nevertheless exhibits itself. This is only the case when we have the human form, because it is the form of the spiritual, and only in it can reality be taken back for consciousness into the simplicity of necessity.

Life generally is this infinitude of free existence, and as what is living is it this subjectivity, which reacts against the immediate determinateness and posits it as identical with itself in feeling. But the life of the animal, that is, the actual existence and externalization of its infinitude, has plainly a merely limited content, is sunk in merely particular conditions. The simplicity to which this determinateness is taken back is a limited and merely formal one, and the content is not adequate to this its form. For thinking man, on the other hand, the spiritual is expressed in his particular conditions also; this expression of it lets us see that man even in any one limited condition is at the same time above it, transcends it, is free, and does not go outside of himself, continues to be at home with himself. We can very easily judge whether a man in the act of satisfying his wants behaves like an animal or like a man. The human element is a delicate fragrance which spreads itself over every action. Besides, man has not only this element of mere life, but has likewise an infinite range of higher ways of expressing himself, of higher deeds and ends, the constituent element of which is just the Infinite, the Universal. Thus man is that absolute reflection into self which we have in the conception of necessity. It properly belongs to physiology to get a knowledge of the human organism, of the human form as the only form truly adequate for Spirit, but as yet it has accomplished little in this regard. Aristotle long ago expressed the truth that it is only the human organization which is the form of the spiritual, when he pointed it out as being the defect in the idea of the transmigration of souls, that according to this theory the bodily organization of human beings was of a merely accidental kind.

The individual actual man still essentially has, however, in his immediate existence the element of immediate natural life, which makes its appearance as something temporary and fleeting, as that which has fallen away from universality. In accordance with this element of finitude, there emerges a discordance or want of harmony between that which man implicitly, in his real nature is, and what he actually is. The impress of simple necessity is not stamped on all the features and parts of the individual man. Empirical individuality and the expression of simple inwardness are mingled together, and the ideality of the natural, freedom and universality are, owing to the conditions of the merely natural life and because of a number of natural needs which come into play, obscured. Looked at from this point of view, from which an "other" appears in man, the appearance of the outward form does not correspond with simple necessity, but the fact that on his existence in all its shapes and parts the stamp of universality, of simple necessity is impressed—which Goethe appropriately called *significance*, as representing the essential character of classic art—renders it necessary that the form should be planned only in Spirit, should be produced only out of it, and brought into existence only by its mediation, that it should in short be ideal and a work of art. This is something higher than a natural product. We are, no doubt, in the habit of saying that a natural product is the more excellent, just because it is made by God, while a work of art is made only by man, as if, forsooth, natural objects did not also owe their existence to immediate natural finite things, to seeds, air, water, light; as if the power of God lived only in Nature and not also in what is human, in the realm of the spiritual. If the real truth is that natural products only flourish under the conditions supplied by what for them are external and contingent circumstances, and under their influence, an influence which comes from without, then in the work of art it is the necessity which appears as the inward soul and as the notion of externality. That is to say, necessity does not here mean that objects are necessary in themselves and have necessity as their predicate, but that necessity is the subject, that which manifests itself in its predicate, in external existence.

If in this process the manifestation belongs to the subjective side, so that God appears as something made by man, still that is merely *one* moment. For this positing of God, the making of His existence dependent on man, is, on the other hand, mediated by the abrogation of the individual self, and thus it was possible for the Greeks to see their god in the Zeus of Phidias. The artist did not give them in an abstract way something which was *his own* work, but presented to them the appropriate and peculiar manifestation of the essential, the outward form of actually existing necessity.

The form given to the god is thus the ideal form. Previous to the time of the Greeks there was no true ideality, nor was it possible for it to appear at any subsequent time. The art of the Christian religion is indeed beautiful, but ideality is not its ultimate principle. We cannot get at the element of defect in the Greek gods by saying that they are anthropopathic, a category of finitude under which we may put the immoral element, as, for example, the stories of the amours of Zeus, which may have their origin in older myths based on what is as yet the natural way of looking at things. The main defect is not that there is too much of the anthropopathic in these gods, but that there is too little. The manifestation and the aspect of the definite existence of the divine do not yet advance so far as immediate actuality, in the form of a definite individual, that is, as this definite man. The truest, most proper form is necessarily this, that the absolute Spirit which exists for itself should advance to the point at which it shows itself as individual empirical self-consciousness. This characteristic, consisting thus in advance to the sensuous definite individual, is not yet present here. The form made by man in which the divinity appears has, it is true, a material side, but this has still such pliability that it can be perfectly adapted to the manifested content. It is only when separation in God advances to its ultimate limit and appears as man, as a particular empirical self-consciousness, that this sensuousness, this externality, is, so to speak, set free as sensuousness; that is to say, the conditionateness of externality and its want of suitability to express the Notion actually come to light in the god. Here matter, the sensuous, has not yet this form. On the contrary, it keeps true to its content. As the god, though spiritual, universal power, issues out of Nature, he must have the natural as the element of his embodiment, and it must be made plain that it is just the natural which is the mode of the expression of the divine. The god thus appears in stone, and the material is still held to be adequate to the expression of the god as god. It is only when the god appears and reveals himself as a definite individual that Spirit, the subjective knowledge of Spirit as Spirit, is seen to be the true manifestation of God, and it is not till then that sensuousness is set free, that is to say, it is no longer blended with the god, but shows itself to be inadequate as his form; the sensuousness, the immediate individuality, is nailed to the cross. In this process of inversion, it is also shown, however, that this self-alienation, or self-emptying of God in the human form, is only one side of the divine life, for this self-emptying, this manifestation, is taken back again in the One who then for the first time becomes Spirit for thought and for the Church. This single, existing, actual man is done away with and taken up into something higher, and appears as a moment, as one of the persons of God in God. Thus only is man as a definite individual man truly in God, and thus the manifestation of the divine is absolute, and its element is Spirit itself. The Jewish idea that God essentially exists for thought alone, and the sensuousness of the Greek form of beauty, are equally contained in this form of the divine, and as being taken up into something higher, are freed from the limitation attaching to them.

At this stage, in which the divine still requires the sensuous for its essential representation, it appears as a multiplicity of gods. In this multiplicity, it is true, necessity presents itself as simple reflection into self, but this simplicity is only form, for the matter in which it exhibits itself is still immediacy, the element of Nature, not the absolute matter, namely, Spirit. It is thus not Spirit as Spirit that is here represented; the truth rather being that the spiritual existence goes ahead of the consciousness of the content, for this latter is not yet itself Spirit.

2. ART AS WORSHIP IN THE RELIGION OF HUMANITY

This is here a very big subject. Worship essentially means that the empirical consciousness elevates itself, and that man gives himself the consciousness and feeling of the indwelling of the divine within him, and of his unity with the divine. If the work of art is the self-revelation of God and the revelation of the productivity of man as the positing of this revelation by the abrogation of his particular knowledge and will, on the other hand, the work of art equally involves the fact that God and man are no longer beings alien to one another, but have been taken up into a higher unity. The positing or bringing out of what is implicit in the work of art is here accordingly worship, and this latter is hence the relationship whereby the external objectivity of God is, relatively to subjective knowledge, abrogated, and the identity of the two set forth. In this way the external divine existence, as something divorced from existence within the subjective spirit, is abrogated, and thus God is, as it were, called to mind within the sphere of subjectivity. The general character of this worship consists in this, that the subject has an essentially affirmative relationship to his god.

The moments of worship are as follows:

a. Inner Feeling or Subjective Attitude

The gods are duly recognized and revered; they are the substantial powers, the essential, real content of the natural and spiritual universe, the Universal. These universal powers, as exempt from contingency, are recognized by man just because he is thinking consciousness. Thus the world no longer exists for him in an external and contingent fashion, but in the true mode. We thus hold in respect duty, justice, knowledge, political life, life in the State, family relationships. They represent what is true, the inner bond which holds the world together, the substantial element in which the rest exists, the valid element, what alone holds its ground against the contingency and independence which act in opposition to it.

This content is the objective in the true sense, i.e., what is absolutely and essentially valid and true, not in the external objective sense, but within subjectivity also. The substance of these powers is the moral element peculiar to men, *their* morality, their actual and valid power, their own substantiality and essentiality. The Greek people are hence the most human people; with them everything human is affirmatively justified and developed, and the element of measure is present in it.

This religion is essentially a religion of humanity, that is, the concrete man, as regards what he actually is, as regards his needs, inclinations, passions, and habits, as regards his moral and political relations, and in reference to all that has value in these and is essential, is in his gods in presence of his own nature. Or, to put it otherwise, his god has within him the very content composed of the noble and the true, which is at the same time that of concrete man. This humanity of the gods is what was defective in the Greek view, but it is at the same time its attractive element. In this religion there is nothing incomprehensible, nothing which cannot be understood; there is no kind of content in the god which is not known to man, or which he does not find and know in himself. The confidence of a man in the gods is at the same time his confidence in himself.

Pallas, who restrained the outbreak of wrath in the case of

Achilles, is his own prudence. Athene is the town of Athens, and is also the spirit of this particular Athenian people; not an external spirit or protecting spirit, but the spirit who is living, present, actually alive in the people, a spirit immanent in the individual, and who in her essential nature is represented as Pallas.

The Erinyes are not the Furies represented in an outward way. On the contrary, they are meant to suggest that it is man's own act and his consciousness which torment and torture him, in so far as he knows this act to be something evil in himself. The Erinys is not only an external Fury who pursues the matricide Orestes, but suggests rather that it is the spirit of matricide which brandishes its torch over him. The Erinyes are the righteous ones, and just because of that they are the well-disposed, the Eumenides. This is not a euphemism, for they really are those who desire justice, and whoever outrages it has the Eumenides within himself. They represent what we call conscience.

In the "Oedipus at Colonus," Oedipus says to his son, "The Eumenides of the father will pursue thee." Eros, love, is in the same way not merely the objective, the god, but is also as power the subjective feeling of man. Anacreon, for instance, describes a combat with Eros. "I also," he says, "will now love; long ago Eros bade me love, but I would not follow his command. Then Eros attacked me. Armed with breastplate and lance, I withstood him. Eros missed, but after that he forced his way into my heart." "But," thus he concludes, "what is the use of bow and arrow? the combat is within me." In thus recognizing the power of the god, and in this reverential attitude, the subject is absolutely within the sphere of his own nature. The gods are his own emotions. The knowledge the subject has of the gods is not a knowledge of them merely as abstractions away beyond the sphere of reality. On the contrary, it is a knowledge which includes the knowledge of the concrete subjectivity of man himself as something essential, for the gods are likewise within him. Here we have not that negative relation, where the relation of the subject to what is above it, even if it is the highest form of relation, is merely the sacrifice, the negation of its consciousness. The powers here are friendly and gracious to men, they dwell in man's own breast; man gives them reality, and knows their reality to be at the same time his own. The breath of freedom pervades this whole world, and constitutes the fundamental principle for this attitude of mind.

But the consciousness of the infinite subjectivity of man is still wanting, the consciousness that moral relations and absolute right attach to man as such, that man, just because he is self-consciousness, possesses in this formal infinitude the rights as well as the duties of the human race. Freedom, morality, is the substantial element in man, and to know this as the substantial element, and to posit in it his own substantiality, is what constitutes the value and the dignity of man. But it is the formal subjectivity, self-consciousness as such, the inherently infinite individuality, and not the merely natural and immediate individuality, which contains the possibility of that value, i.e., the real possibility, and the one on account of which the individual himself has infinite rights. Now, because in the natural morality of the untutored man the infinitude of formal subjectivity is not recognised, man as such does not attain to that absolute value according to which he has worth in and for himself, whatever be his inward qualifications, whether born in this or the other place, whether rich or poor, whether belonging to this people or to that. Freedom and morality have still a special, particular form, and the essential right of man is still affected by what is contingent, so that it is essentially at this stage that slavery is found to exist. It is still a matter of accident whether a man is a citizen of this particular State or not, whether he is free or is not free. And because, further, the infinite opposition is not yet present, and because the absolute reflection of self-consciousness into itself, that climax of subjectivity is not recognized, man as such does not attain to and rational insight is not yet developed.

Nevertheless, in morality, individuality is in a general sense taken up into universal substantiality, and thus there here enters in—if at first only as a faint semblance, and not yet as the absolute demand of Spirit—the idea of the eternal nature of the subjective, individual spirit, the idea of immortality. The demand for the immortality of the soul could not make its appearance at any of the earlier stages already considered, either in the religion of Nature or in the religion of the One. In the former, the immediate unity of the spiritual and the natural is the fundamental idea, and Spirit is not yet self-conscious, or for itself. In the latter, Spirit is, it is true, self-conscious and exists for itself, but it is still unrealized; its freedom is still abstract, and its Being is still a natural form of existence, the possession of a particular land and its welfare. But that is not Being as the determinate existence of Spirit within itself; it does not yet imply full satisfaction in the spiritual. The duration is only the duration of the race, of the family, of natural universality, in short. But here self-consciousness is complete and realized in itself; it is spiritual. Subjectivity is taken up into universal essentiality and is thus known as essentially Idea; and here we meet with the conception of immortality. But this consciousness becomes more definite when morality appears on the scene; self-consciousness goes down into itself, and hence it will recognize that only as good, true, and right which it finds to be in harmony with itself and its thought. With Socrates and Plato accordingly the question of the immortality of the soul is the one expressly raised, while before their day this idea was considered more as a merely general one, and as one which had not absolute value in and for itself.

As infinite subjectivity, the absolute point of the unity of the Notion, is still wanting to self-consciousness, it is still wanting also to its essentialities, to what represents for it real existence. This unity is found within that which we have come to know as its necessity; but this lies outside the circle of the particular, substantial, essential beings. The particular essential beings, like man as such, have no absolute justification, for any justification they have they possess only as a moment of necessity, and as rooted in this absolute unity which is reflected into itself. They are many, though of divine nature, and this their scattered and manifold character is at the same time a limitation, so that divine nature is not attributed to them in any really serious sense. Above the many substantial essential beings there floats the ultimate unity of absolute form—necessity, and self-consciousness, which is in relation to the gods, is at the same time freed by this necessity from them, so that their divinity is at one time taken in a serious sense and at another in an opposite sense.

This religion has, speaking generally, the character of absolute joyousness; self-consciousness is free in relation to its essential beings, because they are its own, though at the same time it is not chained to them, since absolute necessity floats above them too, and they go back into it, just as consciousness with its particular ends and needs also sinks itself in it.

The feeling accordingly of subjective self-consciousness in relation to necessity is this sense of repose which abides in the region of calm, in this freedom, which is, however, still an abstract freedom. It is so far an escape, a flight, but it is at the same time freedom, inasmuch as man is not overcome, weighed down by outward misfortune. Whoever has this consciousness of independence may be indeed outwardly worsted, but he is not conquered or overcome.

Necessity has its own sphere; it has reference only to the particular element of individuality in so far as a collision of spiritual powers is possible, and the individuals are affected by necessity and are brought into subjection to it. Those individuals are in a special way in subjection to necessity and have a tragic interest attaching to them, who raise themselves above the ordinary moral conditions, and who seek to accomplish something special for themselves. This is the case with the heroes who through their own acts of will are separated from others; they have interests which go beyond the ordinary peaceful circumstances in which the government and action of God proceed. They are those who will and act in a special way of their own; they stand above the Chorus, above the calm, steady, harmonious, ordinary moral course of life. This last is exempt from the influence of destiny, restricts itself to the ordinary sphere of life, and rouses none of the moral powers against it. The Chorus, the people, viewed in one aspect, has its particular side too; it is subject to the common lot of mortals, namely, to die, to suffer misfortune and such-like, but an issue of this kind is the common lot of mortal men, and represents the course of justice relatively to the finite. That the individual should suffer some accidental misfortune, that he should die, is something which belongs to the order of things.

In Homer, Achilles weeps over his early death, and his horse weeps over it too. That would be regarded in our day as a silly thing for a poet to mention. But Homer could attribute to his hero this foreknowledge, for it cannot alter anything in his life and actions; it simply *is* so for him, and otherwise he is what he is. The thought can indeed make him sad, but only momentarily; things are so, but this disturbs him no further; he may indeed be sad, but he cannot be vexed or annoyed. Vexation is the sentiment of the modern world; the feeling of vexation or annoyance presupposes an end, a demand on the part of modern free will, which considers itself warranted and justified in indulging this feeling if any such end should not be realized. Thus the modern man easily gets into the mood in which he loses heart with regard to everything else, and does not even seek to reach other things he might quite well have made his aim if otherwise unsuccessful. All else that belongs to his nature and destiny he abandons, and in order to revenge himself destroys his own courage, his power of action, all those ends of destiny to which he might otherwise have quite well attained. This is vexation; it could not possibly have formed part of the character of the Greeks or of the ancients, the truth being that their grief regarding what is necessary is of a purely simple kind. The Greeks did not set before themselves any end as absolute, as essential, any end the attainment of which ought to be warranted; their grief is therefore a grief of resignation. It is simple sorrow, simple grief, which has for this reason the element of serenity in it. No absolute end is lost for the individual; here, too, he continues to be at home with himself, he can renounce that which is not realized. *It is so;* and this means that he has withdrawn himself into abstraction, and has not set his own Being in opposition to what is. The liberation here is the identity of the subjective will with that which *is;* the subject is free, but only in an abstract fashion.

The heroes, as was remarked, bring about an alteration in the course of simple necessity, in this way, namely, that an element of division comes in, and the higher, really interesting element of division, so far as Spirit is concerned, is that it is the moral powers themselves which appear as divided and as coming into collision.

The removal of this state of collision consists in this, that the moral powers which are in collision, in virtue of their one-sidedness, divest themselves of the one-sidedness attaching to the assertion of independent validity, and this discarding of the one-sidedness reveals itself outwardly in the fact that the individuals who have aimed at the realization in themselves of a single separate moral power, perish.

Fate is what is devoid of thought, of the Notion, something in which justice and injustice disappear in abstraction; in tragedy, on the other hand, destiny moves within a certain sphere of moral justice. We find this truth expressed in the noblest form in the Tragedies of Sophocles. Fate and necessity are both referred to there. The destiny of individuals is represented as something incomprehensible, but necessity is not a blind justice; on the contrary, it is recognized as the true justice. And just because of this these Tragedies are the immortal spiritual productions of moral understanding and comprehension, the eternal patterns or models of the moral Notion. Blind destiny is something unsatisfying. In these Tragedies justice is grasped by thought. The collision between the two highest moral powers is set forth in a plastic fashion in that supreme and absolute example of tragedy, "Antigone." In this case, family love, what is holy, what belongs to the inner life and to inner feeling, and which because of this is also called the law of the nether gods, comes into collision with the law of the State. Creon is not a tyrant, but really a moral power; Creon is not in the wrong; he maintains that the law of the State, the authority of government, is to be held in respect, and that punishment follows the infraction of the law. Each of these two sides realizes only one of the moral powers, and has only one of these as its content; this is the element of one-sidedness here, and the meaning of eternal justice is shown in this, that both end in injustice just because they are one-sided, though at the same time both obtain justice too. Both are recognized as having a value of their own in the untroubled course of morality. Here they both have their own validity, but a validity which is equalized. It is only the one-sidedness in their claims which justice comes forward to oppose.

We have another example of collision in the case of Oedipus, for instance. He has slain his father, is apparently guilty, but guilty because his moral power is one-sided; that is to say, he falls into the commission of his horrible deed unconsciously. He, however, is the man who has solved the riddle of the Sphinx; he is the man distinguished for knowledge, and so a kind of balance is introduced in the shape of a Nemesis. He, who is so gifted in knowledge, is in the power of what is un-conscious, so that he falls into a guilt which is deep in propor-tion to the height on which he stood. Here, therefore, we have the opposition of the two powers, that of consciousness and unconsciousness.

To mention still another case of collision. Hippolytus be-comes unfortunate because he pays honour to Diana only, and despises Love, which accordingly revenges itself on him. It is an absurdity to ascribe to Hippolytus another amour, as is done in the French version of the story by Racine, for in that case what he suffers is no punishment of Love with any pathos in it, but is merely a certain misfortune arising from the fact that he is enamoured of one maiden, and gives no heed to another woman; for though the latter is indeed his father's wife, still the moral hindrance implied in this is obscured by the love he has for Aricia. The real cause of his destruction is the injury he has done by his neglect of a universal Power as such; it is nothing moral, but is, on the contrary, something particular and accidental.

The conclusion of this Tragedy is reconciliation, rational ne-cessity, the necessity which here begins to mediate itself; it is justice which is in this way satisfied with the maxim, "There is nothing which is not Zeus," that is, eternal justice. Here there is an active necessity, but it is one which is completely moral; the misfortune endured is perfectly clear; here there is noth-ing blind and unconscious. To such clearness of insight and of artistic presentation did Greece attain at her highest stage of culture. Yet there remains here something unsolved in that the higher element does not appear as the infinitely spiritual power; we still have here an unsatisfied sorrow arising from the fact that an individual perishes.

The higher form of reconciliation would be that the attitude of one-sidedness should be done away with *in the Subject*, that the subject should have the consciousness of his wrongdoing, and that he should in his own heart put away his wrong-doing. To recognize this his guilt, his one-sidedness, and to discard them, is not, however, natural to this sphere of thought. This higher point of view makes the outward punishment, namely, natural death, superfluous. Beginnings, faint echoes of this reconciliation, do undoubtedly make their appearance here, but nevertheless this inward change or conversion appears more as outward purification. A son of Minos was slain in Athens, and its purification was thus rendered necessary. This deed was declared to be undone. It is Spirit which seeks to render what has been done undone.

In the "Eumenides" Orestes is acquitted by the Areopagus; here we have, on the one hand, the greatest possible crime against filial piety, while on the other we see that he did justice to his father, for he was not only head of the family, but also of the State. In one action he both committed a crime and at the same time acted in accordance with perfect and essential necessity. Acquittal just means that something is made undone, made as though it had not happened.

In the case of "Oedipus at Colonus" reconciliation is hinted at, and more particularly the Christian idea of reconciliation. He is taken into favour by the gods, the gods call him to themselves. In the present day we demand more, since with us the idea of reconciliation is of a higher kind, and because we are conscious that this conversion can occur in the inner life, whereby that which is done can be rendered undone.

The man who is "converted" gives up his one-sidedness; he has extirpated it himself in his will, which was the permanent seat of the deed, the place of its abode; that is, he destroys the act in its root. It is congenial to our way of feeling that tragedies should have conclusions which have in them the element of reconciliation.

b. Worship as Service

If the real point accordingly is that subjectivity should consciously pronounce its identity with the divine which confronts it, then both parts must give up something of their determinateness. God comes down from his throne of the universe and delivers Himself up, and man must, in the act of receiving the gift, accomplish the negation of subjective self-consciousness —that is, he must acknowledge God or take the gift with an acknowledgment of the essentiality which is in it. The service of God is consequently a reciprocal giving and receiving. Each side gives up something of the particularity which separates it from the other.

(1) The outward relation of the two sides to one another in its most extreme form is that God has in Himself a natural element, and exists independently relatively to self-consciousness in an immediate definite fashion; or, to put it otherwise, God has His existence in an external, natural manifestation. In this relation the service of God is on the one side an acknowledgment that natural things are an Essence in themselves. On the other side, the deity offers itself up, sacrifices itself in the power of Nature in which it appears, and allows itself to be taken possession of by self-consciousness.

If then the divine powers give themselves up as gifts of Nature and graciously offer themselves for use, the service in which man comes to have a consciousness of unity with his powers has the following signification:—

As for those fruits, those springs, which exist in Nature, they allow themselves to be used and drawn upon without hindrance, or to be laid hold of and used as nourishment. These gifts fall freely into the lap of man; man eats the gifts, drinks the wine, and gets from them invigoration and stimulus, and this invigoration in which they are an element, is their work, the effect they produce. In this relationship it is not a case of mere reciprocal action, the melancholy, continuous, self-producing uniformity of what is mechanical. On the contrary, these gifts are rendered honourable because man eats them and drinks of them; for to what higher honour can natural things attain than to appear as the inspiring force of spiritual action? Wine inspires, but it is man who first exalts it to the rank of an inspiring and power-giving agent. So far the relationship of bare need disappears. In connection with the sense of need man gives thanks to the gods for the receiving of the gifts, and these needs presuppose a separation which it is not in the power of man to do away with. Need, strictly so-called, first makes its appearance owing to property and the retention of something by one will, but man does not stand in such a relation of need to the gifts of Nature; on the contrary, they have to thank him that they come to be something, that anything is made of them; without him they would rot and dry up and pass away in uselessness.

The sacrifice which is connected with the enjoyment of these natural gifts has not here the sense of the offering up of what is inward or of the concrete fullness of Spirit; on the contrary, it is just this very fullness which is affirmed and enjoyed. Sacrifice in this case can only signify that acknowledgment of the universal Power which expresses the theoretical giving up of a part of what is to be enjoyed, i.e., the acknowledgment here is a useless and aimless kind of giving up, a renunciation which is not practical and has not reference to the self; as, for example, the pouring out of a bowl of wine. The sacrifice is itself at the same time the enjoyment of the thing; the wine is drunk, the meat is eaten, and it is the power of Nature itself whose individual existence and external form are offered up and destroyed. Eating means sacrifice, and sacrifice just means eating.

Thus this higher sense of sacrifice and the enjoyment found in it attach themselves to all the actions of life; every occupation, every enjoyment of daily life is a sacrifice. Worship is not renunciation, not the offering up of a possession, of something belonging to oneself, but is rather idealized, theoretical and artistic enjoyment. Freedom and spirituality are spread over the entire daily and immediate life of man, and worship is in short a continuous poetry of life.

The worship of these gods is accordingly not to be called service in the proper sense of the word, as something having reference to a foreign independent will from whose chance decision is to be obtained what is desired. On the contrary, the act of adoration itself already implies a previous granting of something, or, in other words, it is itself enjoyment. It is, therefore, not a question of calling a power back to oneself from its place beyond what is here and now, nor of renouncing what, on the subjective side of self-consciousness, constitutes the separation, in order that man may be receptive of the power. It is thus not a question of deprivation or renunciation, or of the laying aside of something subjective belonging to the individual, nor does the idea of anguish, of self-tormenting, of self-torture come in here. The worship of Bacchus or of Ceres is the possession, the enjoyment of bread and wine, the consumption of these, and is therefore itself the immediate granting of these things. The Muse to which Homer appeals is in the same way his genius, and so on.

The universal powers, however, in this case certainly retire farther into the background again, so far as the individual is concerned. The spring allows itself to be drawn upon unhindered, and the sea allows itself to be freely frequented, but it also rises in storm; it and the stars are not only not serviceable to man, but inspire fear, and are a source of disaster. Nor is the Muse always gracious to the poet either; she goes away and serves him badly, though, properly speaking, the poet really appeals to her only when he is composing his poem, and the appeal to and praise of the Muse is itself Poetry. Even Athene—Spirit, God—is unfaithful to herself. The Tyrians bound their Hercules with chains, so that he should not desert their city, which represented his reality and actual real existence; and yet Tyre fell. But such estrangement on the part of men from their essentiality or embodiment of essential Being does not lead to absolute division, not to that inward laceration of heart which would compel men to draw down their deity, so to speak, by the force of spirit to themselves in worship, and with which the lapse into magic would be connected. The individual cannot go on living in endless opposition to these particular powers, because as particular ends they lose themselves in necessity, and are themselves surrendered in this necessity.

Service hence consists in the fact that the universal powers are given a place of honour on their own account and are duly acknowledged. Thought grasps the essential, substantial element of its concrete life, and hence is neither sunk in a state of torpor in the empirical details of life and dissipated amongst these, nor does it turn from these merely to the abstract One, to the infinite "Beyond." On the contrary, just because Spirit sets before itself the true element, the Idea of its manifold existence, it is, in the very act of acknowledging and doing reverence to this universal, in the state of enjoyment, and remains in the presence of its own nature. This presence of Spirit in its essentialities is on the one hand its truly valuable, thinking, theoretic relationship, and on the other hand is that happiness, joyousness, and freedom which is securely conscious of itself in this state, and is here in presence of its self, or together with its own self.

(2) Service as a certain relationship to the gods on their

spiritual side does not mean either that man appropriates these powers for the first time, or that man for the first time becomes conscious of his identity with them. For this identity is already present, and man finds these powers already realized in his consciousness. The spiritual in a definite form, as right, morality, law, or in the form of universal essential beings, such as Love, Aphrodite, attains actual existence in individuals, moral individuals, who know and love. They are the will, the inclination, the passion of these individuals themselves, their own willing, active, life. Consequently what is left for worship to do is merely to acknowledge these powers, to revere them, and together with this, to raise the identity into the form of consciousness, and to make it into theoretic objectivity.

If we compare this objectivity with our idea, we at the same time lift the universal out of our immediate consciousness and think it. We can also go on to raise these universal powers into the sphere of the ideal and give them spiritual form. But when it comes to offering prayer or bringing sacrifices to such creations, we reach the point at which we abandon the material view referred to. We cannot go so far as to give those images, which yet are no mere fancies but real powers, individual separate independence and ascribe personality to them as over against ourselves. Our consciousness of infinite subjectivity as something universal absorbs those particular powers and reduces them to the level of beautiful pictures of fancy, whose substance and significance we are indeed able to appreciate, but which cannot be held by us to have true independence.

In Greek life, however, poetry, the thinking imagination, is itself the essential Service of God. Viewed from one side, these powers split up *ad infinitum,* and, although they constitute an exclusive circle, just because they are particular powers they themselves come almost to have the infinitude of the qualities belonging to them when they are thought of as actually existing. What a number of particular relations are comprised in Pallas, for instance! Viewed from the other side, again, we see that it is the human, sensuous-spiritual form in which the ideal is to be represented, and as a consequence of all this, this representation is inexhaustible, and must ever continue to go on and renew itself, for the religious sense is itself this continuous transition from empirical existence to the ideal. There is here no fixed, spiritually definite doctrinal system, no doctrine; we have not truth as such in the form of thought; on the contrary, we see the divine in this immanent connection with reality, and hence always raising itself up anew and producing itself in and out of this reality. If this active production is brought to perfection by art, imagination has reached its ultimate fixed form, so that the ideal is set up, and then we find that there is a close connection between this and the decay of religious life.

So long, however, as the productive force which characterizes this standpoint is fresh and active, the highest form of the assimilation of the divine consists in this, that the subject makes the god present through himself, and makes the god manifest in his own self. Because in this connection the recognized subjectivity of the god at the same time remains on one side as a "Beyond," this representation of the divine is at the same time the acknowledgment and the adoration of his own substantial essentiality. Thus accordingly the divine is revered and acknowledged when it is represented in festivals, games, plays, songs—in art, in short. For any one is honoured in so far as a lofty idea is formed of him, and in so far too as this idea is made visible through action and is allowed to appear outwardly in his conduct.

Now since the nation in the productions of art, in the honour paid in songs and festivals, allows the idea of the divine to appear in itself, it has its worship in itself, i.e., it directly shows what is really *its own* excellence; it shows the best it has, that which it has been capable of making itself. Men adorn themselves; pageantry, dress, adornment, dance, song, battle—all are connected with the desire to show honour to the gods. Man shows his spiritual and bodily ability and skill, his riches; he exhibits himself in all the glory of God, and thus enjoys the manifestation of God in the individual himself. This characterizes festivals even yet. This general description may suffice to show that man allows the idea of the gods to appear to him through himself, and that he represents himself in the most splendid possible way, and thus shows his reverential recognition of the gods. High honour was ascribed to the victors in battle; they were the most honoured of the nation; on festive occasions they sat beside the Archons, and it even happened that in their lifetime they were revered as gods, inasmuch as they had given outward manifestation to the divine in themselves through the skill which they had shown. In this way individuals make the divine manifest in themselves. In practice individuals honour the gods, are moral—that which is the will of the gods is what is moral—and thus they bring the divine into the sphere of actual reality. The people of Athens, for example, who held a procession at the festival of Pallas, represented the presence of Athene, the spirit of the people, and this people is the living spirit which represents and exhibits in itself all the skill of Athene and all that is done by her.

(3) But man may be ever so certain of his immediate identity with the essential powers, and may thoroughly appropriate divinity to himself and rejoice in its presence in him, and in the presence of himself in it; he may continue to absorb those natural gods, and represent the moral gods in morality and in the life of the State, or he may in practice live a godly life and bring into view the outward embodiment and manifestation of divinity in festivals in his own subjectivity; still there yet remains for consciousness a "Beyond," that is to say, the entire particular element in action and in the circumstances and relations of the individual, and the connection of these relations with God. Our belief that Providence in its action reaches even to the individual, finds its confirmation in the fact that God has become man, and this in the actual and temporal mode within which consequently all particular individuality is comprehended, for it is owing to this that subjectivity has received the absolute moral justification by which it is subjectivity of the infinite self-consciousness. In the beautiful form given to the gods, in the images, stories, and local representations connected with them, the element of infinite individuality, of particularity in its most extreme form, is doubtless directly contained and expressed, still it is a particularity which in one aspect of it is one of the chief defects charged against the mythology of Homer and Hesiod, while in another aspect these stories belong so specially to the god represented that they have no reference to other gods or men, just as amongst men each individual has his own ticular experiences, doings, circumstances, and history,

belong wholly and entirely to his particular life. The moment of subjectivity does not appear as infinite subjectivity, it is not Spirit as such which is contemplated in the objective forms given to the divine; and wisdom is what must constitute the fundamental characteristic of the divine. This, as working in accordance with ends, must be comprised within one infinite wisdom, within one subjectivity. The truth that human things are ruled over by the gods is thus no doubt involved in that religion, but in an indeterminate, general sense, for it is just the gods who are the ruling powers in all that concerns man. The gods too are certainly just, but justice, so far as it is one Power, is a titanic power and pertains to the ancient gods. The beautiful gods have a valid existence of their own in their particular forms and come to be in collision, and these collisions are only settled by equal honour being given to all—a method, however, which certainly gives no immanent settlement.

From gods such as these, in whom the absolute return into self has not made its appearance, the individual could not look for absolute wisdom and ordered design in connection with what happened to him in life. Man, however, still feels the need of having above his particular acts and particular lot, an objective determining principle. He does not possess this in the thought of divine wisdom and Providence so as to be able to trust it in general, and for the rest to depend upon his own formal knowledge and will, and to await the absolute and entire consummation of these, or else to seek some compensation for the loss and failure of his particular interests and ends, or for his misfortune, in an eternal end.

When the particular interests of man, his happiness or misery, are concerned, we find that this outward element in what happens still depends on whether a man does this or that, goes to this or that other place. This is *his* act, his decision, which he, however, in turn knows to be contingent. As regards the circumstances which I actually know, I can doubtless decide one way or other. But besides these thus known to me, others may exist through which the realization of my end is completely defeated. In connection with these actions I am thus in the world of contingency. Within this sphere knowledge is accordingly contingent; it has no relation to what is ethical, nd truly substantial, to the duties to country, the State, and so on; man cannot, however, get to know this contingent element. The decision consequently cannot so far have anything fixed about it, nor be in any way grounded in the nature of things, but in deciding I know at the same time that I am dependent on what is other than myself, on what is unknown. Now, since neither in the divine nor in the individual is the moment of infinite subjectivity present, it does not fall to the individual to take the final decision of himself, to perform of himself the final act of will, for instance, to give battle to-day, to marry, to travel; for the man is conscious that objectivity does not reside in this willing of his, and that it is formal merely. To satisfy the longing for this completion and to add on this objectivity, a direction from without is required coming from one higher than the individual, that is, the direction of an external, decisive, and definite sign. It is the inner free will which, that it may not be mere free will, makes itself objective, i.e., makes itself inalienably into what is other than itself and accepts the external free will as higher than itself. It is, speaking generally, some power of Nature, a natural phenomenon, which now decides. The man, amazed at what he sees, finds in such a natural phenomenon something relative to himself, because he does not yet see in it any objective essential significance, or, to put it otherwise, he does not see in Nature an inherently perfect system of laws. The formal rational element, the feeling and the belief in the identity of the inward and outward, lies at the basis of his conception, but the inward element of Nature, or the universal to which it stands related, is not the connection of its laws; on the contrary, it is a human end, a human interest.

When, accordingly, any one wills anything, he demands, in order actually to take his resolution, an external objective confirmation or assurance; he asks that he should know his resolution to be one which is a unity of the subjective and objective, one which is assured and ratified. And here this ratification is the unexpected, something which happens suddenly, a materially significant, unconnected change in things, a flash in a clear sky, a bird rising up in a wide uniform horizon, and which breaks in upon the indeterminateness of the inner irresolution. This is an appeal to what is inward, an appeal to act suddenly, and to come to a determination within the mind in

a chance way without a knowledge of the connection and
grounds, for this is just the point at which the grounds or reasons stop short, or at which they are in fact absent.

The outward phenomenon which is nearest at hand for the
accomplishment of the end in view, namely, the finding out
of what is to determine action, is a sound, a noise, a voice,
ὄμφη, whence Delphi has got the name ὄμφαλος, a supposi-
tion which is certainly more correct than that which would
find in it the other meaning of the word, namely, the navel of
the earth. In Dodona there were three kinds of sounds—the
sound produced by the movement of the leaves in the sacred
oak, the murmuring of a spring, and the sound coming from
a brazen vessel struck by rods of brass moved by the wind.
At Delos the laurel rustled; at Delphi the wind which blew
on the brazen tripod was the principal element. It was not till
later on that the Pythia had to be stupefied by vapours, when
in her raving she emitted words without any connection, and
which had first to be explained by the priest. It was the priest,
too, who interpreted dreams. In the cave of Trophonius the
inquirer saw visions, and these were interpreted to him. In
Achaia, as Pausanias relates, there was a statue of Mars, and
the question was spoken into its ear, after which the ques-
tioner went away from the market with his fingers in his ears.
The first word heard by him after his ears were opened was
the answer, which was then connected with the question by
interpretation. To the same class of signs belong also the ques-
tioning of the entrails of sacrificial animals, the signification
of the flight of birds, and several other such purely external
rites. Animals were slaughtered in sacrifice till auspicious to-
kens were got. In the case of the oracles, two things went to
constitute the verdict—the outward word and the explanation.
With regard to the former, the mind took up a receptive attitude, but with regard to the latter, its attitude, as being the
interpreter, was an active one, for the outward element in itself was supposed to be indeterminate. (Αἱ τῶν δαιμόνων
φωναὶ ἄναρθροί εἰσιν.) But even as representing the concrete
expression of the decision of the god, the oracles have a double
meaning. Man acts in accordance with them while taking the
words in *one* of their aspects. The other meaning, however,
appears in opposition to the first, and so man comes into colli-

sion with the oracle. The oracles just mean that man shows himself to be ignorant, and shows that the god has knowledge; as ignorant, man accepts the utterance of the god who has knowledge. He consequently does not represent the knowledge of something revealed, but the absence of the knowledge of this. He does not act with knowledge in accordance with the revelation of the god, which, as being general, has no inherent determinate meaning, and thus, where there is a possibility of two meanings, it must be ambiguous. The oracle says, "Depart, and the enemy will be conquered." Here both enemies are "the enemy." The revelation of the divine is general, and must be general; man interprets it as one who is ignorant, he acts in accordance with it. The action is his own, and thus he knows himself to be responsible. The flight of birds, the rustling of oaks, are general signs. To the definite question, the god, as representing the divine in general, gives a general answer, for it is only what is general, and not the individual as such, that is included in the end aimed at by the gods. The general is, however, indeterminate, ambiguous, capable of a double meaning, for it comprises both sides.

c. Service as Reconciliation

What came first in worship was religious sentiment; then, secondly, we had worship as service, the concrete relationship, where, however, negativity as such has not yet appeared. The third form of the service of God is the divine service of reconciliation. The gods must be realized in the soul, in the subject, which is hypothetically estranged, i.e., negatively determined relatively to the divine, and in opposition to it. The agreement cannot take place in the immediate way characteristic of the foregoing form; on the contrary, it demands a mediation in which that must be sacrificed which was formerly held to be fixed and independent. This negative element, which must be yielded up in order that the estrangement and alienation of the two sides may be removed, is of a twofold kind. In the first place, the soul, in its character as the natural or untutored soul, is negative relatively to Spirit; the second negative element is accordingly the positive-negative element, so to speak, that is, any misfortune whatever, and more definitely, in the third place, a moral misfortune or crime, the extreme alienation of the subjective self-consciousness relatively to the divine.

(1) The soul in its natural state is not as it should be; it ought to be free Spirit, but the soul is Spirit only through the abrogation of the natural will, of the desires. This abrogation, this subjection of itself to what is moral, and the habituation to this so that the moral or spiritual becomes the second nature of the individual, is, above all, the work of education and culture. The thought of this reconstruction of man's nature must accordingly come into consciousness at this standpoint, because it is the standpoint of self-conscious freedom, and come into it in such a way as to show that this change or conversion is recognized as requisite. If this training and conversion are represented as essential moments, and as essentially living, we get the idea of a road which the soul has to traverse, and as a consequence we get the idea of some outward arrangement in which it is supplied with the pictorial representation of this road. But if the course followed by this conversion, this self-negation and dying to self, is to be set forth for perception or pictorial contemplation as absolute and essential, it must be beheld in the divine objects themselves. The need for this has, as a matter of fact, been obviated by means of a process which, in the pictorial representation of the world of the gods, has been carried out in the following way.

It is a fact intimately connected with the adoration of the many divinities,—which, however, just because they are many are limited divine beings,—that there is also a transition to the universality of the divine power. The limited character of the gods itself leads directly to the idea of a transcendence, a rising above them, and to the attempt to unite them in one concrete picture, and not merely in abstract necessity, for the latter is not anything objective. As yet this transcendence cannot here be the absolute inherently concrete subjectivity as Spirit, but neither can it be the return to the pictorial representation or perception of the power of the One and to the negative service of the Lord. On the contrary, the One which is the object for self-consciousness at this standpoint is a unity which is in a concrete fashion all-embracing; it is universal Nature as a whole, or, a totality of gods, the content of the sensuous-spiritual world united in a material fashion. Inasmuch as self-consciousness cannot advance to infinite subjectivity, which as Spirit would be inherently concrete, the perception or picturing of substantial unity is something already present so far as this stage is concerned and preserved from the older religions. For the older original religions are the definite nature-religions, in which this Spinozism, namely, the immediate unity of the spiritual and the natural, constitutes the foundation. But further, the older form of religion, however much it may be locally defined and limited in its outward representation and in the mode in which it is conceived of, is, before it reaches its developed form, still inherently indefinite and general. Each local god in its determination of locality has at the same time the significance of universality, and since this is firmly clung to as against the splitting up and particularization into characters and individualities developed in the Religion of Beauty, it is in what is rude and primitive, in what is unbeautiful and uncultured, that the service of a deeper, inner universal, maintains itself, a universal which is at the same time not abstract thought, but which, on the contrary, retains in itself that external and contingent form.

This older religion may, on account of its simplicity and substantial intensity, be called deeper, purer, stronger, more substantial, and its meaning may be termed a truer one, but its meaning is essentially enveloped in a kind of haze, and is not developed into thought, that is, is not developed into that clearness which marks the particular gods in whom the day of Spirit has dawned, and which have in consequence attained to character and spiritual form. The service of this deeper and universal element involves, however, in it, the opposition of this deeper and universal element itself to the particular, limited, and revealed powers. It is, regarded from one side, a return from these to what is deeper, more inward, and so far higher, the bringing back of the many scattered gods into the unity of Nature, but it also involves the antithesis which is expressed by saying that this deeper element is as opposed to clear self-consciousness, to the serenity of day and rationality, something dull and torpid, unconscious, crude, and barbarous. The perception, or pictorial contemplation, in this kind of worship, is accordingly in one aspect the perception of the uni-

versal life of Nature and of natural force, a return to inward
substantiality; but in another aspect it is equally the perception of the process, of the transition from savagery to a state
of law, from barbarousness to morality, from mental torpor to
the clear growing certainty of self-consciousness, from the Titanic to the Spiritual. It is consequently not a god in his finished
form who is beheld here, no abstract doctrine is propounded;
on the contrary, the content of perception is the conflict of
what is original and primitive, which is brought forth from
its undeveloped state into clearness, into form, into the daylight of consciousness. This idea is already present in many
exoteric and pictorial forms in mythology. The war of the gods
and the conquests of the Titans is just this divine issuing forth
of the spiritual from the overcoming of the rude powers of
Nature.

It is here accordingly that the action of the subjective side
and its movement receive their deeper determination. Worship cannot here be merely serene enjoyment, the enjoyment
of present immediate unity with the particular powers; for
since the divine passes out of its particularity over to universality, and since self-consciousness is reversed or inverted within
itself, opposition is consequently present, and the union starts
from a separation greater than that presupposed by outward
worship. Worship here is rather the movement of an inward
impression made on the soul, an introduction to and initiation
into an essentiality which is for it foreign and abstract, an entrance into disclosures which its ordinary life and the worship
grounded on that do not contain. Just because the soul enters
into this sphere the demand is made that it should give up its
natural Being and essence. This worship is thus at the same
time the purification of the soul, a path to this purification,
and a gradual progress towards it, the admission into the high
mystical Essence, and the attainment of a contemplation in
pictorial form of its secrets, which, however, have for the initiated ceased to be secrets, and can only still remain such in
the sense that the pictures thus contemplated, and this content, are not introduced into the sphere of ordinary existence
and consciousness, that is, into the sphere of ordinary action
and reflection. All Athenian citizens were initiated into the
Eleusinian mysteries. A secret is thus essentially something

known, only not by all. Here, however, there is something known by all, which is merely treated as secret, i.e., secret only to this extent, that it is not made the talk of everyday life, just as we see in the case of Jews, who do not name the name Jehovah, or, to take an opposite case, just as in daily life there are things known to all but of which no one speaks. But these pictures of the divine were not mystical in the sense in which the public doctrines of Christendom have been called mysteries. For in the case of the latter the mystical element is the inward and speculative element. What had been seen by the initiated had to remain secret, mainly because the Greeks would not have been able to speak of it otherwise than in myths, that is to say, not without altering what was old.

But even in this worship, although it starts from a definite opposition, joyousness or serenity still continues to constitute the basis. The path of purification is traversed indeed, but that does not represent the infinite pain and doubt in which the abstract self-consciousness isolates itself from itself in its abstract knowledge, and because of this moves and pulsates merely within itself when in this empty abstract form, is merely a kind of inward trembling, and in this abstract certainty of itself cannot absolutely reach fixed truth and objectivity, nor come to have the feeling of these. On the contrary, it is always on the basis of that unity that this traversing of the path exists and has value as the actually completed purification of the soul, as absolution, and having this original unconscious basis remains rather an external process of the soul, since the latter does not go down into the innermost depths of negativity as is the case where subjectivity is completely developed and attains to infinitude. If terrors, frightful images, forms inspiring dread, and such like, are already employed here, and if, on the other hand, and in contrast to this dark side, bright and brilliant representations, significant pictures full of splendour are made use of to produce a deeper effect on the mind, the initiated is purified in the very process of passing through the experience of seeing these pictorial forms and having these emotions.

These mystical perceptions or pictorial forms accordingly correspond to those pictorial forms of the divine life, the process of which is set forth in tragedy and comedy. The fear, the

sympathy, the grief represented in tragedy, all those conditions
in which self-consciousness is carried away, and in which it
shares, are just what forms that process of purification which
accomplishes all that should be accomplished. In the same way
the pictorial representations of comedy, and the giving up by
Spirit of its dignity, of its value, of its opinion of itself, and
even of its fundamental powers, this entire surrender of all
that belongs to self, is just this worship in which the spirit,
through this surrender of all that is finite, enjoys and retains
the indestructible certainty of itself.

In public worship even the main interest is not so much the
paying of honour to the gods as the enjoyment of the divine.
Since, however, in this worship of mysteries, the soul is on its
own account elevated into an end and is regarded in this condition of contrast as abstract, independent, and, as it were,
sundered from the divine, the idea of the immortality of the
soul necessarily makes its appearance here. The completed
purification raises it above the temporal, fleeting, present existence, and inasmuch as it is made permanently free, the idea
of the passing over of the individual as one dead on his natural
side, into an eternal life, is closely associated with this form
of worship. The individual is made a citizen of the essential,
ideal kingdom of the under world, in which temporal reality is
reduced to the condition of a phantom world.

Since then the mysteries represent the return of the Greek
spirit to its first beginnings, the form of what constitutes these
is essentially symbolical, i.e., the signification is something
other than the outward representation. The Greek gods themselves are not symbolical; they are what they represent, just
as the conception of a work of art means the giving expression
to what is meant, and does not mean that what is inward is
something different from what is outwardly seen. Even if the
beginnings of the Greek god are to be traced back to some
such ancient symbolic representation, still what this is actually
made into has become the work of art which perfectly expresses what it is intended to be. Many have sought, and especially Creuzer, to investigate the historical origin of the Greek
gods, and the signification which lies at the basis of their character. But if the god is a subject for art, that alone is a good
work of art which exhibits him as what he actually is. In the

religions of nature this is a mystery, something inward, a symbol, because the outward form does not actually reveal the meaning which lies in this mystery, the idea rather being that it is merely *intended* to reveal it. Osiris is a symbol of the sun, and similarly Hercules and his twelve labours have reference to the months; thus he is a god of the calendar, and no longer the modern Greek god. In the mysteries, the content, the manifestation, is essentially symbolical. The principal symbols had reference to Ceres, Demeter, Bacchus, and the secrets connected with these. As Ceres, who seeks her daughter, is in the language of prose the seed that must die in order to retain its true essence and to bring it into life, so, too, the seed and the germination of the seed are in turn something symbolical; for, as in the Christian religion, they have the higher signification of resurrection, or they can be taken as meaning that the same holds good of Spirit, whose true essence or potential nature can bear blossoms only through the annulling of the natural will. Thus the meaning changes about; at one time this content signifies an idea, some process, and then again the idea, the signification, may itself be the symbol for something else. Osiris is the Nile which is dried up by Typhon, the fire-world, and is again brought into existence; but he is also a symbol of the sun, a universal life-giving power of Nature. Osiris finally is also a spiritual figure, and in this case the Nile and the sun are in turn symbols of the spiritual. Such symbols are naturally mysterious. The inward element is not clear as yet; it exists first as meaning, signification, which has not yet attained to true outward representation. The outward form does not perfectly express the content, so that the latter remains in a partially expressed shape at the basis of the whole without coming forth into existence. Hence it came about that the mysteries could not give to the self-consciousness of the Greeks true reconciliation. Socrates was declared by the oracle to be the wisest of the Greeks, and to him is to be traced the real revolution which took place in the Greek self-consciousness. This pivot, so to speak, of self-consciousness was not, however, himself initiated into the mysteries; they stand far below what he brought into the consciousness of the thinking world. All this has to do with the first form of reconciliation.

(2) The other negative element is misfortune in general,

sickness, dearth, or any other mishaps. This negative element is explained by the prophets, and brought into connection with some guilty act or transgression. A negative of this kind first appears in the physical world in the shape, for example, of an unfavourable wind. The physical condition is then explained as having a spiritual connection, and as involving in itself the ill-will and wrath of the gods—that ill-will and wrath which are brought upon men by some crime and by some offence against the divine. Or it may be that lightning, thunder, an earthquake, the appearance of snakes, and such-like are interpreted to mean something negative which essentially attaches to a spiritual and moral Power. In this case the injury has to be done away with through sacrifice, and in such a way that he who has shown himself arrogant by committing the crime, imposes a forfeiture on himself, for arrogance is an injury done to a spiritual higher Power, to which accordingly humility has to sacrifice something in order to propitiate it and restore the equilibrium. In the case of the Greeks this idea seems rather to belong to primitive times. When the Greeks wished to depart from Aulis, and unfavourable winds held them back, Calchas interpreted the storm to be the wrath of Poseidon, who demands the daughter of Agamemnon as a sacrifice. Agamemnon is ready to give her up to the god. Diana saves the girl. In the "Oedipus Tyrannus" of Sophocles a certain disease is sent by means of which the deed of the parricide is disclosed. In later times such ideas no longer make their appearance. During the pestilence in the Peloponnesian war we hear nothing of the worship of the gods; no sacrifice was made during this war; we meet only with predictions of its conclusion. The appeal to the oracle implies that such a sacrifice has become antiquated. That is to say, if counsel is asked of the oracle, the result is viewed as determined by the god himself. Thus the result came to be regarded as something which has to happen, as a matter of necessity, a matter of fixed destiny, in connection with which no reconciliation could have a place, which could not be averted and could not be remedied.

(3) The final form of reconciliation implies that the negative is really a crime, and is so regarded and declared to be such; not a crime which is only perceived to be such by the help of the explanation given through some misfortune. An in-

dividual, a state, a people commits a crime; from the human point of view the punishment is the propitiation for the crime either in the form of punishment or in the cruder form of revenge. The free spirit has the self-consciousness of its majesty, whereby it has to make what has happened as if it had not happened, and to do this within itself. An outward act of pardon is something different, but that what has happened can within the mind itself come to be what has not happened, is something which belongs to the higher privilege of free self-consciousness, where evil is not merely act, but is something fixed and settled, and has its seat in the heart, in the guilty soul. The free soul can purify itself from this evil. Faint resemblances of this inward conversion do occur, but the general character of reconciliation here is rather outward purification. With the Greeks this too is something belonging to ancient times. A couple of instances of this are well known in connection with the history of Athens. A son of Minos was slain in Athens, and on account of this deed a purification was undertaken. Aeschylus relates that the Areopagus acquitted Orestes; the rock of Athena stood him in good stead. The reconciliation here is regarded as something outward, not as inward confession. The idea expressed in "Oedipus at Colonus" savours of Christian thought; in it this old Oedipus, who slew his father and married his mother, and who was banished along with his sons, is raised to a place of honour among the gods; the gods call him to themselves. Other sacrifices belong still more to the outward mode of reconciliation. This is the case with the sacrifices to the dead, which are intended to propitiate the Manes. Achilles, for example, slew a number of Trojans on the grave of Patroclus, his intention being to restore the uniformity of destiny on both sides.

3. TRAGEDY AND THE IMPIETY OF SOCRATES

[e]Parallel with the advance in the development of Religious Art and with political growth, we find a progressive strengthen-

[e] *The Philosophy of History*, p. 268.

ing of Thought, its enemy and destroyer. ꜛAnd it was in *Socrates*, that at the beginning of the Peloponnesian War, the principle of subjectivity—of the absolute inherent independence of Thought—attained free expression. He taught that man has to discover and recognize in himself what is the Right and Good, and that this Right and Good is in its nature universal. Socrates is celebrated as a Teacher of Morality, but we should rather call him the *Inventor of Morality*. The Greeks had a *customary* morality; but Socrates undertook to teach them what moral virtues, duties, etc. were. The moral man is not he who merely wills and does that which is right—not the merely innocent man—but he who has the consciousness of what he is doing.

Socrates—in assigning to insight, to conviction, the determination of men's actions—posited the Individual as capable of a final moral decision, in contraposition to Country and to Customary Morality, and thus made himself an Oracle, in the Greek sense. He said that he had a δαιμόνιον within him, which counselled him what to do, and revealed to him what was advantageous to his friends. The rise of the inner world of Subjectivity was the rupture with the existing Reality. Though Socrates himself continued to perform his duties as a citizen, it was not the actual State and its religion, but the world of Thought that was his true home.

When Socrates wishes to induce his friends to reflection, the discourse has always a negative tone; he brings them to the consciousness that they do not know what the Right is. But when on account of the giving utterance to that principle which was advancing to recognition, Socrates is condemned to death, the sentence bears on the one hand the aspect of unimpeachable rectitude—inasmuch as the Athenian people condemns its deadliest foe—but on the other hand, that of a deeply tragical character, inasmuch as the Athenians had to make the discovery, that what they reprobated in Socrates had already struck firm root among themselves, and that they must be pronounced guilty or innocent with him.

ꜛ *The Philosophy of History,* pp. 269–70.

a. The Attacks

[g]The attacks which Socrates experienced are well known, and were from two sources; Aristophanes attacked him in the "Clouds," and then he was formally accused before the people.

Aristophanes regarded the Socratic philosophy from the negative side, maintaining that through the cultivation of reflecting consciousness, the idea of law had been shaken, and we cannot question the justice of this conception. Aristophanes' consciousness of the one-sidedness of Socrates may be regarded as a prelude to his death; the Athenian people likewise certainly recognized his negative methods in condemning him. It is known that Aristophanes brought upon the stage along with Socrates, not only such men as Aeschylus, and more specially Euripides, but also the Athenians generally and their generals —the personified Athenian people and the gods themselves—a freedom which we would not dream of were it not historically authenticated. We have not here to consider the real nature of the Comedy of Aristophanes, nor the wanton way in which he was said to have treated Socrates. As to the first, it should not startle us, nor do we require to justify Aristophanes or to excuse him. The Comedy of Aristophanes is in itself as real a part of the Athenian people, and Aristophanes is as essential a figure, as were the sublime Pericles, the happy Alcibiades, the divine Sophocles, and the moral Socrates, for he belongs as much as any other to this circle of luminaries. Thus much can alone be said, that it certainly goes against our German seriousness to see how Aristophanes brings on the boards men living in the State, by name, in order to make a jest of them; and we feel this specially in regard to so upright a man as Socrates.

By chronological considerations, some have tried hard to refute the fact that Aristophanes' representations had no influence on the condemnation of Socrates. It is seen that, on the one hand, Socrates was treated quite unjustly; but then we

[g] *Hegel's Lectures on the History of Philosophy,* ed. and tr. E. S. Haldane. London, 1955, vol. I, pp. 426–48.

must recognize the merit of Aristophanes, who in his "Clouds" was perfectly right. This poet, who exposed Socrates to scorn in the most laughable and bitter way, was thus no ordinary joker and shallow wag who mocked what is highest and best, and sacrificed all to wit with a view to making the Athenians laugh. For everything has to him a much deeper basis, and in all his jokes there lies a depth of seriousness. He did not wish merely to mock; and moreover to mock what was worthy of honour would be perfectly bald and flat. It is a pitiful wit which has no substance, and does not rest on contradictions lying in the matter itself. But Aristophanes was no bad jester. It is, generally speaking, not possible to joke in an external way about what does not contain matter for joking or irony in itself. For what really is comic is to show a man or a thing as they disclose themselves in their extent; and if the thing is not itself its contradiction, the comic element is superficial and groundless. Hence, when Aristophanes makes merry over the Democracy, there is a deep political earnestness at heart, and from all his works it appears what a noble, excellent, true Athenian citizen he was. We thus have a real patriot before us, who, though it involved the punishment of death, did not fear in one of his works to counsel peace. In him, as one who had a patriotism of the most enlightened kind, we find the blissful self-satisfied enjoyment of a people giving free rein to itself. There is, in what is humorous, a self-security which, though with all seriousness it strives after some particular thing, while the opposite of what it aims at always comes to pass, never has for that reason any doubts nor any reflection about itself, since it remains perfectly certain of itself and of what concerns it. We enjoy in Aristophanes this side of the free Athenian spirit, this perfect enjoyment of itself in loss, this un-troubled certainty of itself in all miscarriage of the result in real life, and this is the height of humour.

In the "Clouds" we do not indeed see this natural humour, but a contradiction with definite intention. Aristophanes in-deed depicts Socrates humorously too, for he brings forth in his moral works the opposite of that from which he starts, and his scholars derive delight from the far-extending discoveries reached through him, which they think are made by their own good luck, but which afterwards turn hateful to them, and become the very opposite of what they intended. The wonderful perception which the followers of Socrates are here represented as having attained is just a perception of the nullity of the laws of the determinate good as it is to the natural consciousness. Aristophanes made fun of the fact that Socrates occupied himself with elementary researches as to how far fleas spring, and of his putting wax on their feet in order to discover this. This is not historic, but it is well known that Socrates had in his philosophy the side which Aristophanes showed up with such acrimony. Shortly, the fable of the "Clouds" is this: Strepsiades, an honourable Athenian citizen of the old school, had great trouble with his new-fashioned extravagant son, who, spoiled by mother and uncle, kept horses and led a life out of keeping with his position. The father thus got into trouble with his creditors, and went in distress to Socrates, and became his disciple. There the old man learned that not this or that, but another is the right, or rather he learned the stronger (κρείττων) and weaker reasons (ἥττων λόγος). He learned the dialectic of laws, and how, by reasoning, the payment of debts can be disregarded, and he then required that his son should go to the School of Socrates; and the latter likewise profited from his wisdom. But we find the result ensuing from the universal which has now through the Socratic dialectic become empty, in the private interest or the wrong spirit of Strepsiades and his son, which spirit is merely the negative consciousness of the content of laws. Equipped with this new wisdom of reasons, and the discovery of reasons, Strepsiades is armed against the chief evil that presses on him, as regards his threatening creditors. These now come one after another to obtain payment. But Strepsiades knows how to put them off with excellent reasons, and to argue them away, for he pacifies them by all sorts of *titulos,* and shows them that he does not need to pay them; indeed he even mocks them, and is very glad that he learned all this from Socrates. But soon the scene changes, and the whole affair alters. The son comes, behaves in a very unseemly way to his father, and finally beats him. The father cries to the supreme power, as if this were the last indignity, but the son shows him, with equally good reasons, obtained by the method derived by him from Socrates, that he had a perfect right to strike him. Strepsiades ends the comedy with execrations on the Socratic dialectic, with a return to his old ways, and with the burning of Socrates' house. The exaggeration which may be ascribed to Aristophanes is that he drove this dialectic to its bitter end, but it cannot be said that injustice is done to Socrates by this representation. Indeed we must admire the depth of Aristophanes in having recognized the dialectic side in Socrates as being a negative, and—though after his own way—in having presented it so forcibly. For the power of judging in Socrates' method is always placed in the subject, in conscience, but where this is bad, the story of Strepsiades must repeat itself.

With regard to the formal public accusation of Socrates, we must not, like Tennemann (Vol. II., p. 39 seq.), say of Socrates' treatment, that "it is revolting to humanity that this excellent man had to drink the cup of poison as a sacrifice to cabals—so numerous in democracies. A man like Socrates, who had made right" (right is not being discussed, but we may ask what right? The right of moral freedom) "the sole standard of his action, and did not stray from the straight path, must necessarily make many enemies" (Why? This is foolish; it is a moral hypocrisy to pretend to be better than others who are then called enemies) "who are accustomed to act from quite different motives. When we think of the corruption, and of the rule of the thirty tyrants, we must simply wonder that he could have worked on to his sixtieth year unmolested. But since the Thirty did not venture to lay hands on him themselves, it is the more to be wondered at that in the reconstituted and just rule and freedom which followed the overthrow of despotism" —in that very way the danger in which their principle was, came to be known—"a man like Socrates could be made a sacrifice to cabals. This phenomenon is probably explained by the fact that the enemies of Socrates had first of all to gain time in order to obtain a following, and that under the rule of the Thirty, they played too insignificant a part," and so on.

b. The Trial

Now, as regards the trial of Socrates, we have to distinguish two points, the one the matter of the accusation, the judgment of the court, and the other the relation of Socrates to the sovereign people. In the course of justice there are thus these two parts—the relation of the accused to the matter on account of which he is accused, and his relation to the competency of the people, or the recognition of their majesty. Socrates was found guilty by the judges in respect of the content of his accusation, but was condemned to death because he refused to recognize the competency and majesty of the people as regards the accused.

(1) The accusation consisted of two points: "That Socrates did not consider as gods those who were held to be such by the Athenian people, but introduced new ones; and that he also led young men astray."[1] The leading away of youth was his casting doubt on what was held to be immediate truth. The first accusation has in part the same foundation, for he made it evident that what was usually so considered, was not acceptable to the gods; and in part it is to be taken in connection with his Daemon, not that he called this his god. But with the Greeks this was the direction which the individuality of judgment took; they took it to be a contingency of the individual, and hence, as contingency of circumstances is an external, they also made the contingency of judgment into something external, i.e. they consulted their oracles—conscious that the individual will is itself a contingent. But Socrates, who placed the contingency of judgment in himself, since he had his Daemon in his own consciousness, thereby abolished the external universal Daemon from which the Greeks obtained their judgments. This accusation, as also Socrates' defence, we wish now to examine further; Xenophon represents both to us, and Plato has also supplied us with an Apology. Meanwhile we may not rest content with saying that Socrates was an excel-

[1] Xenoph. "Apologia Socrat." § 10; "Memorab." I. c. 1, § 1 Plato "Apologia Socrat." p. 24 (p. 104).

lent man who suffered innocently, etc., for in this accusation it was the popular mind of Athens that rose against the principle which became fatal to him.

(a) As regards the first point of the accusation, that Socrates did not honour the national gods, but introduced new ones, Xenophon[2] makes him answer that he always brought the same sacrifices as others to the public altars, as all his fellow-citizens could see—his accusers likewise. But as to the charge that he introduced new Daemons, in that he heard the voice of God showing him what he should do, he appealed to them whether by soothsayers the cry and flight of birds, the utterances of men (like the voice of Pythia), the position of the entrails of sacrificial animals, and even thunder and lightning were not accepted as divine revelations. That God knows the future beforehand, and, if He wishes, reveals it in these ways, all believe with him; but God can also reveal the future otherwise. He could show that he did not lie in maintaining that he heard the voice of God, from the testimony of his friends, to whom he often announced what was said; and in its results this was always found to be true. Xenophon ("Memorab." I. c. 1, § 11) adds, "No one ever saw or heard Socrates do or say anything godless or impious, for he never tried to find out the nature of the Universe, like most of the others, when they sought to understand how what the Sophists called the world began." That is, from them came the earlier atheists, who, like Anaxagoras, held that the sun was a stone.[3]

The effect which the defence against this part of the accusation made on the judges is expressed thus by Xenophon:[4] "One section of them was displeased because they did not believe what Socrates said, and the other part because they were envious that he was more highly honoured of the gods than they." This effect is very natural. In our times this also happens in two ways. Either the individual is not believed when he boasts of special manifestations, and particularly of manifestations which have to do with individual action and life; it is neither believed that such manifestations took place at all,

<hr />

[2] "Apologia Socrat." §§ 11–13; "Memorab." I. c. 1, §§ 2–6; 19.
[3] Plat. "Apol. Socrat." p. 26.
[4] "Apologia Socrat." § 14 (cf. "Memorab." I. c. 1, § 17).

or that they happened to this subject. Or if anyone does have dealings with such divinations, rightly enough his proceedings are put an end to, and he is shut up. By this it is not denied in a general way that God foreknows everything, or that He can make revelations to individuals; this may be admitted *in abstracto*, but not in actuality, and it is believed in no individual cases. Men do not believe that to him, to this individual, there has been a revelation. For why to him more than to others? And why just this trifle, some quite personal circumstances—as to whether someone should have a successful journey, or whether he should converse with another person, or whether or not he should in a speech properly defend himself? And why not others amongst the infinitely many things which may occur to the individual? Why not much more important things, things concerning the welfare of whole States? Hence it is not believed of an individual, in spite of the fact that if it is possible, it must be to the individual that it happens. This unbelief, which thus does not deny the general fact and general possibility, but believes it in no particular case, really does not believe in the actuality and truth of the thing. It does not believe it because the absolute consciousness—and it must be such—certainly knows nothing of a positive kind of trivialities such as form the subject of these divinations and also those of Socrates; in spirit such things immediately vanish away. The absolute consciousness does not know about the future as such, any more than about the past; it knows only about the present. But because in its present, in its thought, the opposition of future and past to present becomes apparent, it likewise knows about future and past, but of the past as something which has taken shape. For the past is the preservation of the present as reality, but the future is the opposite of this, the Becoming of the present as possibility, and thus the formless. From out of this formlessness the universal first comes into form in the present; and hence in the future no form can be perceived. Men have the dim feeling that when God acts it is not in a particular way, nor for particular objects. Such things are held to be too paltry to be revealed by God in a particular case. It is acknowledged that God determines the individual, but by this the totality of individuality, or all individualities, is understood; hence it is said that God's way of working is found in universal nature.

Now while with the Greeks judgment had the form of a contingency externally posited through the flight and cries of birds, in our culture we decide by an inward contingency, because I myself desire to be this contingency, and the knowledge of individuality is likewise a consciousness of this contingency. But if the Greeks, for whom the category of the contingency of consciousness was an existent, a knowledge of it as an oracle, had this individuality as a universal knowledge of which everyone could ask counsel, in Socrates—in whom what was here externally established had become inward consciousness, as with us, though not yet fully, being still represented as an actual voice, and conceived of as something which he separated from his individuality—the decision of the single individual had the form of personality as a particular, and it was not a universal individuality. This his judges could not in justice tolerate, whether they believed it or not. With the Greeks such revelations had to have a certain nature and method; there were, so to speak, official oracles (not subjective), such as Pythia, a tree, etc. Hence when this appeared in any particular person like a common citizen, it was considered incredible and wrong; the Daemon of Socrates was a medium of a different kind to any formerly respected in the Greek Religion. It is so much the more noteworthy, that nevertheless the oracle of the Delphian Apollo, Pythia, declared Socrates to be the wisest Greek.[5] Socrates it was who carried out the command of the god of knowledge, "Know Thyself," and made it the motto of the Greeks, calling it the law of the mind, and not interpreting it as meaning a mere acquaintanceship with the particular nature of man. Thus Socrates is the hero who established in the place of the Delphic oracle, the principle that man must look within himself to know what is Truth. Now seeing that Pythia herself pronounced that utterance, we find in it a complete revolution in the Greek mind, and the fact that in place of the oracle, the personal self-consciousness of every thinking man has come into play. This inward certainty, however, is undoubtedly another new god, and not the god of the Athe-

[5] Plato. "Apol. Socrat." p. 21.

nians existing hitherto, and thus the accusation of Socrates was quite just.

(b) If we now consider the second point of the accusation, that Socrates led youth astray, we find that he first sets against it the fact that the oracle of Delphi declared that none could be nobler, juster or wiser than he.[6] And then he sets against this accusation his whole manner of life, and asks whether by the example that he gave, particularly to those with whom he went about, he ever led any into evil.[7] The general accusation had to be further defined and witnesses came forward. "Melitus said that he knew some whom he advised to obey him rather than their parents."[8] This point of the accusation principally related to Anytus, and since he made it good by sufficient testimony, the point was undoubtedly proved in accordance with law. Socrates explained himself further on this point when he left the court. For Xenophon tells us (Apol. Socr. §§ 27, 29–31) that Anytus was inimical to Socrates, because he said to Anytus, a respected citizen, that he should not bring up his son to the trade of a tanner, but in manner befitting a free man. Anytus was himself a tanner, and although his business was mostly conducted by slaves, it was in itself not ignominious, and Socrates' expression was hence wrong, although, as we have seen, quite in the spirit of Greek thought. Socrates added that he had made acquaintance with this son of Anytus and discovered no evil in him, but he prophesied that he would not remain at this servile work to which his father kept him. Nevertheless, because he had no rational person near to look after him, he would come to have evil desires and be brought into dissolute ways. Xenophon added that Socrates' prophecy had come to pass literally, and that the young man gave himself up to drink, and drank day and night, becoming totally depraved. This can be easily understood, for a man who feels himself to be fit for something better (whether truly so or not) and through this discord in his mind is discontented with the circumstances in which he lives, yet capable of attaining to no other, is led out of this disgust into listlessness, and is thus on the way to the evil courses

[6] Xenoph. "Apol. Socrat." § 14.
[7] Xenoph. "Apol. Socrat." §§ 16–19; "Memorab." I. c. 2, §§ 1–8.
[8] Xenoph. "Apol. Socrat." § 20; cf. "Memorab." I. c. 2, § 49 seq.

which so often ruin men. The prediction of Socrates is thus quite natural.

To this definite accusation that he led sons into disobedience to their parents, Socrates replied by asking the question whether in selecting men for public offices, such as that of general, parents, or those experienced in war, were selected. Similarly in all cases those most skilful in an art or science are picked out. He demanded whether it was not matter of astonishment that he should be brought before a judge because he was preferred to parents by the sons in their aspirations after the highest human good which is to be made a noble man.[9] This reply of Socrates is, on the one hand, quite just, but we see at the same time that we cannot call it exhaustive, for the real point of the accusation is not touched. What his judges found unjust was the intrusion morally of a third into the absolute relation between parents and children. On the whole not much can be said on this point, for all depends on the mode of intervention, and if it is necessary in certain cases, it need not take place generally, and least of all when some private individual takes that liberty. Children must have the feeling of unity with their parents; this is the first immediately moral relationship; every teacher must respect it, keep it pure, and cultivate the sense of being thus connected. Hence, when a third person is called into this relation between parents and children, what happens through the new element introduced is that the children are for their own good prevented from confiding in their parents, and made to think that their parents are bad people who harm them by their intercourse and training; and hence we find this revolting. The worst thing which can happen to children in regard to their morality and their mind, is that the bond which must ever be held in reverence should become loosened or even severed, thereby causing hatred, disdain, and ill-will. Whoever does this, does injury to morality in its truest form. This unity, this confidence, is the mother's milk of morality on which man is nurtured; the early loss of parents is therefore a great misfortune. The son, like the daughter, must indeed come out of his natural unity with the family and become independent, but the separation must be

9 Xenoph. "Apol. Socrat." §§ 20, 21; "Memorab." I. c. 2, §§ 51–55; Plat. "Apol. Socrat." pp. 24–26.

one which is natural or unforced, and not defiant and disdainful. When a pain like this has found a place in the heart, great strength of mind is required to overcome it and to heal the wound. If we now speak of the example given us by Socrates, he seems, through his intervention, to have made the young man dissatisfied with his position. Anytus' son might, indeed, have found his work generally speaking uncongenial, but it is another thing when such dislike is brought into consciousness and established by the authority of a man such as Socrates. We may very well conjecture that if Socrates had to do with him, he strengthened and developed in him the germ of the feeling of incongruity. Socrates remarked on the subject of his capacities, saying that he was fit for something better, and thus established a feeling of dissatisfaction in the young man, and strengthened his dislike to his father, which thus became the reason of his ruin. Hence this accusation of having destroyed the relationship of parents and children may be regarded as not unfounded, but as perfectly well established. It was also thought very bad in Socrates' case particularly, and made a matter of reproach that he had such followers as Critias and Alcibiades, who brought Athens almost to the brink of ruin. For when he mixed himself in the education which others gave their children, men were justified in the demand that the result should not belie what he professed to do for the education of youth.

The only question now is, how the people came to take notice of this, and in how far such matters can be objects of legislation and be brought into court. In our law, as regards the first part of the accusation, divination such as Cagliostro's is illegal, and it would be forbidden as it formerly was by the Inquisition. Respecting the second point, such a moral interference is no doubt more recognized with us, where there is a particular office having this duty laid upon it; but this interference must keep itself general, and dare not go so far as to call forth disobedience to parents, which is the first immoral principle. But should such questions come before the court? This first of all brings up the question of what is the right of the State, and here great laxity is now allowed. Nevertheless, when some professor or preacher attacks a particular religion, the legislature would certainly take notice of it, and it would have a complete right to do so, although there would be an outcry when it did it. There is undoubtedly a limit which in liberty of thought and speech is difficult to define and rests on tacit agreement; but there is a point beyond which we find what is not allowed, such as direct incitement to insurrection. It is indeed said, that "bad principles destroy themselves by themselves and find no entrance." But that is only true in part, for with the populace the eloquence of sophistry stirs up their passions. It is also said, "This is only theoretic, no action follows." But the State really rests on thought, and its existence depends on the sentiments of men, for it is a spiritual and not a physical kingdom. Hence it has in so far maxims and principles which constitute its support, and if these are attacked, the Government must intervene. Added to this, it was the case that in Athens quite a different state of things was present than with us; in order to be able to judge rightly of Socrates' case we must first consider the Athenian State and its customs. According to Athenian laws, i.e. according to the spirit of the absolute State, both these things done by Socrates were destructive of this spirit, while in our constitution the universal of the states is a stronger universal, which last undoubtedly permits of individuals having freer play, since they cannot be so dangerous to this universal. Hence it would undoubtedly in the first place mean the subversion of the Athenian State, if this public religion on which everything was built and without which the State could not subsist, went to pieces; with us the State may be called an absolute and independent power. The Daemon is now, in fact, a deity differing from any known, and because it stood in contradiction to the public religion, it gave to it a subjective arbitrariness. But since established religion was identified with public life so closely that it constituted a part of public law, the introduction of a new god who formed self-consciousness into a principle and occasioned disobedience, was necessarily a crime. We may dispute with the Athenians about this, but we must allow that they are consistent. In the second place, the moral connection between parents and children is stronger, and much more the moral foundation of life with the Athenians than with us, where subjective freedom reigns; for family piety is the substantial key-note of the Athenian State. Socrates thus attacked and destroyed Athenian life in two fundamental points; the Athenians felt and became conscious of it. Is it then to be wondered at that Socrates was found guilty? We might say that it had to be so. Tennemann (Vol. II., p. 41) says: "Though these charges contained the most palpable untruths, Socrates was condemned to death because his mind was too lofty for him to descend to the common unworthy means, by which the judgment of the court was usually perverted." But all this is false; he was found guilty of these deeds, but not for that reason condemned to death.

(2) We here come to the second occurrence in his history. In accordance with Athenian laws, the accused had, after the Heliasts (resembling the English jury) pronounced him guilty, the liberty of suggesting (ἀντιτιμᾶσθαι) a penalty different from the punishment which the accuser proposed; this implied a mitigation of the punishment without a formal appeal—an excellent provision in Athenian law, testifying to its humanity. In this penalty the punishment in itself is not brought into question, but only the kind of punishment; the judges had decided that Socrates deserved punishment. But when it was left to the accused to determine what his punishment should be, it might not be arbitrary, but must be in conformity with the crime, a money or bodily punishment (ὅ, τι χρὴ παθεῖν ἢ ἀποτῖθαι).[10] But it was implied in the guilty person's constituting himself his own judge, that he submitted himself to the decision of the court and acknowledged himself to be guilty. Now Socrates declined to assign a punishment for himself consisting either of fine or banishment, and he had the choice between these and death, which his accusers proposed. He declined to choose the former punishment because he, according to Xenophon's account (Apol. Socr. § 23), in the formality of the exchange-penalty (τὸ ὑποτιμᾶσθαι), as he said, would acknowledge guilt; but there was no longer any question as to the guilt, but only as to the kind of punishment.

This silence may indeed be considered as moral greatness, but, on the other hand, it contradicts in some measure what Socrates says later on in prison, that he did not wish to flee, but remained there, because it seemed better to the Athenians and better to him to submit to the laws. But the first submission

[10] Meier und Schömann: "Der Attische Process," pp. 173–77.

would have meant that as the Athenians had found him guilty, he respected this decision, and acknowledged himself as guilty. Consistently he would thus have held it better to impose his punishment, since thereby he would not only have submitted himself to the laws, but also to the judgment. We see in Sophocles (Antig., verses 925, 926), the heavenly Antigone, that noblest of figures that ever appeared on earth, going to her death, her last words merely stating—

> "If this seems good unto the gods,
>   Suffering, we may be made to know our error."

Pericles also submitted himself to the judgment of the people as sovereign; we saw him going round the citizens entreating for Aspasia and Anaxagoras. In the Roman Republic we likewise find the noblest men begging of the citizens. There is nothing dishonouring to the individual in this, for he must bend before the general power, and the real and noblest power is the people. This acknowledgment the people must have direct from those who raise themselves amongst them. Here, on the contrary, Socrates disclaims the submission to, and humiliation before the power of the people, for he did not wish to ask for the remission of his punishment. We admire in him a moral independence which, conscious of its own right, insists upon it and does not bend either to act otherwise, or to recognize as wrong what it itself regards as right. Socrates hence exposed himself to death, which could not be regarded as the punishment for the fault of which he was found guilty; for the fact that he would not himself determine the punishment, and thus disdained the juridical power of the people, was foremost in leading to his condemnation. In a general way he certainly recognized the sovereignty of the people, but not in this individual case; it has, however, to be recognized, not only in general, but in each separate case. With us the competency of the court is presupposed, and the criminal judged without further ado; to-day the whole matter is also open to the light of day and accepted as an acknowledged fact. But with the Athenians we find the characteristic request that the prisoner should, through the act of imposing on himself a penalty, sanction the judge's sentence of guilt. In England this is certainly not the case, but there still remains a like form of asking the accused by what law he wishes to be judged. He then answers, by the law of the land and by the judges of his country. Here we have the recognition of legal operations.

Socrates thus set his conscience in opposition to the judges' sentence, and acquitted himself before its tribunal. But no people, and least of all a free people like the Athenians, has by this freedom to recognize a tribunal of conscience which knows no consciousness of having fulfilled its duty excepting its own consciousness. To this government and law, the universal spirit of the people, may reply: "If you have the consciousness of having done your duty, we must also have the consciousness that you have so done." For the first principle of a State is that there is no reason or conscience or righteousness or anything else, higher than what the State recognizes as such. Quakers, Anabaptists, etc., who resist any demands made on them by the State, such as to defend the Fatherland, cannot be tolerated in a true State. This miserable freedom of thinking and believing what men will, is not permitted, nor any such retreat behind personal consciousness of duty. If this consciousness is no mere hypocrisy, in order that what the individual does should be recognized as duty, it must be recognized as such by all. If the people can make mistakes the individual may do so much more easily, and he must be conscious that he can do this much more easily than the people. Now law also has a conscience and has to speak through it; the law-court is the privileged conscience. Now if the miscarriage of justice in a trial is shown by every conscience clamouring for something different, the conscience of the court alone possesses any value as being the universal legalized conscience, which does not require to recognize the particular conscience of the accused. Men are too easily convinced of having fulfilled their duty, but the judge finds out whether duty is in fact fulfilled, even if men have the consciousness of its being so.

We should expect nothing else of Socrates than that he should go to meet his death in the most calm and manly fashion. Plato's account of the wonderful scene his last hours presented, although containing nothing very special, forms an elevating picture, and will be to us a permanent representation of a noble deed. The last dialogue of Plato is popular philosophy, for the immortality of the soul is here first brought forward; yet it brings no consolation, for, as Homer makes Achilles say in the nether world, he would prefer to be a ploughboy on the earth.

But though the people of Athens asserted through the execution of this judgment the rights of their law as against the attacks of Socrates, and had punished the injury caused to their moral life by Socrates, Socrates was still the hero who possessed for himself the absolute right of the mind, certain of itself and of the inwardly deciding consciousness, and thus expressed the higher principle of mind with consciousness. Now because, as has been said, this new principle, by effecting an entrance into the Greek world, has come into collision with the substantial spirit and the existing sentiments of the Athenian people, a reaction had to take place, for the principle of the Greek world could not yet bear the principle of subjective reflection. The Athenian people were thus, not only justified, but also bound to react against it according to their law, for they regarded this principle as a crime. In general history we find that this is the position of the heroes through whom a new world commences, and whose principle stands in contradiction to what has gone before and disintegrates it: they appear to be violently destroying the laws. Hence individually they are vanquished, but it is only the individual, and not the principle, which is negated in punishment, and the spirit of the Athenian people did not in the removal of the individual, recover its old position. The false form of individuality is taken away, and that, indeed, in a violent way, by punishment; but the principle itself will penetrate later, if in another form, and elevate itself into a form of the world-spirit. This universal mode in which the principle comes forth and permeates the present is the true one; what was wrong was the fact that the principle came forth only as the peculiar possession of one individual. His own world could not comprehend Socrates, but posterity can, in as far as it stands above both. It may be conceived that the life of Socrates had no need to have such an end, for Socrates might have lived and died a private philosopher, and his teaching might have been quietly accepted by his disciples, and have spread further still without receiving any notice from State or people; the accusation thus would seem to have been contingent. But it must be said that it was through the manner of that event that this principle became so highly honoured. The principle is not merely something new and peculiar to itself, but it is an absolutely essential moment in the self-developing consciousness of self which is designed to bring to pass as a totality, a new and higher actuality. The Athenians perceived correctly that this principle not only meant opinion and doctrine, for its true attitude was that of a direct and even hostile and destructive relation to the actuality of the Greek mind; and they proceeded in accordance with this perception. Hence, what follows in Socrates' life is not contingent, but necessarily follows upon his principle. Or the honour of having recognized that relation, and indeed of having felt that they themselves were tinged with this principle, is due to the Athenians.

(3) The Athenians likewise repented of their condemnation of Socrates, and punished some of his accusers with death itself, and others with banishment; for according to Athenian laws, the man who made an accusation, and whose accusation was found to be false, usually underwent the same punishment that otherwise the criminal would have borne. This is the last act in this drama. On the one hand the Athenians recognized through their repentance the individual greatness of the man; but on the other (and this we find by looking closer) they also recognized that this principle in Socrates, signifying the introduction of new gods and disrespect to parents, has—while destructive and hostile to it—been introduced even into their own spirit, and that they themselves are in the dilemma of having in Socrates only condemned their own principle. In that they regretted the just judgment of Socrates, it seems to be implied that they wished that it had not occurred. But from the regret it does not follow that in itself it should not have occurred, but only that it should not have happened for their consciousness. Both together constitute the innocence which is guilty and atones for its guilt; it would only be senseless and despicable if there were no guilt. An innocent person who comes off badly is a simpleton; hence it is a very flat and uninteresting matter when tyrants and innocent persons are represented in tragedies, just because this is an empty contingency. A great man would be guilty and overcome the great

crisis that ensues; Christ thus gave up his individuality, but what was brought forth by him remained.

c. Socrates and the Tragic End of Greece

The fate of Socrates is hence really tragic, not in the superficial sense of the word and as every misfortune is called tragic. The death of an estimable individual must, in such a sense, be specially tragic, and thus it is said of Socrates, that because he was innocent and condemned to death, his fate was tragic. But such innocent suffering would only be sad and not tragic, for it would not be a rational misfortune. Misfortune is only rational when it is brought about by the will of the subject, who must be absolutely justified and moral in what he does, like the power against which he wars—which must therefore not be a merely natural power, or the power of a tyrannic will. For it is only in such a case that man himself has any part in his misfortune, while natural death is only an absolute right which nature exercises over men. Hence, in what is truly tragic there must be valid moral powers on both the sides which come into collision; this was so with Socrates. His is likewise not merely a personal, individually romantic lot; for we have in it the universally moral and tragic fate, the tragedy of Athens, the tragedy of Greece. Two opposed rights come into collision, and the one destroys the other. Thus both suffer loss and yet both are mutually justified; it is not as though the one alone were right and the other wrong. The one power is the divine right, the natural morality whose laws are identical with the will which dwells therein as in its own essence, freely and nobly; we may call it abstractly objective freedom. The other principle, on the contrary, is the right, as really divine, of consciousness or of subjective freedom; this is the fruit of the tree of the knowledge of good and evil, i.e. of self-creative reason; and it is the universal principle of Philosophy for all successive times. It is these two principles which we see coming into opposition in the life and the philosophy of Socrates.

The Athenian people had come into a period of culture, in which this individual consciousness made itself independent of the universal spirit and became for itself. This was perceived by them in Socrates, but at the same time it was felt that it meant ruin, and thus they punished an element which was their own. The principle of Socrates is hence not the transgression of one individual, for all were implicated; the crime was one that the spirit of the people committed against itself. Through this perception the condemnation of Socrates was retracted; Socrates appeared to have committed no crime, for the spirit of the people has now generally reached the consciousness which turns back from the universal into itself. This meant the disintegration of this people, whose mind and spirit consequently soon disappeared from the world, but yet out of its ashes a higher took its rise, for the world-spirit had raised itself into a higher consciousness. The Athenian State, indeed, endured for long, but the bloom of its character soon faded. It is characteristic of Socrates that he grasped the principle of the inwardness of knowledge, not practically merely, as did Critias and Alcibiades, but in thought, making it valid to thought, and this is the higher method. Knowledge brought about the Fall, but it also contains the principle of Redemption. Thus what to others was only ruin, to Socrates, because it was the principle of knowledge, was also a principle of healing. The development of this principle, which constitutes the content of all successive history, is explicitly the reason that the later philosophers withdrew from the affairs of the State, restricted themselves to cultivating an inner world, separated from themselves the universal aim of the moral culture of the people, and took up a position contrary to the spirit of Athens and the Athenians. From this it came to pass that particularity of ends and interests now became powerful in Athens. This has, in common with the Socratic principle, the fact that what seems right and duty, good and useful to the subject in relation to himself as well as to the State, depends on his inward determination and choice, and not on the constitution and the universal. This principle of self-determination for the individual has, however, become the ruin of the Athenian people, because it was not yet identified with the constitution of the people; and thus the higher principle must in every case appear to bring ruin with it where it is not yet identified with the substantial of the people. The Athenian life became weak, and the State outwardly powerless, because its spirit was divided within itself. Hence it was dependent on Lacedaemon, and we finally see the external subordination of these States to the Macedonians.

We are done with Socrates. I have been more detailed here because all the features of the case have been so completely in harmony, and he constitutes a great historic turning point. Socrates died at sixty-nine years of age, in Olympiad 95, 1 (399–400 B.C.), an Olympiad after the end of the Peloponnesian war, twenty-nine years after the death of Pericles, and forty-four years before the birth of Alexander. He saw Athens in its greatness and the beginning of its fall; he experienced the height of its bloom and the beginning of its misfortunes.

APPENDIX

A. C. BRADLEY:
HEGEL'S THEORY OF TRAGEDY[1]

[a]Since Aristotle dealt with tragedy, and, as usual, drew the main features of his subject with those sure and simple strokes which no later hand has rivalled, the only philosopher who has treated it in a manner both original and searching is Hegel. I propose here to give a sketch of Hegel's theory, and to add some remarks upon it. But I cannot possibly do justice in a sketch to a theory which fills many pages of the *Aesthetik*; which I must tear from its connections with the author's general view of poetry, and with the rest of his philosophy;[2] and

[1] See, primarily, *Aesthetik*, iii. 479–581, and especially 525–81. There is much in *Aesthetik*, i. 219–306, and a good deal in ii. 1–243, that bears on the subject. See also the section on Greek religion in *Religionsphilosophie*, ii. 96–156, especially 131–36, 152–56; and the references to the death of Socrates in *Geschichte der Philosophie*, ii. 81 ff., especially 102–5. The works so far cited all consist of posthumous redactions of lecture-notes. Among works published by Hegel himself, the early essay on 'Naturrecht' (*Werke*, i. 386 ff.), and *Phaenomenologie d. Geistes*, 320–48, 527–42, deal with or bear on *Greek* tragedy. See also *Rechtsphilosophie*, 196, note. There is a note on *Wallenstein* in *Werke*, xvii. 411–14. These references are to the second edition of the works cited, where there are two editions.

[a] A. C. Bradley, *Oxford Lectures on Poetry*, London, 1950, pp. 69–95.

[2] His theory of tragedy is connected with his view of the function of negation in the universe. No statement therefore which ignores

which I must try to exhibit as far as possible in the language of ordinary literature. To estimate this theory, therefore, from my sketch would be neither safe nor just—all the more because, in the interest of immediate clearness, I have not scrupled to insert without warning various remarks and illustrations for which Hegel is not responsible.

On certain characteristics of tragedy the briefest reminder will suffice. A large part of the nature of this form of drama is common to the drama in all its forms; and of this nothing need be said. It will be agreed, further, that in all tragedy there is some sort of collision or conflict—conflict of feelings, modes of thought, desires, wills, purposes; conflict of persons with one another, or with circumstances, or with themselves; one, several, or all of these kinds of conflict, as the case may be. Again, it may be taken for granted that a tragedy is a story of unhappiness or suffering, and excites such feelings as pity and fear. To this, if we followed the present usage of the term, we should add that the story of unhappiness must have an unhappy end; by which we mean in effect that the conflict must close with the death of one or more of the principal characters. But this usage of the word 'tragedy' is comparatively recent; it leaves us without a name for many plays, in many languages, which deal with unhappiness without ending unhappily; and Hegel takes the word in its older and wider sense.

Passing on from these admitted characteristics of tragedy, we may best approach Hegel's peculiar view by observing that he lays particular stress on one of them. That a tragedy is a story of suffering is probably to many people the most obvious fact about it. Hegel says very little of this; partly, perhaps, because it is obvious, but more because the essential point to him is not the suffering but its cause, namely, the action or conflict. Mere suffering, he would say, is not tragic, but only the suffering that comes of a special kind of action. Pity for mere misfortune, like fear of it, is not tragic pity or fear. These are due to the spectacle of the conflict and its attendant suffering, which do not appeal simply to our sensibilities or our instinct of self-preservation, but also to our deeper mind or spirit (*Geist*, a word which, with its adjective, I shall translate

his metaphysics and his philosophy of religion can be more than a fragmentary account of that theory.

'spirit,' 'spiritual,' because our words 'mind' and 'mental' suggest something merely intellectual).

The reason why the tragic conflict thus appeals to the spirit is that it is itself a conflict of the spirit. It is a conflict, that is to say, between powers that rule the world of man's will and action—his 'ethical substance.' The family and the state, the bond of parent and child, of brother and sister, of husband and wife, of citizen and ruler, or citizen and citizen, with the obligations and feelings appropriate to these bonds; and again the powers of personal love and honour, or of devotion to a great cause or an ideal interest like religion or science or some kind of social welfare—such are the forces exhibited in tragic action; not indeed alone, not without others less affirmative and perhaps even evil, but still in preponderating mass. And as they form the substance of man, are common to all civilised men, and are acknowledged as powers rightfully claiming human allegiance, their exhibition in tragedy has that interest, at once deep and universal, which is essential to a great work of art.

In many a work of art, in many a statue, picture, tale, or song, such powers are shown in solitary peace or harmonious co-operation. Tragedy shows them in collision. Their nature is divine, and in religion they appear as gods; but, as seen in the world of tragic action, they have left the repose of Olympus, have entered into human wills, and now meet as foes. And this spectacle, if sublime, is also terrible. The essentially tragic fact is the self-division and intestinal warfare of the ethical substance, not so much the war of good with evil as the war of good with good. Two of these isolated powers face each other, making incompatible demands. The family claims what the state refuses, love requires what honour forbids. The competing forces are both in themselves rightful, and so far the claim of each is equally justified; but the right of each is pushed into a wrong, because it ignores the right of the other, and demands that absolute sway which belongs to neither alone, but to the whole of which each is but a part.

And one reason why this happens lies in the nature of the characters through whom these claims are made. It is the nature of the tragic hero, at once his greatness and his doom, that he knows no shrinking or half-heartedness, but identifies himself wholly with the power that moves him, and will admit the justification of no other power. However varied and rich his inner life and character may be, in the conflict it is all concentrated in one point. Antigone *is* the determination to do her duty to her dead brother; Romeo is not a son or a citizen as well as a lover, he is lover pure and simple, and his love is the whole of him.

The end of the tragic conflict is the denial of both the exclusive claims. It is not the work of chance or blank fate; it is the act of the ethical substance itself, asserting its absoluteness against the excessive pretensions of its particular powers. In that sense, as proceeding from an absolute right which cancels claims based on right but pushed into wrong, it may be called the act of 'eternal justice.' Sometimes it can end the conflict peacefully, and the tragedy closes with a solution. Appearing as a divine being, the spiritual unity reconciles by some adjustment the claims of the contending powers (*Eumenides*); or at its bidding one of them softens its demand (*Philoctetes*); or again, as in the more beautiful solution of the *Oedipus at Colonus*, the hero by his own self-condemnation and inward purification reconciles himself with the supreme justice, and is accepted by it. But sometimes the quarrel is pressed to extremes; the denial of the one-sided claims involves the death of one or more of the persons concerned; and we have a catastrophe. The ultimate power thus appears as a destructive force. Yet even here, as Hegel insists, the end is not without an aspect of reconciliation. For that which is denied is not the rightful powers with which the combatants have identified themselves. On the contrary, those powers, and with them the only thing for which the combatants cared, are affirmed. What is denied is the exclusive and therefore wrongful assertion of their right.

Such in outline is Hegel's main view. It may be illustrated more fully by two examples, favourites of his, taken from Aeschylus and Sophocles. Clytemnestra has murdered Agamemnon, her husband and king. Orestes, their son, is impelled by filial piety to avenge his father, and is ordered by Apollo to do so. But to kill a mother is to sin against filial piety. The spiritual substance is divided against itself. The sacred bond of father and son demands what the equally sacred bond of son and mother forbids. When, therefore, Orestes has done the deed, the Furies of his murdered mother claim him for their prey. He appeals to Apollo, who resists their claim. A solution is arrived at without a catastrophe. The cause is referred to Athene, who institutes at Athens a court of sworn judges. The votes of this court being equally divided, Athene gives her casting-vote for Orestes; while the Furies are at last appeased by a promise of everlasting honour at Athens.

In the *Antigone*, on the other hand, to Hegel the 'perfect exemplar of tragedy,' the solution is negative. The brother of Antigone has brought against his native city an army of foreigners bent on destroying it. He has been killed in the battle, and Creon, the ruler of the city, has issued an edict forbidding anyone on pain of death to bury the corpse. In so doing he not only dishonours the dead man, but violates the rights of the gods of the dead. Antigone without hesitation disobeys the edict, and Creon, despite the remonstrance of his son, who is affianced to her, persists in exacting the penalty. Warned by the prophet Teiresias, he gives way, but too late. Antigone, immured in a rocky chamber to starve, has anticipated her death. Her lover follows her example, and his mother refuses to survive him. Thus Antigone has lost her life through her absolute assertion of the family against the state; Creon has violated the sanctity of the family, and in return sees his own home laid in ruins. But in this catastrophe neither the right of the family nor that of the state is denied; what is denied is the absoluteness of the claim of each.

The danger of illustrations like these is that they divert attention from the principle illustrated to questions about the interpretation of particular works. So it will be here. I cannot stay to discuss these questions, which do not affect Hegel's principle; but it will be well, before going further, to remove a misunderstanding of it which is generally to be found in criticisms of his treatment of the *Eumenides* and the *Antigone*. The main objection may be put thus: 'Hegel talks of equally justified powers or claims. But Aeschylus never meant that Orestes and the Furies were equally justified; for Orestes was acquitted. Nor did Sophocles mean that Antigone and Creon were equally right. And how can it have been equally the duty of Orestes to kill his mother and not to kill her?' But, in the first place, it is most important to observe that Hegel is not discussing at all what we should generally call the moral quality of the acts and persons concerned, or, in the ordinary sense, what it was their duty to do. And, in the second place, when he speaks of 'equally justified' powers, what he means, and, indeed, sometimes says, is that these powers are *in themselves* equally justified. The family and the state, the bond of father and son, the bond of mother and son, the bond of citizenship, these are each and all, one as much as another, powers rightfully claiming human allegiance. It is tragic that observance of one should involve the violation of another. These are Hegel's propositions, and surely they are true. Their truth is quite unaffected by the fact (assuming it is one) that in the circumstances the act combining this observance of one and violation of another was morally right, or by the fact (if so it is) that one such act (say Antigone's) was morally right, and another (say Creon's) was morally wrong. It is sufficient for Hegel's principle that the violation should take place, and that we should feel its weight. We do feel it. We may approve the act of Antigone or Orestes, but in approving it we still feel that it is no light matter to disobey the law or to murder a mother, that (as we might say) there is much justice in the pleas of the Furies and of Creon, and that the *tragic* effect depends upon these facts. If, again, it is objected that the underlying conflict in the *Antigone* is not between the family and the state, but between divine and human law, that objection, if sound, might touch Hegel's interpretation,[3] but it would not affect his principle, except for those who recognise no obligation in human law; and it will scarcely be contended that Sophocles is to be numbered among them. On the other hand, it is, I think, a matter for regret that Hegel employed such words as 'right,' 'justified,' and 'justice.' They do not mislead readers familiar with his writings, but to others they suggest associations with criminal law, or our everyday moral judgments, or perhaps the theory of 'poetic justice'; and these are all out of place in a discussion on tragedy.

Having determined in outline the idea or principle of trag-

---

[3] I say 'might,' because Hegel himself in the *Phaenomenologie* uses those very terms 'divine' and 'human law' in reference to the *Antigone*.

edy, Hegel proceeds to give an account of some differences between ancient and modern works. In the limited time at our
disposal we shall do best to confine ourselves to a selection
from his remarks on the latter. For in speaking of ancient
tragedy, Hegel, who finds something modern in Euripides,
makes accordingly but little use of him for purposes of contrast, while his main point of view as to Aeschylus and Sophocles has already appeared in the illustrations we have given of
the general principle. I will only add, by way of preface, that
the pages about to be summarised leave on one, rightly or
wrongly, the impression that to his mind the principle is more
adequately realised in the best classical tragedies than in modern works. But the question whether this really was his deliberate opinion would detain us too long from weightier
matters.[4]

Hegel considers first the cases where modern tragedy resembles ancient in dealing with conflicts arising from the pursuit of ends which may be called substantial or objective and
not merely personal. And he points out that modern tragedy
here shows a much greater variety. Subjects are taken, for example, from the quarrels of dynasties, of rivals for the throne,
of kings and nobles, of state and church. Calderon shows the
conflict of love and honour regarded as powers imposing obligations. Schiller in his early works makes his characters defend the rights of nature against convention, or of freedom of
thought against prescription—rights in their essence universal.
Wallenstein aims at the unity and peace of Germany; Karl
Moor attacks the whole arrangement of society; Faust seeks
to attain in thought and action union with the Absolute. In
such cases the end is more than personal; it represents a power
claiming the allegiance of the individual; but, on the other
hand, it does not always or generally represent a great *ethical*
institution or bond like the family or the state. We have passed
into a wider world.

But, secondly, he observes, in regard to modern tragedy,
that in a larger number of instances such public or universal
interests either do not appear at all, or, if they appear, are
scarcely more than a background for the real subject. The real

[4] See Note at end of lecture.

subject, the impelling end or passion, and the ensuing conflict, is personal,—these particular characters with their struggle and their fate. The importance given to subjectivity—this is the distinctive mark of modern sentiment, and so of modern art; and such tragedies bear its impress. A part at least of Hegel's meaning may be illustrated thus. We are interested in the personality of Orestes or Antigone, but chiefly as it shows itself in one aspect, as identifying itself with a certain ethical relation; and our interest in the personality is inseparable and indistinguishable from our interest in the power it represents. This is not so with Hamlet, whose position so closely resembles that of Orestes. What engrosses our attention is the whole personality of Hamlet in his conflict, not with an opposing spiritual power, but with circumstances and, still more, with difficulties in his own nature. No one could think of describing Othello as the representative of an ethical family relation. His passion, however much nobility he may show in it, is personal. So is Romeo's love. It is not pursued, like Posa's freedom of thought, as something universal, a right of man. Its right, if it could occur to us to use the term at all, is Romeo's right.

On this main characteristic of modern tragedy others depend. For instance, that variety of subject to which reference has just been made depends on it. For when so much weight is attached to personality, almost any fatal collision in which a sufficiently striking character is involved may yield material for tragedy. Naturally, again, characterisation has become fuller and more subtle, except in dramas which are more or less an imitation of the antique. The characters in Greek tragedy are far from being types or personified abstractions, as those of classical French tragedy tend to be: they are genuine individuals. But still they are comparatively simple and easy to understand, and have not the intricacy of the characters in Shakespeare. These, for the most part, represent simply themselves; and the loss of that interest which attached to the Greek characters from their identification with an ethical power, is compensated by an extraordinary subtlety in their portrayal, and also by their possession of some peculiar charm or some commanding superiority. Finally, the interest in personality explains the freedom with which characters more or less definitely evil are introduced in modern tragedy. Mephistopheles is as essentially modern as Faust. The passion of Richard or Macbeth is not only personal, like that of Othello; it is egoistic and anarchic, and leads to crimes done with a full knowledge of their wickedness; but to the modern mind the greatness of the personality justifies its appearance in the position of hero. Such beings as Iago and Goneril, almost portents of evil, are not indeed made the heroes of tragedies; but, according to Hegel, they would not have been admitted in Greek tragedy at all. If Clytemnestra had been cited in objection as a parallel to Lady Macbeth, he would have replied that Lady Macbeth had not the faintest ground of complaint against Duncan, while in reading the *Agamemnon* we are frequently reminded that Clytemnestra's husband was the sacrificer of their child. He might have added that Clytemnestra is herself an example of the necessity, where one of the principal characters inspires hatred or horror, of increasing the subtlety of the drawing or adding grandeur to the evil will.

It remains to compare ancient and modern tragedy in regard to the issue of the conflict. We have seen that Hegel attributes this issue in the former to the ethical substance or eternal justice, and so accounts for such reconciliation as we feel to be present even where the end is a catastrophe. Now, in the catastrophe of modern tragedy, he says, a certain justice is sometimes felt to be present; but even then it differs from the antique justice. It is in some cases more 'abstract': the end pursued by the hero, though it is not egoistic, is still presented rather as his particular end than as something rightful though partial; and hence the catastrophe appears as the reaction, not of an undivided ethical totality, but merely of the universal turning against a too assertive particular.[5] In cases, again, where the hero (Richard or Macbeth) openly attacks an ethical power and plunges into evil, we feel that he meets with justice, and only gets what he deserves; but then this justice is colder and more 'criminalistic' than that of ancient tragedy. Thus even when the modern work seems to resemble the ancient in its issue, the sense of reconciliation is imperfect. And partly for this reason, partly from the concentration of our interest on individuality as such, we desire to see in the individ-

[5] This interpretation of Hegel's 'abstract' is more or less conjectural and doubtful.

ual himself some sort of reconciliation with his fate. What shape this will take depends, of course, on the story and the character of the hero. It may appear in a religious form, as his feeling that he is exchanging his earthly being for an indestructible happiness; or again, in his recognition of the justice of his fall; or at least he may show us that, in face of the forces that crush him to death, he maintains untouched the freedom and strength of his own will.

But there remain, says Hegel, many modern tragedies where we have to attribute the catastrophe not to any kind of justice, but to unhappy circumstances and outward accidents. And then we can only feel that the individual whose merely personal ends are thwarted by mere particular circumstances and chances, pays the penalty that awaits existence in a scene of contingency and finitude. Such a feeling cannot rise above sadness, and, if the hero is a noble soul, it may become the impression of a dreadful external necessity. This impression can be avoided only when circumstance and accident are so depicted that they are felt to coincide with something in the hero himself, so that he is not simply destroyed by an outward force. So it is with Hamlet. 'This bank and shoal of time' is too narrow for his soul, and the death that seems to fall on him by chance is also within him. And so in *Romeo and Juliet* we feel that the rose of a love so beautiful is too tender to bloom in the storm-swept valley of its birth. But such a feeling of reconciliation is still one of pain, an unhappy blessedness.[6] And if the situation displayed in a drama is of such a kind that we feel the issue to depend *simply* on the turn the dramatist may choose to give to the course of events, we are fully justified in our preference for a happy ending.

In this last remark (or rather in the pages misrepresented by it) Hegel, of course, is not criticising Shakespeare. He is objecting to the destiny-dramas of his own time, and to the fashionable indulgence in sentimental melancholy. Strongly as he asserted the essential function of negation throughout the universe, the affirmative power of the spirit, even in its profoundest divisions, was for him the deepest truth and the most

[6] Hegel's meaning does not fully appear in the sentences here condensed. The 'blessedness' comes from the sense of greatness or beauty in the characters.

inspiring theme. And one may see this even in his references to Shakespeare. He appreciated Shakespeare's representation of extreme forms of evil, but, even if he was fully satisfied of its justification, his personal preference lay in another direction, and while I do not doubt that he thought *Hamlet* a greater work than *Iphigenie,* I suspect he loved Goethe's play the best.

Most of those who have thought about this subject will agree that the ideas I have tried to sketch are interesting and valuable; but they suggest scores of questions. Alike in the account of tragedy in general, and in that of the differences between ancient and modern tragedy, everyone will find statements to doubt and omissions to regret; and scarcely one of Hegel's interpretations of particular plays will escape objection. It is impossible for me to touch on more than a few points; and to the main ideas I owe so much that I am more inclined to dwell on their truth than to criticise what seem to be defects. But perhaps after all an attempt to supplement and amend may be the best way of throwing some part of Hegel's meaning more into relief. And I will begin with the attempt to supplement.

He seems to be right in laying emphasis on the action and conflict in tragedy rather than on the suffering and misfortune. No mere suffering or misfortune, no suffering that does not spring in great part from human agency, and in some degree from the agency of the sufferer, is tragic, however pitiful or dreadful it may be. But, sufficient connection with these agencies being present, misfortune, the fall from prosperity to adversity, with the suffering attending it, at once becomes tragic; and in many tragedies it forms a large ingredient, as does the pity for it in the tragic feeling. Hegel, I think, certainly takes too little notice of it; and by this omission he also withdraws attention from something the importance of which he would have admitted at once; I mean the way in which suffering is borne. Physical pain, to take an extreme instance, is one thing: Philoctetes, bearing it, is another. And the noble endurance of pain that rends the heart is the source of much that is best worth having in tragedy.

Again, there is one particular kind of misfortune *not* obviously due to human agency, which undoubtedly may affect us

in a tragic way. I mean that kind which suggests the idea of
fate. Tragedies which represent man as the mere plaything of
chance or a blank fate or a malicious fate, are never really
deep: it is satisfactory to see that Maeterlinck, a man of true
genius, has now risen above these ideas. But, where those factors of tragedy are present which Hegel emphasises, the impression of something fateful in what we call accident, the
impression that the hero not only invites misfortune by his exceptional stature and exceptional daring, but is also, if I may
so put it, strangely and terribly unlucky, is in many plays a
genuine ingredient in tragic effect. It is so, for example, in the
Oedipus Tyrannus. It is so even in dramas like Shakespeare's,
which exemplify the saying that character is destiny. Hegel's
own reference to the prominence of accident in the plot of
Hamlet proves it. Othello would not have become Iago's victim if his own character had been different; but still, as we say,
it is an extraordinary fatality which makes him the companion
of the one man in the world who is at once able enough, brave
enough, and vile enough to ensnare him. In the *Antigone* itself, and in the very catastrophe of it, accident plays its part:
we can hardly say that it depends solely on the characters of
Creon and Antigone that the one yields just too late to save
the life of the other. Now, it may be said with truth that Hegel's whole account of the ultimate power in tragedy is a ra-
tionalisation of the idea of fate, but his remarks on this particular aspect of fate are neither sufficient nor satisfactory.

His insistence on the need for some element of reconciliation
in a tragic catastrophe, and his remarks on the various forms
it assumes, have the greatest value; but one result of the omissions just noticed is that he sometimes exaggerates it, and at
other times rates it too low. When he is speaking of the kind
of tragedy he most approves, his language almost suggests that
our feeling at the close of the conflict is, or should be, one of
complete reconciliation. This it surely neither is nor can be.
Not to mention the suffering and death we have witnessed, the
very existence of the conflict, even if a supreme ethical power
is felt to be asserted in its close, remains a painful fact, and, in
large measure, a fact not understood. For, though we may be
said to see, in one sense, how the opposition of spiritual powers arises, something in us, and that the best, still cries out

against it. And even the perception or belief that it must needs be that offences come would not abolish our feeling that the necessity is terrible, or our pain in the woe of the guilty and the innocent. Nay, one may conjecture, the feeling and the pain would not vanish if we fully understood that the conflict and catastrophe were by a rational necessity involved in the divine and eternally accomplished purpose of the world. But this exaggeration in Hegel's language, if partly due to his enthusiasm for the affirmative, may be mainly, like some other defects, an accident of lecturing. In the *Philosophy of Religion*, I may add, he plainly states that in the solution even of tragedies like the *Antigone* something remains unresolved (ii. 135).

On the other hand, his treatment of the aspect of reconciliation in modern tragedy is in several respects insufficient. I will mention only one. He does not notice that in the conclusion of not a few tragedies pain is mingled not merely with acquiescence, but with something like exultation. Is there not such a feeling at the close of *Hamlet, Othello,* and *King Lear;* and that although the end in the last two cases touches the limit of legitimate pathos? This exultation appears to be connected with our sense that the hero has never shown himself so great or noble as in the death which seals his failure. A rush of passionate admiration, and a glory in the greatness of the soul, mingle with our grief; and the coming of death, so far from destroying these feelings, appears to leave them untouched, or even to be entirely in harmony with them. If in such dramas we may be said to feel that the ultimate power is no mere fate, but a spiritual power, then we also feel that the hero was never so near to this power as in the moment when it required his life.

The last omission I would notice in Hegel's theory is that he underrates the action in tragedy of what may be called by a rough distinction moral evil rather than defect. Certainly the part played by evil differs greatly in different cases, but it is never absent, not even from tragedies of Hegel's favourite type. If it does not appear in the main conflict, it appears in its occasion. You may say that, while Iago and Macbeth have evil purposes, neither the act of Orestes nor the vengeance of the Furies, neither Antigone's breach of the edict nor even Creon's insistence on her punishment, springs from evil in them; but

the situation with which Orestes or Antigone has to deal, and
so in a sense the whole tragedy, arises from evil, the murder
of Agamemnon, and the attempt of Polyneices to bring ruin
on his native city. In fact, if we confine the title 'tragedy' to
plays ending with a catastrophe, it will be found difficult to
name great tragedies, ancient or modern, in which evil has not
directly or indirectly a prominent part. And its presence has an
important bearing on the effect produced by the catastrophe.
On the one hand, it deepens the sense of painful awe. The
question why affirmative spiritual forces should collide is hard
enough; but the question why, together with them, there
should be generated violent evil and extreme depravity is
harder and more painful still. But, on the other hand, the element of reconciliation in the catastrophe is strengthened by
recognition of the part played by evil in bringing it about; because our sense that the ultimate power cannot endure the
presence of such evil is implicitly the sense that this power is
at least more closely allied with good. If it rejects the exaggerated claims of its own isolated powers, that which provokes
from it a much more vehement reaction must be still more
alien to its nature. This feeling is forcibly evoked by Shakespeare's tragedies, and in many Greek dramas it is directly appealed to by repeated reminders that what is at work in the
disasters is the unsleeping Ate which follows an ancestral sin.
If Aristotle did not in some lost part of the *Poetics* discuss
ideas like this, he failed to give a complete rationale of Greek
tragedy.

I come lastly to the matter I have most at heart. What I
take to be the central idea in Hegel's theory seems to me to
touch the essence of tragedy. And I will not assert that his
own statement of it fails to cover the whole field of instances.
For he does not teach, as he is often said to do, that tragedy
portrays only the conflict of such ethical powers as the family
and the state. He adds to these, as we have seen, others, such
as love and honour, together with various universal ends; and
it may even be maintained that he has provided in his general
statement for those numerous cases where, according to himself, no substantial or universal ends collide, but the interest
is centred on 'personalities.' Nevertheless, when these cases

come to be considered more fully—and, in Hegel's view, they are the most characteristically modern cases—we are not satisfied. They naturally tend to appear as declensions from the more ideal ancient form; for how can a personality which represents only itself claim the interest of one which represents something universal? And further, they are sometimes described in a manner which strikes the reader, let us say, of Shakespeare, as both insufficient and misleading. Without raising, then, unprofitable questions about the comparative merits of ancient and modern tragedy, I should like to propose a restatement of Hegel's general principle which would make it more obviously apply to both.

If we omit all reference to ethical or substantial powers and interests, what have we left? We have the more general idea —to use again a formula not Hegel's own—that tragedy portrays a self-division and self-waste of spirit, or a division of spirit involving conflict and waste. It is implied in this that on *both* sides in the conflict there is a spiritual value. The same idea may be expressed (again, I think, not in Hegel's own words) by saying that the tragic conflict is one not merely of good with evil, but also, and more essentially, of good with good. Only, in saying this, we must be careful to observe that 'good' here means anything that has spiritual value, not moral goodness alone,[7] and that 'evil' has a similarly wide sense.

Now this idea of a division of spirit involving conflict and waste covers the tragedies of ethical and other universal powers, and it covers much besides. According to it the collision of such powers would be one kind of tragic collision, but only one. *Why* are we tragically moved by the conflict of family and state? Because we set a high value on family and state. Why then should not the conflict of anything else that has sufficient value affect us tragically? It does. The value must be sufficient—a moderate value will not serve; and other characteristics must be present which need not be considered here. But, granted these conditions, *any* spiritual conflict involving spiritual waste is tragic. And it is just one greatness of modern art that it has shown the tragic fact in situations of so many and such diverse kinds. These situations have not the peculiar

---

[7] Hegel himself expressly guards against this misconception.

effectiveness of the conflicts preferred by Hegel, but they may have an equal effectiveness peculiar to themselves.

Let me attempt to test these ideas by choosing a most un-favourable instance—unfavourable because the play seems at first to represent a conflict simply of good and evil, and so, according both to Hegel's statement and the proposed restate-ment, to be no tragedy at all: I mean *Macbeth*. What is the conflict here? It will be agreed that it does not lie between two ethical powers or universal ends, and that, as Hegel says, the main interest is in personalities. Let us take it first, then, to lie between Macbeth and the persons opposing him, and let us ask whether there is not spiritual value or good on both sides—not an equal amount of good (that is not necessary), but enough good on each to give the impression of spiritual waste. Is there not such good in Macbeth? It is not a question merely of moral goodness, but of good. It is not a question of the use made of good, but of its presence. And such bravery and skill in war as win the enthusiasm of everyone about him; such an imagination as few but poets possess; a conscience so vivid that his deed is to him beforehand a thing of terror, and, once done, condemns him to that torture of the mind on which he lies in restless ecstasy; a determination so tremendous and a courage so appalling that, for all this torment, he never dreams of turning back, but, even when he has found that life is a tale full of sound and fury, signifying nothing, will tell it out to the end though earth and heaven and hell are leagued against him; are not these things, in themselves, good, and gloriously good? Do they not make you, for all your horror, admire Macbeth, sympathise with his agony, pity him, and see in him the waste of forces on which you place a spiritual value? It is simply on this account that he is for you, not the abstraction called a criminal who merely 'gets what he de-serves' (art, like religion, knows no such thing), but a tragic hero, and that his war with other forces of indubitable spir-itual worth is a tragic war.[8]

[8] The same point may be put thus, in view of that dangerous word 'personality.' Our interest in Macbeth may be called interest in a personality; but it is not an interest in some bare form of self-consciousness, nor yet in a person in the legal sense, but in a per-sonality full of matter. This matter is not an ethical or universal

It is required by the restatement of Hegel's principle to show that in the external conflict of persons there is good on both sides. It is not required that this should be true, secondly, of both sides in the conflict within the hero's soul; for the hero is only a part of the tragedy. Nevertheless in almost all cases, if not in all, it is true. It is obviously so where, as in the hero and also the heroine of the *Cid*, the contending powers in this internal struggle are love and honour. Even when love is of a quality less pure and has a destructive force, as in Shakespeare's Antony, it is clearly true. And it remains true even where, as in Hamlet and Macbeth, the contest seems to lie, and for most purposes might conveniently be said to lie, between forces simply good and simply the reverse. This is not really so, and the tragic effect depends upon the fact. It depends on our feeling that the elements in the man's nature are so inextricably blended that the good in him, that which we admire, instead of simply opposing the evil, reinforces it. Macbeth's imagination deters him from murder, but it also makes the vision of a crown irresistibly bright. If he had been less determined, nay, if his conscience had been less maddening in its insistence that he had thrown the precious jewel of his soul irretrievably away, he might have paused after his first deed, might even have repented. Yet his imagination, his determination, and his conscience were things good. Hamlet's desire to do his duty is a good thing, but what opposes this desire is by no means simply evil. It is something to which a substantial contribution is made by the qualities we most admire in him. Thus the nature of tragedy, as seen in the external conflict, repeats itself on each side of this conflict, and everywhere there is a spiritual value in both the contending forces.

In showing that *Macbeth*, a tragedy as far removed as possible from the *Antigone* as understood by Hegel, is still of one nature with it, and equally answers to the account of tragedy proposed, it has been necessary to ignore the great difference between the two plays. But when once the common essence of all tragedies has been determined, their differences become

end, but it must in a sense be universal—human nature in a particular form—or it would not excite the horror, sympathy, and admiration it does excite. Nor, again, could it excite these feelings if it were not composed largely of qualities on which we set a high value.

the interesting subject. They could be distinguished according
to the character of the collisions on which they are built, or of
the main forces which move the principal agents. And it may
well be that, other things being equal (as they never are), the
tragedy in which the hero is, as we say, a good man, is more
tragic than that in which he is, as we say, a bad one. The
more spiritual value, the more tragedy in conflict and waste.
The death of Hamlet or Othello is, so far, more tragic than
that of Macbeth, that of Macbeth than that of Richard. Below Richard stands Iago, a figure still tragic, but unfit for the
hero's part; below him persons like Regan or, in the very depth,
Oswald, characters no longer (at least in the dramatic sense)
tragic at all. Moral evil, that is to say, so greatly diminishes
the spiritual value we ascribe to the personality that a very
large amount of good of some kind is required to bring this
personality up to the tragic level, the destruction of evil as
such being in no degree tragic. And again, it may well be that,
other things being equal, the more nearly the contending forces
approach each other in goodness, the more tragic is the conflict; that the collision is, so far, more tragic in the *Antigone*
than in *Macbeth,* and Hamlet's internal conflict than his struggle with outward enemies and obstacles. But it is dangerous
to describe tragedy in terms that even appear to exclude *Macbeth,* or to describe *Macbeth,* even casually or by implication,
in terms which imply that it portrays a conflict of mere evil
with mere good.

The restatement of Hegel's main principle as to the conflict
would involve a similar restatement as to the catastrophe (for
we need not consider here those 'tragedies' which end with a
solution). As before, we must avoid any reference to ethical
or universal ends, or to the work of 'justice' in the catastrophe.
We might then simply say that, as the tragic action portrays
a self-division or intestinal conflict of spirit, so the catastrophe
displays the violent annulling of this division or conflict. But
this statement, which might be pretty generally accepted,
would represent only half of Hegel's idea, and perhaps nothing
of what is most characteristic and valuable in it. For the catastrophe (if I may put his idea in my own way) has two aspects,
a negative and an affirmative, and we have ignored the latter.
On the one hand it is the act of a power immeasurably su-

perior to that of the conflicting agents, a power which is irresistible and unescapable, and which overbears and negates whatever is incompatible with it. So far, it may be called, in relation to the conflicting agents,[9] necessity or fate; and unless a catastrophe affects us in ways corresponding with this aspect it is not truly tragic. But then if this were all and this necessity were merely infinite, characterless, external force, the catastrophe would not only terrify (as it should), it would also horrify, depress, or at best provoke indignation or rebellion; and these are not tragic feelings. The catastrophe, then, must have a second and affirmative aspect, which is the source of our feelings of reconciliation, whatever form they may assume. And this will be taken into account if we describe the catastrophe as the violent self-restitution of the divided spiritual unity. The necessity which acts and negates in it, that is to say, is yet of one substance with both the agents. *It* is divided against itself in them; they are *its* conflicting forces; and in restoring its unity through negation it affirms them, so far as they are compatible with that unity. The qualification is essential, since the hero, for all his affinity with that power, is, as the living man we see before us, not so compatible. He must die, and his union with 'eternal justice' (which is more than 'justice') must itself be 'eternal' or ideal. But the qualification does not abolish what it qualifies. This is no occasion to ask how in particular, and in what various ways in various works, we feel the effect of this affirmative aspect in the catastrophe. But it corresponds at least with that strange double impression which is produced by the hero's death. He dies, and our hearts die with him; and yet his death matters nothing to us, or we even exult. He is dead; and he has no more to do with death than the power which killed him and with which he is one.

I leave it to students of Hegel to ask whether he would have accepted the criticisms and modifications I have suggested. Naturally I think he would, as I believe they rest on truth, and am sure he had a habit of arriving at truth. But in any case their importance is trifling, compared with that of the

[9] In relation to *both* sides in the conflict (though it may not need to negate life in both). For the ultimate agent in the catastrophe is emphatically not the finite power of one side. It is beyond both, and, at any rate in relation to them, boundless.

theory which they attempt to strengthen and to which they owe their existence.

Why did Hegel, in his lectures on Aesthetics, so treat of tragedy as to suggest the idea that the kind of tragedy which he personally preferred (let us for the sake of brevity call it 'ancient') is also the most adequate embodiment of the idea of tragedy? This question can be answered, I think, only conjecturally, but some remarks on it may have an interest for readers of Hegel (they are too brief to be of use to others).

One answer might be this. Hegel did not really hold that idea. But he was lecturing, not writing a book. He thought the principle of tragedy was more clearly and readily visible in ancient works than in modern; and so, for purposes of exposition, he emphasised the ancient form. And this fact, with his personal enthusiasm for certain Greek plays, leads the reader of the *Aesthetik* to misconstrue him.

Again, we must remember the facts of Hegel's life. He seems first to have reflected on tragedy at a time when his enthusiasm for the Greeks and their 'substantial' ethics was combined, not only with a contemptuous dislike for much modern 'subjectivity' (this he never ceased to feel), but with a certain hostility to the individualism and the un-political character of Christian morality. His first view of tragedy was thus, in effect, a theory of Aeschylean and Sophoclean tragedy; and it appears in the early essay on *Naturrecht* and more fully in the *Phaenomenologie*. Perhaps, then, when he came to deal with the subject more generally, he insensibly regarded the ancient form as the typical form, and tended to treat the modern rather as a modification of this type than as an alternative embodiment of the general idea of tragedy. The note in the *Rechtsphilosophie* (p. 196) perhaps favours this idea.

But, whether it is correct or no, I believe that the impression produced by the *Aesthetik* is a true one, and that Hegel did deliberately consider the ancient form the more satisfactory. It would not follow, of course, from that opinion that he thought the advantage was all on one side, or considered this or that ancient poet greater than this or that modern, or wished that modern poets had tried to write tragedies of the Greek type. Tragedy would, in his view, be in somewhat the same position as Sculpture. Renaissance sculpture, he might say, has qualities in which it is superior to Greek, and Michael Angelo may have been as great an artist as Pheidias; but all the same for certain reasons Greek sculpture is, and probably will remain, sculpture *par excellence*. So, though not to the same extent, with tragedy.

And such a view would cohere with his general view of Art. For he taught that, in a sense, Classical Art is Art *par excellence*, and that in Greece beauty held a position such as it never held before and will not hold again. To explain in a brief note how this position bears upon his treatment of modern tragedy would be impossible: but if the student of Hegel will remember in what sense and on what grounds he held it; that he describes Beauty as the '*sinnliches* Scheinen der Idee'; that for him the new idea that distinguished Christianity and Romantic Art from Greek religion and Classical Art is that '*unendliche* Subjektivität' which implies a negative, though not merely negative, relation to sense; and that in Romantic Art this idea is not only exhibited in the religious sphere, but appears in the position given to personal honour, love, and loyalty, and indirectly in what Hegel calls 'die formelle Selbstständigkeit der individuellen Besonderheiten,' and in the fuller admission of common and un-beautiful reality into the realm of Beauty,—he will see how all this is connected with those characteristics of modern tragedy which Hegel regards as necessary and yet as, in part, drawbacks. This connection, which Hegel has no occasion to work out, will be apparent even from consideration of the introductory chapter on 'die romantische Kunstform,' *Aesthetik*, ii. 120–35.

There is one marked difference, I may add, between ancient and modern tragedy, which should be considered with reference to this subject, and which Hegel, I think, does not explicitly point out. Speaking roughly, we may say that the former includes, while the latter tends to ignore, the accepted religious ideas of the time. The ultimate reason of this difference, on Hegel's view, would be that the Olympian gods are themselves the '*sinnliches* Scheinen der Idee,' and so are in the same element as Art, while this is, on the whole, not so with modern religious ideas. One result would be that Greek tragedy represents the total Greek mind more fully than modern tragedy can the total modern mind.

INDEX

Abel, 117

Absolute spirit, xvi–xvii, 261. *See also* Spirit

Accidents. *See* Misfortune

Achaia, 336

Achilles, 72, 100–1, 130, 140, 142, 154–55, 157, 194–95, 203, 220, 312–13, 319–20, 323–44, 345, 362

Action, 124–27, 131, 238, 243–44, 291; dramatic, 1–7, 10–13, 15–17, 27, 31, 36, 53, 54, 131, 155, 208–9; tragic, 27, 52–54, 59, 63, 80, 87, 128–30, 274–75, 291–92, 296, 336, 368; comic, 52–54; epic, 129–30, 289–91; ethical, 274–86

Actor and Acting, 34–42, 58, 299, 301

Acts and Scenes, 14, 16

Aeschylus, 37, 57, 63, 83, 177–78, 184, 185, 197, 347, 370, 386; and unities, 10, 16; tragic conflict in, 68, 177–78, 192. *See also* names of plays and characters: e.g., Orestes; *Eumenides*

Admetus, 115, 307

Agamemnon, 83, 129, 142, 154–55, 202, 220; as epic hero, 72, 100–1; as tragic hero, 125, 344, 380

Agamemnon (Aeschylus), 68, 375

Ajax (Sophocles), 10, 124–25, 155

Aleestis (Glück and Euripides), 115

Alcibiades, 347, 357, 365

Alexander, 219, 366

Alexandrine, 21–22

Amphitro (Plautus), 56

Anabaptists, 361

Anacreon, 320

Anaxagoras, 352, 360

Andromache, 155

Antigone, 14, 68, 73–74, 133, 147, 178, 197, 202, 279–80, 283, 360, 370, 379–80

Antigone (Sophocles), 186, 269, 280, 283, 378, 379; Hegel's estimate of, xi, xxv, xxvi, 73–74, 178, 325, 371–72; conflict in, 68, 133, 178, 360; contrasted with *Macbeth*, 383–84

Antilochus, 154

Antistrophes, 37

Antony and Cleopatra, 231, 383

Anytus, 355

Aphrodite, 197, 201, 331

Apollo, 57, 74, 137–38, 140, 170–71, 185, 297, 307–8, 312, 370

Architecture, xvii, xix–xx, xxii, 31

Areopagus, 57, 74, 185, 327, 345

Argus, 137

Ariosto, xii

Aristophanes, 38, 63, 78, 192, 300, 347; and Athenians, 29, 30, 55, 77–79, 347, 348; comic genius of, 55, 76–79, 93; and Shakespeare, 95–96; and Socrates, 347–50

— *Birds,* 185; *Clouds,* 300, 347–50; *Ecclesiazusae,* 54; *Knights,* 300

Aristotle, 15, 22, 27, 223, 315, 380; and Hegel, xiv, xxix, 367; on unities, 10–13; on fear and pity, 49–50, 123

Arlecchino, 42

Art, xvi, 28, 29, 99, 119, 315, 345–46; classical or ideal, xii–xx *passim,* xxv–xxvii, xxix, 38, 65–72 *passim,* 79, 99–100, 104, 132, 139, 166–71, 178–84, 189, 192–93, 198–99, 223–24, 305, 313–18, 380, 387–88; death of, xv–xvi, 345–46; origin of, xvi–xviii, 132, 286, 303–4; defined, xvi–xviii, 19, 62, 112, 114, 139, 232, 234–36, 287, 305, 315–16; symbolic, xvii, xix, 167–68; romantic or modern, xvii–xviii, xxi–xxii, 62, 127–28, 137–38, 145–46, 166, 194–96, 198–99, 213,

316, 332, 374, 387; subject matter of, 98–99, 115–16, 127–28, 131, 134–35, 145–46, 149, 167–69, 178–80, 184, 194–96, 318, 342–43

Artemis, 307

Artist, 40, 141, 167, 193, 315–16

Aspasia, 360

Ate, 380

Athene (Pallas), 74, 142, 143, 174, 184–86, 305–6, 313, 319–20, 330–33, 345, 371

Athens and Athenians, xvi, 74, 319, 327, 333, 345, 365–66; in Aristophanic comedies, 29, 55, 77–79, 347; mysteries of, 183–84, 304, 340–41; and Socrates, 346, 354–64 *passim*

Audience, 2, 22–29, 34, 37, 42, 93, 291–92

Augaean stables, 100

Aulis, 344

Bacchus, 66–67, 78, 184, 192, 329, 343

Ballet, 43

Bas-reliefs, 192

Beatrice, 198

Beauty, xvii, xxiv, 131–34, 143, 166, 188, 305, 321–24, 339, 387; and Greek art, 66, 113–14, 132, 165, 313–18; and Ideal, 114, 300, 313–16 *passim*

Benedict, Ruth F., xiv

"Beyond," The, 330, 332–33

Boccaccio, xii, 198

Bombast, 22

Bosanquet, Bernard, xii, xiii, xviii, xxiv

Bradley, A. C., xi, xii, xxiv–xxv, xxix

Bradley, F. H., xiii

Brahman, 24

Bravery, 194

Briareus, 172

Bride of Messina (Schiller), 107, 117

Briseis, 154

Brontes, 172

Brutus (*Julius Caesar*), 229–30

Cain, 117

Calchas, 312–13, 344

Calderon, 22, 24, 82, 222, 373

Carl Moor (Schiller), 81–82, 110–11, 373

Cassirer, Ernst, xiii

Cassius (*Julius Caesar*), 229–30

Caste, 119

Ceres, 173, 329, 343

Cervantes, 112

Chaos, 172, 179

Character, 36–54 *passim*, 93, 152–54, 157, 208–9, 215–16, 275, 281, 295, 311; in Shakespearean drama, xvii, xxviii, 21, 26, 39, 83–91 *passim*, 107–8, 117–18, 123–26, 135, 146–47, 156–58, 162, 204–17 *passim*, 229–30, 294–96, 370, 374–79, 382–84; and action, 4–7, 12–13, 27, 54, 131, 155; dramatic, 12–13, 27, 45–77 *passim*, 155, 291–92; in modern drama, 26, 39, 57, 60–62, 80, 82–88, 93–95, 206, 208–9, 215–16, 374–75; epic, 27, 102–4, 110, 154–55, 157; in classical drama, 47, 58–59, 65, 74–79, 83–84, 93, 102, 117, 125, 156, 209, 374; and pathos, 70, 74–75, 84, 153, 157, 280–83. *See also* names of plays and characters: e.g., Macbeth; *Antigone; Macbeth*

Charles the Great, 101, 205

Charmian (*Antony and Cleopatra*), 231

China, xvi, 59

Chivalry, 67, 92, 106, 112, 204–5

Choephorae (Aeschylus), 68, 83

Chorus, 19–20, 37–38, 42, 66–67, 292–300 *passim*, 323; ancient, 19, 37, 65–67, 107; modern, 19, 37, 65, 67

Christ, 80, 97, 145, 364

Christendom, 101, 193, 201, 341

Christianity, xvi, 75, 106, 139, 145, 193, 316. *See also* Art: Romantic; Religion

Chronos, 306, 172, 179

Church, 80, 106, 317

Cicero, 43, 235

Cid (Corneille), 101, 158–59, 205, 383

Clairvoyance, 161

Clandestine Revenge for Clandestine Insult (Calderon), 24

Claudius, 151–52

Cleon, 78

Cleopatra (*Antony and Cleopatra*), 231

Clouds (Aristophanes), 300, 347–50

Clowns: in Shakespeare, 157–58

Clytemnestra, 69, 74, 83, 125, 202, 370, 375

Cohen, Morris R., xiii

Collision, 14, 48–49, 62, 69, 73, 83–84, 114–34 *passim*, 170–71, 213–14, 274–75, 326, 334; and action, 2, 4, 15, 16, 87, 128–29, 274–75; forces in, 45, 64, 67, 72, 115–29, 199, 200, 214, 237, 274–75, 323–25, 362, 364; and con-

Collision (*cont'd*)
    flict, 80, 113, 115–29, 325–
    26, 368; and Socrates, 362,
    364
Comedy, 59, 77, 93–95, 232,
    298–301, 341–42; defined,
    xv, xxiv, 1–2, 13, 45–46, 52–
    53, 56–57, 77, 91–92; reso-
    lution in, 9, 54, 76; modern,
    22, 24–25, 93–95; and poet,
    30, 39; characters in, 36, 39,
    53–54, 93–96; ancient, 38–
    39, 55, 76–79, 93, 298–99;
    content of, 52–54, 79, 107,
    299–300
Commedia dell'arte, 41–42
Community, 265–67, 282–84
Conceits, 236
Conflict, 69, 113–14, 250–53,
    368; resolution of, 2–3, 8, 13,
    370, 375; defined, 10, 15, 37,
    51, 113, 369; in modern
    drama, 13, 67–68, 84, 205–6,
    237, 250–53, 373, 375, 383;
    in ancient drama, 37, 48, 57–
    64, 67–68, 178, 185, 281–82,
    370, 375; sources of, 48, 67–
    68, 178, 185, 205–6, 237,
    250–53, 254–55, 281–82,
    289–91, 369, 370, 373, 383
Conscience, 320, 361
Consciousness, 63–64, 69, 76,
    275, 279, 294–98, 301, 325–
    26
Content, xviii, 7–8, 10, 24, 63–
    64, 76, 295; of art, xix–xxi,
    98–99, 104–5, 108–10, 167,
    193–94, 201, 231; religious,
    7, 80, 150; of tragedy, 46–
    51, 63–64, 67, 69, 76, 80–83,
    105, 113, 192, 293–94; of
    comedy, 52–54, 79; histori-
    cal, in Shakespeare, 105, 118;
    of epic, 192, 288, 292

Contingency, 46
Cordelia (King Lear), 135
Corneille, 158–59
Corybantes, 173, 181
Creon, 39, 68, 73–74, 133, 186,
    197, 202, 325, 372, 378, 379
Creuzer, 303–4, 342
Crime, 68–69, 247, 277–80,
    337–38, 343–45, 359–60,
    362; in modern drama, 61,
    81, 83–84, 89, 92, 117–18,
    230; in ancient drama, 75,
    102, 279–80, 327; in Shake-
    speare's plays, 117–18, 230.
    See also Evil; Guilt; Wrong
Crime (Müllner), 61
Critias, 357, 365
Croce, Benedetto, xiii, xv
Crusades, 3
Cult, 301
Curse, 310
Custom, 118, 238–39, 261, 278
Cybele, 307

Daemon: of Socrates, 351, 354,
    358
Damayanti, 125–26
Dance, 31–32, 36, 38, 41
Dante, xii, 198, 234
Death, 263–67, 296–97, 323–
    24, 326–27; of ancient he-
    roes, 75, 83, 186, 323–24; of
    Shakespeare's heroes, 90, 231,
    376, 384; of Socrates, 351–
    52, 359, 361–62, 366
Declamation, 31, 36–38, 232–
    33
Dei inferi, 178
Delos, 169, 336
Delphi, 169, 294, 336
Demeter, 184, 343
Democracy, 190, 348
Demos, 299–300
Demosthenes, 223

Denmark, 13

Dénouement, 51, 71, 89, 117, 123, 134, 214

De Sanctis, Francesco, xii

Destiny. *See* Fate

Deus ex machina, 57, 74–75, 94, 140, 209

Dewey, John, xiii

Dialectic: of Socrates, 300–1, 349–50

Dialogue, 9, 17–20, 37, 40, 70

Diana, 129, 143, 186, 326, 344

Diction, 34, 221–24, 226, 231–36, 257; dramatic, 9, 17; classical, 18–19, 223; modern, 22, 226, 235–36; Shakespearean, 86, 224–31. *See also* Language

Diderot, 18

Dike, 176, 181

Dilthey, Wilhelm, xiii

Diomedes, 155

Dithyramb, 66

Divine, The, 7, 314–15, 332–33, 342; in Greek literature, 47, 138–39, 142, 306; *en negligée,* 161

Dodona, 169, 303, 336

Don Carlos (Schiller), 111

Don Quixote (Cervantes), 112

Dottore: in *commedia dell'arte,* 42

Drama: defined, xxiii, 1–2, 9, 18, 28, 30–32, 45, 66, 113–14; tragic, comic, and intermediary type distinguished, xxiv, 44–46, 51, 56–58, 91–93; distinguished from epic and lyric, 1–4, 6–29 *passim,* 104, 155, 225; performance of, 1–2, 16, 22–25, 30, 32, 34–42, 58, 229, 301, 332; language of, 9, 16–21, 31–32, 35, 223–27, 326–27; uni-

ties of, 10–13; classical (ancient) and romantic (modern) distinguished, 13, 17, 19, 35, 40, 45, 58–62, 66–68, 79, 85, 90, 208–9, 237; English, 16, 22, 85–86, 226; German, 16, 22, 33, 37, 42, 92, 215, 226, 375; Spanish, 16, 21, 24–25, 85, 94–95, 182, 198, 224, 226, 235–36; French, 16, 21–22, 26, 41–42, 85, 93–94, 135, 156, 159, 216–17, 226, 230; Greek, 18–19, 33, 37, 60–63, 156, 165–66, 171, 324; Italian, 41–42, 85, 226; Roman, 43, 56, 63, 85, 93, 95; Oriental, 59, 62. *See also* Comedy; Intermediary type drama; *and under* authors, titles, characters

Dramatis personae, 3–6, 18, 20, 25–26, 35, 56, 227

Dreams, 336

Duncan (*Macbeth*), 117–18, 375

Duty, 92, 201, 274–75, 319

Ecclesiazusae (Aristophanes), 54

Egypt, 169, 182, 187, 303–5

Electra (Sophocles), 68–69; contrasted with *Hamlet,* 83

Elegies, 192

Eleusinian mysteries, 340–41

Eliot, T. S., xxii–xxiii

Eloquence, 257. *See also* Rhetoric

England, 360–61

English jury, 359

English literature, 16, 22, 85–86, 226

Ephesus, 307

Epic, xxiii, 14–15, 28, 45, 59,

63, 66, 72–73, 128, 140, 155, 288–92; defined, 1–2, 4, 6, 8–9, 11, 14–15, 27, 45, 73, 116, 155, 225, 301; and national existence, 3, 9, 28; language of, 17, 20, 227, 235, 288–92

Epigram, 192

Epimetheus, 173

Epopaea and Epos. See Epic

Erebus, 172

Erinyes. See Eumenides

Eros, 320

Eteocles, 117, 281

Ethical life, 47, 63–64, 92, 98–100, 271; in tragedy, 7, 47–49, 51, 76, 102–3, 269, 273, 275, 279, 293–98; human conduct and, 143, 237–86 passim, 335–37. See also Morality; State

Eumenides, xxvi, 14, 141–42, 177–78, 185–86, 307; distinguished from furies, 75, 176–77, 320. See also Furies

Eumenides (Aeschylus), 10, 57, 74, 179, 185–86; conflict in, 68, 177, 185, 370; reconciliation in, 74, 185, 327

Euripides, 71, 78, 86–87, 143, 347, 373

— Alcestis, 115; Heraklidae, 185; Hippolytus, 326; Iphigenia in Aulis, 33, 68, 123, 125, 129, 133–34; Iphigenia in Tauris, 33, 57, 129, 143–45, 377; Phaedra, 201

Eurystheus, 100

Eve, 75

Evil, 67, 75, 115, 134–35, 310, 345, 364, 369; in drama, 71, 208–9, 297, 379–80; in Shakespeare, 86, 135, 230,

377, 382–83. See also Crime; Wrong; Guilt

Fall: in Bible, 365

Falstaff, xii, 216

Family and Family relations, 46, 117, 201, 262, 299–300, 319; in tragedy, 68–69, 129, 178, 293, 295–96; claims of, 262–70, 274, 281–84

Fancy, 223–24

Fatality, 62, 103–4, 208–9

Fate, 97, 308, 364–66; in tragedy, 62, 69, 71, 209, 294, 297, 325, 377–78; defined, 103–4, 139, 244–45, 310–11; in comedy, 298–99, 301. See also Necessity

Faust (Goethe), 81, 242, 373, 375

Fear: Aristotle on, 49–50, 123

Ferdusi, 101

Feridu, 117

Feudalism, 101, 112

Fidelity, 205–6; defined, 203–5; in King Lear, 204

Fiesco (Schiller), 111

Folk songs, 212

Forces, 7, 8, 45–46, 199–200, 237, 323–25, 362–64; ethical, 48, 63–64, 67–68, 273; spiritual, 115–29, 214–15

Fortinbras (Hamlet), 13

Freedom, 329; and art, 29, 59, 77, 98–99, 106, 119, 167, 176, 193–94, 201, 323–24; and individual, 46, 139, 312, 321, 338; significance of, 103–4, 139, 143, 199, 287, 309–12, 321, 364; and Greeks, 165, 321, 364

French literature, 10, 16, 22–23, 26, 41–42, 85, 93–94,

French literature (*cont'd*) 135, 150, 156, 159, 198, 216–17, 226, 230, 235

Friar Lawrence (*Romeo and Juliet*), 157

Friedrich, Carl J., xii–xiii

Furies, 75, 135, 141, 176–77, 220, 279–80, 295–98, 320, 371. *See also* Eumenides

Gaia, 172, 179, 306

Gentile, Giovanni, xiii

German literature, 16, 19–23, 29, 37, 150, 155, 159–60, 198, 206, 215, 226

Gessner, Salomon, 105–6

Ghosts, 145–47, 214, 295–96

Gloster (*King Lear*), 88

Glück, 115

God, 97, 134, 139, 150, 186, 317–18, 327, 330, 333, 337

Gods, 49, 136, 268–69, 307–8, 319–20, 330–32, 334; in epic poetry, 64–65, 136–37, 140, 142–43, 168, 289–91, 303–4, 333; in comedy, 77–79, 298–300; character of, 97, 136, 138–43, 148, 153, 171–72, 176–77, 182, 188, 205, 306–45 *passim*, 387; origin of, 141–43, 153, 168, 183, 187, 303–4, 312–13, 342; in art, 183, 315–16, 318, 331, 342–43; in tragedy, 295–97, 325

Goethe, xii, 20, 110–12, 143, 144, 181, 213; language of, 18–20, 151, 213, 224; characterizations of, 26, 86–87, 159; and Schiller, 26–27, 86, 111–12, 151; and art, 29, 35, 42, 92, 215, 315; and Shakespeare, 86, 146

— *Faust*, 81, 242, 373, 375; *Götz von Berlichingen*, 89,

92, 111–12; *Hermann and Dorothea*, 106; *Iphigenia in Tauris*, 26–27, 33, 57, 143–45; *Stella*, 87

Goneril (*King Lear*), 375

Good, 92, 190, 300, 346, 369; and evil in tragedy, 75, 297, 364, 369; in Shakespeare, 382–83

Götz von Berlichingen (Goethe), 89, 92, 111–12

Greece, 3, 60, 303–4; religion of, xxix, 150, 166–69, 303–6, 312–13, 319–20, 331, 334, 344, 354; heroes and men of, 70, 84, 99–102, 193, 305, 324; politics of, 79, 165–66; spirit of, 181, 304–6, 309–10. *See also* Art; Drama

Grief, 324

Guilt, xi, 277–78, 326–27, 343–45, 377–80; ancient view, 70–71, 102–4, 129, 202, 237, 279, 297, 325–26, 359–60, 363–64; modern view, 70, 102–4

Gyges, 172

Haemon, 73–74, 186, 197

Hamlet, 83, 146–47, 162; death of, 90–91, 376, 384; beautiful soul of, 90–91, 214, 294–95, 379; and Orestes, 125, 294–95, 374; and Oedipus, 294–95; and Macbeth, 214, 294–95; conduct of, 295–96, 383

Hamlet, xii, 13, 83, 125, 377–79; Hegel's high estimate of, xxviii, 294–96; compared with *Choephorae* and *Electra*, 83

Hartmann, Eduard von, xiii

Hartmann von der Aue, 133–34

Haute comédie, 41

Heaven, 297, 307

Hebrews, xvi. *See also* Jews

Hector, 72, 154–55, 157, 220

Hegel: and Bradley, xi–xii; influence of, xii–xiv; aesthetic system, xiv–xxii, xxiv–xxvii; and Aristotle, xiv, xxix, 367; his preferences, xxiv–xxviii, 370, 376–77

Heidegger, Martin, xiii

Helen of Troy, 125, 129

Heliasts, 359

Helios, 138, 172, 186, 306–7

Hellenes. *See* Greece

Henry Bolingbroke (*Richard II*), 229

Henry IV, 228

Henry VIII, 229, 230

Hephaestos, 174–76, 184–85

Hera, 142, 306

Heraklidae (Euripides), 185

Hercules, 33, 57, 100, 115, 173, 185, 304, 330, 343

Herder, J. G. von, 235

Hermann and Dorothea (Goethe), 106

Hermes, 140

Herodotus, 168, 303, 312–13

Heroes, 237, 291–92, 295–98, 323–24, 334–35; classical, 47, 99–102, 193, 323, 354, 362–63, 370; romantic, 93, 106–8, 193–94; Eastern, 101

Heroic Age, 99, 103–4, 110

Hesiod, 168, 179, 303–4, 312–13, 333

Hexameter, 21

Heyne, 221

Hindoos, 24, 59, 171–72

Hippel, 215

Hippolytus, 326

Hoffmann, Theodore, 135

Holy Maid (Schiller), 87

Homer, xii, xv, 130, 142, 192, 312–13, 329–30, 362; characters of, 26, 100–1, 154–55; gods of, 64–65, 136–38, 142–43, 168, 182, 290–91, 303–4, 312–13, 333; language of, 220, 223, 234, 236

Honour, 81–83, 85, 94, 194–96, 199, 383

Hook, Sidney, xiv

Horace, 235, 307

Humour, 215

Husserl, Edmund, xiii

Iago (*Othello*), 375, 378–79, 384

Iambic meter, 21–22

Idea, 314–15, 340

Ideal, 98–100, 105–7, 114, 121–22, 128, 132, 139, 152, 162, 189

Idyllic, 105–6

Iffland, 42, 92–93

Iliad, 130, 142, 154

Ilium, 72. *See also* Troy

Imagery, 86, 217–18, 235–36

Images, 331

Imagination, 128, 177–78, 218, 220, 225, 231, 312

India, xvi, 119, 126, 303–4

Individual, 20, 64, 67, 238–42, 274, 346

Individuality, 84, 101, 103–4, 110, 152–53, 179, 183, 240, 244–46, 256–59, 286, 305, 307–8

Innocence, xi, 70, 278, 346

Inquisition, 357

Intermediary Type Drama, xxiv, 45–46, 56–58, 91–93

Intrigue, 13, 67, 94–95

Iphigenia, 123, 125, 129, 133–34, 145

Iphigenia in Aulis (Euripides), 33, 68

Iphigenia in Tauris (Euripides), 33, 129, 143–45

Iphigenia in Tauris (Goethe), 26–27, 33, 57, 143–45, 377

Irony, 284, 298–99

Isis, 187

Italian literature, 41–42, 85, 198, 226, 236

Ithaca, 72

Jacobi, F. H., 159–60

Jaspers, Karl, xiii

Jean Paul, 215, 224

Jehovah, 182, 186, 341

Jews, 118, 121, 182, 317, 341

Juliet (*Romeo and Juliet*), 90–91, 126, 156, 211–12

Julius Caesar, 229

Jupiter, 101

Jury, 359

Justice, 49, 51, 73, 89, 98–99, 176–77, 199, 272, 307, 319, 325, 334, 372, 375

Kabale und Liebe (Schiller), 82, 89, 111

Käthchen von Heilbronn, 199

Katherine (*Henry VIII*), 229

Kent (*King Lear*), 204

Kierkegaard, Soren, xiii

King James, 118

King Lear, 88–89, 135, 204

King Lear, xii, 135, 204, 379

"King of Thule" (Goethe), 213

Kleist, Heinrich von, 161, 208

Knight Errantry, 112. *See also* Chivalry

Knights (Aristophanes), 300

"Know thyself," 354

Knowledge, 281, 294–95, 307, 319, 364–65

Knox, Israel, xi–xii, xxv

Kotos, 172

Kotzebue, August F. F. von, 42, 55, 92–93, 208

Kronos, 172, 179, 306

Lacedaemon, 365–66

Lady Macbeth (*Macbeth*), 162, 207, 209, 375

Laertes (*Hamlet*), 90, 214

Lafontaine, August, 149

Laius, 14

Language, xiii–xiv, 217, 298–301; and poetry, 17, 31, 38, 86, 119, 150–51, 217–18, 229, 231–36, 282–98. *See also* Diction

Latin literature, 43, 56, 63, 85, 93, 95, 235, 307

Law, 98–99, 118, 199, 238–39, 254, 271, 276–78, 331, 335, 340, 357–61; of the heart, 246–54, 271; divine and human, 260–61, 265–71, 273, 293–94, 325

Leda, 129

Lessing, G. E., 18, 29

Lethe, 296–97

Libretto, 42

Lives of Saints, 127

Love, 81–83, 85, 94, 120–21, 123, 196–202, 265, 326, 383

"Lovely soul," 159–61, 214, 294–95, 376, 379

Lyric, 4, 17, 19–21, 28, 45, 59, 63, 66, 192; compared with epic and drama, xxiii–xxiv, 1–4, 8–9, 14, 27, 155

Macbeth, xxviii, 207, 209, 375, 384; good and evil in, 85, 89, 117–18, 379, 382–83; and witches, 146, 216, 294; compared with Hamlet, 214, 294–95

Macbeth, xii, xxviii, 117–18, 146, 207, 230, 294, 382; contrasted with *Antigone,* 383–84
Macedonians, 360
Machiavelli, xii
Maeterlinck, Maurice, 378
Magic, 161
Magic Flute (Mozart), 43
Magnetism, 161
Mahâ-Bhârata, 125–26
Mahomet (Voltaire), 42
Maid of Orleans (Schiller), 43, 200
Manes, 345
Margaret, 207
Marriage, 201, 273
Mars, 138, 336
Marxism, xiii
Masks, 37, 39
Medicean Aphrodite, 197
Meleager, 192–93
Melitus, 355
Melody, 31
Menelaus, 129
Menschenhass und Reue (Kotzebue), 92
Mephistopheles, 374–75
Mercury, 56, 137
Metaphor, 221–24
Michelangelo, 387
Middle Ages, 111–12, 117, 127, 194, 206. *See also* Chivalry
Minerva, 142
Minnesingers, 198
Minos, 327, 345
Minstrel, 288–91
Miranda, 212
Misanthrope (Schiller), 149
Miser, The (Molière), 94
Misfortune, 50, 90–91, 116, 309, 377–78
Mnemosyne, 288
Mohammedan literature, 59,

101, 224, 236
Mohammedans, xvi
Moirai, 176
Molière, xii, 93–94
"Mona Lisa," xxvii
Monologue, 17, 19–20
Morality, 29, 66, 92–93, 165–66, 199, 241–42, 321, 331, 340, 346. *See also* Ethical life; State
Morality plays, 67
Mozart, 43
Müller, 307
Müllner, 61
Muse, 157, 172–73, 192, 307, 329, 330
Music, xxi–xxii, 31–32, 37–39, 42, 156, 217; and drama, 36–39, 41; and mysteries, 67, 183–84, 301, 304, 340–43
Mythology and Myths, 104, 173–76, 187, 212–13, 306, 340, 341; in art, 13–14, 108–10, 127, 129–30, 168–69

Naiads, 307
Nalas, 125–26
Nathan (Lessing), 29
National Spirit, 238–39, 261, 278, 283, 285; and art, 9, 29, 285–87
Naturalism, 18–19, 42
Nature, 64, 115–16, 236, 264–65, 327, 334–35, 338–39; religion of, 171–72, 186–87, 315–16, 321–22, 327, 339–41; and art, 177–83, 313–18; and Greek spirit, 181–83, 186–87, 304–6, 313–18, 340–41
Near East, xvi
Necessity, xxii–xxix, 271, 290–91, 307, 311, 326; defined, 8, 244–45, 308–14, 325; in

Necessity (*cont'd*)
tragedy, 209, 244–47, 298, 311, 323–24, 344. *See also* Fate

Nemesis, 72–73, 176–77, 309; and Oedipus, 176

Neoptolemos, 57

Neptune, 186

Nestor, 154, 312

Nether World, 271–72, 293, 325

Nicias, 39

Northumberland (*Henry IV*), 228

Notion, 314, 376

Oceanus, 138, 172, 180, 306

Ode, 66

Odysseus, 72, 140, 155, 204

Odyssey, 142

Oedipus, xxvi–xxviii, 69, 76, 117, 124–25, 133, 202, 279, 294, 325–26; sense of guilt of, 14, 69, 75, 102–3, 279, 325–26; reconciliation and death of, 75–76; and Hamlet, 294–95

Oedipus at Colonus (Sophocles), 69, 75, 141–42, 184, 281, 320, 375; Hegel's high estimate of, xxvi, 75; Christian elements in, 327, 345

Oedipus Rex (*Tyrannus*) (Sophocles), 69, 344

Old Testament, 186

Olympus, 49, 78, 135, 142, 153, 175, 185, 304, 308, 387

One, The, 330, 338–39

One-sidedness, 8, 49, 52, 71, 73, 237, 276–77, 315–16, 325–27, 370

Opera, 42–43, 150

Oracles, 169–71, 179, 294, 336–37, 343–44, 346, 354–55

Orestes, 69, 74, 125, 143, 145, 201, 272, 294, 370; suffering and acquittal of, 122–23, 134, 147, 170–71, 345, 379–80; and furies, 177, 320

Oriental despotism, 165

Oriental Spirit, 59, 62, 190, 306

Osiris, 187, 343

Oswald (*King Lear*), 384

Othello, 123, 207, 375, 378, 384; jealousy of, 85, 374

Othello, xii, 123, 207, 379

Oxford Idealism, xiii

Paean, 66

Painting, xxi–xxii, 38, 148–49, 156; and poetry, 113–14, 217

Paladins, 205

Pallas. *See* Athene

Pantheon, 308

Pantomime, 44

Paris (Count), 157

Paris (of Troy), 129

Parsees, 169

Past and Present in art, 104–5, 108–10, 157

Pataeci, 173

Pathos, 20, 36, 39, 49, 64, 73, 148–51, 153, 157, 162–63, 227, 280–83, 286–89, 291–92, 297–98; and content of art, 8, 48, 70, 147–52; defined, 17, 147–52; in ancient tragedy, 21, 37, 40, 48–49, 70, 73–75, 147, 171, 201, 280–81, 326; in modern tragedy, 21, 83–84, 92–93, 149, 151; in Shakespeare, 21, 149

Patroclus, 72, 140, 154, 203, 345

Pausanias, 179, 336

Peloponnesian War, 29, 344, 346, 366

Penates, 262, 268–69, 284

Percy (*Henry IV*), 228

Pericles, 347, 360, 366

Persian War, 3

Personality, 5, 99–105, 139, 208–9

Petrarch, xii, 198

Phaedra (Euripides), 197, 202

Phèdre (Racine), 159

Pheidias (Phidias), 168, 316, 387

Philoctetes, 33, 57, 74–75, 116, 140, 209, 377

Philoctetes (Sophocles), 57, 115, 370; *deus ex machina* in, 57, 74–75, 140

Philosophy, xv–xvii, 233, 347

Phoebe, 179

Phoebus, 179, 294

Phoenix, 154

Physical pain, 377

Physician of his own Honour, The, or, *The Intrepid Prince* (Calderon), 24

Piccolomini, 40, 89

Pindar, 179

Pistol, 216

Pity: in Aristotle, 49–50, 123

Place: unity of, 10

Plastic Arts, 31, 114, 301

Plato, xv, 173–76, 182, 190, 223, 261–62, 322

Plautus, 56, 93

Pleasure, 243–46, 248–49, 271

Plutarch, 187

Poet, 8, 27–30, 34–35, 38, 104–5, 127, 193, 220, 227, 235

Poetics: of Aristotle, xiv, xxix, 380

Poetry, 40, 42, 101, 330–31; defined, xvii, xxii, 30, 36,

218–20; epic, dramatic, lyric distinguished, xxii–xxiv, 1, 6, 43, 45, 58; content of, 29, 114, 193–94, 201, 231, 329; relation to other arts, 30–32, 114, 156; language and style of, 38, 119, 218, 229, 231–36. *See also* Drama; Epic; Lyric

Polonius, 214

Polynices, 117, 281, 380

Poor Henry (Hartmann von der Aue), 133–34

Poseidon, 143, 306–7, 344

Priam, 140, 154, 228

Prince von Homburg (Heinrich von Kleist), 161, 208

Princes, 106–7, 109

Prometheus, 173, 175–76, 180–81, 184–85

Prose, 223, 232, 234–35

Prospero, xvii

Protagoras (Plato), 174–76

Providence, xxiv, 62, 71–72, 333–34. *See also* Fate

Pylades, 203

Pythia, 169–70, 179, 336, 352, 354

Quakers, 361

Racine, xii, 159, 326

Realism, 18, 42, 98–99, 226

Reality, 246–47, 251

Reason, 271

Recitation, 32, 36

Reconciliation, 21, 72, 297, 343–44, 378–79, 380; defined, 49, 51; forms of, 51, 72–73, 75–76, 296–97, 326–27, 337–38; in ancient tragedy, 51, 71–76, 80, 326–27; in modern tragedy, 57, 80, 89, 91–92, 209, 326–27, 375

Redemption, 365

Regan (*King Lear*), 384

Reinecke Fuchs, 101, 205–6

Religion, xxix, 149–50, 303–4, 319–22; and art, xv–xix, 29, 80, 168, 188, 201, 232, 293–94, 301, 315–16, 332; of spirit, xvi–xvii, 201, 343; of beauty, 150, 303–4, 319–24; of nature, 171–72, 186–87, 303–4, 315–16, 321–22, 339–41; and Socrates, 346, 354, 358. *See also* Gods

Renaissance, xvi

Renunciation, 329

Resolution, 2, 8, 9, 15, 45, 49, 54, 91; in Aeschylus and Sophocles, 57, 186

Responsibility, 102–3, 337

Resurrection, 343

Rhetoric, 18, 21, 70, 85, 226, 232–36; of Shakespeare, 36; and virtue, 257

Rhythm, 37

Richard II, 228

Richard III, 89, 207, 375, 384

Richard III, 207

Rickert, Heinrich, xiii

Right, 69, 175, 177–78, 237, 281–83, 296–97, 331; and Socrates, 346

Romans, 99–100, 187, 360

Romeo, 90–91, 126, 156, 370, 374

Romeo and Juliet, 13, 156–57, 211, 215, 376

Russell, Bertrand, xiv

Russia, 122

Sacrifice, 329, 344

Sakontala, 24

Santayana, George, xiv

Saracens, 101

Sartre, Jean Paul, xiii

Satyric drama, 56

Scenery and Scenic representation, 1–2, 16, 22–25, 30, 32, 34–42, 229, 301, 332

Scenes and Acts, 14, 16

Schiller, xii, 21, 23, 83, 87, 110–11, 373; language of, 18, 86, 224, 235; pathos of, 21, 149, 151; and Goethe, 26–27, 86, 151; characterizations of, 82, 111, 212; and Shakespeare, 86

— *Bride of Messina*, 107, 117; *Carl Moor*, 81–82, 110–11; *Don Carlos*, 111; *Fiesco*, 111; *Kabale und Liebe*, 111; *Maid of Orleans*, 43, 200; *Misanthrope*, 149; *William Tell*, 161–62

Schlegel, A. W. and F., von, 23

Schopenhauer, Arthur, xiv

Science, xvi, 149, 232, 304, 335–37

Sculpture, xvii, xx, xxii, 31, 36, 38, 47, 113–14, 156, 171, 192, 217, 387

Scythian mountains, 180–81

Selene, 306

Self-consciousness, 41, 333, 345; and ethical life, 238, 240–42, 254, 257–60, 271, 276–78, 321, 354–55; and tragedy, 279, 297–98, 342–45; and comedy, 299, 301

Seneca, 85

Sentimentalism, 105–6

Service, 329–31

Seven Before Thebes (Aeschylus), 68

Sexes, 270–71

Shah-Rameh, 101, 117

Shakespeare, xvi, xxv, xxix, 11, 13, 204, 215, 380; unrivalled genius of, xii, xxvii–xxviii,

Shakespeare (cont'd)
21, 24–25, 40, 85–86, 95–96, 162, 234–35, 376–77; and ancient tragedy, xviii, 25; characterizations of, xxvii–xxviii, 21, 25–26, 39, 83, 85–86, 88–91, 107–8, 117–18, 123, 125–26, 135, 145–47, 149, 156–57, 162, 206–9, 211–12, 216–17, 230, 374; unities in, 11, 13; language of, 19, 86, 224, 226, 228–31; and Spanish tragedians, 24–25; and Goethe, 86, 146; and Schiller, 86; treatment of crime and evil in, 86, 135, 162, 207, 230; and Aristophanes, 95–96; historical sources of, 105, 118; witches and ghosts in, 145–47, 295–96; and Voltaire, 151–52; clowns of, 157–58, 216; imitators of, 208; and French, 216–17. See also names of plays and characters: e.g., Hamlet; Macbeth

Shame, 115–16

Sickingen, Franz von, 111–12

Simile, 86, 224–31

Sisyphus, 181

Sleep-walking, 161

Social Drama. See Intermediary type drama

Social Order, 237–41

Socrates, 173–74, 304, 322, 343, 350; trial and death of, xxix, 346–47, 350–66; and Aristophanes, 39, 78, 300–1, 347–50; and Athenians, 190, 346–47, 350–57; wisdom of, 343, 346–47, 354, 360–61; daemon of, 346, 351, 354; as tragic hero, 360, 362–63,

364–66

Song, 31, 151, 332

Sophists, 352

Sophocles, xi, xxvi, xxlx, 37–38, 57, 63, 69, 75, 115–16, 133, 140, 184, 186, 344; unities in, 13–14; characterizations of, 26, 70, 83, 156, 386; themes of, 68–69, 141–42, 192, 197, 325; language of, 223; and Aristophanes, 347; and Aeschylus, 370. See also names of plays and characters: e.g., Philoctetes; Antigone

Soul, 193–94, 223, 227, 309, 337–38, 340; immortality of, 182, 315, 322, 361–62; silent, lovely, noble, 159–61, 210–16, 294–95, 311, 376, 379; evil in, 230, 345

Spanish literature, 16, 21, 24–25, 82, 85, 94–95, 198, 224, 226, 235–36

Speech: art of, 32, 34–42, 131, 218, 231–34

Sphinx, 294, 305, 325

Spinozism, 339

Spirit, xvi–xvii, 115, 286–87, 304–6, 309–10, 314–15, 317, 330–31, 340–41; Absolute, xv–xvii, 261; in art, 8, 77, 167, 179–83, 286–87, 305; in tragedy, 48, 123–29, 293–94, 369, 381–82; in comedy, 76–79, 95–96; and freedom, 77, 167, 176, 190, 259–60, 304, 312, 334, 338–39, 345

Spiritualism, 329

Spondee, 21

Stage, 35, 42, 85–86

State, 111, 165, 189–90, 261, 266–67, 318–19, 321, 333, 361; and art, 7, 68, 80, 98–

State (*cont'd*)
99, 119, 172–73, 178, 200–1, 293, 325; and Socrates, 190, 346, 357–58, 361. *See also* Ethical life; Morality

Stella (Goethe), 87

Stephano, 216

Steropes, 172

Strepsiades, 78, 349–50

Strophes, 37

Style, 86, 223–24, 230, 235–36, 257

Styx, 140

Subjectivity, 334, 339, 346; in art, 80, 137–38, 374; as subject matter, 25, 60, 81, 94, 106–8, 113, 115, 127–29, 145–46, 149–50, 233

Sublime, The, 171–72

Suffering, 368, 377

Sun, 343

Symbolik (Creuzer), 304

Symbolism, 211–12

Symbols, 343

Syria, 303–4

Tancred (Voltaire), 42

Tantalus, 129, 181

Tartarus, 172, 181

Tartuffe (Molière), 93–94

Tasso, xii

Tasso (Goethe), 26–27, 57

Teiresias, 371

Telchines, 173

Telemachus, 142

Tennemann, 350, 359

Terence, 93

Theatre, 18, 33–34, 38–44. *See also* Drama: performance of

Theban myths, 13–14, 129–30

Thebes, 75, 117, 133

Thecla, 212

Themis, 179, 181

Theogony, 178–79, 187, 303.

See also Gods

Thespius, 100

Thetis, 154, 312

Thirty, The, 350

Thoas, 122, 143–45

Thought, 345–46

Thousand and One Nights, The, 43

Thucydides, 223

Tieck, Ludwig, 23–24, 29

Timon, 149

Titans, 172–73, 180, 182, 306, 340

Toynbee, Arnold, xiii

Transcendence, 338–39

Trilogies, 113. *See also* names of plays and characters

Trinculo, 216

Trochaic tetrameter, 21

Trojan War, 3, 72, 181, 345

Troy, 57, 72, 228

Truth, 7, 305, 354

Tybalt, 157

Typhon, 343

Tyre, 330

Ugliness, 114, 133–35

Unities, The, 10–13

Uranos, 172, 179, 306

Venus, 138, 192

Verbal expression, 37

Verse measure, 9, 17, 21–22

Vexation, 309, 324

Virgil, xii, 235

Virtue. *See* Ethical life

Voltaire, 29, 42, 151–52

Wallenstein (Schiller), 40, 82, 89, 111

War, 181, 266–67, 306, 340, 344, 366, 369

Weber, Max, xiii

Weimar stage, 42

Werther, 159
Wickedness, 135. *See also* Evil
Will, 324, 375
William Tell (Schiller), 161–62
Windelband, Wilhelm, xiii
Witches, 145–46, 216, 294
Woldemar (Jacobi), 159–60
Wolsey, Cardinal, 230
Wonder, xviii, 71
World, 14, 98, 256–59
Worship, 318–33, 340–42

Wrath, 72, 194–95
Wrong, 283; in tragedy, 49, 69, 81, 89, 237, 296–97. *See also* Crime; Evil; Guilt

Xenophon, 190, 351–56, 359

Zeus, 101, 168, 173, 316; epic character of, 137, 179, 185, 205, 304–8, 316; in tragedy, 294–98, 326
Zodiac, 304